The Mad Fragger and Me

Leading an Infantry Rifle Platoon in Vietnam

Tom Dolan

Copyright © 2013-2016 Thomas E. Dolan

ISBN: 978-1-62646-332-5

All rights reserved. No part of this publication may be reproduced, stored in a retrieval system, or transmitted in any form or by any means, electronic, mechanical, recording or otherwise, without the prior written permission of the author.

Published by Booklocker.com, Inc., St. Petersburg, Florida.

Printed on acid-free paper.

Booklocker.com, Inc.
2016

Second Edition

Dedication

This book is dedicated to the memory of the following fallen soldiers from Bravo Company, 1st Battalion, 20th Infantry Regiment, 11th Light Infantry Brigade, Americal Division:

Corporal James Califf, 3rd Platoon, Killed In Action - 2/21/71

PFC Frederick Young, 3rd Platoon, Killed In Action - 2/21/71

PFC Steven Ast, 3rd Platoon, Died Of Wounds - 3/3/71

SGT Joseph Johnson, 1st Platoon, Killed In Action - 4/6/71

SP/4 Alexander Quiroz, 3rd Platoon, Killed In Action - 5/10/71

AND

THE MAD FRAGGER:

SP/4 Gary Smith, 2nd Platoon, B Company, 11th LIB, Americal Division, Died 8/24/11, From Agent Orange Exposure

Contents

FORWARD 1

CHAPTER 1: INDUCTION, BASIC COMBAT TRAINING AND ADVANCED INDIVIDUAL TRAINING 13

Chapter 2: INFANTRY OFFICER CANDIDATE SCHOOL, FORT BENNING, GEORGIA 27

Chapter 3: TROOP DUTY IN THE SECOND ARMORED DIVISION, FORT HOOD, TEXAS 55

Chapter 4: FOUR DEUCE PLATOON, 1st BATTALION 20th INFANTRY 77

Chapter 5: GOING TO THE BUSH WITH BRAVO COMPANY 101

Chapter 6: THE EASTER SUNDAY MASSACRE 129

Chapter 7: ROLLING UP THE BODY COUNT 155

Chapter 8: MORE ADVENTURES IN THE BUSH 189

Chapter 9: REAR AREA FOLLIES 229

Chapter 10: SOLDIERS AND DOGS 253

Chapter 11: PEANUT BUTTER FRAGS 293

Chapter 12: GOING HOME 337

Epilogue 343

Glossary of Terms 357

FORWARD

My mother told me that a family history (researched and compiled by one of her relatives) revealed that many of my ancestors fought in the armed forces of the United States, going back at least to the Revolutionary War. In more recent generations, Pvt. Richard Dey, a great-great grandfather on my mother's side, fought in the Union Army during the Civil War. He belonged to Company C, 39th Regiment, New Jersey Volunteer Infantry, 1st Brigade, 21 Division, 9th Army Corps, which was mustered in to U.S. service on October 8, 1864 in Newark. Company C was commanded by Captain Edwin W. Hedges and the Regimental Commander was Colonel Abram C. Wildrick, according to a family document. The 39th Regiment fought in the bloody Petersburg Virginia Campaign, under General Ulysses S. Grant, in April 1865. Pvt. Dey participated in the pursuit of The Army of Northern Virginia when it retreated from Petersburg and he may have witnessed General Robert E. Lee's surrender, because his regiment was at the Appomattox Courthouse. This information was gleaned from historical records, but we have no information which came directly from Private Richard Dey. A note in Grandmother Andrews' handwriting which is attached to an old military blanket indicates that her father (my Great-grandfather Dey) also served a hitch in the U.S. Army, probably in the 1880s.

My maternal grandfather, Elmer F. Andrews enlisted in the Army during WWI and attained the rank of Master Sergeant. He detested his given name and was known to all his friends as "Andy". Andy Andrews entered the Army on May 8, 1917 and spent most of his enlistment in a Texas training camp, eventually serving as the Regimental Supply Sergeant for the 57th Infantry Regiment. I have a ceramic dish he owned marked "Logan Rifles", suggesting that he was stationed at Camp Logan, in what is now Houston. This is consistent with an inscription on his grave marker indicating that he was in the 15th Division, which was based at Camp Logan during

WWI and demobilized in February 1919, the same month/year he was discharged. He was proud of his military service, but I don't know very much about his experiences in the Army. My Grandfather Andrews was delighted when I enlisted in the Army, shortly before he died in 1968. He told me, "You will get back from the Army exactly what you put into it. If you make no effort, you will get nothing back. But if you make a maximum effort, you will be rewarded by your Army experience for the rest of your life." Part of my grandfather's joy with my Army enlistment arose from him gaining a big point in the ongoing competition between him and his son-in-law (my father) about the merits of the Army vs. the Marine Corps.

Andy's wife, my Grandmother Andrews, lost her older brother, Claude M. Dey, in The Great War. "Nana" Andrews worshipped her big brother and never fully recovered from his death. When WWI started, Claude enlisted in the Marine Corps. He was killed in action as a USMC Corporal on 6 June 1918, in the Battle of Belleau Woods. We have his medals and two lithographed certificates from the Marine Corps, but we don't really know anything about Great Uncle Claude's military experiences.

My other grandfather, Thomas E. Dolan, Sr., was promoted to General Foreman of the Blast Furnace Department at Republic Steel (later Bethlehem Steel Corporation) at the age of 21 in 1913. His civilian job was considered to be essential to the war effort, so he was assigned an occupational deferment which prohibited his entry into military service. One of his brothers, my Great Uncle Dan, enlisted in the Army and was sent overseas during WWI. In one of my Grandfather Dolan's favorite stories, he described a large family dinner which was held at his home on a major holiday in 1918. His oldest son, my Uncle Pat, was a toddler and he was just learning to speak in complete sentences. Pat was seated at the table in his high chair, surrounded by a crowd of adult relatives. Daniel Dolan was Patrick's favorite uncle and someone asked him, "What are you going to say to the Kaiser, when your Uncle Dan captures him?"

The Mad Fragger and Me

Little Pat thought for a moment and responded, "I'm going to say, 'Goddamn and that's good for you, you son of a bitch'", using perfect pronunciation and inflection. All the adult relatives were horrified, delighting my grandfather. I have a doughboy helmet which belonged to Great Uncle Dan, but I don't know anything at all about his wartime adventures.

Another Great Uncle, John Fox, aka "Unc", Grandmother Dolan's brother, fought as an Army Infantry sergeant in WWI and he was severely wounded by mustard gas. He was also bayoneted in the leg by a German soldier, who Unc then killed with his .45 sidearm. As an Army enlisted man, he boxed against Gene Tunney, later World Heavyweight Champion, who was representing the Marine Corps in an inter-service competition. Needless to say, Unc lost that match, knocked out in the third round according to family legend. Unc was discharged after WWI, but he was a true warrior, so he reenlisted in the Army to also fight in WWII. I wish I knew more about Unc's military history, but that part of the family is now gone. He must have been pretty tough to go even one round with Gene Tunney.

My father's military history is better known, because he was an inveterate story-teller. Thomas Edward Dolan, Jr. dropped out of college after his 3rd year at the University of Virginia, to enlist in the U.S. Marine Corps. After boot camp at Parris Island, he was assigned to the Philadelphia Navy Yard. While there, he served under Colonel Anthony J. Drexel Biddle, who later was the subject of a 1967 Walt Disney movie, *The Happiest Millionaire*. Colonel Biddle, about 69 years old when Dad knew him, was an eccentric Philadelphia socialite. He was an expert on various methods of unarmed combat, including boxing, jujitsu and French foot fighting. Colonel Biddle developed the USMC methods of knife and bayonet fighting, using predetermined moves similar to fencing techniques for parrying, thrusting, slashing, and stabbing. These methods were described in the USMC manuals on knife and bayonet fighting, which were written by Colonel Biddle. He was famous in the Corps for being a spry elderly officer who demonstrated unarmed combat techniques by lying down on the ground, in front of a youthful marine armed with rifle and bayonet. Colonel Biddle would order the marine to stick him with the bayonet and then toss him head-over-heels when he attempted to comply. Because of Colonel Biddle's influence, my father became interested in knife fighting and seriously trained in it. As a PFC, Dad entered the 1944 All-Navy Bowie Knife Fighting Contest and won the competition. As first prize, he was awarded an autographed copy of a book written by Colonel Biddle, *Do or Die: A Supplemental Manual on Individual Combat*. More significantly, Colonel Biddle obtained a waiver for approval of Dad's application for Officer Candidate School. A waiver was necessary, because my parents had already been married in the Philadelphia Navy Yard's chapel. Married junior officers were not wanted in the Marine Corps because of the high casualty rates for lieutenants in the Pacific Theater. After OCS and commissioning as a 2nd Lieutenant, Dad was sent overseas, first to Guam and then to occupied Japan.

There wasn't any real combat going on in Guam when Dad arrived, but Japanese holdouts occasionally came out of the jungle to take potshots at the Americans. This occurred one day when 2LT Thomas Dolan found himself to be unarmed, so he threw rocks at the sniper. The other marines saw this as a great joke and kidded him endlessly about the incident. Dad's quarters caught fire one night, but his houseboy Yoshiuko "Suki" Watanabe entered the burning building and awakened him, saving his life. The building burned to the ground, so all of my father's uniforms and personal belongings were lost. He was issued some enlisted-men's uniforms as an emergency measure, but officers' insignia were not available. He had a good time for awhile, telling other lieutenants and ensigns to go to hell, whenever they attempted to admonish him for not saluting them. This entertainment came to an end because his commanding officer became tired of the complaints and arranged for special procurement of some lieutenant's bars.

The Mad Fragger and Me

He did some exploring on Guam and one day came upon a dead Japanese soldier in the jungle, whose body was mostly a skeleton. Dad picked up the soldier's rifle, bayonet and helmet and brought them home as souvenirs. The rifle, a Type 99 Arisaka, cleaned up nicely and it proved to be quite accurate. The helmet has the soldier's surname painted inside the back edge in Japanese characters, which translate to "Kodou". An anchor insignia is painted on the front of the helmet, denoting that Private Kodou belonged to the Imperial Japanese Special Naval Landing Force, the so-called Japanese marines. During another exploration in Guam, Dad came upon the ruins of a Shinto temple and he found a ceremonial dagger with a handle which was covered in snakeskin. He later attempted to ship this home, but his footlocker was broken into and the contents were looted, including the dagger.

Lieutenant Dolan was reassigned to Japan, as part of the occupation force. Shortly after his arrival, he was sent to the city of Nagasaki, where he viewed the destruction from the atomic bomb. He made this trip only a short time after the bomb was dropped, traveling alone on a civilian train. He had no idea what the purpose of this tour was, because he was given no clear instructions or explanation for it. Nagasaki was barricaded, but he somehow did not notice the signs forbidding entry and he explored the devastated city on foot. Years later, his civilian doctors suspected that some of his chronic medical problems were probably attributable to radiation exposure in Nagasaki, but Dad never bothered to apply for VA benefits as an "Atomic Veteran".

2LT Dolan was assigned to the War Crimes trials in Japan, which were similar to the Nazi trials at Nuremburg. The defendants were accused war criminals, not POWs. Dad's selection for this duty was based upon his 6' 3" stature. Tall marines were assigned to the war crimes detail, in an effort to impress the prisoners with American superiority. The structure of the courtroom was also intended to intimidate the Japanese war criminals. Military judges were seated behind a long paneled bench, constructed high above the courtroom. When prisoners were brought before them, the accused therefore had to look up at an acute angle to address the judges far above them. Formal courtroom protocol was followed, including a requirement for everyone to rise when the military judges entered. One day when Lieutenant Dolan was OIC of the courtroom guard detail, the judges came in and everyone stood, except one Russian newspaper reporter, who remained slouched in his seat. This display of insolence infuriated Dad, who moved quickly to the reporter, grabbed him by the lapels and forcefully jerked him to his feet. He glared silently at the Russian for a moment, before letting go of his suit jacket. He had not received instructions on how to manage such an incident, so he was afterwards concerned that his rough intervention might be questioned. But there were no repercussions, so my father concluded that his solution to the problem was satisfactory to the judges.

The prisoners were kept in a prison compound, the cell blocks surrounded by a heavy mesh fence topped with barbed wire. The marine guard detachment dreamed up various ways to cause loss of *mentsu* ("face") among the accused war criminals, consistent with boot camp tradition and GI humor. Whenever a marine officer appeared at a cell door, the inmate, regardless of relative rank, was required to post himself at the position of attention, salute crisply and formally report: "SIR! Admiral Tashahari, Damned Imperial Japanese Swabjockey, reports everything shipshape in cell number four, SIR!" Japanese Army officers were self-described as "Damned Imperial Japanese Dogface" during these recitations. Dad enjoyed taking visiting U.S. officers on tours and watching their reactions when the higher ranking Japanese officers reported to him, a mere second lieutenant. Whenever there was a full moon, the prisoners were roused from their beds at midnight and roughly assembled in the prison compound's courtyard for a "Moon Dance". During the Moon Dance ceremony, the Japanese prisoners were required to loudly sing *The Marines Corps Hymn*, which produced a comic effect because many of them did not speak English or pronounce it very

The Mad Fragger and Me

well. On one occasion, an American-educated Japanese officer tried to draw 2LT Dolan into a debate by asking, "How can you persecute us like this, lieutenant?" Dad said it was because they were war criminals. The Japanese officer responded that American troops had done things just as bad as what the Japanese were accused of doing. Dad said, "Maybe, but YOU lost. So that's just tough".

The accused war criminals had been indicted for various atrocities and crimes against humanity. Most notoriously, some members of the Japanese garrison on the island of Chichi Jima were charged with beheading captured American flyers and cannibalizing their livers in a perverted Spirit Warrior ceremony. Dad came to know these Japanese officers, but he said that not all of the inmates were actually war criminals, rather some were guilty only by association. One of these was Major Horie, with whom he became friendly. He described another, Major Matoba, as "insane" and as an authentic war criminal. Major Matoba attempted to escape from the prison compound one night. It took six or seven marines to pull him off the fence and subdue him, because he seemed to be possessed of some form of diabolical superhuman strength. During the struggle, Dad bashed Major Matoba repeatedly in the head with the butt of his M1 Carbine, but he later commented, "It did not seem to bother him very much". Matoba was eventually convicted and hanged. The full story of the Chichi Jima war criminals, including photos, is contained in the book *Flyboys*, by James Bradley, which I highly recommend.

Dad was being transported a long distance over the Pacific Ocean on an aircraft which developed engine trouble, later attributed to sabotage. The plane lost both engines and went down, but the pilot managed to pancake it off the water and bounce it up onto an uninhabited rocky atoll, where it broke apart. Several people were killed and several others were seriously injured. There was an incredible crescendo of noise, chaos and violence when the plane struck the rocks and wrenched apart, baggage and people flying in all directions. This was followed by several seconds of complete silence, then a muffled voice, emanating from under a big pile of rubble and wreckage, incredulously said, "Son of a BITCH!!" Everyone still alive then started laughing. Dad was seriously hurt, with internal injuries which plagued him for the rest of his life. After the rescue of crash survivors, Dad spent considerable time recuperating in a Navy hospital, so his war injuries were well-documented. But he did not apply for disability benefits, because he felt that his injuries were just a small price he paid for the privilege of serving his country.

    Dad's unit acquired several Japanese military trucks, which the enlisted men were allowed to use, to meet their recreational transportation needs. There were other items which were also acquired, above and beyond what was on the unit's property books. They learned that the Navy had received a shipment of propane-powered refrigerators. The Marines clearly needed a few of these refrigerators to keep their beer cold. Dad had his men stencil some phony bumper numbers on one of their trucks. He assembled a small detail of enlisted men and they drove to the Navy warehouse which had received the refrigerators. As they entered the warehouse compound, 2LT Dolan leaned out the window of the truck, so that the guard at the gate could see the lieutenant's bars on his khaki cap and collar. Once inside the warehouse yard, clipboard in hand, he made notations on some forms and put on a show of supervising the loading of several refrigerators onto the truck. They drove out unchallenged and returned to their unit, where they repainted the real bumper numbers on the truck. One of the stolen refrigerators was given to their Navy Chaplain, perhaps to assuage guilty consciences. Later, area USMC units underwent a "strict accountability" inventory. They had to get rid of the refrigerators, Japanese trucks and all other extra acquisitions which were not authorized by the Table of Organization and Equipment. The Japanese army trucks were run off a cliff into the ocean. In the confusion and excitement about the strict inventory, no one remembered to tell the Chaplain to get rid of his refrigerator. Dad rationalized this oversight, commenting that the Chaplain answered to a higher authority than anyone in the Navy.

He also spoke about witnessing a tsunami. The marines were notified that a "tidal wave" was coming, in time to move to high ground. They saw it strike from the top of some cliffs and the view was apparently quite spectacular.

Dad was discharged to the USMC Reserve after WWII, but he was recalled to active duty in 1951 and assigned to Camp Lejeune in North Carolina. 1st Lieutenant Dolan was able to take his growing family with him and although I was only 5 years old, I have a few vivid memories of the trip South, living in Kinston NC and visits to the marine base. While there, 1LT Dolan commanded one of the last segregated USMC units, a motor transport (truck) company. He sometimes referred to his African-American marines as "my night-fighters"... and they reciprocated by referring to him as "The Great White Father". After this stint on active duty, my father returned to reserve status, drilling with a Volunteer Training Unit in Baltimore and attending annual training periods each summer. He retired after 35 years total service, as a lieutenant colonel.

I know almost nothing about the military adventures of my ancestors, except my father. Although my own military history consumed only a few years of my life, those years were vivid and memorable, far outshining other life experiences. I suspect that this was also true for my ancestors who were veterans, but their memories are now lost forever. I initially decided to write this memoir to preserve my experiences, primarily for the benefit of my relatives and descendants, but the project evolved somewhat as it progressed.

In the late 1960s, the network news programs were always full of coverage about the Vietnam War and the campus antiwar demonstrations. I did not have strong feelings about the controversial war, because the opposing arguments were difficult to sort out. There was obvious merit in the notion that the U.S. should refrain from meddling in the political affairs of another sovereign nation, so I did not entirely disagree with the antiwar faction. But antiwar proponents began to lose credibility with me when they dodged the draft, engaged in violent protests, disparaged the military services, insulted our soldiers or abetted the enemy. I was also puzzled by the peaceniks' references to the Vietnam War as "immoral" and "meaningless", as if it was somehow different from other wars. Because of the dubious tactics of the antiwar crowd and the strong tradition of military service within my family, I leaned toward the belief that America's reasons for being in Vietnam were probably honorable. I also recognized the hypocrisy of those who pretended that they were following a higher moral path, by burning their draft cards and running away to Canada. The promotion of lofty moral values was not really the motivation of most draft evaders and radical war protesters. They were really opposed to the *draft*, not to the war, usually because they knew that if they got drafted they might also get killed. Many of them simply did not wish to have their lives interrupted by several years of military service. It was well known that a young man could avoid going in harm's way, but still serve the country honorably, by enlisting for an extra year or two to obtain a noncombatant job in the Army, Navy or Air Force. Joining the Coast Guard, National Guard or Peace Corps were additional options for providing honorable service to our country. But many of the war protesters did not WANT to serve the country in ANY capacity. So to avoid looking like cowards or hedonists and to maintain an illusion of good citizenship, they pretended to be against the Vietnam War on moral grounds. Antiwar activists and Jody-types from the Vietnam era are still doing that and it still irritates me. There were also some folks who got caught up in campus protests because protesting the war was trendy among college students, or because of the social aspects of belonging to a protest group. These people were usually not introspective enough to recognize and acknowledge their true motives, but there were exceptions. 2LT Gerald O'Malley, a friend of mine at Fort Hood, was doing troop duty there before going to Vietnam. One day, O'Malley

The Mad Fragger and Me

told me he had to get a waiver to enter Officer Candidate School, because he had a criminal record. I asked what he had done and Gerry said he was arrested for trespassing in a college ROTC building, protesting against the Vietnam War. Lieutenant O'Malley was a proud and committed Infantry officer, so I asked him why he had been protesting the war. He said it was a great way to meet girls.

I seldom talk very much to friends or family about my war experiences, even though I live with vivid memories of those events every day. My reluctance to talk about it usually extends to other veterans. Vietnam veterans who spent their tours in safe rear areas have often convinced themselves that their war experiences were fraught with hardship and danger, so their war stories always give me the heebie-jeebies. Flights of fantasy by former combat soldiers can be equally cringe-worthy, such as conversations (or memoirs) in which facts and fiction are obviously being used interchangeably. The bleak truth is that combat infantrymen in Vietnam were usually mired in drudgery and violence. We were almost never off duty. We were normally exhausted, sweaty and filthy, from toiling in the cruel tropical climate. Our only creature comforts were those which we could carry on our backs, but we had a more urgent need to carry enough water and ammunition. It is difficult to fully appreciate the primitive nature of our existence, or the mental exhaustion which came from 24/7 combat exposure. The stress of coping with omnipresent booby traps and the frequent casualties from them is hard to for the uninitiated to comprehend. Grunts in Vietnam lived in a different world than the rest of American military forces, one that was exponentially more primeval and violent, but the average person doesn't understand this. This lack of proper context is the reason why I'm not comfortable talking about what I did during the war, except with the soldiers who served alongside me... they know how far we managed to rise above our dismal circumstances, with good humor and strong camaraderie, which is our *real* story. I decided that writing about my experiences might be better than talking, because this would provide some control over context, as well as more influence on the reader's perspective. In doing this, I was determined to stick to the exact truth, without any waffling or embellishment.

The 2013 edition of *The Mad Fragger and Me* was criticized by some reviewers as being too lengthy and detailed. I recognized the validity of that feedback and I revised *TMF&M* accordingly. This 2nd Edition also contains some corrections and morsels of new information. Other reviewers thought I was too harsh in commenting about rear area denizens and other military groups, but I did not significantly change those passages because my original observations were accurate. A few critics gave *TMF&M* low marks because of their own biases, such as antipathy towards commissioned officers. I applaud all reviewers for exercising our right of free expression, which American military veterans have always protected with our service. But to those detractors who just didn't like my point of view or my conclusions, I cheerfully recite my Great-Grandmother Dolan's favorite Irish toast: *Here's to you and here's to me, but if we should ever disagree, then to hell with you and here's to me.*

Some of my experiences so long ago in combat now seem incredible. I was hesitant to describe things which may sound like exaggeration or bragging to folks who were not there, even though they are the truth. Nevertheless, here is my story. This narration begins with a description of my training, because readers should have some understanding of how I learned about military operations and leadership, before I was sent into the Vietnam meat grinder.

CHAPTER 1:

INDUCTION, BASIC COMBAT TRAINING AND ADVANCED INDIVIDUAL TRAINING

I graduated from Mount Saint Mary's College in Emmitsburg, Maryland in 1968, with a BA in English. When I looked for jobs after graduation, it seemed that every potential employer first asked about my draft status and I had been newly reclassified to 1-A after four years of receiving a student draft deferment. Most potential employers told me to come back, after taking care of that problem. I didn't have a specific career goal, so a few years of military experience began to look attractive. I had no interest in trying to finagle a 4-F draft rating, or going to graduate school, or starting a teaching career, or just hoping for a high draft number, which was how most of my friends were dealing with this dilemma. So I decided to just get it over with and I signed up for a two year hitch in the U.S. Army. The enlistment contract included an option to attend Officer Candidate School (OCS), on the strength of my bachelor's degree. Basic Combat Training (BCT) was projected to take 8 weeks, followed by 8 weeks Advanced Individual Training (AIT) and 24 weeks of OCS, provided that I was not "recycled" because of illness or a training injury, for a minimum total of 10 months as an enlisted man. If I was successful in completing OCS, I agreed to accept a commission as a U.S. Army Reserve Second Lieutenant and to perform two additional years of active duty military service as a commissioned officer, followed by a stint in the inactive reserves, for a total of 6 years active duty and reserve service combined. If I washed out of OCS, I was obligated to serve a total of two years active duty as an enlisted man from the date of original entry on active duty, with the same 6 year total active/reserve commitment.

Tom Dolan

I was inducted at age 22 at Fort Holabird in Dundalk, Maryland, under the Delayed Entry Program, to allow time for the Army to coordinate consecutive dates for my BCT, AIT, and OCS classes. I officially joined the Army for pay purposes on September 9, 1968, but I did not go on active duty until December 27, 1968. As part of the screening process, I had to take the usual physical exam, batteries of Army aptitude/ qualifying tests and I also went for an interview before an OCS screening board at Fort Holabird. The ongoing tradition in my family had been to sign up for the wars and most of my ancestors were ground-pounders. I also knew I was going to do this only once, I saw it as an opportunity for the adventure of a lifetime at government expense, and I did not want to be ashamed later in life of the choices I made. So, what the heck, I enlisted for the Infantry branch, including OCS. On the enlistment contract, I was required to specify 1st, 2nd and 3rd choices for OCS, including one non-combat arm, so I specified Infantry, Artillery and Adjutant General Corps. The Fort Holabird OCS Selection Board was comprised of three officers, one from the Armor branch, one from the Artillery and an Infantry major, who chaired the panel. They asked me predictable interview questions about why I wanted to be an officer, what I thought I could contribute to the Army, and so forth. One of them noticed that I had listed Adjutant General Corps last and he commented that most enlistees put down a non-combat arm as their first OCS choice, asking if I had made a mistake on the form. I told him I really wanted to be in the Infantry and I put down the other two choices only because the recruiter told me I had to. There was a pregnant silence, so I asked if they thought I'd have trouble getting into the Infantry. The war in Vietnam was raging in 1968 and they burst out laughing. I could tell that the Infantry major, who was wearing lots of ribbons and a Combat Infantryman's Badge, was my ally after that. The Selection Board approved my OCS application.

I reported back to Fort Holabird two days after Christmas 1968 and they put a large group of recruits on a train for Fort Dix, New

Jersey. The train ride was exciting, because we were all buzzing with anticipation. There was an element of anxiety too, but I felt like I was embarking on a great adventure. I was right.

I don't remember much about the Reception Station at Fort Dix, except that there was a lot of yelling and very little sleep, apparently intended to disorient us. One young kid started whimpering and crying for his momma and they immediately took him out and we never saw him again. They gave us the obligatory shaved heads and some ill-fitting uniforms, still screaming at us the whole time, which was more annoying and tiresome than intimidating. The facilities were primitive, consisting of WWII era "temporary" barracks with peeling paint, but we were not there long before we were sent to our BCT Company. I was assigned my "RA" (Regular Army) number, which was soon replaced by SSAN (Social Security Account Number) as my service number, but I can still rattle off the original one, RA11582555.

Basic Combat Training (BCT) was unremarkable, probably no different for me than it was for the thousands of other guys who went through it. The only hard part about it was the pain involved in getting into really good physical shape. My muscles were sore all the time and my weight dropped from the constant exercise. This seemed to run me down and build me up at the same time. It was winter in New Jersey and with a bunch of guys living in close proximity, we seemed to constantly pass around the same upper respiratory infection (URI) and everyone was usually sick. This didn't result in any slackening of the physical conditioning, however. Over time, I found that I became able to do more pushups and other standard exercises than I ever dreamed possible.

When we were in garrison, we had to negotiate a "horizontal ladder" before going into the mess hall for each meal. This contraption looked the way it sounds. It was a heavy welded steel ladder about 20 feet long which was suspended horizontally 8 feet above and parallel to the ground. Each trainee had to mount a step, grab the first rung overhead and then swing his dead weight to grab the next rung a couple of feet away with the other hand, and so on, to the other end. If a recruit couldn't negotiate the obstacle after a couple of tries, the Drill Sergeant would allow him to go in the mess hall to eat, but he would first have to endure a whole lot of verbal harassment and do many extra pushups. Also, it was very cold and trainees had to develop enough hand strength to negotiate the obstacle while wearing gloves, otherwise skin would be left on the metal rungs. It was harder than it looked and I just couldn't do it at first. I practiced on my own and finally figured out that the horizontal ladder required timing and coordination more than strength. When I got the rhythm down and my hand strength up, it was fairly easy. The point of this wasn't just harassment. The horizontal ladder was part of the Army Physical Training (PT) Test in those days and we all had to be able to negotiate it. The official name of the PT test was the "Physical Combat Proficiency Test", but I don't know of anyone who ever had to negotiate horizontal ladders in combat. To pass the Horizontal Ladder portion of the PT Test, a trainee had to travel a certain minimum number of rungs within a specified time, so each recruit also had to develop the skill of turning around at the end of the ladder and coming back again, to meet the standard. The other PT Test requirement I remember as inordinately difficult was the "150 Yard Man-Carry". On that test, a soldier picked up another man in the Fireman's Carry who was supposedly the same weight (I ALWAYS got someone heavier) and ran with him for 150 yards within a specified time. It too was harder than it sounds. There were a number of other PT Test requirements too, like the "Mile Run" and the "Run, Dodge and Jump", but they weren't as difficult. Other PT testing requirements replaced the Horizontal Ladder and the 150 Yard Man Carry after I completed BCT and AIT.

    There was representative diversity in our company, probably because of the equalizing effects of the draft. One of my platoon buddies was an Asian-Indian kid named Mohammed, who I later bumped into in Vietnam. I also remember a humorous, slightly

The Mad Fragger and Me

eccentric, stocky, round faced, black guy from Baltimore, who was nicknamed "Buddha" because of his physical appearance. (About ten years later, Buddha amazingly landed in my National Guard outfit as a Staff Sergeant.) We also had the stereotypical hillbilly recruit who never showered, until we threatened to throw a blanket over his head in the middle of the night and scrub him down with a long handled brush and a cake of strong yellow G.I. soap. There were a surprising number of guys who were slated for OCS with me. Because of this, our Company Commander, a First Lieutenant Vietnam returnee, came in one night and held an informal OCS briefing and Q&A session. This was helpful, because we were all anxious about it, but nobody had told us anything. Someone asked him how difficult should we expect the OCS program to be? He said that an Officer Candidate *really* had to want to get through it, in order to complete the program. He nailed it.

The training in BCT was so boring that it was mind-numbing. It was mostly about basic military subjects, like rank structure, General Orders, military courtesy, The Code of Conduct, guard mount procedures, dismounted drill, and so forth. The subjects were not very interesting to begin with and the NCO instructors only cared that we passed the Army proficiency tests. They had absolutely no interest in entertaining us while we learned the material. It was also clear that the training was geared to the slowest recruit, because it was simplistic and repetitive. We finally got out to the rifle ranges, where we spent considerable time. I enjoyed the actual shooting, but there was a whole lot of "hurry up and wait", always in bitterly cold weather. We qualified with the old M14 rifle, which I learned to appreciate as a powerful, accurate and reliable weapon. The M16 was still being phased in throughout the Army, but it had a mixed reputation.

I have a vivid memory of miserably standing on a Fort Dix rifle range in a swirling white-out, my fingers and toes freezing, while I tried to eat stone-cold baked beans and boiled hot dogs, covered with snow on a flimsy and disintegrating paper plate. I just read that last sentence again, but it does not begin to describe the misery I felt. On the other hand, I have an equally clear recollection of spending a night at a bivouac site, in a huge canvas squad tent. The tent was lined with double bunks and heated at both ends by gargantuan coal-burning pot bellied stoves, with a blizzard raging outside. The inside of that tent smelled like a herd of camels had been living in it and it was hard to get up in the middle of the night to take my turn on fire watch. But I have never felt as secure and warm and cozy and comfortable as I did when I climbed back up in my bunk and snuggled down into my goose down and feathers GI sleeping bag, listening to the wind and snow howling outside. That was probably the soundest night's sleep I've had in my life.

    I was lucky in being assigned to Drill Sergeant Grooms' platoon in BCT. He was a Staff Sergeant (SSG), slightly less than average height, in his late 20s, very wiry, fit and physically tough. SSG Grooms was a relentless taskmaster, never cutting us any slack, but he always displayed a positive and patient, although stern, disposition. He was very professional in his appearance, military bearing and knowledge. He was the first of a long list of Army NCOs I learned to respect, setting a personal example and strong leadership standard for me to later try to meet as a junior officer. Although he usually kept it carefully concealed, he also had a wry and deadpan sense of humor. This was sometimes displayed through a series of running chants with droll lyrics, about the many merits of *Thunderbird*, a cheap and awful wine. Although Drill Sergeant Grooms was hard on us, we appreciated what he did for us. When we graduated from BCT, the platoon took up a collection and we gave him a half pint of *Thunderbird* wine, with a $100 dollar bill taped to it. That was a lot more money in 1969 than it is now, for example my base pay for a month was about $97. He laughed when he was presented with the half pint of wine, then he turned the bottle over and saw the bill taped to the back. He said, "I can't accept this, you guys will have me in jail". Somebody said it was really for his wife and she deserved a lot more, for putting up with him. So he smiled and put the little bottle in his pocket. I hope he is still alive and well.

On 8 March 1969, SSG Grooms was left behind and I reported to C Company, 2nd Battalion, 1st AIT Brigade, also at Fort Dix, for an additional 8 weeks of Advanced Individual Training as a Light Weapons Infantryman, Military Occupational Specialty (MOS) 11Bravo. There, the cast of characters expanded considerably. My existence was now controlled by three buck-sergeants who ruled the platoon I was in, at least in the barracks. All three sergeants were "Shake 'N Bakes", that is recent graduates of the Army's NCO Academy. They worked hard to do a good job, but their lack of experience sometimes showed. Next up the ladder was Staff Sergeant Coleman, our "Field First Sergeant", who accompanied us to all training, while the buck sergeants stayed behind in garrison doing paperwork. SSG Coleman was an experienced, tough and lanky NCO of indeterminate age. He basically functioned like a Drill Sergeant, but for the whole AIT Company instead of just one platoon. To assist SSG Coleman in the field, which is where we spent most of our time, trainee leaders were appointed. We also had a cadre Training Officer who accompanied us to all training. He was a First Lieutenant and a Vietnam returnee, whose name I unfortunately don't remember. It could have been Arthur Fonzarelli, though, because he was very cool and self-possessed. There was also a cadre Executive Officer, another Vietnam veteran, who was a swashbuckler. Whenever we saw the XO, he was tooling around post in his flashy Jaguar XKE roadster, the top down, with some stunning blond or dazzling brunette next to him. I'm not sure if this sight was good for our morale, or bad for our morale. The Company Orderly Room was presided over by First Sergeant Meños, quickly nicknamed "Meanie", which tells you all you need to know about him. Our Company Commander, 1LT Creston Cathcart did not wear a Combat Infantryman Badge or a unit combat patch on his right shoulder like the other two lieutenants. But he must have been senior to them by date of rank, because he was the CO and they occupied lesser slots. My most clear recollection of Lieutenant Cathcart was his odd gait, slightly bow-legged, with his toes pointed outwards. He walked like a duck.

The intermittent upper respiratory infection from BCT stayed with me into AIT and I couldn't shake it off. I tried to tough it out for quite awhile and I continued going to training, but I finally felt so terrible that I went on Sick Call. The medics treated me with contempt at the Troop Medical Clinic (TMC) on the apparent assumption that everyone who showed up there was goofing off. They gave me some G.I. Gin (wonderful stuff!) for cough and APCs (all purpose capsules, i.e., aspirin) for fever and marked me for regular duty. When I got back to my unit, Meanie Meños saw the Regular Duty notation, which of course confirmed his suspicion that I was malingering. So he gave me a hard time and put me on a crappy extra duty fatigue detail, which was far worse than usual because I felt so miserable. We had an overnight pass the following weekend and I was still sick, so I started taking some antibiotics a doctor had prescribed for my wife. By the time I resumed training on Monday, I was feeling much better. Two days later I received an order to report to the Orderly Room ASAP, where they told me I had an urgent message to report back to the TMC right away. They had taken a throat culture during my first visit to the clinic and the results had come back from the lab showing that I had a serious strep infection. Of course, I was over it by then, no thanks to the Army's medical personnel. This is the flip side to, "Fall out for Sick Call, all you sick, lame and lazy… blind, crippled and crazy!"

The training in AIT involved more potentially useful subjects than BCT, although the slow pace and repetition continued to be annoying. I especially enjoyed the Land Navigation classes and the Communications training, which were very good. I paid close attention in those classes, as I did in First Aid and all weapons training. We were taught basic tactics, like movement formations, field fortifications, fire & maneuver, patrolling, ambush techniques and counter-guerrilla operations, practicing the related techniques in field training areas. We unmasked in the gas chamber, crawled through mud under barbed wire while live machine gun ammo was fired over our heads in a night infiltration course, and we ran confidence/obstacle courses. We spent a lot of time practicing bayonet fighting, while screaming "KILL! KILL! KILL!" which was clearly intended to instill aggression. If we were going to distant training sites, we were sometimes transported in "cattle trucks" as we had been in BCT, but most of the time we force-marched, which built up our legs and wind. A force-march pace was about 4 MPH and actually involved quite a bit of running to catch up, because of the accordion effect which always results from marching in a long column, especially over unpaved terrain. This whipped us into superb physical condition.

We spent a great deal of time learning about infantry weapons and shooting them on multiple ranges. The weather was starting to moderate and I loved the range time. There were three ascending levels of weapons qualification, Marksman, Sharpshooter and Expert. I had already qualified as Expert with the 7.62mm M14 rifle in BCT and I was determined to do the same with all the rest of the infantry weapons. We had begun using M16s in AIT, carrying them everywhere we went. I shot Expert with the M16 rifle and the M60 machine gun, firing near-top of the Company scores with both. I was already a pretty good shot with a rifle, shotgun and pistol before I entered the Army, but on my father's advice I paid very close attention to the NCO instructors. I took careful notes when they taught adjustment of sights, zeroing, effective ranges, trajectories and aiming techniques for all the different weapons. I then focused on doing it all exactly the way they taught it. I qualified as Expert with the hand grenade, by throwing for distance and accuracy. We also fired the M79 grenade launcher, M1911A1 .45 pistol, the M72 LAW, the M2 Browning .50 caliber heavy machine gun and the 90mm & 106mm recoilless rifles, but only for "familiarization". My downfall was record-fire with the Automatic Rifle (AR) which was the M16 in rock 'n roll mode. In practice sessions on the rifle range, we were instructed to "educate" our trigger fingers, to fire short (2 or 3 round) bursts. I again focused on doing everything exactly as the instructors told us to do it, but I couldn't hit anything with the M16 on full auto. Despite my best efforts, I barely qualified as Marksman. Everyone else had exactly the same experience with Automatic Rifle qualification. This convinced me that the M16 was worthless on full auto except at bayonet-fighting distances, so in later Vietnam combat I fired my rifle almost exclusively on semi-automatic.

One soldier in AIT was light years ahead of the rest of us, with regard to military bearing and appearance. I suspect he may have had had some ROTC training, or perhaps personal coaching from a relative who had been in military service. I remember when this trainee reported for a Guard Mount inspection I was also in. He turned out in heavily starched and impeccably tailored fatigues, with pegged pant legs and a cut-down shirt with "military creases". He was wearing jump boots with a blinding spit-shine and his web gear, weapon and everything else were perfect. He was immediately picked as the Guard Mount Supernumerary. This meant that he was released to go back to the barracks on stand-by and he essentially got the night off from guard duty. He was also selected as our Trainee Company Commander and he did a good job in that role. He was a quiet guy, not showy or pretentious, but our Field First Sergeant quickly noticed him. Like Drill Sergeant Grooms in Basic Training, SSG Coleman was an African-American and he took an obvious interest in mentoring this young black soldier, teaching him the nuances of dismounted drill and coaching him in leadership skills.

Toward the end of our AIT cycle, we were taken to a remote area of Fort Dix for Escape and Evasion (E&E) training. We were told that this was new and experimental training, which would include realistic exposure to a simulated North Vietnamese Army (NVA) prison camp. The E&E instructors were burly senior NCOs, supervised by a Captain OIC, who had an Irish surname, like Duffy or

The Mad Fragger and Me

Murphy. They read a training scenario to us, describing how we supposedly became fugitives. The training problem required us to travel on foot through a long wooded area which was bordered by dirt roads, while evading capture by the Aggressor force. The exercise boundaries and the Rules of Engagement were rigged to make it very difficult to avoid being captured. If we were caught by Aggressors, we would be taken to a mock NVA Prison Camp, where we were expected to resist interrogation. The exercise was to be run twice, the first time in daylight and the second time after dark. I traveled several hundred meters in the daylight phase, before I was spotted and challenged, then I surrendered in accord with the Rules of Engagement. I was tied up by cadre, blindfolded and thrown on the back of a 2 ½ ton truck with other trainees for transport to the POW compound. I knew at this point that something was wrong, because we were handled so roughly. When we arrived at the mock POW camp, the violence escalated. We were thrown off the truck, still trussed, a distance of about 5 feet to the hard ground. The E&E cadre cursed us, beating our legs and buttocks with short lengths of heavy rubber garden hose. We were dragged into the prison compound and thrown into a deep sandy pit, which was difficult to climb out of without assistance. Various medieval-style torture machines had been set up to use for "interrogations". They periodically took one of the trainees out of the pit and tortured him under the guise of questioning him. We were supposed to provide only name, rank and serial number, but there wasn't any real information to give up anyway, which made the exercise pointless. The NCOs doing the interrogations were obviously enjoying it too much, i.e., they were a bunch of sadists. They dragged my friend Mike Garber, a mild mannered and inoffensive little guy, out of the pit. They stretched and rolled him over a barrel until he puked and started crying. They also stretched our Trainee Company Commander on a torture rack until he cried and screamed for mercy; we later learned that the SOBs broke his leg.

I almost immediately lost my spectacles, as a result of the tossing and battering I'd received. I felt vulnerable and disoriented because I couldn't see very well, but I could clearly hear my buddies screaming and I became progressively more outraged by the cruelty. With no other real options for resistance, I scrambled out of the pit and ran for it. I managed to squiggle under the barbed wire and out of the compound, but they sent a soldier we derisively called "Drill Corporal" after me. Drill Corporal was a tall and flamboyant soldier of about my age, who did not suffer in the least from low self-esteem. He usually worked as a clerk in our unit Supply Room, but for some reason he went out to training with us that day and he was recruited by the E&E instructors to help them. He caught me about 150 yards from the compound and brought me down with a well executed football tackle. I whupped-up on Drill Corporal pretty good, using my feet, knees, elbows and fists. I don't think I hurt him much, but he was furious that a lowly trainee would attempt to put knots on his head. Several E7s came puffing up and they dragged me back to the POW compound. I was in a rage after the scuffle and no longer cared about consequences, so I tried to hurt everyone within reach. The NCOs manhandled me inside a building, where Captain Duffy/Murphy sternly ordered me to stand at attention. CPT Duffy/Murphy told the NCOs to leave and he spoke to me at length in quiet and jocular tones, asking questions about my upbringing and telling me that my terrible Irish temper was going to be my undoing. I didn't think his comments were amusing and I was shaking uncontrollably, afraid that my voice would betray me if I tried to answer him. I was left alone for awhile and I calmed down somewhat. They put me back in the pit, but no one really messed with me again. I wasn't the only person who lost it. SSG Coleman was trying to disrupt the "training" to the extent possible, by encouraging the trainees and making disparaging comments about the instructors. But he had a grim look on his face and at one point I saw tears in his eyes. I also saw Captain Duffy/Murphy bracing our Training Officer. I am certain that

The Mad Fragger and Me

Lieutenant Fonzie had confronted him about what was going on. The Fonz was standing at attention while the Captain barked at him, but he looked cool as usual and not at all repentant. He tried to intervene for us when we were being treated badly and he obviously did not mind getting chewed out for it. So I filed that memory away in my brain, under "How Infantry Officers Ought to Act". That night, we were required to negotiate the E&E Course again. I still couldn't see because my glasses were long gone but I compensated by teaming up with Mike Garber and a couple of other buddies. We were determined not to be victimized again and we deliberately violated all the Rules of Engagement. We picked up pieces of tree limbs and rocks to use as weapons, then we marched straight through the woods, not trying to evade the Aggressors. Whenever one of them challenged us, we answered him with threats and verbal abuse. There was nothing they could do about it and we knew that we were not recognizable in the darkness.

Somebody filed a complaint with his congressman about this loony training, because an officer later came out to a training area and talked to all of us about the resulting Congressional Inquiry. It was a very ambiguous briefing and nobody could figure out what the officer was trying to tell us. Did the Army expect us to cooperate with the Congressional Inquiry or not? I never heard any more about it. The Escape and Evasion (E&E) training label was later stretched to "Survival, Escape, Resistance and Evasion" (SERE), probably to satisfy the Army's insatiable need for more complex acronyms. I later became aware that students in Special Forces or other elite training had to endure sleep deprivation and water-boarding, plus they were placed in claustrophobic sweat boxes during SERE courses. But those guys volunteered to undergo that treatment and even water-boarding doesn't sound quite as brutal as being beaten with rubber hoses, or tortured on medieval stretching racks until bones broke. SERE training was presumably structured to have some training value. The E&E training at Fort Dix taught me that there were sadistic bullies in the U.S. Army, but there were also righteous leaders like SSG Coleman and 1LT Fonzarelli who tried to take care of their subordinates.

We had completed all training and we were cleaning the barracks, our TA50 gear and weapons for final turn-in, when I got a message from home, informing me that my Grandfather Dolan had died. Following my father's instructions, I asked to see the CO about skipping the graduation parade so I could attend his funeral. Meanie Meños wouldn't let me see Lieutenant Cathcart and he scoffed at my request, implying that the graduation ceremony was more important than my grandfather's funeral; what could I do for him *now,* after all? I was pretty upset about Pop's death, even though he had been wasting away for several years in a nursing home. I couldn't sleep and stayed up all night smoking cigarettes in the stairwell, trying to decide if I should go AWOL to attend the funeral and fantasizing about what I would say to 1SG Meños if I ever found him after OCS. I was still pretty dumb about Army protocol, but I had put the funeral request in writing. At the last minute, they let me go a day early and skip the graduation ceremony. I caught a train to Baltimore and I did make it to the funeral.

Chapter 2:

INFANTRY OFFICER CANDIDATE SCHOOL, FORT BENNING, GEORGIA

After a brief period of leave, I reported for OCS at Fort Benning on 9 May 1969. I flew to Georgia a day early and linked up with several friends who had been in AIT with me at Fort Dix. We pooled resources to get an inexpensive motel room in Columbus and we stayed up late talking about what we thought OCS would be like. There were four of us who shared that room. Six months later, I was the only one who graduated OCS and was commissioned, because the other three had washed out.

The OCS operation was large in those days, to meet the manpower demands of the Vietnam War. The Officer Candidate School consisted of a Student Brigade, comprised of three Battalions. At that time, there were about five OCS Companies in each of the three Battalions. I reported in to Officer Candidate Class Number 37 of 1969 (OC 37-69) in the 97th Company, 9th Student Battalion. There were approximately 150 Officer Candidates in the 97th Company when we started, in 6 Platoons of 25 guys each, assigned alphabetically by last name.

There was mass confusion at the 97th Company when I got out of a cab there, most of it deliberately generated by six Second Lieutenant Tactical Officers, who seemed to be tireless in inflicting unrelenting harassment and punishment. I also remember their uncompromisingly STRAC appearance, with their tailored and heavily starched fatigue uniforms and impeccably spit-shined boots. The harassment started on the lawn outside the three story cinder block building and continued into the stairwells, halls and student rooms. Unlike the verbal abuse from the NCOs in BCT and AIT, there was never any vulgar language used by the "Tacs", but they were far worse than any Drill Sergeant when it came to imposing rigid military discipline and physical punishment in the form of pushups and grass drills. We were supposed to be moving into the barracks and getting squared away the first day, but the Tacs interfered with this process in every way possible, yelling and dropping guys for pushups in all directions. They could actually generate confusion just by walking through the barracks, because we were required to immediately hit a section of bare wall at rigid attention whenever we encountered an officer in a hallway. We had to hit the wall audibly, the source of the "Smack" nickname, by which Tac Officers often addressed us. We quickly learned to produce this sound by slapping the wall with our palms and heels as we snapped to attention. Our heels, buttocks, elbows, shoulders and heads had to be in direct contact with the wall and we were required to look straight ahead. The Tacs would engage in all sorts of antics to make us look at them and when we did, this was called "Eyeballing", a most serious offense which would result in much berating and many pushups. An even more serious offense than Eyeballing was "Skulking", which occurred when a Tac caught a Smack peering at him from around a wall corner or other barrier. Proper Skulking technique required a Smack to keep his head in a defilade position, just sending one eyeball around a corner to watch and pulling it back instantly when a Tac started to turn his head. "Quibbling" was another egregious offense and it occurred whenever a candidate questioned any pronouncement by a Tac Officer. Eyeballing, Skulking and Quibbling were mortal sins, according to OCS doctrine. Our first day in OCS was totally exhausting, as were all the other days during the following six months.

    We were each issued a thick book called "The SOP", or Standard Operating Procedure. This contained incredibly detailed instructions and diagrams about everything in our new world, most notably, in the first days, the uniform expectations and inspection standards for our rooms. For example, our wall lockers had to have certain items on the shelf, arranged a certain way, each a specific number of inches from the front edge and sides. Uniforms on hangers all had to be facing to the left, all laundry tags and staples removed, all buttons buttoned and zippers zipped, khaki uniforms on the left and fatigue uniforms on the right. There could be no loose threads ("ropes") on any uniform. All sleeves had to be displayed as if they were marching forward, kept in place by a horizontal "sleeve board" of specific dimensions, including the height and color of the lettering showing the Officer Candidate's name. Sleeve boards could not be purchased anywhere, nor could the name plaques we were required to hang outside the room door, so we had to fabricate these to SOP specs in the post carpentry shop. The set-up of our beds, desks and bureaus were similarly described in exquisite detail by the SOP. This provided a rich source for the gigs (demerits) the Tacs would hand out liberally in our daily inspections. The SOP also contained information on the numerous OCS regulations, many of which had been contrived for harassment purposes. For example, we had to stop whatever we were doing and stand at attention singing *The Alma Mater*, whenever someone else started to sing that silly song. The Tacs frequently did this in the mess hall to disrupt our meals. The SOP contained detailed information on the demerit system and how they could accrue to become "Class I" and "Class II" offenses, which could only be expunged from a candidate's record by marching "Punishment Tours". The SOP described the disciplinary penalties for getting a ticket from the Military Police, or having a book overdue at the post library, and everything else imaginable. We were told to learn The SOP and abide by it. So we did.

THE ALMA MATER
Far across the Chattahoochee, to the Upatoi,
Stands our loyal Alma Mater, Benning's School for Boys.
Forward ever, backward never, faithfully we strive,
To the ports of embarkation, follow me with pride.
We like it here! We like it here!!
YOU BET YOUR ASS, WE LIKE IT HERE!

Tom Dolan

We had several students in the 97th Company who had been regular Army E6s (Staff Sergeants). A few others were hard-stripe E5s (Sergeants), one of them a former Marine. The rest of us were E2 PVTs or E3 PFCs, but college graduates. We were told that the company was experimental and unusual because it was comprised of mostly college grads. All of us who were below pay grade E5 were given an immediate promotion to Specialist/5. This was done because the uniform maintenance requirements in OCS were so expensive. We started working on our wardrobes immediately, although it took several weeks to get them up to expectations. All fatigue and khaki uniforms were custom tailored, by pegging the baggy pant legs and taking in the shirts to closely fit the torso. The standard printed nylon U.S. Army and name tapes on fatigues were replaced with new embroidered cotton tapes, and "Follow Me" patches were sewn on the left sleeves. Most of us had the flaps on our shirt pockets sewn shut, so the corners would not curl up when sweat began to dissolve the starch. All uniforms had to have HEAVY starch, to the extent that they were as stiff as heavy cardboard and very difficult to get into. Except when we were in field training, we had to 'break starch" - put on a clean fatigue uniform – at least twice each day, to maintain a proper appearance in the fierce Georgia summer heat. Daily laundry runs became a way of life and we found that we had to have at least 15 sets of tailored fatigues to meet daily uniform needs and laundry turn-around. Fatigue uniforms were purchased at the nearby Quartermaster Sales store and taken to the PX Tailor Shop for customizing. We were allowed to use one hip pocket, to carry a wallet. All other pockets had to remain starched shut, flat and empty. Cigarettes and a Zippo lighter were carried in a rigid plastic slip-case inside our shirts. A handkerchief was carried inside the helmet liner, to dust boots or polish brass during the course of the day. Uniforms were expected to present an impeccable appearance throughout the day, especially in cantonment areas or classrooms. Fatigue shirts and pants had to be matched, i.e., equally aged and faded. A slightly darker olive drab shirt worn with more faded fatigue pants (or the reverse) was called a "golf suit", which would inspire harassment and punishment from the Tac duty officer.

We usually wore black helmet liners with fatigues, except during tactical and weapons training, when we wore soft caps or steel helmets with camouflage covers. The black gloss helmet liners had OCS decals on the front and "Follow Me" decals on the sides. They gave us some slightly dinged helmet liners from a prior class for immediate use, but it was understood that these were substandard and had to be replaced ASAP. We took new ones to a civilian auto body shop, to be professionally sanded, gloss painted, and to have the decals applied. We kept them polished to a high shine with Turtle Wax and they were never touched on the outside, because the fingerprints would show. We took them off and put them on by sliding our fingers up the sides of our heads, placing four fingers between the headband and the inside surface. Indoors, they were always carried upright by the inside webbing. If helmet liners were dropped or otherwise scarred, they had to be replaced, so we were very careful with them.

Each Officer Candidate purchased two or more pairs of Corcoran paratrooper boots, which had taller shafts and were made of better leather than the standard-issue combat boots. Jump boots also had enlarged hard leather toe caps which took a better spit shine. Corcoran boots were difficult to break in, but very comfortable when that was accomplished. The boots, including the tongues, were spit-shined daily with Kiwi paste polish, water and cotton balls, to a high gleam. A thin layer of Johnson's Glo-Coat wax was then applied over the spit shine on the heel and toe caps. After a good base of Kiwi polish was established, a new spit shine could be put on in very little time. On both pairs of my Corcorans, so much polish was applied that the decorative holes and stitching across the edge of each toe cap eventually disappeared completely. The jump boots were worn daily and the two pairs were rotated for the benefit of foot health. We were not allowed to walk for the first 18 weeks of OCS. We always had to run everywhere in the "airborne shuffle", even when we were not on duty, and this took a toll on boot soles. When my jump boots were rebuilt by the PX Cobbler Shop towards the end of OCS, I had them double-soled, with sanded and squared edges. They looked like an early version of Earth Shoes, higher in the front than at the heel, very sharp looking and comfortable. Most OCs also had a pair of "boonie boots", worn during field training.

    The time and amount of work that was devoted to uniform and boot maintenance each day could not be avoided. We learned to pay great attention to our appearance and after the first weeks there was no such thing as a slovenly or non-uniform Officer Candidate. The same requirements for attention to detail and high standards of appearance also applied to our living quarters, but we found that we could devise shortcuts and faster ways of getting the multiple jobs done. OCS barracks were deliberately designed and built to maximize the amount of time required to maintain their appearance. The floors were all covered with shiny BLACK linoleum tiles, which had to be cleaned, waxed and buffed to a mirror-like gloss each day. This included floors in all hallways, all rooms and all offices. All the pipes and fittings for the sinks and toilets were made of un-plated solid brass, which were polished daily with Brasso. Tac Officers carried dental mirrors, to inspect under sinks and toilet rims. The floors in the latrines were grouted white ceramic tile, which also required a lot of maintenance. In cases where high maintenance requirements weren't already designed into the building, the slack was picked up by imposing additional requirements. Every new class was expected to redecorate the building's interior. Our Dayroom was completely renovated, to include the construction of a separate room for the pool table, even though only cadre were permitted to use it. Every Tac's office had to be redone to suit that particular 2LT. I was assigned to paint a mural on one cinder block wall of my Tac's office. 2LT Crutchfield wanted a Roman army motif, so I found an illustration of an ancient battle scene in a *National Geographic* magazine at the post library and reproduced it on his wall. This included a life size image of a Roman officer. It turned out well and the cinder blocks gave the acrylic paint a nice texture.

The OCS program was designed to require us to accomplish an overwhelming number of tasks simultaneously in our "spare" time, of which there was none. They threw more requirements at us than it was humanly possible to accomplish and then observed how we handled that, in a state of continuous physical and mental stress. Several guys cracked under the pressure and quit or were removed from the 97th Company. No matter how many requirements the Tacs threw at us, we found ways to get them done. We always had a very long and full training day. We rose early each morning and fell out for PT in the dark, which consisted of "The Daily Dozen" Army exercises and a two mile run around the Airborne Track, across the road from our barracks. We then took care of morning ablutions, put on clean uniforms, had breakfast at 0600, got the barracks ready for daily inspection, stood in-ranks inspection in the company street and then double-timed to training in Infantry Hall or another training site. Sometimes we ran back to the barracks for lunch or a uniform change and we were usually there in the mess hall for dinner, after which our formal training day generally ended, unless we were in the field somewhere. The evening hours were partially spent in maintenance of our quarters and uniforms, but we also had to do a lot of studying to keep up with school academic requirements. Formal study hours were designated from 8-10:30 PM, lights out at 11:00. The academic requirements were stringent and resulted in a number of wash-outs, probably secondary only to dismissals for leadership deficiencies.

We discovered, as the Army intended, that we could accomplish a lot more if we were highly organized and worked in teams. For daily maintenance of the black tile floors, they were first cleaned with dust mops, then with wet mops. As soon as a section of floor dried, one man, equipped with a can of Butchers' Bowling

Alley Wax, a steel mess kit fork and a Zippo would go through the area. He'd pick up a gob of wax with the fork, light it and rapidly scatter the melted wax over the floor with a lateral wrist motion. He was immediately followed by another OC with an electric buffer, who would buff out the still warm wax with a standard buffer brush. The first buffing was followed by a second buffing, using a square piece of wool military blanket under the brush. Then a couple of guys on hands and knees would finish up, buffing by hand with cotton baby diapers moistened with rubbing alcohol, to put on the final high-gloss shine. While this was going on, everyone else stayed out of the way of the work detail. Working in this organized fashion, a floor team could get the job done in a remarkably short time. Periodically, the built-up bowling alley wax had to be stripped, which was a major job. Everyone hustled and we all became adept at each of these tasks. Other work details were set up in a similar fashion whenever possible.

Our plywood footlockers were the only pieces of furniture which were not subject to regular inspection or SOP requirements. The footlockers were where we kept our cigarettes, lighter fluid, boonie boots, cotton balls, Johnson's Glo-Coat, Brasso, Kiwi boot polish, and personal items. The footlockers were not sacrosanct and were checked periodically for pogey-bait or other contraband. One day, for a reason I don't recall, probably for no reason except harassment, our Tac conducted "footlocker drill". He required us to carry our loaded footlockers to the company street and perform the manual-of-arms with them, as if they were M14 rifles: "Right shoulder footlockers! Or-der footlockers!" The loaded footlockers were bulky and heavy, but tossing them around in a mock rifle drill also played havoc with their contents. On another occasion, the 97th Company Tacs held a "bunk drill", as a consequence of some trivial infraction. This required us to take all beds, mattresses, pillows, sheets and blankets up and down the stairs several times. We took the bunks outside and made them up on the lawn, lining them up exactly, the alignment checked by the Tacs with a tape measure and

The Mad Fragger and Me

a stretched length of cord. The Tacs then re-inspected the beds and found them to be unsatisfactory, so we broke them down and took them back to our rooms and made them up again. This was done several times, accompanied by lots of yelling. A key element to this exercise was the very short amount of time they gave us to take the bunks outside, and back inside again. The chaos this produced in the stairwells is impossible to describe. And like everything else, it was done in scorching Georgia heat.

Despite the organizing and coordinating, we were never able to get everything done during the hours available. We had a strict "lights out" deadline each night, but most of us learned to get by on much less sleep than we were accustomed to. I got up in the middle of every night and went to the latrine to polish my boots, write brief letters home and take care of anything else I hadn't gotten to that day. There was always a Tac OD (Officer of the Day) who would roam through the barracks at night trying to catch guys doing this, but he had to get some sleep too and I quickly discovered the hours during which I could turn nocturnal in relative safety.

The TAC Officers were recent OCS graduates who knew all the tricks. A few new Tacs were carefully selected from each graduating class, using unknown but highly effective criteria. The Tac originally assigned to 2nd Platoon was 2LT Crutchfield, but he unfortunately did not complete the cycle with us. "Crutch" always tried to be very stern with us, but he was a genuinely nice guy and it was easy for the clowns in our platoon to crack him up. Crutch was an exception to the norm, because most Tac officers were surly, showed no signs of good humor and were consistently adversarial toward all OCs. A Tac who was unrelentingly hardnosed was known as "Iron Mike". I never saw him smile. He was not my Tactical Officer, but I did many more pushups and grass drills for Iron Mike than I ever did for Crutch. The first thing Iron Mike wanted to know from everyone in the 97th Company was "Who is from Maryland?" Iron Mike's second question was "Do you know anyone who went to Towson State College?" I got special treatment from Iron Mike, because I made the mistake of admitting that my sister Judy, two years younger than me at 21, was a student at Towson State. Iron Mike didn't recognize her name, so I was required to send home for a photo. Judy was always pretty, but her graduation portrait made her look like a drop-dead-gorgeous movie star. Iron Mike required me to carry Judy's glamour photo at all times and to immediately produce it for his inspection upon demand. This put me in very frequent contact with him. My New Best Friend's favorite form of physical torture was grass drills, sometimes called "Up-Downs", so I did a lot of those.

The Tacs constantly gathered information on all of us. Some of this came from their observations and notes. Some of it came from the demerits from daily barracks and in-ranks inspections, or from disciplinary actions, school tests, or training committee feedback. A primary source of information was other Officer Candidates. We rotated student leadership positions, from Squad Leaders to Company Commander, every few days. Each time the student chain of command changed, everyone was required to fill out a "PDOR" form on our outgoing leaders. That was a Personal Deficiency Observation Report, also called a "Bayonet Sheet" for short. There was a little OCS ditty, to the tune of *It's Howdy Doody Time*: "It's PDOR time, it's PDOR time, so get your bayonet shined, it's PDOR time... It's not ability, it's not agility, it's personality, most every time." PDORs had been cunningly designed to ferret out information on everyone's leadership weaknesses. We were required to rate every student leader on multiple leadership attributes, such as "Personal Integrity", "Professional Knowledge", "Leads by Example" and so forth. The diabolical aspect to the PDOR was that all student leaders were listed on the same form, and they had to be ranked numerically from first place to last. First and last places on a rating were justified by a brief description of specific observations. This protocol always resulted in someone being ranked highest and someone being ranked lowest in leadership qualities. Over a period of time, clear patterns and trends emerged

The Mad Fragger and Me

for each individual, not unlike data-driven "Quality Improvement" schemes used years later in the business world. This data was used to "Panel" a group of the lowest ranking Officer Candidates every six weeks, to determine whether they would be retained or dismissed from OCS for leadership deficiencies. The Retention Panel was a board of higher ranking officers, mostly captains, from outside of the OCS company to ensure objectivity. They did a group interview with each referred OC and then "counseled" him one-on-one. They were experts and they really put these candidates through the wringer. I know first-hand, because I was Paneled at the end of the 6th week, for not being sufficiently Forceful/Assertive. This was an entirely valid criticism from my peers and it had resulted from a deliberate effort on my part to maintain a low profile. There was an OCS saying, "Cooperate and Graduate". One of my college friends had attended the Marine Corps' Platoon Leaders' Class, which was a summer program similar to Army OCS; my college buddy told me the best way to get through the PLC program was to never be noticed by the cadre, and to always cooperate with everyone. That sounded logical to me, so that's what I did, resulting in the low PDOR rating for forcefulness. But the humiliation of having to appear before the Retention Panel cured me permanently. Later, my Tac Officer told me I received consistently high Bayonet Sheet evaluations for being Forceful/Assertive, but I needed to work hard on improving my Tact, which was seriously substandard. I didn't really try to do that, but I was not Paneled again. I intuitively knew that Tactfulness wasn't that important for an Infantry officer.

    The daily in-ranks inspections on the company street were stressful. The Tacs were uncanny in smelling out deficiencies. If you had neglected to polish the inside of your brass belt buckle, or the backs of your OCS collar brass, you could be almost certain that the Tac would tell you to take that item off so he could inspect it. During in-ranks inspections we were subject to questioning on any military subject imaginable. If you could not state the maximum effective range of the M60 machine gun, or perfectly recite the Fifth General Order, or answer whatever else the Tac asked, you were going to pay a penalty in demerits and/or pushups. They constantly changed the inspection criteria, at one point instituting a "nickel check". Demerits were assessed to all candidates who could not immediately produce a five cent piece with the specified minting date, e.g. 1962.

If there was a little extra time, the Tacs used in-ranks formations to harass us unmercifully. The Company Street was a 20 foot wide concrete-paved area, bordered by grass on both sides, between our barracks and the 96th Company's building. We were on the Company Street in the broiling sun at noon one day and the Tactical Officer of the Day ordered us to assume the Front Leaning Rest (pushup) position. The Student Company Commander repeatedly asked for permission to "recover" and the Tac kept denying permission. This went on for a long time and despite our superb physical conditioning, we began to wilt in the hot sun. Finally, from the ranks, somebody started singing, "Far across the Chattahoochee, to the Upatoi…" and we all jumped to our feet and sang with him, in accord with The SOP mandate. The Tac OD did not "drop" us again, because he knew someone would start singing *The Alma Mater* again. We learned that we could get away with a lot if we all did it together. What were they really going to do to ALL of us, after all? This aspect of the OCS program was surely intended to reinforce the absolute military need for cohesiveness and teamwork.

"Hang together so we do not hang separately" was a principle which permeated all phases of the OCS program. It became clear that we were expected to break certain rules, but not others. All civilian food ("pogey-bait", or just "pogey") was prohibited in the barracks, but it was an OCS tradition to break this rule by making "Pogey Runs". If we were caught there would be punishment, but they couldn't expel an entire platoon from OCS. Any platoon which did not make a regular Pogey Run was considered to be hopelessly nerdy and lacking in esprit de corps. Pogey Runs were organized and operated in a military manner. Everyone in the platoon had to receive the same food items, to preserve military uniformity, for example each guy might get a cheeseburger, French fries and a Coke. The menu was selected by committee and no concessions were made to someone who preferred root beer, or to an oddball OC who didn't like cheese on his 'burger. Tactical deception was entirely appropriate, because the Tac ODs always tried to catch us in the act. Sometimes a noisy diversion was created at one end of the building to draw the OD's attention, while the pogey-bait was brought in the other end. Pogey Run plans could be simple or complicated, but the key element was not getting caught. (For example, two OCs might run outside with the platoon's heavy steel trash can to empty it, immediately after our mandatory study hours; this was a routine event and not likely to draw attention. They would be met at the dumpster by a couple of candidates' wives, who brought the food at a prearranged time. They'd put the pogey in the empty trash can and double-time back in to the building with it.) Whenever we did a successful Pogey Run, we would leave evidence, maybe a hamburger, or some food wrappers, on our Tac's desk, so he would find it the next morning and know we'd pulled one off. There were no repercussions as long as we were not caught in the act. If a platoon was caught with pogey-bait it would often produce hilarious results, because the Tacs were creative in coming up with punishments. One platoon stupidly got a whole pizza for each guy one night. Everybody knew they had done it, including the Tac OD, because we could smell pepperoni pizza throughout the building. When the OD went to their area to confront them, sentries alerted the platoon and they sailed all the pizza boxes out the windows like frisbees, all over the company lawn. The platoon not only had to pick up the pizzas, but they also spent a couple of hours in the dark on hands and knees, cutting the grass with the little scissors from their sewing kits. Another platoon was caught with hamburgers, fries and milk shakes. There was no air conditioning, so each platoon area had a giant exhaust fan with blades about 6 feet in diameter, behind a heavy mesh screen at the end of the hallway. The Tac OD reversed the exhaust fan's rotation so it was blowing in and he turned it up to high speed. He made the platoon throw all the 'burgers, fries and chocolate shakes into the roaring fan. They were then told to clean up the mess before Lights Out.

    The Tac Officers harassed us all the time, day and night, seven days a week, but the dining room harassment was particularly odious. This started outside the mess hall, which was located on one end of our barracks building. We got in line, at parade rest, coming to attention and moving forward one step at a time, as the line advanced toward the entrance. We were required to do a specified number of pull-ups or push-ups before requesting permission to enter, from a Tac Officer who was standing on the stoop. If he was in the mood for conversation, we sometimes had to undergo mind-blowing interrogations by him. If granted permission to enter, the Smack had to throw open the heavy screen door so it banged loudly against the wall, then speed-walk to the end of the serving line inside, where he went through the parade rest/attention/ parade rest routine as the line advanced. All the other Tacs sat at a long table near the entrance door and if a Candidate didn't bang the door loudly enough, or walk fast enough, they would yell at him to get out of the mess hall. If that happened, he had go out the exit door, run around the building and go through the entry rigmarole again. When a Candidate got his tray of food, he went to a four-man table and stood at attention until an OC was standing behind every chair. The last person to arrive shouted, "Take seats!" and everyone would sit down together. We were required to arrange our tableware in a uniform way on our trays, as specified in The SOP. Except when we were cutting food, only one utensil could be picked up at a time. A Candidate had to put his fork back in its place, after putting food in his mouth, before he could begin chewing. Everyone sat at attention looking straight ahead and there was no talking. When a candidate finished eating, he could leave and someone else could sit down at that place, if other OCs were already seated at the table. Sometimes a Tac came and sat down at a four person table with only 2 or 3 OCs, in which case everyone stopped eating and jumped to attention, as required in The SOP. When the Tac stood up, everyone sat down again, per The SOP. So the Tac would rapidly sit down and stand up repeatedly, to confuse them and provide an excuse for their ejection from the mess hall. The Tacs would roam around the mess hall, looking for people who chewed before putting their forks down, who were Eyeballing, or who committed some other SOP infraction. It was easy for the Tacs to create total pandemonium in the mess hall and they did this occasionally. If the Tacs used up too much time by harassing us, they would declare Pig Privileges. They ran around yelling, "You have Pig Privileges, eat up, eat up, Pig Privileges!" This meant that we had to eat as fast as possible with both hands, shoveling in the food with spoons and forks simultaneously. The Tacs then screamed at individuals to get out of the mess hall, because they were eating too slowly so they must not be hungry. The mess hall harassment was particularly bad during the first 12 weeks of OCS, but we were learning to stick together. During one meal when the Tacs were going too far, an Officer Candidate suddenly shouted, "AIR RAID!!!" One of the Tacs apparently knew what was coming, because he jumped up from the cadre table and ran around yelling, "Negative! No Air Raid! Negative on the Air Raid!", but It was too late. The air raid had been planned in advance and four designated candidates picked up a fifth guy. They held him horizontally above their heads, "flying" him around the mess hall, with his arms spread out to simulate wings, while all five of them made loud airplane and bombing noises. All other candidates "took cover" under the dining tables, shouting and banging the chair legs rapidly on the floor to simulate machine gun fire. The racket and chaos created during this mess hall rebellion were wonderful. We didn't finish eating that meal, but it was worth it. The Tacs continued to harass us in the mess hall after The Great Air Raid, but not as badly.

Planning and carrying out social functions was integral to the OCS program. Two parties were held, at the 12th week and the 18th week, planned entirely by the Officer Candidates. We were to be evaluated on these parties and it was made clear that expectations were high. The 12th Week Party was held in the 97th Company's Day Room and mess hall, which adjoined through double doors. It was basically a semi-formal dance with nonalcoholic refreshments. Committees were formed to plan everything from decorations to music to entertainment. The theme for party decorations was based on *2001-A Space Odyssey* and the results were mind boggling. The Decorations Committee totally transformed the Day Room and created a transitional entry into the mess hall with multicolored transparent plastic sheeting, movie-like props, flashing strobes and psychedelic lighting, so that we really felt like we were entering another dimension. The entertainment included a humorous roasting of our Tac Officers, one of whom did not appreciate being skewered. His angry reaction of course greatly enhanced our appreciation of the jokes about him.

Some guys were not married and could not bring their girlfriends from home, but everyone was expected to attend both the 12th and 18th Week Parties. So a Date Committee was formed of two guys with strong social skills (i.e., our best pick-up artists). They went to area colleges and sororities to recruit blind dates and they also coordinated Army bus transportation. Regardless of a blind date's physical appearance, it was understood that her military escort was expected to be gracious and attentive, treating her like the most desirable female he had ever met. We were in training to be officers and gentlemen, after all, and later OCS classes would also need blind dates from the same colleges and sororities. So the girls were treated like queens and it was obvious that they were having a glorious time. But a candidate would occasionally whisper discreetly into his buddy's ear, "I think you have a winner", or some similar sentiment. This was because another OCS tradition required us to establish a Pig Pool. Everyone kicked in two bucks prior to the party and a vote was taken afterwards. The guy with the ugliest date won the pot. An OCS Urban Legend was that the Pig Pool in another company was won by a married candidate who came with his wife. Officers and gentlemen were expected to be completely honest at all times, you know, including Pig Pool voting.

The 18th Week Party was held at the Fort Benning Officers' Club. It was an elegant old-fashioned facility built in 1934, so elaborate decorations were not required. That party, too, was meticulously planned and executed. The Commanding Officer of the Candidate Brigade was a courtly geezer named Colonel Robert Piper, of the "Piper Cub" family, and he was our guest of honor. Colonel Piper was known to love chain-dancing to *The Saints Come Marching In*, so we did that throughout the entire Officers' Club, up and down the stairs and around the balustrades, laying on plenty of FE (False Enthusiasm) in the process. This pandering to Colonel Piper was so blatant and so wildly exaggerated that it became a parody of itself and a hilarious entertainment in its own right. The highlight of our 18th Week Party was a lengthy slide show with sound track, which was featured as the main entertainment. Candidate David Greene had worked as a professional photographer for *National Geographic* and he always carried a big Nikon 35mm SLR everywhere with him. Dave made a comprehensive photographic record of our company's training, spanning the 6 months of OCS. The slide show was supplemented by a sound track of our marching sounds, which was recorded with a portable tape deck. We had two excellent bass and snare drummers, plus a superb baritone cadence caller. Candidate Bill Dawson had been a high school music teacher and he wrote two really punchy 97th Company marching songs, one of them to the tune of Perry Como's *Round and Round*: "Follow me, follow me, I am the In-fan-try, Queen of Battle, 97th Com-pan-y... Follow me, follow me, it's on courage we stand, to protect our nation's homeland..." Each subsequent stanza contained references to the Infantry throughout U.S. history: "Follow me, follow me, we pushed with wagon trains, led an empire far across the western plains"... and so forth. While marching, we would often harmonize between platoons, with songs like *Johnnie Comes Marching Home*. We sounded like a well-rehearsed professional choir. The slide show and the sound track were outstanding.

The OCS program was divided into three distinct phases. The first 12 weeks we were "Basic" candidates, so this was when the most intense harassment occurred. More guys quit or were dropped during this phase than the others, but attrition continued throughout the program. There was no time off during the Basic phase and we were harassed around the clock, 7 days a week, with only one memorable exception. We were told toward the end of the Basic phase that we were going on a bivouac and that we were to fall out the next morning with "full field pack". This included all field equipment, including shelter-half, tent stakes, sleeping bag, air mattress, mess kit, canteen, full web gear, pack, helmet, C-rations, bayonet and our heavy M14 rifles. The next morning, there was the usual torment during the in-ranks inspection. When we started marching out, we knew we were in trouble because 4 or 5 jeep field ambulances pulled in behind us. The Tac OD ordered us to double-time and he ran us all the way out past the Fort Benning airfield, then for miles down a road that parallels the Chattahoochee River. It was July in Georgia and the temperature was about 100°, with 90%+ humidity. We ran the whole way, carrying all that equipment, and we didn't stop for a break at all. Several guys fell out with heat injuries, the medics picking them up along the road. I stubbornly decided I wasn't going to quit, no matter what, and I got my mind in that zone. The Tac duty officer wasn't carrying anything except a pistol belt and canteen, but his heavily starched uniform became drenched with sweat and towards the end of the run he began to look like he wasn't going to make it. It was by far the worst forced march I've ever been on, but we eventually turned off the hardball onto a dirt road, then into a pretty little shady campsite next to the Chattahoochee River, where the rest of the Tacs were waiting. We each partnered with another candidate, making sure we both had either buttons or snaps (older veterans know what I'm talking about) to set up our tents and blow up air mattresses. The harassment continued, with the Tacs stretching commo wire and breaking out tape measures, making us move our pup tents because they weren't exactly in line, or equal distances apart. But the harassment took on a jovial tone and we began to think that maybe we were there to have a good time. The Tacs found a dead tadpole and made us concoct an elaborate ceremony to give it a "burial at sea" in the Chattahoochee with full military honors. After the tadpole's burial, the harassment ceased and the Tac Officers disappeared. We slathered on mosquito repellant, heated up some C-rations and had a fine time relaxing and camping out. That was the only break we ever got during the Basic phase.

After the 12th Week Party, we were given an overnight off-post pass, from Saturday afternoon until noon on Sunday. That was the first actual day off we'd had in 3 months! At the 12th week interval, we "turned Black", entering the second OCS phase. Intermediate Candidates were distinguished by the black felt tabs we began wearing under our OCS collar brass. The harassment diminished only slightly and we gained a few carefully delineated "privileges", but the Intermediate phase wasn't really very different from the Basic phase. "Black" status was essentially something the Tacs could take away from us, at the same time revoking the nominal privileges, which they did regularly. When we turned Black, we began to get an occasional overnight pass on Saturdays. One Saturday afternoon, we were standing on the company street dressed in fresh khaki uniforms, anxious to be released to go into Columbus. The Tactical Officer of the Day came out and told us to change back into fatigues. He announced that all overnight passes had been cancelled, because "Candidate Gibbons engaged in an unauthorized public display of affection with his wife". This alleged act of indiscretion had occurred outside the OCS barracks, after the Tuesday evening Family Visiting Hour. Bob Gibbons' wife, Penny, was a former professional model who was shapely and striking in appearance, so I had an instant mental vision of Gibbons suddenly losing control, throwing Penny down on the company lawn and ravishing her. Candidate Gibbons was a hard-nosed former Staff Sergeant and he immediately erupted, forcefully demanding an explanation from the Officer of the Day. Gibbons did this so loudly and so assertively that it visibly shook the Tac Officer's composure, which the rest of us greatly appreciated. It was then revealed that a Tactical Officer had seen Bob grasp Penny's arm, when he escorted her across the street to her car after the visiting hour. So much for Intermediate Candidate "privileges".

We "turned blue" or gained Senior Candidate status at the 18th week. We began wearing "infantry blue" felt tabs under our OCS collar brass and dorky looking white neck ascots with embroidered OCS logos. Actual privileges went with Senior status. The mess hall harassment stopped and we were permitted to walk when we went to the barber shop or PX, instead of always running everywhere. We still had to keep a sharp eye out for officers, even in their cars, and render a sharp salute to each. The officers' cars had blue parking stickers on the right front bumper and the enlisted men's were red. A crisp salute was rendered and held until it was returned, to every car with a blue sticker. Sometimes we were saluting an officer's wife or teenage kid, but that didn't matter, because the driver might be a WAC in mufti or a young looking 2LT. Some of the younger officers' wives waved at us or clumsily returned our salutes, which was always cute and funny.

Senior Officer Candidates were expected to bring instant smoke on any junior OCs who were slovenly in appearance or otherwise substandard. After 18 weeks on the receiving end, we knew how to do that. We were sometimes assigned to supervise lower level OCs, particularly in marching Sunday Punishment Tours. The candidates receiving punishment were usually guys who were on the ropes due to demerits accruing to higher class disciplinary violations, sometimes on the threshold of being bounced from the program. We put them through a very rigid inspection of their uniforms and weapons. If they passed inspection, they were required to march each Tour on the concrete company street of a vacant OCS barrack. They marched from one end to the other at a rapid Quick Time, their weapons at Right-Shoulder Arms. At the end of the street, they halted, smartly executed Order Arms, then About Face and Right-Shoulder Arms. Then they sharply marched back to the other end of the street. They continued to do the same thing, over and over again. Each Punishment Tour was 55 minutes. An Officer Candidate receiving punishment often had to march several Tours on the same day. They were given a 5 minute break between each Tour, during which they were allowed to stand in any available shade and drink warm water from their canteens. In the scorching summer months, marching Tours was true discipline, no doubt far exceeding the legal definition of "cruel and unusual punishment".

As noted previously, the Tacs were continually adversarial and demanding, but we began to find little ways to get back at them without incurring too much of their wrath. For example, one nice guy in our company was a quiet OC named John Whipple. Whenever something got screwed up, the guys in his platoon started kidding him by attributing it to "The Whipple Effect" and the rest of us picked it up. This was just a silly inside joke among the candidates, but a Tac overheard some OCs talking about The Whipple Effect, stimulating his curiosity. Everyone clammed up and played dumb when questioned, which of course created an impression that The Whipple Effect was a lot more significant than it really was. After that, The Whipple Effect was regularly mentioned within earshot of the Tacs, in a variety of confusing circumstances so they could not deduce its meaning, which was really *nothing*. The brief but notorious OCS career of Candidate Crenshaw provides another example of scant revenge by OCs. We had guys leaving regularly because they quit or were kicked out, but also new guys coming in, which sometimes made it hard to keep the company roster straight. The new guys usually had been put back in training from other OCS companies because of illness or injuries. Candidate Crenshaw was a recycled OC whose orders got changed, so he briefly appeared on the 97th Company's Morning Report, but he never really showed up in person. The cadre First Sergeant knew this, of course. Student leaders also were immediately aware because of the emphasis on accountability, but it was quickly noticed that the Tacs did not realize that Crenshaw was a ghost. So for several days, we were able to blame Candidate Crenshaw for everything that went wrong or didn't get done. Why wasn't the grass cut? "Sir, Candidate Crenshaw was in charge of the grass cutting detail". When the Tac OD then asked "Where is Candidate Crenshaw?" someone shouted out from the ranks that he had an appointment with the Chaplain, or he was at Post Finance taking care of an allotment for his wife, or something like that. When the Tacs finally figured it out, they didn't want to admit we'd gotten away with stringing them along, so there were no repercussions.

Bill Borah was a classmate in the 97th Company. We both had red hair and about the same complexion. We were the same age/height/weight/build and we both wore glasses. We could have passed for twin brothers, although not identical ones. There was a very tall Tac Officer in 97th Company who was nicknamed "Lurch", because his uneven gait resembled that of the butler character on *The Addams Family* TV show. Lurch could not tell us apart. He regularly addressed me as "Candidate Borah" and just as often he referred to Bill as "Candidate Dolan". At first we gave our correct names whenever Lurch did this, but then we started reporting to him using the other guy's name, to confuse him. He'd call me over as "Borah" and I'd say, "Sir, Candidate Borah reports". One time I did this and Lurch looked at my name tape, catching me in the deception, so I said, "Sir, Candidate Dolan did not wish to contradict the Tactical Officer, Sir!" I then did a lot of pushups, of course. This game seemed to pique Lurch's interest in actually figuring out which of us was which, so he began to call one of us over to him regularly, apparently to see if he got the name right. The first thing he'd then do is look at the shirt's name tape. So one day when Lurch was duty officer, my doppelganger and I traded fatigue shirts to further confound him. (Lurch, aka Lieutenant Neil Hayes, was killed in action on 22 May 1970, at age 24 in Quang Ngai Province, Vietnam, while assigned to 198th Light Infantry Brigade, Americal Division.)

The training in OCS was generally excellent. All formal training was done by various Infantry School "Committees". We received instruction in Hand-to-Hand Combat, Bayonet Fighting, Physical Training and some tactical subjects such as Ambush, Raid and Patrol techniques, from The Ranger Committee, always outdoors. The Ranger Committee also put us through the obstacle and confidence courses. The Ranger Physical Training classes were geared toward teaching us how to instruct and lead P.T. with troops. It also included unusual exercises, such as "Log Drills", group weight training using telephone poles. There were other discrete Infantry School Committees for subjects such as Land Navigation, Weapons, Leadership, Communications and Tactics. Most classroom instruction was given in Infantry Hall, which was a huge air conditioned building that served as the instructional and administrative hub of The Infantry School. The classrooms there were auditorium style, with 200 or more comfortable seats arranged in tiers and a wide stage in the front. There were all sorts of projectors, drop-down screens and large TVs mounted on the side walls... very high tech classroom equipment, circa 1969.

One Sunday, we were told that we were being taken to Camp Darby for a special Ranger training indoctrination. Camp Darby was the location where the Ranger Confidence Course and their rappelling towers were located. I've always been afraid of heights because my balance was poor, so some of this training represented a special challenge for me. I did not mind the rappelling too much, after I got up the gumption to make a first attempt, because I had ropes to hold on to. We rappelled down a 40 foot wooden wall and we also rappelled out of a fixed helicopter mock-up. The "Slide for Life" also involved height. Trainees were suspended by hanging from an inverted "T" bar attached to a roller-block under a long cable which ran from a high tower to a lower fixed point across a pond. The contraption went pretty fast and riders lifted their legs to a horizontal position and let go, slamming into the water butt-first before they hit the far bank. I had the bar to hold onto and I could swim pretty well, so the Slide for Life was not too scary. But there was another obstacle which took every bit of my willpower to negotiate. It featured three telephone poles set vertically into the ground, equal distances apart. Two additional telephone poles were laid horizontally on top of the upright poles. A 2x4 was nailed across the top of the horizontal poles to provide flat footing. Halfway across the horizontal poles there were 3 steps up to a very narrow platform, then 3 steps down. There was hard ground under the lateral telephone poles. The 3rd upright pole was set at the edge of a pond, with a cable running horizontally from it over the water to another vertical telephone pole. A large Ranger tab mock-up hung from the middle of the cable. We climbed up the pole farthest from the water, using spike steps which projected from both sides. We then had to get up on top somehow, stand up, balance ourselves, walk across the top of the 1st horizontal pole, negotiate the steps, walk across the 2nd horizontal pole, grab the cable and monkey-crawl out to the Ranger tab. Students then hung from the cable by both arms, slapped the tab and requested permission to drop. When the Ranger instructor said "Drop", we'd let go, dropping into the water 20 feet below, then swim to shore wearing fatigues and boots. The worst part of this was walking across the wobbly horizontal poles over dry land, because if we fell, there was no doubt that we would be seriously injured or killed. While a student was trying to walk across the horizontal poles, someone was climbing the first vertical pole behind him and someone else was crawling out on the cable, which caused the whole apparatus to sway and shake. This thing was truly dangerous and worse than my worst nightmare. Nevertheless, I somehow managed to climb up the first pole, get on top, and walk across, giddy with fear and vertigo the whole time. After that, monkey-crawling out on the cable, dropping in the water and swimming to shore was easy. One guy in our company chickened out of negotiating this obstacle, but this was extra/voluntary training and he was not required to do it.

OCS companies were on the march or running throughout the central post area all day, every day. OCS companies were exempt from the "Category IV" heat restrictions, which routinely curtailed all running and modified outdoor training activities for the other schools at Fort Benning. When a Cat IV was called, all other trainees un-bloused their boots, pulled out their shirt tails and walked at route-step. OCS companies just drove on, tightly uniformed as usual, no matter how hot the weather became. The Senior OCS companies all marched with complete precision like very sharp drill teams, usually with drummers. The Intermediate and Basic companies looked good double-timing around post too, because they also strived for perfection. OCS companies therefore always stood a very visible cut above all other troops at Fort Benning. We held daily evening Retreat formations on the 9th Battalion Street and there were occasional Command Retreat ceremonies on the Fort Benning Parade Field. For the latter, we carried M14s and wore starched khakis with bloused jump boots and white gloves. Command Retreat also featured the post band playing martial music, plus a reviewing stand filled with wives and military dignitaries. Command Retreat was always carried out with great ceremonial detail and perfection.

Our tactical training in OCS culminated in a field training exercise called "Ranger Week". We were warned that this would be an ordeal and we should prepare ourselves mentally for that. We would be pushed to the limits of physical endurance and we needed to take an absolute minimum of field equipment with us, leaving behind shelter halves, sleeping bags and air mattresses. Ranger Week was supposed to give us an opportunity to apply the patrol, raid, ambush and night defensive techniques we had been taught, but it was really a seven day long practical exercise in exhaustion, protracted misery and sleep/ food deprivation. There were a few officers on the Ranger Committee, but most of the instructors were NCOs. A key technique we used to keep the Rangers happy was False Enthusiasm, but everyone ran out of FE by the end of Ranger Week. We were issued only one C-Ration meal each day, which we ate cold when we could find time. We got maybe an hour of sleep at a time, two or three times in each 24 hour period. It was also beginning to get quite cold at night. Sleep and food deprivation, in combination with physical discomfort, is amazingly effective in producing exhaustion, stress and disorientation, so the evaluators could observe how well we functioned under extreme duress. We were continually on the move, or digging in with our entrenching tools, then moving again, because the Ranger controllers with us carried radios and they constantly told the Aggressors exactly where we were located. As soon as we got a defensive position set up, an Aggressor jeep would drive through our perimeter, with Rangers firing blanks from a swivel-mounted M60 machine gun, throwing artillery simulators and tear gas. We would then have to move in the dark to our rally points, get a head count and move to a new night defensive position, where the same thing would happen again as soon as we were dug in. This became very frustrating, adding to the other stresses. Our student leaders got practice in land navigation and we did plenty of tactical movement, but that was about it for actual training value. After a few days of this, exhaustion took over and tempers flared. The Rangers on foot with us worked in shifts, so it was not so exhausting for them, and the other Rangers were riding around in gun jeeps, probably also working in shifts. They did not play fairly. For example if we managed to ambush a gun jeep, the Rangers would just drive through the ambush shooting blanks, instead of properly playing dead. This of course offended our sense of justice and propriety. So when the pattern had been well established and the Rangers steered us into an NDP right next to a dirt road, we knew what was coming and the direction it would be coming from. We sent out a patrol carrying their entrenching tools, but the Ranger cadre who were with us did not notice the shovels. The patrol dug a hasty vehicle trap which spanned part of the dirt road and camouflaged it with natural materials. When the gun jeep later came ripping down the road, it hit the trap and turned over, throwing Rangers all over the woods. The jeep was wrecked, some of the Rangers were hurt and all of them were really, really angry about this. But at that point we did not care and in fact, we thought it was rather amusing. Ranger Week could have been good training in small unit tactics, and just as tough, if it had been planned and executed slightly differently. But as it was, it was a week-long endurance test, with extra training in how to be miserable.

Tall tales told by older OCS graduates always alleged that "The *Old* Program" from the 1950s was so impossibly tough that none of us 1960s softies would have survived it. Despite those yarns, the Vietnam-era 24 week Officer Candidate School was the most grueling officers' training program ever run by the U.S. Army, as demonstrated by its 6 month duration and the extremely high attrition rate. The Army's later decision to reduce the length and difficulty of the Infantry OCS program was a poor one, because the high standards were also downgraded. The remnant Officer Candidate School is now only 12 weeks long and it is "branch immaterial", meaning that graduates must also attend Infantry Officers' Basic Course, or a similar MOS school. This also resurrected the WWII label of "Ninety Day Wonders", the original length of the OCS course in the 1940s.

By the end of the cycle, I no longer knew everyone in the company, because we received so many replacements in the final weeks. Our company attrition rate was around 50%, which was apparently normal, but as a result of "recycles" joining our company, 147 graduated in the end. Most of the classmates I knew were terrific guys, radically better than the scruffy pot heads and war protesters who seemed to dominate the youth "culture" in the late 1960s. In August 1969, while we Infantry Officer Candidates of

OC 37-69 were about half way through six grueling months of incredibly stressful leadership training in the scorching Georgia heat, drug addled dropouts of our age were skinny dipping and frolicking at the Woodstock music orgy. Yet the liberal media still gushes in admiration when they reminisce about the antics of the spaced-out attendees of the Woodstock rock concert, while simultaneously condemning the "immoral" or "meaningless" war in Vietnam, and by extension and inference, its participants. Go figure.

I invited my father to attend OCS Graduation, to personally swear me in as a U.S. Army officer, which was permitted because he was a Lieutenant Colonel in the USMC Reserve. He was thrilled at this invitation, lost about 30 pounds so he'd look good in uniform, and drove down to Fort Benning to swear me in. This is the oath Dad administered to me on the morning of 5 November 1969: "I, Thomas E. Dolan 3rd, do solemnly swear that I will support and defend the Constitution of the United States, against all enemies, foreign and domestic; that I will bear true faith and allegiance to the same; that I take this obligation freely, without any mental reservation or purpose of evasion; and that I will well and faithfully discharge the duties of the office on which I am about to enter. So help me God." I took this oath seriously then and I still do. Please note that it has no expiration date.

The Infantry OCS program at Fort Benning was extremely well designed, organized and operated. It was much more intense, focused and effective than any other training course I've ever taken. Completing it was one of the most arduous and difficult things I've ever done. In six stressful months, it gave me a good start in my transformation into a professional military officer. OCS did not equip its graduates to manage battalions, brigades or divisions, but it taught us the basic skills we needed to become company-level leaders. With the addition of actual experience in pushing troops and guidance from experienced mentors, most of us would soon become fully qualified to lead soldiers in combat.

Chapter 3:

TROOP DUTY IN THE SECOND ARMORED DIVISION, FORT HOOD, TEXAS

All newly fledged 2LTs were assigned to perform a 6 to 9 month period of "Troop Duty", which was intended to reinforce the theoretic principles taught in leadership classes at Officer Candidate School, ROTC and West Point. I was assigned to the 2nd Armored Division/"Hell On Wheels" for my Troop Duty. Following a period of leave, I drove to Killeen, Texas with my wife Suzanne, pulling all our belongings in a U-Haul cargo trailer behind our '66 Mustang coupe. We went earlier than my due date, because I had been warned that on-post housing was not available at Fort Hood for married junior officers and civilian apartments were scarce. That information proved to be accurate. We checked in to a cheap motel and began our housing search at the Post Housing Office. They were not at all helpful, so we began searching classified ads for rentals in Killeen and surrounding communities. Nothing was available. This went on for several days. In desperation, we began driving around, looking for rental signs. There were none of those either, but while driving through a residential area, we saw a small sign, which said "Orville Bay, Realtor". I knocked on the door and, eureka, yes, Mr. Bay knew of an available one bedroom apartment in Killeen. It turned out to be modern, clean and affordable. We moved in, had the utilities turned on and I checked in to my new unit, 2nd Battalion, 41st Infantry (Mechanized) on 1 December 1969.

I was initially assigned as a Liaison Officer at 2/41 Infantry Battalion HQ, which I hated. There was nothing meaningful for me to do, so they gave me busy work, researching and writing the unit history, among other things. I was assigned to teach a number of classes in the battalion classroom on contrived and boring subjects, for unduly long periods of time. I was also sent to untangle a range-guard fiasco out in the post impact area, which was an ordeal lasting for several days. I was stressed out and miserable during my first month with 2/41 Infantry.

After about a month of busy work at battalion HQ, a line slot opened up and I was reassigned to Charlie Company as a platoon leader. In addition to about 40 soldiers, I was responsible for the care and maintenance of four M113 armored personnel carriers (APCs) or "tracks". Three of my vehicles were the older gasoline powered M113s, while the fourth was a diesel-powered M113A1. I was required to sign a hand-receipt for the four APCs and all related equipment, such as radios, .50 caliber machine guns, pioneer tools and mechanics' tool sets. Two out of my four E5 Squad Leaders were short-timers, combat veterans who were waiting for discharge; two had re-upped and were considering Army careers. Each of them was required to sign secondary hand-receipts for one M113 and a complete set of accessories, but this did not entirely relieve me of responsibility. Keeping track of all that stuff was a never-ending headache. Pilferage of mechanics' tools was especially a problem, with APC crews often stealing from each other to cover shortages. A common trick was to replace Army-issued tools with cheap Taiwanese knock offs and the high quality government tools sometimes disappeared into personal tool boxes. The TO&E only specified "Adjustable Wrench, 12 Inch, One Each", so a pot metal copy of a *Crescent* wrench would pass muster when tools were inventoried. Maintenance of the tracked vehicles was difficult because of inadequate manpower resources. We had a limited number of automotive mechanics who were assigned to the Motor Pool's Maintenance Platoon, but they were not highly motivated. Most routine maintenance work fell on infantrymen, who usually had no significant mechanical knowledge. I'd had only one day of maintenance training in OCS, but it was limited to inspection techniques, fluid levels and maintenance paperwork. I had not been taught to work on an engine, remount a thrown APC track, replace a road wheel, put on the swim shrouds, or the other things I suddenly needed to know. Somehow we made it work and kept the APCs running, but the situation was generally difficult.

I started off with a good platoon sergeant, SSG Hershel Higgins, who was a reliable roughneck. He had been an orphan who turned into a street hoodlum. As a youthful offender, a Baltimore judge gave him a choice of the Army or prison. Higgins chose the Army and found a home in it, making the best of the opportunities it offered. Unfortunately, he was soon reassigned to be Company Training NCO, a waste of his leadership talent in my estimation. I briefly had an older SFC to replace SSG Higgins, but he was burned out and operating under the ROAD concept (Retired On Active Duty). Our troops were a mix of Vietnam returnees waiting to get out of the Army, new graduates from AIT and short-timers who had come back from 18 month tours in Korea or Germany. This troop mixture made company level leadership fairly challenging and I still had a lot to learn about that. One day I ran into a former AIT classmate and casual friend, who was now a SP/4. He had been newly assigned to another line company in 2/41 Infantry. I didn't recognize him at first, because he had terrible facial scars from wounds he received in Vietnam. His jarring appearance reminded me that I was in a serious business, despite the sometimes surreal training environment at Fort Hood.

My first Commanding Officer in Charlie Company was an insufferable clown, whose name I long ago erased from my memory, but I'll call him Captain Wanker. After going through college at taxpayer expense on an ROTC scholarship, he was commissioned in the Infantry branch, so he extended his contract and signed up for an 18 month tour in Germany to avoid combat in Vietnam. Wanker was in a mechanized infantry unit in Germany and in those days they trained incessantly in the field. For this reason, the Captain became technically proficient in conventional tactical operations, but he was seriously deficient in leadership ability. He was arrogant and he took an authoritarian approach to supervising C Company, ruling by the authority of his rank, supplemented with bullying. Like many weak leaders, he was convinced that rank has its privileges. He also epitomized the "Do as I say, not as I do" School of Supervision. We had an in-ranks inspection each Saturday morning in the cantonment area, followed by a barracks inspection. The uniform of the day was usually fatigues, but our Company Commander often turned out in wrinkled Class A greens which looked like he'd slept in them, with dandruff flakes all over his shoulders. He would go through the ranks wearing the wrong uniform, and criticize the EM for their appearances, apparently oblivious to his own. He did this one Saturday and one of my soldiers later asked me how Wanker could jack him up for a poor shine on his boots, when the Captain's low-quarters looked like they'd been polished with a Hershey bar. I told him to look at my boots (which had a dazzling spit shine) and I said, "Your boots don't meet *my* standards, so don't worry about the Captain". But even when the CO showed up in the correct uniform of the day, he looked like crap. None of his fatigues were tailored, he'd often wear the same uniform for two or three days and his best boots looked worse than my boonie boots.

The Troop Duty concept worked well, in providing general military seasoning and reinforcement of leadership principles. I am thankful that I was sent to a TO&E Infantry unit, because it offered at least some exposure to problems I would encounter later. I tried hard, but I made lots of dumb 2LT-type mistakes. My biggest shortcoming was in land navigation. Our 2nd Armored Division did its tactical field training in winter months and the 1st A.D. did theirs in summer. So I was thrown directly into field training when I was assigned to Charlie Company on January 6th, 1970. We usually went to the field for about a week at a time and the company was typically attached to a tank battalion during the conventional tactical training. Conventional mechanized infantry tactics are not that complicated at platoon level, so I got more or less up to speed by reading the field manuals and educating myself on what I was expected to do. But I was <u>lost</u> all the time. I had been taught to

The Mad Fragger and Me

The Mad Fragger and Me

navigate primarily by shooting azimuths with a compass, always walking and keeping track of distances through pace counts. Those methods couldn't be used on top of a tracked vehicle, moving cross-country at 20 MPH. Eleven tons of steel surrounded the commander's hatch of my track, so a magnetic compass always gave erratic readings. We had been given some training in terrain analysis in AIT and OCS, but not enough to navigate by terrain analysis at high speed, or in the dark. So I'd be sent out on a recon mission, or whatever, and promptly get lost. My own technical deficiency was made more painful by the fact that CPT Wanker was quite skilled in land navigation, probably because of the extensive field practice he received during his 18 month tour in Germany. I blundered around whenever my platoon was sent out alone and my perpetual confusion about where I was located really provoked my Company Commander. This should have made me happy because I detested Wanker anyway, but I was too young and dumb to relax and laugh about it. Instead, my anxiety escalated and I began to worry that I'd never be able to get my act together.

Captain Wanker reached his ETS date and he was discharged. Captain John Pinkston was assigned as his replacement. CPT Pinkston was old for a Captain, in his early thirties. Unlike his predecessor, my new CO had two tours in Vietnam under his belt, one as a Special Forces NCO and one as an Infantry lieutenant. He was a Master Parachutist and a Ranger. He had attended OCS as a Sergeant First Class/E7. Somewhere along the way he picked up a bootstrap college degree. I have often reflected that I learned as much about what *not to do* as a leader from CPT Wanker, as I did about what *to do* from CPT John Pinkston, and the stark contrast between them drove all the lessons home. CPT Pinkston regularly demonstrated all the principles they had talked about in the Leadership classes at Fort Benning. CPT Pinkston set high standards and he demanded that they be met. He led by example in everything he did. He took care of his soldiers, but he never compromised the mission under the guise of troop welfare. He was knowledgeable, dynamic, resourceful, innovative and hard. He was fiercely determined and he had personal courage. He did not particularly care whether the enlisted men *liked* him, but he always treated them with dignity, while demanding excellent performance from them.

At the Fort Hood Officers' Club over drinks, CPT Pinkston told the C Company lieutenants that his troops had nicknamed him "Shane" when he was an infantry officer in Vietnam, which was perfect. Like Alan Ladd's movie character, Shane Pinkston was somewhat slight in stature, but he had the soul of a gunfighter. He would never back away from any fight and he cheerfully courted violence as he led his lieutenants in wild forays through honky-tonks, saloons and pool halls in Texas and Oklahoma, partying and raising hell everywhere we went. We got away with this slightly antisocial behavior and never got into serious trouble, mostly because of Shane's winning personality. CPT Pinkston's basic dogma was that *real* Infantry officers are warriors and all warriors love a good fight. He was an intriguing combination of wild man and professional Infantry officer. I quickly decided that I wanted to be a hard-ass Infantry officer like Shane, not a candy-ass like Wanker. Under CPT Pinkston's guidance, I began to relax and enjoy my leadership role. Even my land navigation skills somehow began to improve.

As was the case everywhere I went in the Army, I met other interesting people. We had two notable ROTC graduates in Charlie Company while I was there, who were at opposite ends of the leadership spectrum. 2LT Wayne Romagosa, was a nice guy and highly competent, earning him the respect of his soldiers. 2LT Paul Oddfellow (not his real name) was a nice guy too, but sadly incompetent. Paul had approximately the same appearance and command presence as the Wally Cox character, *Mister Peepers*. He was really as helpless as his appearance suggested. I was walking through the barracks one day and I overheard part of a dialog between 2LT Oddfellow and an enlisted soldier in one of the rooms,

The Mad Fragger and Me

through an open door. Paul sounded upset, so I lingered in the hallway long enough to get the drift of it. The soldier kept addressing Lieutenant Oddfellow as "Odd-o" and Paul kept telling him, "You can't call me that... you have to call me 'Sir'". Then the enlisted guy would say, "Okay Odd-o", whereupon Paul would tell him again and the soldier would say, "OOO-KAAY, ODD-O!" There was an audience of two other EM, who were laughing. I went into the room and rescued Paul by jacking up the enlisted men. I could relate other stories about this lieutenant too, but the theme is the same, he was hopelessly inept. He is the only Infantry officer I ever heard of who received orders for Vietnam, which were then rescinded prior to his departure from CONUS. This must have been devastating to his self esteem and I felt sorry for him, but I was beginning to understand that we were in a deadly business. The troops deserved better leadership and the Army should have done a more efficient job of screening potential officers prior to commissioning.

Peter Zierden was a 2LT in Charlie Company, source of commission, OCS. Pete had an overbearing personality, which rubbed me the wrong way from the first day we met. He was a very big guy, about 6'5". Zierden was the Charlie Company Executive Officer, because of his seniority as a 2LT. This was an administrative job, not a command slot, but Pete thought that his XO status entitled him to order around the other company lieutenants. I rejected that notion, in accord with an Army saying that "Rank among lieutenants is like chastity among whores". We were drinking heavily and we got into a confrontation at a party in John and Sandy Pinkston's home, about Pete's authority to tell me what to do. This was the kind of macho dispute that Shane loved to egg on, so he didn't try to be a peacemaker. It was decided that we would meet in the post gym and settle our differences wearing boxing gloves, but we sobered up and apologized to each other in a half-assed way the next morning.

Fellow platoon leader 2LT Mike McGovern was a West Point graduate and Shane despised him for it, the only major flaw I ever saw in CPT Pinkston. I later learned to share Shane's prejudice against West Point lieutenants, but 2LT McGovern did not deserve to be condemned with some of the others. Mike had grown up in a coal mining town in Pennsylvania and he was admitted to West Point through the USMA Prep School in Virginia. McGovern became the Leadership Graduate, i.e., the student Brigade Commander in the West Point Class of 1969. He never forgot where he came from and he was not the least bit arrogant or entitled, unlike too many other Military Academy lieutenants. Mike was a charming playboy who loved the ladies and he compulsively hit on every attractive woman he met, including some of the other officers' wives. Pinkston had a somewhat similar personality (and an appreciation for handsome women) which may have been the source of some of the conflict between them. McGovern liked to party, he was sometimes a little loose with attention to detail and CPT Pinkston was always ready to burn him for his casual attitude. On one occasion, I discovered a shortage in the company's arms room count, when I was the Officer of the Day. This was a big deal and it turned out that Mike had been the OD on the prior day, but he had done a cursory inventory. We eventually found the missing weapon, but that wasn't the point to Shane. He fully expected all West Point graduates to perform their duties in a slipshod manner, because of their privileged culture. On another occasion, Mike got a DWI citation from the Fort Hood Military Police. This was usually an absolute career-breaker, but it could have happened to any of us because we wallowed in an alcohol-fueled warrior culture. Pinkston had no sympathy for McGovern and didn't try to help him. We had a very professional battalion Command Sergeant Major who everyone called "John Wayne", but respectfully, not in a pejorative way. The CSM was highly protective of all young fools, but especially buck sergeants and second lieutenants. He knew influential people

The Mad Fragger and Me

at Fort Hood and he made some phone calls, fixing 2LT McGovern's DWI problem.

Jane Fonda put in an appearance at Fort Hood while I was there, protesting against the Vietnam War at the main gate, with some of her lackeys. I saw a news report about the protest on the Waco TV channel, but I don't remember very many demonstrators or spectators. No one I knew was interested or curious enough to go see Hanoi Jane in person, even though the event was well publicized. There was a lot more interest in seeing Donald Sutherland's new movie, *M*A*S*H*. That film had been banned at the Fort Hood Theater, by the Post Commanding General, because of its satirically anti-military humor. No Hollywood advertising genius possibly could have cooked up better publicity for a movie than *that* on an Army post and we all went to see it, when the ban was lifted. *Patton* came out shortly afterwards, which was a very good film, but it provided unnecessary inspiration for some of the nuttier Armor branch officers. I encountered one of the screwballs, a very hostile full-bird Colonel from 2nd Armored Division Headquarters, who was accompanied by a surly Master Sergeant, in our company barracks. No one else was around and I discovered them conducting an unannounced inspection of the quarters. I properly and formally reported to the Colonel, but he was a martinet and a George Patton wannabe who had worked himself into a snit about something he'd already found. He immediately jumped all over me and he continued to do so as I accompanied them on their tour. At that early point in my military career, I was a compliant young lieutenant who was never impertinent toward superiors. But this upbraiding was unfair and I realized that Colonel Wannabe was showing off for his toady at my expense. We went into one of the latrines and he found the letters "FTA" scratched into the paint on a toilet stall door. This was universally understood to mean F_ _ _ The Army, but COL Wannabe rhetorically shrieked, "F-T-A!!! What does *THAT* mean, Lieutenant?!" I brightly answered,

"Fun, Travel and Adventure, Sir!" Colonel Wannabe looked like he was having a heart attack, bless his rotten soul.

2/41 Infantry was sent to Fort Sill, Oklahoma on a TDY (Temporary Duty) basis, to support an ROTC Summer Camp. We were to leave all APCs behind and operate as a light infantry unit, great news to me. Army buses were laid on to transport the troops. We also drew 2 ½ ton trucks to transport our equipment and to ferry troops while at Fort Sill. Junior officers were required to ride in convoy with the troops, so if we wanted to bring our POVs (privately owned vehicles) we had to arrange for NCOs to drive them to Fort Sill. Several weeks before we departed for Oklahoma, I was assigned a new Platoon Sergeant, SSG Arthur "Butch" Kraut. SSG Kraut was raised in the community of Maryland Line, which is on the MD/PA border, not far north of where I grew up. SSG Kraut was in his early 30s and he had been in the Army a long time. He was experienced in Infantry operations and strong on leadership. Butch was generally reliable about taking care of business, unless he got too heavily into drinking and partying, which he did periodically. He had been busted a couple of times because of his foibles and then promoted again later, but that didn't bother him. He always addressed each of our soldiers as "Homie", as if he was a childhood friend. His favorite expression to verify the validity of any situation, or to affirm the truthfulness of any statement, was "I want to shit in your mess kit, Sir". I really liked him, his off-the-wall sense of humor and his hell raising. SSG Kraut was also helpful to me, providing sound guidance in the form of subtle suggestions, so as to preserve my youthful ego. During the convoy to Fort Sill, SSG Kraut drove another junior officer's POV and he initially did not show up for duty, the car unaccounted for too. But our First Sergeant knew where to look and soon found him in the custody of the Lawton Police Department. Butch had arrived early, gotten drunk and into a saloon brawl with some artillery soldiers in The Impact Area, which was a few blocks of civilian bars and strip joints just outside of Fort Sill. The First Sergeant found Butch before he could really be considered AWOL.

The Mad Fragger and Me

This incident set the tone for our whole sojourn in Oklahoma. Butch meant well, but he was a wild-child and he later had to be liberated from jail a second time, following a fracas with the husband of a floozy he'd picked up in an Okie honky-tonk. The husband was not very open minded about the fun, when he discovered Butch skinny dipping with his wife in Lake Elmer Thomas, so he attempted to express his displeasure with a baseball bat. Even unarmed, drunk and naked, SSG Kraut was a formidable opponent, thanks to his umpteenth-degree black belt in *Tae Kwon Do*. When our First Sergeant again picked up Butch from the police, he was mostly uninjured but clothed only in a blanket. After being brought back to Charlie Company in that state of *dishabille*, SSG Kraut was contrite: "I don't know what came over me, Lieutenant Dolan, Sir." Butch had been gone for more than 24 hours, so he was considered to be AWOL. As a former noncommissioned officer himself, Shane had high expectations for senior NCOs and he said he intended to bust SSG Kraut down to buck sergeant. I barely persuaded him not to do that.

Our battalion was assigned to Camp Eagle, outside of the Fort Sill main post. Our new home consisted of neat rows of GP Large tents, pitched on concrete pads. The ROTC group we were supporting was set up in a similar tent city nearby. We had to provide aggressors for ROTC field training and personnel for various fatigue details, like ammo delivery or trash removal. It was easy duty, usually with regular hours and time off. We set up volleyball courts, horseshoe pits and played lots of softball, to keep the EM occupied. There were frequent beer parties and company cookouts in the cantonment area, using charcoal cookers manufactured in the motor pool from 55 gallon drums cut in half lengthwise. The food came from our regular mess hall rations draw and the beer was purchased from the post Class VI store and resold at cost to maintain the coffers.

Command Sergeant Major "John Wayne" retired and a new Sergeant Major was assigned to replace him just before we moved to Fort Sill. He had a Hispanic accent and he therefore reminded me of "Meanie" Meños in AIT. The new Command Sergeant Major immediately began to show hostility towards SSG Kraut, so I asked Butch about it. They had gotten into a beef back in Texas, because the CSM made a crude pass at Butch's girlfriend in a Goat-Roper saloon. No blows had been exchanged, only words, but even though that incident occurred off duty, the new Sergeant Major tried to use his rank and authority to punish SSG Kraut. I was naturally protective of my trusty platoon sergeant, so the CSM and I were on a collision course. Unlike most of our other senior noncoms, the Sergeant Major was somewhat overweight and untidy in appearance. He was sometimes unprofessional in other ways too. For example, he would often come into our company area and say, "Good morning, lieutenant" to me or to one of my peers, but he never saluted. He always addressed junior officers as "lieutenant", never "sir", telegraphing that 2nd Lieutenants were inferior to His Command Sergeant Majorship. He regularly did this, so I had time to think about how to handle it. One morning after not receiving a salute, I casually asked him if he had seen the new Department of Army Directive which stated that senior NCOs were no longer required to salute junior officers. He said no, he had not seen it. I loudly responded, "That's because there *isn't* one, Sergeant Major... so I expect you to show proper military courtesy to me in the future". A small audience of C Company enlisted men and NCOs were present when I said this. He complained to LTC Moore that I was busting his chops, so CPT Pinkston counseled me, telling me to knock it off: "Yes Tom, Second Lieutenants technically outrank all NCOs, including E9s. But Lieutenant Colonels outrank Captains. *AND* Captains outrank Second Lieutenants. So Captains get to tell Second Lieutenants what to do, and then Second Lieutenants get to do it." At least I had the satisfaction of knowing that the Sergeant Major could not handle me and had to go tattling to the Battalion Commander.

The Mad Fragger and Me

Captain Pinkston went out one night and he did not come back. He still hadn't shown up in the morning and we hadn't heard from him. LTC Moore held a "Commanders' Call" meeting on most weekday mornings right after breakfast, with company commanders and primary staff. 2LT Zierden had departed with orders for Vietnam and a new XO had not been appointed. The First Sergeant told me I'd have to go to Commanders' Call in place of CPT Pinkston, because he hadn't shown up and nobody knew where he was. I went, but I was sweating bullets because I knew the Battalion Commander would ask me why CPT Pinkston hadn't come to the meeting. I am a terrible liar and I know that guilt always shows in my face when I'm telling a whopper, so I have found that it is always simpler to just tell the truth and take my lumps. In this case, I *couldn't* tell the Battalion CO that Shane was gone and we didn't have any idea where he was. On the other hand, if he later turned up injured or something, I would get burned for lying. I sucked it up and lied through my teeth. I told the battalion commander that CPT Pinkston had gotten wind of a possible problem in a remote training area and he had gone out in a jeep to check on it. I'm sure my face was burning as I said that, but maybe they thought it was sunburn. Shane showed up an hour or so later and wanted to know if anyone had missed him, so I told him about Commanders' Call. He was evasive about where he'd been, but I wouldn't accept that after the sweating and lying I'd done for him. He had been arrested by civilian police and spent the night in jail.

Battalion HQ received a requirement for one company to move from Camp Eagle to another tent village at the Fort Sill Range Area, to support weapons firing by the ROTC cadets. Company officers were to serve as Range OICs and Safety Officers, backed up by unit NCOs. Drivers and general muscle were also needed for ammo details. Charlie Company was selected to do this, probably because CPT Pinkston was the senior company commander. This assignment removed us almost entirely from battalion HQ's supervision, because the Range Area was a long distance from Camp

Eagle. A bird colonel was assigned to C Company as the post liaison officer. Fort Sill is an Artillery post, but this O-6 was Infantry branch and it soon became obvious that he enjoyed coming out to the range bivouac and hanging out with other infantrymen. Following Shane's lead, we always made a big fuss over him, invited him to pitch horseshoes or play softball, gave him coffee, beer or cookout grub, and generally welcomed him as one of our own. He just loved this comradeship and Pinkston's boisterous mojo, so anything Shane did was OK with the Colonel. One drizzly day shortly after we moved into the tents, Colonel Snuffy got out of his sedan wearing a raincoat and he walked up to CPT Pinkston with his hands in his pockets. CPT Pinkston saluted him, shook his hand and asked, "Are you going on leave, Colonel?" The colonel answered, "No, why?" Shane said, "Why don't you unpack your pockets? You're setting a bad example for my troops". They both laughed, but I couldn't believe Shane got away with that remark.

    I went to see CPT Pinkston one day, because one of my soldiers had a problem with his clothing records. He was a married PFC who had several kids. He was in severe financial straits because of his low pay and a bad credit history. The clothing records problem was fairly common. Enlisted men would receive a basic issue of clothing when they were inducted. If they were later sent to Vietnam, some of them were told (improperly) to turn in all their uniforms and footwear, but unknown to them, the turn-in was not reflected on their clothing records. Some stateside supply sergeants were making up clothing shortages through this scam. Tropical uniforms and jungle boots were issued in Vietnam, but they were not authorized for wear in CONUS. If a returning soldier had any active duty obligation remaining, he needed stateside uniforms, but these then had to be purchased at his personal expense. The same story came up often enough that I knew the problem was authentic. My PFC was a "black cloud person"... bad things always happened to him. He seemed to have a dark storm cloud hovering over his head all the time, like the Joe Btfsplk character in the old *Li'l Abner* comic strip. PFC Btfsplk had one set of fatigues and a pair of old boots, which had been given to him by somebody, but they were in poor shape and didn't fit properly. He washed the uniform by hand on weekends and wore it all week. He did not have Class A greens or khaki uniforms and he was always unsatisfactory in inspections. He was really not able to purchase replacement uniforms. When I went to Shane with this problem, I told him I had been to see the Company Supply Sergeant, who told me nothing could be done. Captain Pinkston said that the soldier was assigned to me, not to the Supply Sergeant. And why was I coming to Shane with a problem I was supposed to solve? Infantry officers *always* take care of their troops, no matter what obstacles are put in their paths. Shane expected his platoon leaders to be resourceful and creative. If I couldn't find a solution within military channels, then I needed to do whatever was necessary outside of channels. If I still couldn't solve the problem, I could come back to CPT Pinkston and he'd take care of it. But it was clear that he did not expect that to happen.

    I pondered the clothing records problem and it was clear that no solution existed within normal channels. It occurred to me that we had previously turned in uniforms after a soldier went AWOL for long enough to be considered a deserter. This had only happened once or twice in Charlie Company, but I knew how it was handled at unit level. The platoon leader and Supply Sergeant used a bolt cutter to cut the padlocks off the AWOL soldier's footlocker and wall locker, then jointly inventoried the contents and created a written record. Uniforms, TA 50 web gear and any other government-issue stuff were turned in through supply channels. I knew that used uniforms were never reissued, but I had no idea where they went. I thought that this might be a relatively frequent occurrence at a post as large as Fort Sill. Starting with our Supply Sergeant, I traced turned-in of uniforms through the system, ending up at a Fort Sill disposal facility run by a Warrant Officer. I explained my problem to him. He said that the turned in uniforms were shredded and sold by the pound for recycling. Anything which could not be recycled was thrown away. Uniforms were carefully accounted for, up to the point where they came in to his facility, before they were shredded. I asked if some of them could go missing, after he had counted them in, but before they were shredded. He told me that he would give me some uniforms for Joe Btfsplk and the date to come back. I came back with a jeep and a list of the sizes Btfsplk needed, plus a bottle of scotch for the Warrant Officer. The bottle of scotch resulted in the acquisition of much more than what PFC Btfsplk needed. I returned to C Company with a load of used but serviceable uniforms and accessories. After we outfitted Joe Btfsplk, I gave out the remaining uniforms to any soldiers who wanted them.

PFC Btfsplk acted like he had expected me to solve his problem all along, which was probably the correct attitude for him to take. Although he was indifferent to my efforts, the other soldiers in my platoon became aware of what I'd done. Another young man in my platoon encountered a relatively minor problem with his uniforms being misplaced by the Post Laundry facility, just prior to a major inspection. I went out of my way to fix the problem and he was appreciative to the point that it was almost embarrassing. He became my biggest fan and most ardent supporter after I helped him out. This leadership principle now seems simple and obvious, but it was an epiphany at the time. I reaped huge loyalty and unit cohesiveness benefits from applying the concept that an officer always takes care of his troops, regardless of obstacles.

After we returned to Fort Hood from Fort Sill, we didn't do much with the APCs, except routine maintenance in the motor pool, because of a gasoline conservation and budget austerity program. I thought this was great, because I hated the tracks and their continuous mechanical problems. The field training we did was in light infantry subjects. We were doing this one day in an outlying training area and Shane returned to garrison early to attend a meeting, leaving me in charge of the company. The training schedule called for instruction in patrolling and ambush techniques.

The Mad Fragger and Me

Several of our junior NCOs team-taught this class, using their Vietnam experience to impart useful knowledge, primarily through demonstrations and practical exercises. The troops really got into it and it turned out to be one of the best field training sessions I had ever experienced. The battalion training schedule called for the last several hours of the day to be spent on "Forced Road March Techniques" back to the cantonment area, which was quite a long distance. This was just a training schedule time-filler and I thought it would be a morale buster, after the good training day we'd had. The Field First Sergeant thought so too, when I asked his opinion. So I sent several guys who owned vans and pickup trucks back to the cantonment area in the available jeeps, to bring back their POVs. We convoyed the troops back to the barracks, ditching the forced march on the training schedule. Somebody saw us coming back from the field in civilian vehicles and reported it to Battalion HQ. Shane called me into his office the next day and told me he had been instructed to discipline me..."so consider yourself to have been verbally reprimanded". He commented that this was a case of good initiative and poor judgment, especially the poor judgment I used in getting caught. His demeanor made it clear that he was amused by the incident.

    I had submitted a DA Form 1049 Request for Reassignment to volunteer for Vietnam, even though I knew I'd probably be going anyway. When my orders for Vietnam came through, CPT Pinkston called me into his office to give some advice. He said if I was very lucky I'd get a good platoon sergeant, but they were scarce. When I arrived in my new rifle platoon, I should expect that the troops would try to tell me that I needed to do everything they told me to do, until I got my act together. He predicted they'd say, "Don't worry lieutenant, we know what we're doing and we'll take care of you". Shane said I should not pay any attention to that, because it was just a common fantasy among enlisted men. The troops would often test a new platoon leader in other ways too. They might try to persuade him to "sham" patrols, night ambushes or other things they didn't want to do, claiming that it was the way things were always done in Vietnam. Or they might try to hold a vote on compliance with an order they perceived as too difficult or too dangerous. If I fell into any of those traps, there would be no possibility of going back to revisit the decision later. Shane said, "I know you think you don't know anything, but you already know a *whole* lot more than the enlisted men do. The first time a situation goes really bad, every one of them will be looking at you with a 'What do I do now?' look in their eyes. And you had *better* know what to do." This advice made a strong impression on me and those are very close to CPT Pinkston's exact words. It later happened exactly the way he predicted.

When I left Fort Hood, my wife and I moved back to Maryland. I was on a lengthy period of leave, before I was scheduled to report for Jungle Warfare School en route to Vietnam. For some reason, my pay got interrupted and I made two futile trips to the Post Finance Office at Fort Meade, trying to straighten out the problem. This resulted in a couple of emergency partial back-pay advancements, but the amounts were limited by Finance branch regulation. The Army owed me a considerable amount of back pay when I really needed it.

The two week Jungle Warfare School in the Panama Canal Zone was operated by Army Special Forces and consisted of training in survival, jungle living and jungle warfare. The tropical climate was almost unbearable and the gear they issued us was in various stages of decomposition and rot. Even the stucco buildings at Fort Sherman were dank, with sweaty walls, and they seemed to be decaying too. There was no air conditioning anywhere. Small lizards were deliberately given the run of the steamy screened-in BOQ, to keep the mosquitoes down. The O-Club had a tiny black and white TV as its only form of entertainment. There was only one channel on the TV and it was always playing Three Stooges shorts, with Larry, Moe and Curly speaking dubbed Spanish. Fort Sherman was the only U.S. Army post in the world that maintained its own zoo, with panthers and other jungle mammals, plus assorted reptiles, which were incorporated into the survival classes. There was a little beach surrounded by a shark net, but swimming was not recommended because the net had holes in it. Many of the instructors were Latino NCOs with thick Hispanic accents, so they were often difficult to understand. Some of the janitors and other civilian employees were San Blas Indians, who spoke neither English nor Spanish.

Jungle Warfare training was generally similar to Ranger Week in OCS, except for Panama's harsher climate, more difficult terrain and denser foliage. The Jungle Warfare School's Night Land Navigation exercise lasted from dusk to sunrise and it was by far the most difficult one I've ever done. It became so dark that I could not see my hand when I held it directly in front of my face. The course ran through heavy jungle, in a training area which the cadre said had not been used for more than a decade. We had to cut through the tangled foliage with machetes and the terrain was incredibly rough. We spent the night walking off of cliffs and falling in deep ravines in the dark. Miraculously, no one was seriously injured. A lieutenant in our class lost his M14 after falling in a deep, water-filled pit. We had tied our rifles to our web harnesses using improvised lanyards, but the LT abandoned his web gear, canteens and weapon to avoid drowning. The school was still trying to pressure him into agreeing to pay for the lost M14 and TA50 gear when I left. He was still refusing, on the grounds that it was an unavoidable accident and the M14 was an old piece of junk anyway. The lieutenant knew that the equipment could be "surveyed" to take it off the property books, but the school cadre did not wish to initiate a Report of Survey because the tedious and lengthy procedure required a huge amount of paperwork.

They transported us on an ancient LCM (Landing Craft, Medium) to a training area on the Chagres River, which is a fairly wide body of water. We constructed poncho rafts as instructed and swam across the river with our M14s and gear, only finding out later that the Chagres was shark-infested. They had built a long zip-line across the Chagres River, from a platform very high up in a tree on a tall hillside, to the base of another tree on the opposite bank. It was a cable arrangement, like the Slide-for-Life at Camp Darby, but much longer and higher. Trainees dangled below the steel cable under roller-blocks, with rope loops under their armpits and around their backs. The ride was very fast until the zip-line came to an abrupt stop at a shackle on the far bank of the river. Several SF enlisted men were detailed to slow down students before they hit the shackle, with a braking device made of ropes, but whenever they saw an officer coming, they would just go through the motions. The sudden stop jerked many of us up and over the cable, which was excruciatingly painful. At the same location, we did some rappelling, down a slippery waterfall and off of a tall wooden tower. I was one of the few students who chose to try the Australian Commando Rappel. The Commando Rappel was designed to allow attacking soldiers to fire their weapons while they rappelled down cliffs or buildings. This required the student to go over the edge of the tower facing straight down, with the rappel rope attached by a D-ring to a waist rope at his lower back. The "commando" would wrap the rappel rope across his chest and control it with his weak arm while he ran face-first down the wall. I ended up tangled in the rope, hanging upside down, halfway down the 40 foot wall. I somehow managed to lower myself the rest of the way without killing myself. The Green Beret instructor invited me to come back up and give it another go, but I thanked him and declined.

  We were tested on everything and I scored high enough to receive a certificate as a "Jungle Expert". I wasn't sure what I was supposed to do with that… carry it in my rucksack and show it to the Viet Cong if I was captured? The Jungle Warfare School in Panama started acclimatizing us to the tropics, which takes about 6 weeks according to Army doctrine. Even better, my 12 month Vietnam tour officially began on the date I reported to Fort Sherman, 3 October 1970.

The Mad Fragger and Me

Because my pay was messed up, I borrowed a hundred bucks from my parents, which was about how much it cost to fly by commercial military rates to Seattle/Tacoma airport. I reported to Fort Lewis and they put me on a charter flight to Vietnam, via Flying Tiger Airlines, which featured geriatric stewardesses. I had a large flask with two shot glasses in a zippered bottom compartment, a gift from my sister Judy. The flask was filled with bourbon, what was left of a quart of *Jim Beam* my father gave me as I was leaving home. I was seated next to an older Chief Warrant Officer helicopter pilot, who was going back for his second or third tour. He commented that the bad thing about military flights was that you could not get a drink of alcohol. I said you could, if you knew who to ask. I retrieved the flask from my grandfather's old leather shaving kit and we had some shooters. When we stopped to refuel in Anchorage, the plane was parked far out on the tarmac. We had a long walk to the terminal, wearing only TWs (tropical weight khakis) and it was very cold in Alaska. Several of us started drinking boilermakers in the terminal's bar, shots of *Old Grand Dad*, chased by draft beers. We didn't notice the cold so much when we staggered back to the plane. After we re-boarded, an elderly stewardess saw the CWO and me passing the flask. She told us it was against regulations to drink on a military charter flight. If we didn't put the booze away, she would have us put off the plane when we refueled in Yokota, Japan. The flask was empty by that time anyway. It was otherwise an uneventful 18 ½ hour flight to Vietnam.

Chapter 4:

FOUR DEUCE PLATOON, 1st BATTALION 20th INFANTRY

I don't recall the exact date I arrived in the Republic of Vietnam (RVN), but it was in the latter half of October 1970. I clearly remember the blast of superheated air and the strange odors which assailed me when I stepped off the Flying Tiger Airlines flight in the Cam Ranh Bay airport. All of Vietnam had the same peculiar smells. By then, I was 24 years old. I had traveled light, at the recommendation of other soldiers who had already been to Vietnam. I carried my Grandfather Dolan's old Dopp kit, but I had stupidly checked in my "AWOL Bag" as hold baggage at the Fort Lewis airport. Because of a mechanical problem, we changed planes at the Yokota Airport in Japan and my bag was left behind. The canvas AWOL Bag, which was the size of a small carry-on, contained a set of used jungle boots and fatigues, a going away gift from one of my guys at Fort Hood. There was a towel, an OD baseball cap, underwear, some cushion sole socks, a heavy duty D-cell flashlight embossed "Bethlehem Steel Corp-Work Safely" and my *Puma Folding Hunter* knife. The lost AWOL bag also contained a GI .50 caliber machine gun headspace and timing gauge, which I had been told was hard to get in Vietnam. Because my bag was lost, I actually arrived for war with the clothes on my back, my toothbrush and shaving gear. What else do you really need?

We were sent to the Replacement Center (Repo-Depot) at Cam Ranh Bay, where we were required to turn in all our greenbacks and silver coins. We were given Military Payment Certificates (MPC) to replace the real money. This military script looked like money from a Monopoly game and it was issued in denominations ranging from 5 cents to $20. It was intended to avoid ruining the RVN economy by flooding it with U.S. dollars. We were instructed to exchange MPC for piastres (aka, dong), the South

Vietnamese currency, at a military base and to keep a stash of that for local purchases. We quickly learned that the South Vietnamese would not accept piastres, always demanding MPC. On roads at the Repo-Depot, I noticed some unfamiliar Army trucks, which had a quaint archaic look. They were three-quarter ton tactical trucks, derived from the original Dodge Power Wagons. They had been built in the early 1950s, but taken out of mothballs and shipped to Vietnam, to replace the newer but unreliable AMC/Jeep "five-quarter" ton trucks. The elderly Dodge trucks burned a lot of oil, but they were monotonously dependable. At the Repo Depot, we filled out a "dream sheet" to request our units of choice. I requested the 101st Airborne Division (Airmobile) and the 1st Cavalry Division as my first and second choices, because they were reputed to be the best infantry units still in Vietnam. I was instead assigned to the Americal (23rd Infantry) Division, but I felt a wave of relief that I was not sent to the 5th Mechanized Infantry Division, which was also on the list. We were issued jungle boots and four sets of new tropical fatigues. On a street in Cam Ranh, I ran into my Basic Combat Training classmate, Mohammed. He had been promoted to Spec/5 by then and was a senior clerk in an Army finance office. I described my pay problem and asked if he could straighten it out. Mohammed said he could and he wrote down my Social Security number and the allotment information for my wife. The problem which had existed for months was entirely fixed prior to the next payday and I got all my back pay, plus the allotment was started. I never saw Mohammed again to thank him.

We were shipped out almost immediately to our major units and I attended the Americal Division's Combat School in Chu Lai, for one week. It was an abbreviated combat orientation course and it was very well done. While there, I saw a demonstration of NVA sapper capability. They had a former sapper who was a Hoi Chanh, an enemy soldier who came over to our side. He was dressed only in gym shorts. They had set up a "demonstration" multiple strand barbwire perimeter entanglement, reinforced with concertina razor wire, with trip flares and cans with rocks in them as noisemakers. You would swear that a mouse could not get through the barrier. The ex-sapper went through it in seconds, like a greased eel contortionist, the most amazing demonstration of physical agility I ever saw. There was a Filipino-American, Major Rodriguez, in my class at the Combat School, with whom I became friendly. He was such a nice guy that the school retained him as its Executive Officer. I was talking to him in the Combat School's club one night and I mentioned my lost AWOL Bag. He took down my name and unit, commenting that he would see what he could do, although I had not asked him to do anything.

I was sent to the 11th Light Infantry Brigade ("The Jungle Warriors") at LZ Bronco, in Duc Pho Province. The 1st Battalion 20th Infantry Regiment's rear area was on the same base. I arrived on 3 November 1970 during the monsoon season, which had started a month earlier. LZ Bronco occupied a large piece of real estate, larger than a grid square. The base was dominated by a small mountain in the middle of it, named "Montezuma" by the U.S. Marines who had originally occupied LZ Bronco. At $1/20^{th}$ Infantry Headquarters, I learned that I was being assigned to Echo Company, as the Battalion Heavy Mortar Platoon Leader. I met the E Company First Sergeant, Robert Moore, a first rate NCO. There was a helicopter flight leaving soon for LZ Liz, the battalion's forward firebase. I was rushed through the E Company supply room, where I was issued an M16, magazines and ammo, a rucksack with frame and TA50 gear. I was then hustled to the helipad. 2LT Sidney Hopfer, an OCS classmate and friend, had come in from Chu Lai with me and he was on the same chopper ride to LZ Liz. Sid had been assigned to D Company 1/20 Infantry as a rifle platoon leader. At Landing Zone Liz, we met our battalion commander, LTC Gordon Lynch. Colonel Lynch had a reputation as a totally professional soldier and he looked the part, trim, well groomed and courtly in his bearing.

At "Four-Deuce", I met my Platoon Sergeant, SFC Hugh Morris, who was pleasant, knowledgeable and straightforward. SSG Earl

Willard was the Chief-of-Smoke, an unofficial but traditional title in mortar platoons. SSG Willard supervised all technical operations in the FDC (Fire Direction Center) and the laying-in of the guns. He was an Appalachian mountain man, gruff, rough as a cob, hardnosed and plain-spoken. SSG Willard was probably in his early to mid thirties, but he looked much older and the troops called him "Pop", usually behind his back. There was nothing about mortars that SSG Willard did not know. My new job as platoon leader was almost ceremonial, because I had never received any significant training on mortars. I settled in to learn the technical aspects of mortar gunnery and FDC procedures from SSG Willard and SFC Morris, who were willing teachers. I also studied field manuals, but the subject was complex enough that I never got fully up to speed. I learned to lay in the guns by rote, using the Aiming Circle instrument (similar to a surveyor's transit) but I did not fully understand the math involved. The precision artillery charts which SSG Willard fabricated for the FDC crew to use in lieu of standard mortar Plotting Boards were also somewhat mysterious. It didn't matter, because SFC Morris and SSG Willard were already running the Heavy Mortar Platoon quite nicely, thank you, and they really didn't need any help from a butter-bar lieutenant. They were always courteous and deferential towards me, but I soon realized that my main function was to keep other officers off their backs. I was not accustomed to allowing NCOs to run all operations, but it was clearly in everybody's best interest, especially mine, to not interfere with what they were already doing. I was scheduled for promotion to First Lieutenant on 5 November 1970, two days after I arrived. I did not receive any notice of promotion and I didn't bother to change my rank insignia to black bar, because I really didn't care about it. When Morris and Willard found out about this, they had a fit, insisting that I change my rank insignia immediately. I thought it was funny they reacted that way, but I guess they preferred to have a 1LT as their nominal leader.

    I soon learned that the notorious Lieutenant William Calley had also been a member of my new unit. In 1968, Calley and his

The Mad Fragger and Me

troops from Charlie Company, 1st Battalion 20th Infantry had committed the monstrous atrocities at My Lai-4 (aka, Pinkville) in the northern part of our Area of Operations (AO). I also learned that Calley's Company Commander, CPT Ernest L. Medina, had been one of my predecessors as leader of the Four Deuce Platoon, because I found an old 4.2 Inch Mortar field manual with his name hand-written inside the front cover.

At the 4.2 Inch Mortar Platoon I had a choice of either moving into a relatively spacious bunker with SFC Morris and SSG Willard, or occupying a tiny vacant bunker which had the platoon's Aiming Circle surveyed-in on its roof. I took the small bunker for privacy, even though it was in disrepair. It had been dug down partially into the ground, a feature I liked. I had worked as a carpenter's helper in a construction company during college summers and I enjoyed that work, so I immediately began renovations. After cleaning out the bunker, I modified it to get some fresh air flowing by cutting small ventilation openings and stalling screens. I fashioned a screened window in the door, which I louvered with basswood splints obtained from the medics. I scrounged some light green paint for the interior plywood walls and red paint for the door. I also found a can of "Electrical Varnish", which I used to put a gloss finish on the interior framing timbers. I fabricated a gun rack for my M16, a towel bar and a shelf for my shaving gear. There was room inside for only two pieces of furniture, a GI bed with mosquito bar and a footlocker, which I also used as a table. When I was finished, the little bunker was a cozy and watertight abode, which I occupied throughout the rest of the monsoon season.

Shortly after I arrived at the Heavy Mortar Platoon, we received a soldier as an in-country transfer from another division which had stood down. He brought a dog with him, a Vietnamese mongrel unimaginatively named Dink. ("Dink" was generally a racial slur, but when the word was used by grunts, it usually meant an enemy soldier.) Dink was a spayed female who showed affection toward her master, but she growled and snapped at everyone else who came near her. I had always liked dogs and I tried to make friends with Dink, to no avail. Her keeper soon went home and left her behind, because there was no practical way to take a dog back to CONUS. We had a contact fire mission in the middle of one night. When I ran into the FDC (Fire Direction Center), Dink was lying on the floor just inside the doorway and she snapped at my leg when I stepped over her. Her snarling and snapping startled me, so I cussed her, stamped my feet loudly and kicked her out the door. From that moment on, Dink was my slave and my body guard. One of the braver guys used to tease her by pretending to attack me with a rolled up newspaper and Dink would go after him with bared fangs, snarling ferociously and generally going berserk. Whenever I said, "SIC 'EM!", she transformed into a canine raging lunatic, whether she saw a threat or not. I did not feed her, except special treats, but she went to the mess hall to eat with the troops every day. A few other soldiers on LZ Liz had pet dogs, notably a rambunctious puppy called Crowbar, who was somehow appropriately named. The Four Deuce Platoon already had another dog as their official platoon mascot, a poor old soul named Skippy. The guys used to brag about how dumb Skippy was, for example they had to literally drag him in out of the rain. Skippy had a peaceful but perpetually vacant look in his eyes and he may have been brain-damaged. He was an extremely gentle and friendly animal, but Dink gave him a good thrashing about once a week, apparently to remind him that she was the big dog on the porch. Dink became amazingly affectionate towards me, but no one else could really do much with her, except SSG Willard. He talked roughly to her in his mountain twang, so she probably recognized him as an Alpha-Male. But it was clear that she merely tolerated Willard, whereas she adored me. She followed me everywhere and she began sleeping in my bunker. I made a collar for her out of an old leather belt and a pull-ring from a hand grenade to attach her rabies vaccination tag. She gradually became more civilized towards the guys in the platoon, but she allowed only a few of them touch her. A line company walked into the firebase through our area one day, leading a military-aged Vietnamese male prisoner in black pajamas who was blindfolded and bound by the wrists. Dink merely snarled at the strange GIs, but she attacked the detainee and I had to drag her away. She knew who the enemy was.

Life was good in the Four Deuce Platoon. SFC Morris was creative about projects to keep the troops busy and out of trouble, but it was paced so nobody killed themselves with work. We had a full complement of soldiers, 53 men, to operate the FDC and four 4.2 inch mortar tubes. We had so many guys because the line companies were never filled up with their authorized numbers of mortar men. Each rifle company was allowed an 81mm mortar platoon with four tubes, but they operated on foot. The weapons and ammo were so heavy that they could carry only one mortar cannon, a base plate, a bipod and a few rounds of ammo. For this reason, there were many extra 81mm mortars within the battalion. SFC Morris and SSG Willard came up with the idea of creating an 81mm Squad within the 4.2 Inch Mortar Platoon, to use for firebase defense. Four Deuce mortars were not well suited for this, because they were heavy long range weapons, actually slightly larger in bore diameter than a 105mm howitzer. So we acquired three surplus 81mm mortars. We built a spacious firing pit, living quarters and an ammo bunker in our area to accommodate the new squad. We were able to operate three 81mm tubes because the new squad consisted of three gunners with a skeleton crew of assistant gunners/ammo bearers. The same FDC plotters were able to serve both the 81mm and the 4.2 inch crews. Constructing the new 81mm bunkers with only hand tools was a major undertaking.

When we got the 81mm Squad up and running, word quickly got around. There were two artillery batteries on LZ Liz, a 105mm battery on one end and a 155mm on the other end. Our battalion's Artillery Liaison Officer asked if we would shoot "service practice" for the artillery Forward Observers (FOs) using the new 81mms and I agreed to do so. Whenever we did this, the Liaison Officer "cleared" a grid square about 500 meters out, within sight of our tubes. We fired a few white phosphorous smoke rounds into the grid, to chase civilians out of the area. Then the art'y FOs picked out a tree or another object as a target and shot at it with the 81mms, adjusting fire as the rounds were observed. This was a relatively cheap way for the FOs to practice and it provided "live fire" crew drill for our 81mm Squad. It also gave our mortar crews a rare opportunity to see the results of their efforts.

We plotted 81mm "Delta Tangos" (DTs/defensive targets) and FPFs (Final Protective Fires) around each of the bunkers on the LZ Liz perimeter. These preplanned targets were shown on a chart inside each perimeter bunker. Grunts defending the bunker during a ground attack could just look at the chart and call in a target number on the field phone, without going through the lengthy "call for fire" rigmarole. The Delta Tangos covered a broad area in front of each bunker, but an FPF was the last line of defense, fired when a bunker was about to be overrun by enemy. SSG Willard plotted the FPFs to land within 25 meters of the bunkers. I was skeptical that they could really be shot that close, but Pop Willard said it was possible with 81mms. The only problem with plotting FPFs so close to the bunkers was that they also had to be shot in for verification. SSG Willard and I spent several days doing that at every bunker, all around the perimeter. The universal Forward Observer SOP was to call in a cautionary "Danger-Close" for any indirect fire target less than 100 meters away from the observer. Twenty-five meters is very, very close, so this was quite dangerous. We were shooting in the FPFs from inside the perimeter bunkers, but it was still hairy when an HE (high explosive) round landed about 50 meters away and Willard would calmly say into the radio "Round observed, direction same, proximity five-zero, drop two-five, repeat". The guns were shooting from a short distance away, so the mortar rounds were going almost straight up and coming almost straight down, propelled by minimum charges. There was absolutely no margin for error. The 81mms are smoothbore weapons and I never trusted their accuracy very much, but SSG Willard knew exactly

The Mad Fragger and Me

what he was doing. We completed the DT/FPF project without incident.

After a month or so, I received my lost AWOL Bag, along with a nice note from my friend Major Rodriguez at the Americal Division Combat School, who had tracked it down somewhere in Asia. I had not really expected to see the bag again, but all my stuff was still inside. I gave away the .50 headspace and timing gauge to a Quad .50 crew which visited LZ Liz and they were delighted to get it. We had received instructions to "jump" an 81mm tube to the radar outpost on Nui Vong (Hill 103), and I ran into Pete Zierden, my rival from Fort Hood, when I went there to check on my crew. Pete commanded "Q Company" on Nui Vong, a provisional unit comprised of soldiers on light duty medical profiles. In a photo of Pete and me snapped on Nui Vong, I am wearing my recovered "stateside" jungle fatigues and my salty old baseball cap from the found AWOL bag. Those fatigues were distinctive, because the embroidered U.S. Army tape and name tape had been sewn on horizontally at the Fort Hood tailor shop, instead of along the slanted pocket lines as was always done in Vietnam.

After 30 days in the unit, I was eligible to receive the coveted Combat Infantryman's Badge (CIB) and I was presented with one at an awards ceremony on LZ Liz a short time later. I had not really earned the CIB when I received it because I was not engaged in active close combat at LZ Liz. But I know that I did truly earn it later.

The Army distributed a glossy "PACEX" (Pacific Exchange) catalog for the benefit of troops who did not have access to the PX stores at the major bases. It was like a Sears & Roebuck mail order catalog, only better. PACEX was based in Japan and the catalog was jammed with all the goodies for which the orient was famous, duty-free and sold at bargain basement prices. Some stuff, like intricate ivory carvings or similar Asian artifacts, were always in short supply, but the other merchandise was readily available. I had a checkbook from the Maryland National Bank (now-defunct), which was the only banking institution which would agree to do all my transactions by mail from halfway around the world. Most of my pay went home to my wife through an allotment, but $100 per month was deposited in my checking account. PACEX purchases were one of the few options for spending my allowance. Most guys had to get money orders for PACEX purchases, but money orders were available only from the payroll officer once a month, or from the PXs at the larger bases, so my checkbook was a real asset. One of the first things I bought from PACEX was an Olympus "Penn" 35mm point & shoot camera. Most soldiers had plastic Kodak-110 cameras, which were cheap, compact and light. But they didn't take very good pictures and 110 film cartridges became difficult to find because of high demand. My little Japanese Olympus was about the same size, but it was all-metal, of much higher quality and it came in a nice soft leather case. The 35mm film was easy to get and I could take 72 photos on a 36 frame roll, because the camera was a "half-frame" model. The Olympus took very good pictures and I carried it everywhere in a thigh cargo pocket, until it was stolen later in my tour. I did not get around to replacing it, but I took several hundred pictures before it went missing. I bought some other neat things from PACEX, but I had all of them shipped directly home. My wife loved it when one of these unexpected packages arrived, because unpacking it was like a mini-Christmas for her. The items I remember sending included a full sized Panasonic stereo system with receiver, speakers and turntable; a supplemental stereo component 12 cassette automatic tape deck; a 12-place setting of gold-rimmed Noritaki china; a Petri 35mm SLR camera; a pair of 4' tall brass table lamps; a Seiko lady's watch; a large Lazy Susan which was hand-carved from Filipino Monkey Pod wood.

    Mail delivery was regular and surprisingly efficient, considering the distances involved. All postal delivery was by air mail, which was a premium and separate service in 1970. Outgoing letters were written on flimsy onionskin stationary and placed in lightweight "air mail envelopes" with identifying blue and red colored borders. G.I.s in a combat zone did not have to fool with postage; we merely

The Mad Fragger and Me

printed "FREE" in the place where stamps usually went. As long as the return address contained an Army Post Office (APO) Number, an envelope would go right through the U.S. Postal System without stamps. Mail was the only regular and reliable way of communicating with home. The Army also operated a Rube Goldberg telephone party line called "MARS" (Military Affiliate Radio System) but it was rarely accessible on the forward firebases. MARS consisted of a TA312 field telephone, linked to a military switchboard, which was connected by land line to another switchboard, which was linked to volunteer HAM radio operators, one of whom (in the U.S.) was connected to long distance Ma Bell lines. All calls were "collect" and time zones had to be considered when placing calls. The HAM operators monitored the conversations in order to switch back and forth between "receive" and "transmit", so both parties had to say "over" at each break in the conversation to signal them to do that. The MARS system was complicated and subject to atmospheric limitations. On the rare occasions when it was available on LZ Liz, there was always a long wait for soldiers who wanted to try to get a call through to home. There was a single telephone line and of course a strict time limit on the length of calls. I never bothered, because MARS was too much hassle.

We did a lot of partying in Four Deuce. Somebody acquired a key to the battalion mess hall's meat reefer, by methods I didn't want to know about. A standard menu item at that time was roast beef, served in the mess hall so frequently that the troops always complained about it..."Oh no, water buffalo AGAIN!" My guys would raid the reefer in midnight forays and bring back huge roasts of beef, which we cut into steaks and cooked on a charcoal grill in the Four Deuce area, making the meat much more palatable. OCS pogey runs and other rule-bending high jinks in Texas made it easy for me to rationalize this thievery, but Battalion HQ took it much more seriously. The pilferage was noticed and I began hearing about it during the Battalion Commander's Briefings I attended every day.

The battalion staff could not figure out when or how it was being done, which was amusing. The unit cooks were high on the list of suspects, reminding me of the missing strawberries in *The Caine Mutiny*. We had to tone down the midnight reefer sorties for awhile.

    For the convenience of the E Company Commander, I became the company's S.L.J.O., or Shitty Little Jobs Officer. I was appointed as Payroll Officer, Firebase Reaction Force Commander, Acting Executive Officer and various other extra duties. Payroll Officer was the worst extra job. In those days, everyone was paid in cash. After the money was counted and signed for at the Brigade Finance Office, any later discrepancies came out of the Payroll Officer's pocket. The Payroll Officer had to go to wherever each soldier was located to pay him, even if he was in the hospital or at some other remote location. There was also a deadline for completing the pay-out and returning all paperwork to Finance. The Recon Platoon usually operated together, but Four Deuce had the "jump" detachment at Nui Vong and the snipers were always attached individually to line companies, so I typically had to visit a number of different locations to pay all E Company troops. There was a lot of paperwork, because the Payroll Officer was required to process changes to dependant allotments, money orders, U.S. Savings bonds, bank deposits and other transactions. I found an olive drab case for a large Starlight Scope which I used as a briefcase, to carry the cash, payroll signature roster and banking forms. I also carried a canteen and a bootleg M1911A1 .45 pistol for personal defense, but nothing else. I might have to go to a specific line unit to pay just one sniper, but if I didn't get the paperwork done, or if "backhaul" was cancelled, I'd have to wait until the next day to find transportation to wherever I had to go next. I would usually have to spend a night or two in the bush, carrying up to $20,000 in cash. I always had to beg for C-Rations from the line company grunts when I got stuck somewhere overnight. Payroll Officer duty was a pain in the neck.

The Mad Fragger and Me

I became friends with 1LT Roger Mackintosh, who was the Battalion Recon Platoon Leader. Mac was an avid big game hunter and a rifle nut. He had probably been on a college rifle team, because he did his troop duty at the U.S. Army Marksmanship Training Unit at Fort Benning. When he departed for Vietnam, the USAMTU gunsmiths fixed him up with a nice hunting scope in a hand-made mount which attached to the carrying handle of his M16, a very unique accessory in those days. I quizzed Mac about life in the bush, because I expected to go to a rifle company at some point. Mac asked if I had done any big game hunting or backpack camping and I said that I had. He commented that life in the bush was about the same and I'd have no problem. At the other end of the spectrum was OCS classmate Sid Hopfer, who came to my hootch and drank a few beers whenever D Company rotated to LZ Liz for perimeter security duty. Sid hated the bush. He told me horror stories about incidents like the night his platoon sergeant ("My only friend out there") was blown up by a booby trap as they moved into a night defensive position. Sid's stories made it sound like life in the bush was pure hell, a continuous series of shocking, terrifying events and unrelenting casualties. I wasn't sure who to believe, but I knew Sid to be truthful. His stories seemed to be confirmed by the battalion's continual casualties.

I had to go into the battalion "rear" at LZ Bronco regularly, to pick up a payroll or take care of some other chore, usually traveling in the Company Commander's jeep. 1SG Robert Moore maintained a couple of bunks in a room behind the Orderly Room office, for E Company officers to use. There was an adjacent bunker, which no one ever entered because it was so tiny, airless and claustrophobic. I was sleeping in one of those backroom bunks one night in November, when Super Typhoon *Patsy* made landfall in Vietnam. I remember the horrendous screeching sounds, when the high winds wrenched off part of the Orderly Room building's metal roof. I got up and looked outside, where I saw roofing tin and other debris blowing around like tissue paper. I tried to go back to sleep, without much success because of the racket from the wind and from buildings coming apart. I walked around our battalion area the next morning and observed the wreckage. Most buildings were damaged in varying degrees and I saw some perimeter bunkers which had collapsed completely.

    E Company had two young and pretty hootch maids, Lei and Mai. 1SG Moore treated them exactly like they were his own daughters. They were paid to clean the company buildings and to do laundry. They were both very nice girls, but they had opposite personalities. Lei was shy, demur and quiet, usually averting her eyes if you even spoke to her. Mai was funny, vivacious and feisty. Because I'd had a habit of torturing my sisters but they were not around, I often teased Mai, just to watch her flip out. I'd say, "You go to bunker with El Tee now, yes?"… then leer at her and wiggle my eyebrows up and down like Groucho Marx. Mai would always fly into a fit of temper, sputtering "You talk Number TEN!! Me tell First Sergeant!!" The two girls were convinced that Top Moore walked on water and outranked everyone else in the rear area. He really was their protector and no one dared to hit on them in a serious way.

    LZ Bronco had amenities like a Stand Down compound, clubs, a PX complex with barber shop, massage parlor and steam baths, and a fairly large airport. The rear area orderly rooms and supply rooms for the numerous combat arms and support units in the brigade were also located there. Bronco was surrounded by a perimeter road and bunkers which had to be manned 24/7. I wondered how the Army could commit so many resources to maintain such a large rear area. I have read that fewer than 10% of the Army troops in Vietnam were in the Infantry, but infantrymen also manned bases like LZ Bronco and the sprawling Division HQ at Chu Lai. Even though LZ Liz was categorized as a "Forward Fire Base", in reality it was a pretty secure area and every infantry battalion maintained a firebase similar to it. Troops based at LZ Liz were killed occasionally by mines on the access road or other mishaps, but they did not regularly go in harm's way like the rifle company grunts. What percentage of in-country troops were actually involved in infantry ground combat? My guess is that it was somewhere around 3%-5%.

There was a significant drug problem, mostly in rear areas. Troops usually smoked dope to alleviate boredom. Despite SFC Morris' and SSG Willard's best efforts to keep our troops fully occupied, drugs turned up in the 4.2 Inch Mortar Platoon. This was probably a reflection of general society, because the so-called drug culture had taken a strong hold throughout the United States in the 1960s. Morris and Willard told me that they suspected drug use within the platoon, especially in one squad. I'd had some experience with this at Fort Hood and I knew what we legally could and could not do. If we had evidence which constituted "probable cause", we could advise the culprit(s) of that and read them their rights under Article 31 (similar to Miranda) of the Uniform Code of Military Justice (UCMJ). We could then conduct a search for a specific item of contraband. If we then found that item, the miscreant could be charged criminally. I told Morris and Willard that we had "reasonable suspicion", but not enough evidence for "probable cause". The only action we could really take was an unannounced shakedown inspection. We could confiscate whatever contraband we found, but we could not initiate court martial charges. We conducted a shakedown inspection and came up with a sandbag full of mostly marihuana, but also some smack (heroin). Most of it came from the squad the NCOs suspected, but we also found some drugs in other areas. Dope was cheap and easy to get in the villes along QL1. Heroin was so inexpensive that it was usually smoked like grass. The packaging came as a surprise to me, especially the "Duc Pho One Hundreds". These were long, professionally rolled marihuana cigarettes, which were prepackaged in sealed clear plastic packs of five. They looked like regular 100mm cigarettes, but without filters. We read the riot act to the dopers and we burned the drugs.

The drug epidemic was destructive to discipline. The Army's other major sociological problem was racial conflict, another reflection of troubles within our larger society. The loudest and most obnoxious agitators on both sides of the racial problem were in the rear areas, where people had too much time on their hands. Younger black soldiers usually hung out together and they displayed signs of solidarity and youthful rebelliousness, such as the "dap" (an elaborate fist-bumping handshake). They often sported regulation-bending Afro hairstyles and symbolic braided bracelets or necklaces, but this was not very different from the hippy-like hair/attire deviations of younger white soldiers, who also tended to congregate by race. The more mature soldiers and NCOs tried to keep a lid on things, but friction between the two groups seemed to be constantly escalating and agitators on both sides of the problem were too often successful in stirring up trouble. This was a serious problem on a practical level, because it disrupted the absolute military need for teamwork. Many entire books have been written about the race problem, so my comments here will not begin to address it. To me at the time, racial conflict was mostly an unfortunate fact of human nature which I was forced to contend with as a white junior officer. Racial prejudice against the Vietnamese was blatant among too many GIs, both white and black.

    I was required to attend the Battalion Commander's Briefing every day. This was held in a briefing room/ bunker next to the TOC (Tactical Operations Center) at the top of Liz's main hill. Except for receiving occasional instructions about special things I was expected to do, it was a waste of time. The S2 (Intelligence), S3 (Operations), S5 (Civil Affairs) and a secondary staff officer or two would stand up in turn and give briefings about their areas of responsibility, using a long pointer, maps and charts. The battalion's body count ratio, by company, was updated daily on a chart board. It was always a Dog and Pony Show, but even more so if there was a VIP visitor present. The S3 was a busy man, but I think the other staff officers spent most of their time preparing for the daily briefing. I began to get a cynical attitude about the battalion staff after watching their daily performances. They were obviously detached from the casualties

The Mad Fragger and Me

being inflicted upon the line companies, most of which came from enemy mines and booby traps. They would casually mention the too-frequent rifle company KIAs, DOWs and WIAs, but then demonstrate their preoccupation with mundane problems and trivial events at LZ Liz. The Intelligence Officer's briefing was especially worthless, because it was about enemy activity "last week" or "two days ago". He never developed local intelligence and his information was always extrapolated from Brigade, ARVN, MACV or other reports. Occasionally, some of the briefing was amusing. I recall them talking about a Military Police raid on "Alice's Restaurant" in a ville along QL1. "Alice" was a Vietnamese black marketeer and her shop was called that because of the Arlo Guthrie song lyrics... "You can get anything you want...at Alice's Restaurant". Alice was notorious as a drug dealer, but the Military Police confiscated a complete and fully functioning U.S. M2 .50 caliber Browning machine gun from Alice's Restaurant!

I was invited to the 11th Brigade Officers' "Dining-In" at LZ Bronco during the 1970 Christmas season. It was a Command-Performance event, so my attendance was mandatory. Dress was informal, jungle fatigues, but the dinner party itself was ceremonious and somewhat stuffy. I was strongly admonished during the cocktail hour at the Dining-In, by a distinguished looking but pompous staff Lieutenant Colonel, regarding an offhand comment I made about "dinks". He loudly accused me of using racist language. I told him I used the word only as a shorthand term for enemy soldiers and not as a disparaging racial label... but that explanation didn't satisfy him. He lectured to everyone within earshot that "dink" was a pejorative and offensive term, so enemy soldiers should be properly and exclusively referred to as "HIPs", which he said stood for Hostile Indigenous Personnel. Friendly Indigenous Personnel were to be referred to as "FIPs". As he probably intended, I was slightly embarrassed by the LTC's stern reprimand, but I really didn't understand why I should be concerned about saying anything which might offend the VC and NVA. After my later reassignment to a rifle company, I deliberately offended the enemy *with extreme prejudice*, every chance I got. If that Lieutenant Colonel is still alive, I imagine he is a committed Progressive, who rails on in his dotage with astute opinions about HIPs and FIPs, formulated during his observation of the Overseas Contingency Operation in Vietnam. I'd like to tell him that I still refer to my former enemies as "dinks" and I didn't sit out *my* war as a Field-Grade pogue, making politically correct pronouncements at rear-area officers' cocktail parties.

The Fire Direction Center crew threw a New Year's Eve party. We were gathered in the FDC bunker, listening to music and drinking beer. I had found an experimental illumination flare in a footlocker, which looked exactly like an M26 fragmentary hand grenade, except for the markings. Pretending to be inebriated, I took the "frag" out of my cargo pocket and pulled the pin, causing much consternation and yelling. I let the safety handle fly off, opened the FDC bunker door and casually tossed the "grenade" outside to "celebrate New Year's". I thought this was a great joke, but I forgot there was a deuce 'n half parked outside in the dark. The flare landed in the uncovered back of the truck and set the wooden seats on fire. The FDC crew thought *that* was funny. They were laughing so hard that none of them were able to help me put out the fire.

The TOC called for a "Mad Minute" periodically, when all soldiers on the bunker line would fire their weapons into and beyond the perimeter wire at cyclic rates for 60 seconds, changing magazines or ammo belts as fast as possible. This was always done at night and at a preplanned time, but "start" and "stop" for the Mad Minute were signaled by star cluster rockets. It was SOP to load a tracer as every fifth round in M16 magazines and M60 ammo belts were set up the same way. The grunts often loaded several magazines with all tracers in preparation for a Mad Minute, to produce a better light show. A Mad Minute was a demonstration of firepower, intended to discourage infiltration or ground attacks.

The Mad Fragger and Me

Once in awhile, the VC/NVA would lob one or two 82mm mortar rounds, or a 122mm rocket, into LZ Liz. There was a somewhat more serious mortar attack on 1 February 1971. That night, Dink woke me up around 1:35 AM by growling ferociously. It was quiet outside, but Dink had apparently either heard something or she'd had a doggy premonition. I let her out of the bunker and she ran downhill to the west perimeter wire. The perimeter was illuminated by spotlights and I could see Dink running up and down the wire, growling, with the hair standing straight up on her back. Within a minute or two, CHICOM 82mm mortar rounds started coming in, about 20 of them in all, most of them landing in or just west of the Four Deuce Platoon area. One of them hit a 2½ ton truck parked in our area and wrecked it. Everybody got up and went to fighting positions or to the mortar pits. I knew the general direction the enemy mortar fire was coming from because of Dink's antics, but I could not spot any muzzle flashes. We put up illumination and fired some 81mm Delta Tangos on that side of the perimeter. I remember that the art'y battery next to us was also shooting at something. The mortar attack did not last very long, but it certainly got the TOC Commandos buzzing for a few days. The mortar shower was apparently intended to distract us from an all-out ground attack on a Regional Force/Popular Force (RF/PF) compound at LZ Max, about four klicks North of LZ Liz. We could see that firebase from our location and they really took a pounding. We saw streams of tracers going back and forth, then gunships pouring it on. The fire fight went on for a long time. We heard later that the outpost was overrun by NVA and that the RF/PFs had multiple KIAs/WIAs, with several MACV advisors also wounded.

My first company commander in E Company was 1LT Timothy Capps. He seemed okay but we did not have much direct contact and did not really become friends. 1LT Capps was replaced in December by an officer I'll call Tobias Macadamia. Captain Macadamia was a slightly built and vertically challenged little man from Hawaii, who suffered severely from Short Man's Syndrome. He always carried an equally diminutive Walther PPK .380 in a waistband holster under his shirt, very James Bond-ish, you know. At first, I really tried to get along with him, but it was impossible to do that. Our first major run-in was at an awards ceremony on the helipad at the top of the hill next to the TOC. Some of my guys were receiving "I was there" medals, so I went to watch the ceremony and Dink followed me. There is a photo of this in my album and Dink can be seen walking around on the asphalt. CPT Macadamia loudly said, "Lieutenant Dolan, get that dog out of here." I tried to call Dink over to me quietly, so as to not disrupt the awards ceremony, but I apparently didn't move fast enough to suit Macadamia. He screamed," GOD DAMN IT, LIEUTENANT DOLAN, I TOLD YOU TO GET THAT @#%$! DOG OUT OF HERE! DO IT NOW!" I did that, with my cheeks burning from being called down and cursed in front of my troops, the Battalion Commander and several staff officers. There were other such incidents too. When Macadamia criticized me, he often did it in the presence of others and he always expressed his dissatisfaction in ways which were personally insulting. He treated everyone of lower rank with similar contempt and rudeness. Macadamia was a nasty little creep and he quickly became universally despised, by EM and officers alike. The troops referred to him by various sobriquets, including "Captain Pineapple". SGT Edgardo Rodriguez-Velez, our Puerto Rican humorist, usually referred to him as *Capitan Maricon.*

One day, I took a phone call from CPT Macadamia in the Fire Direction Center. SGT Jerry Ford, the FDC Chief, was the only other person in the bunker. Macadamia began giving me some instructions, in an obnoxious and bullying fashion. I was talking to him on a TA312, which is a battery operated field phone with a push-to-talk switch on the handset. Because he was speaking to me in a demeaning way, I began saying "Yes, Sir"… then letting go of the push-to-talk button and continuing "…you jerk"… or "… you little runt". This went on for awhile and at one point Macadamia asked, "What did you say?" so I repeated it, including the insult. SGT Ford

The Mad Fragger and Me

had initially ignored the telephone conversation, but then he started listening and he began shaking his head "No" and making a "cut it off" gesture with his hand, under his chin. After I hung up, Ford said, "Sir, if you were talking to CPT Macadamia, he could hear what you were saying. He is just up at the top of the hill and that is a battery operated phone... you can still hear what is being said when the phones are that close to each other, even if the button is not pushed, it just sounds faint and far away". SGT Ford and I looked at each other for a moment and then we both burst out laughing. Accordingly, my relationship with Macadamia continued to deteriorate. I heard scuttlebutt about a possible fragging of his quarters at one point. I was not certain if the threat was serious, but I still intervened and I may have saved his sorry butt.

We were shooting 4.2 inch service-practice on February 11th and CPT Macadamia came down to the platoon area to observe it. We had wrapped up the firing session and a group of us were standing outside the Fire Direction Center bunker, which was part way up a slope, overlooking the gun pits. Having finished plotting, SGT Ford came out of the FDC bunker with several guys from his crew, including SGT Rodriguez-Velez and SP/4 Jerry Gillespie. Skippy, the platoon's dimwitted mascot, came wandering up the slope towards us, vaguely wagging his tail. Macadamia picked up a heavy rock the size of a baseball and threw it at Skippy, striking him in the head. The dog went down, dazed severely, then he struggled to get up, and he staggered around bawling and howling. Macadamia started laughing uproariously at the clever joke he had played on Ol' Skip. Skippy finally got his feet organized and he ran away, yelping and crying. The FDC guys were standing behind Macadamia, so he did not see Jerry Gillespie, who doted on Skippy, start coming for him with fire in his eyes. SGT Ford, SGT Rodriguez-Velez and a third guy grabbed Gillespie, clamped a hand over his mouth and dragged him into the FDC bunker, his arms and legs flailing, the door slamming shut behind them. I was shocked by Macadamia's behavior and stunned that Jerry Gillespie, who was an easy going kid, had fully intended to attack him. Choking down my anger, I finally managed to say, "You really are a *sorry* son of a bitch", and I turned and walked away. Macadamia started yelling about me being disrespectful, come back here, stand at attention, that's a direct order, and all that kind of stuff. He said he was going to court martial me for insubordination. I continued walking away and I answered over my shoulder, "Good luck finding a witness around *here*, asshole".

The day after that confrontation with Macadamia, I received a message to report to our new battalion commanding officer, LTC Thomas Brogan, in his quarters. Colonel Brogan said, "I understand that you are not getting along too well with CPT Macadamia", smiling as he said it. I'm sure he had gotten an earful about me, but I'm also sure he knew that Macadamia was a complete idiot. I confirmed that I wasn't getting along with him and LTC Brogan told me Macadamia had recommended that I be sent to the bush, immediately, with a rifle company. He asked how I felt about that and I said it suited me just fine. I was told to go down to the bunker line and report to CPT James Davidson, the CO of Bravo Company, which was leaving LZ Liz for the bush in the morning. I did that and found that CPT Davidson was obviously a nice guy, so I looked forward to working for him. My friend 1LT Roger Mackintosh was now in B Company too, and I met the other two rifle platoon leaders, 1LT Greg Studdard and 1LT Frank Korona. Greg had 1st Platoon, Frank had 2nd and Mac had 3rd. There seemed to be strong camaraderie among the B Company officers. I was to be attached to the 2nd Platoon, under Frank, who would show me the ropes as a platoon leader. I would get my own platoon at some future date. It was obviously a rushed reassignment, because I was transferred to B Company before they had a slot for me, so I wondered what CPT Davidson had been told about me and my conflicts with *Capitan Maricon*. I was told what time to report in the morning and I went back to my little bunker and packed my rucksack, with some trepidation. After hearing the tales of violence from line platoon leaders and the continuous rifle company casualty numbers in daily briefings, I wasn't sure what to expect in Bravo Company, but it sounded like it was going to be dangerous out there. My last day in Four Deuce was 12 February 1971, so I had been there almost 4 months.

Chapter 5:

GOING TO THE BUSH WITH BRAVO COMPANY

I got up early on 13 February 1971 and walked up the hill to CPT Davidson's CP (Command Post) in the dark. There had been several trucks blown up recently by land mines on the LZ Liz Access Road, and troops on them killed or wounded. For this reason, we foot-marched about two klicks (2,000 meters) along the Access Road, out to the hard ball, QL 1, for pickup by a convoy of deuce 'n halfs. I had asked SSG Willard to keep Dink for me, but she must have gotten loose, because she found me as we were starting off from the firebase entrance around daybreak. I scolded her and threw clumps of dirt at her, but she would not go back and she happily followed me all the way out to the hard ball. We climbed on the trucks and headed North on QL 1. Dink urgently wanted to go with me and she chased the convoy for quite a long distance, probably a half mile or more, through the villes along Highway 1, until the trucks finally picked up speed in open country and left her behind. I was seriously worried about her, because she was wearing a leather collar with a rabies vaccination tag attached to it, and dog meat was high on the Vietnamese list of desirable cuisine. Native dogs never wore collars and were regarded as a source of protein, not as pets. Dink would have to make her way back to the firebase through a long and contiguous gauntlet of villages which were teeming with unfriendly humanity, while dodging vehicular traffic on Highway 1. But I couldn't take her to the bush with me and there was nothing I could do about her having gone AWOL from LZ Liz.

The convoy took us about 5 miles north to LZ Dragon, a long elevated helicopter landing zone, from which we made a CA (Combat Assault) by helicopters into the mountains west of Dragon Valley. The remnants of an old road ran through Dragon Valley, from Highway 1 to the mountains. The road had deteriorated into a heavily used footpath and it was universally known as "VC Highway". There were no hamlets in the valley, but plenty of VC/NVA. CPT Davidson and his CP group were traveling with Mac's 3rd Platoon on the other side of the valley. I watched Frank Korona plan his operations for two days and I went on several patrols. That was the extent of the orientation Frank was able to give me. On February 15th, at 1700 hours (5:00 PM) the 3rd Platoon hit an explosive booby trap, which we heard detonate. An "urgent" dust-off was called for two WIAs (Wounded In Action) with multiple shrapnel wounds. The two wounded were CPT James Davidson and 1LT Roger Mackintosh. They were initially taken to the 91st Evacuation Hospital, but their wounds were severe enough that they were then flown to a medical facility in Japan. I never saw either of them again, but we heard later that they both survived, although not whether they were permanently disabled. Frank Korona was appointed as CO of B Company. He went to the 3rd Platoon's location to assume command of the CP group and to direct the 3rd Platoon, which no longer had a platoon leader. I was designated to lead the 2nd Platoon. So much for being oriented gradually by an experienced rifle platoon leader, but I needn't have worried. As Shane Pinkston had predicted, the troops in 2nd Platoon assured me that I didn't have anything to be concerned about. They all knew what they were doing. All I had to do was to follow their instructions and do everything they told me to do until they had me broken in.

    B Company continued to find more booby traps in the VC Highway/Dragon Valley area. On February 16th, we were extracted from that AO (Area of Operations) and we were picked up for a CA into the Song Ve River Valley. The troops said that the Song Ve area was known for its bad juju and it was considered to be "Indian Country". Four months earlier, on 12 October 1970, Bravo Company had made an Eagle Flight (one of a series of "cold" helicopter insertions) into the Song Ve area and had landed on top of a large NVA unit, which was occupying a group of old French concrete bunkers there. Four B Company soldiers were killed in action, including the Company Commander, and seven others were wounded. That had been LT Frank Korona's first day in the field, and the Song Ve Valley was where he began to establish his reputation as a warrior. The 2nd Platoon guys said that El Tee Korona had saved the day, after CPT Francis Powers was killed. Frank received an impact award of the Silver Star for valor, because of his actions on 12 October 70. (He later also received two Bronze Star Medals with "V"/valor devices, for his actions on 30 October 70 and 12 January 71. He was additionally awarded an Army Commendation Medal with "V", for his actions on 4 May 71. That makes a total of four awards for conspicuous bravery in combat, a remarkable record. It was unusual for a lieutenant to be decorated in rifle platoons which operated autonomously, because it seldom occurred to an enlisted man to recommend his lieutenant for a decoration and an officer of higher rank was rarely present to observe a brave act. Frank Korona was our battalion's answer to Audie Murphy.)

The troops were angry about 1LT Mackintosh and CPT Davidson being blown up. They were also not happy about being sent into the Song Ve Valley. The villagers there were openly hostile towards us and we could see it in their faces, eyes and body language. We picked up multiple detainees, most of them adult females or middle aged men, and we sent them back to the rear for interrogation. We would look for irregularities in their ID cards (*can cuoc*), pack strap marks on their shoulders, soft hands and things like that. Or just bad attitudes, which were prevalent. Part of the attitude problem resulted from my soldiers being unnecessarily brutal towards the Song Ve villagers. The 2nd Platoon started by torching hootches when my back was turned. This was done arbitrarily and maliciously. It made me angry, even more so because while I was trying to stop it, the Battalion S3 (or CO?) was flying around at 2,000 feet in a C&C bird, transmitting radio messages such as, "I see that Zippo Squad moving through that ville", and "Watch where you drop those cigarette butts, ha ha!". I really lost it when I saw an elderly Mamma-San wailing because her forehead had been laid open by a rifle butt and I had our medic patch her up. Like the burning hootches, nobody knew who butt-stroked Mamma-San. I went ape with the troops, reaming them out and making plenty of nasty threats. At least they probably got the message that their new El Tee would not meekly go along with whatever they felt like doing. I asked one of the more senior and steady guys, Roger Steward, "What the hell is wrong with these people?" He answered, "You will understand it after you've been out here for awhile." He was wrong. I never did learn to understand or accept that kind of behavior. I was seething mad to the extent I couldn't eat or sleep for several days. I sensed that some of the 2nd Platoon soldiers agreed with my point of view, but they would not talk about who was responsible. I understood that a few jerks might do that kind of stuff, but I could not understand why nobody else had enough courage to speak up against it. In hindsight, it was probably peer pressure and fear of the few thugs who were doing it.

We moved around in the Song Ve Valley for about four days, changing day laagers and NDPs, so as to not set any patterns. While moving to a new PB on the morning of February 19th, Squad Leader Roger Steward was walking "point" and he tripped a fresh booby trap. The fuse was from a U.S. smoke grenade and it popped like a firecracker. Fortunately, the main charge, a large #10 mess hall can packed with petna (properly, PETN), a high explosive used in artillery rounds, did not go off. The exploding fuse startled SGT Steward and he cursed, then ripped the device out of the tall grass in a display of temper. I was walking right behind him and if the main charge had exploded, it probably would have killed both of us. We destroyed the booby trap and I called the incident in. This mishap was my fault and I knew it. We should not have been walking on a trail in a place where we did not have to do it. That night and the next day, 2nd Platoon moved around a large mountain, hugging the east side of the Song Ve River, moving north towards Nui Vong/Hill 103. There was an old French Foreign Legion outpost

The Mad Fragger and Me

on Hill 103 which 1/20 Infantry had occupied and used as a ground radar site.

On February 20th, a new lieutenant was sent out to 3rd Platoon, to replace Roger Mackintosh. The 3rd Platoon also made a CA to the opposite side of the Song Ve River and they began to move along the west side of the river parallel to my 2nd Platoon. The 1st Platoon was on our side of the river, but I don't remember if they were in front of or behind us.

The same day, February 20th, we were taking a break at the base of the mountain and I saw an M26 U.S. fragmentary hand grenade loft up out of a clump of brush into the midst of us. The frag looked like it was coming in slow motion, but the dink who threw it must have cooked it off because it exploded immediately after it hit the ground. A couple of other guys also saw it, we all yelled "FRAG!" and everyone hit the ground. It landed about 15 feet from me and exploded, but I wasn't touched. Another soldier near me, SP/4 Charles Beavers, was painfully wounded by shrapnel in his abdomen. The guys had started shooting into the brush automatically after the frag exploded. The second part of Shane's prediction then came true, because the troops were all looking at me with that "What do we do now?" look in their eyes. Fortunately, after a nanosecond of near panic, I knew what to do. I had been rehearsing various contingencies in my mind almost continuously for several days as we moved, and I had also mentally rehearsed the "call for fire". I called for a priority MEDEVAC and then got artillery coming, rattling off the call for fire into the radio. I started to adjust the art'y fire, but lifted it as the dust-off chopper came in for Beavers. We moved through and searched the area from which the frag was thrown. We found a little ground depression the enemy soldier had been occupying, with grass matted down like a deer's bed, but that was all. The dink who threw the grenade didn't hang around after he tossed it, but the artillery was intended to interdict his escape and clear any possible booby traps. A standard VC/NVA tactic was to booby-trap an area, then shoot at GIs or take some other action to draw them into the mines. I knew this anecdotally, even though I was inexperienced.

The next day, February 21st, the 3rd Platoon tripped a booby trapped 155mm artillery round which was suspended chest high in a tree. We heard the explosion from across the Song Ve River and saw a huge plume of smoke go up. There were two immediate KIAs, CPL Jim Califf and PFC Fred Young. Seven more guys were wounded, some of them grievously, including the new Platoon Leader, who had been in the bush for just one day. The lieutenant did not come back, nor did I ever meet him. (One of the wounded, PFC Steve Ast, later died of wounds on March 3rd.) After the dead and wounded were dusted off, the survivors, leaderless, refused to move and demanded helicopter extraction. 1LT Greg Studdard had previously been assigned to 3rd Platoon. He waded across the waist-deep Song Ve River, which was about 200 meters wide at that point, accompanied only by an RTO. After crossing the river, Studdard found some VC booby trap warning signs, a boot upside down on a stake and tall grass tied in knots, but the 3rd Platoon had not seen the warnings because they had followed a different route prior to hitting the trap. Lieutenant Studdard got the survivors moving, leading them back across the river.

On 22 February 1971, we humped out to Nui Vong/ Hill 103, which we then helped a Combat Engineer outfit close down as a 1/20 Infantry outpost. I had a tough time keeping up with the unit when we walked out from the bush, even though I was probably carrying the lightest rucksack in 2nd Platoon at that point. I had put on weight but had not been getting any serious exercise, during my three months with Four Deuce. All that beer drinking and those steak cookouts had taken their toll. At only 24 years old I was able to tough it out, otherwise I might have been left behind. Grunts did not pay much attention to the personal problems of newbies, such as having trouble keeping up during a foot march. After helping to destroy the bunkers and perimeter wire at Nui Vong, B Company returned to LZ Liz. The first thing I did was check on Dink and she was there, safe and sound with SSG Willard. She gave me an enthusiastic greeting.

One thing that occurred to me after this first mission was that there might not be much future in the job of Rifle Platoon Leader. Each rifle company usually had four Infantry officers in the field on each mission, but Bravo Company had lost three such officers or 75%, two lieutenants and a captain, in ten days. One of the lieutenants only lasted one day in the bush. We'd also had 3 enlisted men tragically killed and 7 more wounded (including my guy) out of a probable total of about 80 EM, during the same 10 day period, which comes out to a 12.5% casualty rate for the enlisted personnel. I had come uncomfortably close to being blown away by both a booby trap and a hand frag during that same brief period of time. What the hell had I gotten myself into?

It may appear that I have a phenomenal memory for the sequence of events, names and dates, but that is not the case. Some experiences, such as seeing that M26 hand grenade coming, were burned into my brain and are still vivid. The sequence of events and dates were provided by CPT Chuck Sekeda's website, www.1-20infantry.org and a feature on it called *A Daily Recap of Operations*. It contains transcribed summaries of the Battalion's S2/S3 journal, by year, date and company. Some of this material is not accurate, for example it lists another soldier as WIA from the frag on February 20th, but I vividly remember SP/4 Beavers grimacing in agony (he recovered and was given a rear job). Nevertheless, the *Recap* provided a fine chronological outline and was a wonderful memory-jogger while I was writing this memoir. The S2/S3 log also provides insight into the trivial incidents at LZ Liz which the TOC Commandos thought were important, because they documented them for posterity.

You may have noticed that I have not mentioned a Platoon Sergeant who might have assisted me in the above adventures. Do not jump to the conclusion that I did not have one assigned to me. *Au contraire*, Staff Sergeant John Warrior (a pseudonym) was assigned to 2nd Platoon as the Platoon Sergeant. Alas, Sergeant Warrior's presence in 2nd Platoon was not helpful to me. SSG Warrior was a burly African-American with a sour and resentful demeanor. When I picked an NDP or PB, he often grumbled about the location to the troops and there was intermittent griping about other operational issues, usually behind my back. When I issued orders he didn't like, he made disparaging comments to other black soldiers which implied that my decisions were influenced by racial bias. He did not attempt to support me in discouraging the ville arsons or the abuse of the civilians. I suspected that he knew who the perpetrators were but withheld that information from me. I quickly noticed his subversive behavior, but SSG Warrior was either not aware that I was on to him, or he did not think that I could do anything about it. In spite of his deficiencies, Warrior was a physically impressive man, both large and intimidating. As a result, he had a fair amount of influence over at least some of the troops in 2nd Platoon, but his lousy attitude prevented that influence from producing positive results. This situation set up a direct conflict between us. As a result of Shane Pinkston's leadership coaching, I had no inclination to defer any of my command authority to an NCO, so the problem was only going to be resolved by the departure of one or the other of us. SSG Warrior had been in the bush for a long time and he had been through at least two other platoon leaders before I was assigned to 2nd Platoon. 1LT Korona told me that SSG Warrior had acted heroically during the battle in the Song Ve Valley four months earlier, saving two young soldiers from probable death, so there had been another side to him in the past. Warrior was long overdue for a rear job. He may have been overstressed and burned out as Platoon Sergeant, but the 2nd Platoon and I needed someone in that slot who was functional and effective. However, I would deal with SSG John Warrior soon enough.

Despite the sudden exposure to violence and the high casualties during my first mission with B Company, by far the most

The Mad Fragger and Me

stressful aspect of going to the bush was the rebelliousness of some of my troops and the noncooperation of my Platoon Sergeant. I understood my soldiers' hesitancy to accept a new and unproven lieutenant. I also fully understood that I was responsible for their welfare and this responsibility weighed heavily on me. I could not allow them to do as they pleased, so I had to either persuade or force them to comply with my orders. I have read several accounts by Vietnam veterans about the sense of alienation they felt as newbie enlisted men, when first joining a rifle platoon. As they entered their new and violent world, they discovered it was inhabited by indifferent strangers, who didn't seem to be interested in becoming friends, or teaching them how to survive on the battlefield. Those accounts are unquestionably truthful, although perhaps not accurate in identifying the reasons for the uncaring attitudes. But cherry enlisted men did not have their new comrades working *against* them, as seemed to always occur with Infantry platoon leaders. This problem of establishing leadership credibility in combat units is an ancient one which will never change as long as mankind engages in warfare.

Our general operations followed the pattern described above. There were four rifle companies, A through D, which took turns manning the defensive perimeter at LZ Liz. Firebase security duty would generally last 3 or 4 days, then the company on Liz would return to the bush and another company would come in from the field to replace it, with some overlap on the day when the units were coming in/out. Stints in the bush would therefore usually last about 12-14 days.

Whenever we came in from the boonies, we had been wearing the same uniforms for about two weeks and we were pretty gamey by then, although everyone made an effort to stay reasonably clean in the bush. When I first joined Bravo Company, Battalion Headquarters always set up a "Circus" at the bottom of the hill, outside of the LZ Liz entrance. They had a field shower unit there, which consisted of eight 5 gallon canvas bags with shower heads attached to the bottoms, suspended from an open steel frame on a trailer. We were required to strip off all our clothes and take cold showers. They gave us towels to dry off with and then we got in line, naked, for a medical exam. The medics set up an open air aid station at the Circus under the direction of the Battalion Surgeon and they gave everyone a good going over, especially checking feet/groins for jungle rot and bodies for any open sores. Treatment, care instructions and medications were issued on the spot. Then the EM tried to find clothes that would fit them by rummaging through the bags of clean uniforms which had been brought out from the rear area at LZ Bronco. These ragged uniforms were stripped of name tapes and other insignia. They were faded, well-worn and some had been repaired a number of times, or needed repair when they were handed out. There always seemed to be plenty of spectators around, just like at a real circus. The only thing missing was popcorn and cotton candy. There is no modesty among grunts, but that doesn't mean they enjoyed being stared at like carnival side show geeks. I thought that these troops, the small percentage of soldiers who were really fighting the war, were being treated like animals. They were not allowed to enter the firebase until they had been deloused and inspected like cattle, and they were then dressed in faded cast-off rags. The officers fared slightly better, because the First Sergeant brought out a clean personal uniform for each, with his rank and name affixed. The Company Supply Sergeant also brought a truck full of field gear to the Circus, so equipment could be issued or exchanged. This was no doubt seen as an efficient way to handle the refitting of a rifle company coming in from the field, but it was unnecessarily demeaning. It also preempted the responsibility of platoon medics and leadership personnel to monitor and care for their troops. A short time after I joined B Company, the Circus operation was dropped and we were allowed to move directly into the bunkers and get cleaned up/refitted there. I never saw the slightest difference in outcomes

The Mad Fragger and Me

for the troops, except that they were treated with the dignity that they deserved.

As soon as we came in to Liz, we were given perimeter assignments by bunker number, so each platoon had responsibility for a segment of the bunker line, about five bunkers per platoon. The bunkers were fairly primitive and looked like they had probably been built by grunts. There was no standard in design or dimensions. They were framed with timbers, with plywood interior walls and steel PSP roofs. The walls and roofs were covered with sandbags, which had an overlay of cement or tar as a preservative. They had rough concrete floors and wooden double bunks built in, with wooden slats, no springs or mattresses. There were spotlights which illuminated the perimeter wire. Some bunkers were wired for a single light bulb, but many of them only had candles. There were vertical timbers from which jungle hammocks could be hung. There was no furniture, except sometimes a few wooden boxes. Some of the bunkers had firing ports and some did not. Guard duty was pulled outside, often from a fighting position on the roof. There were additional fighting positions around each bunker, usually simple ones with sandbagged culvert halves as overhead cover, sometimes with chain link RPG Screens to provide "stand-off" of B40 rockets. The perimeter bunkers were usually dirty and poorly maintained, except for the structural basics. There were permanent claymores and FUGAS drums (55 gallon drums filled with a mixture of JP4 aviation fuel and diesel, with an explosive charge on the bottom) placed to the front of the bunker line. The barbed wire and other defenses were generally in marginal shape. The enemy could have penetrated the perimeter without too much difficulty if they had made a determined attack on LZ Liz. The bunkers were widely separated and lightly manned, grass had grown up in the wire and there were areas where some dead space existed. There was a system of field telephones, between bunkers and CP, with battalion switchboard access. We supplemented the defenses with our own radios, trip flares and claymores.

Tom Dolan

One persistent problem in the perimeter bunkers was rats, which came in extra large size only. We had plenty of those, but rat traps were always in short supply for some reason. I usually slept outside under the stars, unless the weather was bad. One night I was sleeping inside a perimeter bunker and something woke me up, by scurrying down my hammock rope to my feet. I was wide awake instantly and of course I knew what it was. A jungle hammock wraps around you like a cocoon, so I couldn't do anything but lay there on my back with my eyes closed and let the rat run over my legs, body and face, then up the other rope. While I was in Four Deuce, we sometimes shot rats inside the bunkers with "soap rounds" in our M16s. These were 5.56mm cartridges which had the bullets pulled and replaced with wads of soap or candle wax, so they could be fired indoors with relative safety. Jujubes were sometimes used as projectiles, which was a good use for them because they tasted like crap. At close range, soap rounds had enough punch to kill rats. But rats are smart and when you start shooting them, they quickly become wary and totally nocturnal. In 2nd Platoon we improvised our own rat traps when we were at Liz, which were patterned after the "Mechanical Ambush", which I will describe in more detail later. These traps were set up outside the bunkers, inside steel ammo cans turned on their sides. Our improved rat trap featured an electrical blasting cap, attached to a short section of claymore firing wires with a triggering device, hooked up to a battery, so the trap was trip-detonated. When the rat grabbed the bait and tripped the trigger, he would blow himself to Kingdom Come. A blasting cap alone generated enough shrapnel to kill a rat inside the confines of an ammo can, but molding a small ball of C4 plastic explosive around the tip of the blasting cap produced a more spectacular assassination of Mr. Rat. These improvised traps actually worked better than factory-made rat traps. It was always satisfying to hear one go bang in the middle of the night.

When we were at LZ Liz, we were able to eat regular hot rations in the firebase mess hall. The mess hall was a large and airy

The Mad Fragger and Me

building enclosed all-around by screens, nicely built, probably by Army Engineers or Seabees. The food was pretty good by Army standards, but it would have been considered swill in Navy or USAF mess halls. Unlike the troops assigned to the firebase, the grunts never complained about the frequency of roast beef. When I was in the Heavy Mortar Platoon, I usually ate in the Battalion Commander's Dining Room, which was a small building which could seat about 16 officers at a time. It sported a small window A/C unit and was the only air conditioned place on LZ Liz. That option was still open to me, but in B Company I often ate with my troops in the mess hall. Line companies were required to provide KPs while they were on Liz. The Four Deuce Platoon pulled KP duty on days when line companies were rotating in/out, but all other firebase enlisted men were exempt from KP. This was an example of how the grunts were always treated like second class citizens in any rear area, even at a so-called Forward Firebase, like LZ Liz.

B Company left LZ Liz after my first stay there with B Company, on 26 February 1971. We humped out on foot about 3 klicks to an area west of LZ Liz, which was known as "The 515 Valley", named after the route number of an old road that ran through it from QL 1. I was to later spend a lot of time in The 515 Valley and it became my favorite place for combat operations. The area was pretty well pacified and the villagers were usually friendly. There were always a lot of kids present and they liked to hang out with us. The troops sometimes called this area "Happy Valley". There were very few booby traps, which facilitated night operations, and we could sneak around and be "tactical". The VC/NVA seemed to use Happy Valley as an R&R area and there were always enough enemy around to keep things interesting.

Because of the leadership void, the 1st and 3rd Platoons were initially combined under Greg Studdard, until a new platoon leader (1LT Doug Knight) joined us later during this mission. Frank Korona accompanied me and the 2nd Platoon, probably because I was still a rookie. This was Greg's last tour in the bush as a rifle platoon leader, so I did not get to know him very well. The S2/S3 log entries repeatedly refer to the 4th Platoon, but there was no such platoon, only a small group of 11 Charlie mortarmen, with one 81mm mortar tube. They had a lieutenant assigned to them only briefly (1LT Jim Waugh) and they were usually led by SSG Larry Spangler. The mortar group went with whichever rifle platoon the CO was with. The general pattern in the bush was that the three rifle platoon leaders operated independently within assigned AOs and the Company Commander accompanied one of them.

The day we went out, a 2nd Platoon patrol suddenly came upon and captured a suspected VC/NVA, estimated to be 40 years old, who was carrying a map of North Vietnam and Laos. He was sent back to the rear for interrogation. We also killed a Viet Cong soldier at grid 736437. I remember the event clearly, but the S2/S3 journal entries about this incident are totally inaccurate. Frank Korona had ordered 2nd Platoon to search a ville at that location and he described how he wanted it done. We went in very rapidly and quietly, one squad wrapping around the outside of the ville to block on the left, and a second squad encircling to block on the right side. The third squad went high-diddle-diddle, straight-up-the-middle. This was the classic "Cordon and Search" maneuver, but executed at high speed. I was with the middle squad near the front of the file and I saw a military aged male, 25 to 30 years old, dressed in black pajamas, playing with a small boy, next to a dwelling. He spotted us, jumped up and ran into the hootch. SP/4 Keith Moore was walking point and he yelled "Chieu hoi!" (Vietnamese for "open arms"… roughly meaning "surrender and come over to our side".) Keith ran up on top of a bunker mound which was attached to the back of the hut and his "slack" man followed the dink inside, an impressive demonstration of instinctive teamwork. Moore saw the guy come out of a tunnel into the hedgerow behind the hootch and he hosed him with a long burst from his M16. The hedgerow was very thick and we could hear the dink moving around and groaning, but we could not see him. We did not know whether he was armed or not

The Mad Fragger and Me

and I did not want to risk sending one of my men in there. So I pulled the pin on a frag and tossed it into the brush in the direction of the noise, which finished him off. Two of the guys went in and dragged him out, his brains spilling out of his skull as they pulled the body out by the feet. The little boy, about five years old, had seen the whole thing and he was screaming bloody murder. The new widow had also appeared and she was wailing while trying to console the kid. It was a very ugly scene, one which is forever tattooed on my brain. The casual brutality and the stark finality of the killing were shocking, but I realized that the dead person could have just as easily been one of us. We searched and found a stash of trip wire, blasting caps, fuses and petna, i.e., booby trap materials. I've sometimes thought about this incident and wished we'd let the guy go, instead of killing him in front of his son, but he shouldn't have tried to run. *Xin loi.* (Pronounced "sin loy", Vietnamese for "too bad" or "sorry"; but when said by a G.I., it always meant "tough shit.")

Two nights later, 28 February 1971, we moved a relatively long distance into a Night Defensive Position, which was located along a major trail leading into the mountains. The NDP was in a small abandoned rice paddy, with old dikes which could be used as defilade positions. We went in quietly after dark. Frank Korona's idea was to set up a platoon-sized night ambush and NDP combination on the trail. I verified that the squad leaders were setting up their positions, then went back to my ruck and started to roll out my bedroll. Frank came up to me and whispered that he wanted me to go with him to inspect the defensive positions. Thinking that we would remain inside the NDP, I stupidly left my rifle leaning on my rucksack, a thoughtless act that my Grandfather Dolan would have called "A Dumb Irish Trick." I followed Frank Korona to the far side of perimeter, where we talked to the squad leader in whispers. Frank decided that he wanted to go outside our perimeter, to check for dead space and possible approaches to the NDP. We walked out about 50 meters and were looking around, when all hell broke loose in the perimeter behind us. The guys on the far side lit up somebody with full automatic M16 fire and a machine gun quickly joined in, streams of tracers going out. Then they started sending up white parachute illumination flares and we could hear "bloop-CRUMP", "bloop-CRUMP", "bloop-CRUMP" from 40mm grenade launchers. We crouched and watched the action for a minute or two and Frank calmly said, "I think we'd better go back in there", which was such a nice understatement that I kidded him about it later. I was unarmed and I asked Frank if he had a frag. He said, "Where is your pistol?" I usually carried the .45 around at night in my hip pocket, but it was still in an outside pocket of my rucksack. He handed me a frag. By this time our guys were really bringing pee on whoever they were shooting at. We started running in, yelling "FRIENDLIES COMING IN!" As I was running, I pulled the pin and threw the grenade off into the dark as far as I could, not at anything in particular. We somehow got back inside the NDP without getting shot and my adrenalin was really pumping by then. Frank called for gunship support and one came out pretty quickly, but it was really all over when the gunship arrived. We later questioned the troops and found out that everyone had been busy setting up their bedrolls, so they were not paying as much attention as they should have to what was going on outside of the perimeter. SGT Roland "Roop" Ruppert, from the CP group, heard some voices chattering in Vietnamese and he turned around to see a large NVA rice carrying party standing there in the dark, talking. Roop picked up his M16 and blasted them, gunning down two right there, about 25 meters out. The rest of 2nd Platoon and CP group joined in as the other dinks dropped their packs and scattered.

After the gunship shot up the nearby woods, we called for more illumination, then went out and checked the area, finding more bodies and packs. The S2/S3 log says that we got two KIAs and Saber 40 got three, but that was just the result of Frank Korona buying goodwill from the aviation unit, by giving them credit for some of our kills. In reality, 2nd Platoon and the CP group probably got all five KIAs that night. We found 7 very large NVA packs full of rice and salt. We did not find any weapons, although a couple of people in each rice-carrying party were usually armed, so we thought they probably got away. It took awhile for all the commotion to die down and then we packed up and moved out to a new NDP, arriving around midnight. We booby-trapped two of the bodies with grenades that night, before we moved to the new NDP. The frags did not go off and we came back at first light to neutralize them, so no villagers would be hurt burying the corpses. It was a little dicey to reach under the bodies and remove armed frags, so we dragged the corpses with claymore wire, blowing the grenades. One of the dead soldiers was unusually large, causing speculation that he might be Chinese. Two days later, on March 2nd, we found another body and rice pack nearby. The KIA was dressed in a khaki uniform like some of the others and he had been shot to death, either by us or by the gunship. That brought the total bag for February 28, 1971 to 6 KIAs.

1LT Doug Knight joined B Company sometime during this period. Doug took over the 1st Platoon. The entire company consolidated into a single large patrol base one day and for some reason we received a double or triple issue of Class A rations on the resupply bird (roast beef again). We decided to feed all the neighborhood kids, to get rid of the large amount of leftover food. Word went out to the surrounding villes and a large crowd of young children quickly showed up. We tried to get them into an orderly chow line to serve them, but the excited little boys kept pushing and shoving each other. We finally gave up and Frank Korona took them all about 20 yards away in a mob. We gave each of them a paper plate, then Frank pointed to the line of mermite cans and shouted "SOUVENIR!" I got some good pictures of the ensuing food fight. Our company officers and NCOs were able to manage and maneuver three platoons of combat infantrymen, but we could not control a gang of hungry children.

We found and blew up some bunkers, and picked up some detainees, sending them back for questioning, as a result of patrols. But I also began to realize what a wild and crazy guy 1LT Frank Korona was. I guess he was worried that 1st and 3rd Platoons were feeling left out of the action, so he led some of them in a "Rat Patrol" in a ville on March 6th. A "Rat" was a night raid on a ville. The troops did not have much enthusiasm for them, because they were pretty scary and no one got much sleep the night that one was done. The 81mm mortar section was set up to fire illumination over the selected ville and preplanned artillery fire was laid on around it, with Delta Tangos plotted on expected escape routes. The raiders would walk to the ville after it got really dark, call for the illumination, then move in quickly and go door to door, trick or treating with dim flashlights and M16s. Night vision goggles had not yet been invented. American-made BA30s (D cell batteries) were almost impossible to get through supply channels and Vietnamese batteries purchased along QL 1 would only last a few minutes. We never had many flashlights anyway. It is amazing to me now that we were able to make-do then, with the little we had. The idea behind a Rat Patrol was to catch the VC/NVA taking their R&R breaks in the villes, during times when they did not expect GIs to show up to spoil the fun. The troops told me that 2nd Platoon had caught a VC/NVA in a hammock with his wife or girlfriend on a prior Rat Patrol and shot/killed both of them *in flagrante delicto*, when he reached for his weapon. Frank Korona loved doing that kind of stuff, but his zeal for it was not very contagious. He led another Rat Patrol with some of my 2nd Platoon troops two nights later. Neither of the two Rat Patrols produced any results, except to keep Frank pumped up, but he was always gung-ho anyway.

The 1st Platoon spotted 10 VC/NVA just before dark on March 9th and engaged them with artillery and a helicopter gunship. They searched the area and found two KIAs, which were credited to Saber 40, the same gunship which shot for us on February 28th. They also found 3 bunkers, which were blown, and 15-20 fighting positions. They finally got into their NDP at 5 minutes after midnight. We were feeling pretty good about getting revenge for our casualties on the prior mission. Nine VC/NVA were killed in the 515 Valley on this trip, of which 2nd Platoon and the CP Group probably got seven. The crew members of Saber 40 were no doubt our friends for life.

On this mission I started to notice something about my troops, which was confirmed during subsequent operations. The 2nd Platoon sometimes appeared to be an undisciplined mob, especially during down-time. But whenever a firefight started, the 25 to 30 individual delinquents magically transformed into a well oiled fighting machine, usually needing only general direction from me. My primary jobs were to provide daily operational planning and to call for fire support when the action began. My other normal role was to nag my soldiers about basics, because they sometimes tended to bunch up in movement, cluster in groups when halted, or do other dumb things when the action was slack, i.e., when they had relapsed into the rabble mode.

Bravo Company returned to LZ Liz for perimeter duty on March 10th, so we had been in the bush for 13 days.

We went out again on March 13th, making a CA from LZ Dragon into the mountains near the VC Highway. When we got off the helicopters on a mountaintop, we saw several cardboard signs with Vietnamese words written on them in grease pencil. A Kit Carson Scout (KCS) said the signs indicated we had landed in a VC/NVA minefield. There was a lot of thick waist high brush surrounding the small LZ clearing on the mountaintop, making it impossible to see any trip wires which might have been there. This gave everybody pause, except Frank Korona, who did not hesitate. He said, "We'd better get out of here... follow me" and started bulling his way through the brush, leading the company out of the LZ and walking "point" down the mountain. Like I said, he was a wild and crazy guy.

We split up and Frank went with Doug Knight's 1st Platoon. We spent most of the next 14 days moving around on the high ground between various NDPs and PBs, running patrols in random directions downhill. The terrain was very rough and the jungle was dense, so the area was too confining to suit me. There was only one main trail running down a very long ridgeline, which channelized our movements and I began to worry about the VC/NVA patterning and exploiting us. One afternoon from our day laager, my Kit Carson Scout, Huynh The Hy (pronounced "when-tay-hi") saw an Indochinese Tiger on a distant mountainside and he pointed it out to me. I could barely see the tiger with the help of binoculars and I have no idea how he spotted it with bare eyeballs. On March 19th, we were reconning an NDP location and I heard something in the jungle next to the main trail. I squatted to try to look under foliage and got a flash-glimpse of a moving black object, maybe a man, evading down the mountain. So I pointed my rifle and blasted off a whole magazine, the only time I remember ever firing my weapon on full automatic, except to test fire it. We searched the area in cursory fashion, but it was getting late, the undergrowth was very thick and we didn't find anything. The next day, the 3rd Platoon, which was on the next ridgeline to the west, found sandal tracks and followed them to a fresh grave. They also found a bloody hammock and a long pole, which had apparently been used to carry it, at the gravesite. They opened the grave, which they estimated to be 8 to 10 hours old. It contained a dead VC dressed in black pajamas, with multiple gunshot wounds, to the head, face, chest and thigh. The S2/S3 log attributed the kill to the action the evening before. I was the only person who fired his weapon in anger that evening, so I guess I got my first kill, not counting the "assist" I had given Keith Moore in The 515 Valley.

While we were operating in the mountains I had a clash with B Company's Artillery Forward Observer (FO). The artillery lieutenant had plotted some Delta Tangos (defensive targets) around my Night Defensive Position one night and he called for the DTs from his location with the Company CP Group, but without me requesting them. He probably did that on the theory that firing artillery near our NDP would keep the enemy away from us, but that was not properly his tactical decision to make. The artillery fire landed dangerously close to 2nd Platoon's NDP on a mountain slope and I urgently called for a check-fire. I initially had trouble getting through on the radio and the art'y kept coming in. When the Forward Observer finally answered and I complained about the close proximity of the artillery, he scoffed at my protest. His comments implied that I was just a timid cherry-boy, who didn't have any idea what "too close" meant. But I had already commanded the Battalion Heavy Mortar Platoon for 3+ months, whereas the FO had never commanded anything in Vietnam. SSG Willard had also thoroughly schooled me on spooky-close indirect fire when we shot in the LZ Liz FPFs, which was an experience I doubted the FO could match. He called in the Delta Tangos from another location in the dark, so he had no idea how close the impact was to 2nd Platoon. After I objected, he then tried to blow smoke up everyone's skivvies at my expense. I had met a number of Artillery FOs on LZ Liz and I was not impressed. Some of them had a haughty demeanor and I had also become aware that FO duties in a rifle company were pretty trivial. I therefore regarded all Artillery FOs as dilettantes and Feather Merchants. Because of this bias, I was probably angrier about being razzed by a redleg lieutenant than I was about the near miss friendly-fire incident. I was still seething when we came in from the bush and I had made up my mind to confront our FO and pick a real fight, but he apparently left B Company before we returned to LZ Liz.

During the ensuing days, 2nd Platoon found 5 NVA bunkers in two locations and various items of food and equipment, which we destroyed. I had to dust off one soldier for a medical problem, a rectal fissure according to my new medic, Tommy "Doc" Wright. (Doc actually called it a "wrecked 'em fish-hook", but I figured out what he meant.) On another day, the NVA crept up on us along the jungle's edge and they attempted to shoot down the S3's LOACH as it was trying to land at to our day laager. We then had a guy slightly wounded by friendly-fire, a 40mm grenade that someone fired too close, in the ensuing firefight. When we were checking the area after that engagement, I found a stash of spanking new NVA web equipment, including a pack, a complete mess kit, a canteen, a pistol belt with a red star on its metal buckle and an unusual olive drab bush hat. I carried the enemy gear in my rucksack until we went to LZ Liz, intending to take it home to my little brother. I sent it to the B Company Supply Room for storage, but like <u>all</u> my battle souvenirs, it was later stolen by REMFs. (RE stood for "Rear Echelon" and MF stood for what it usually means.) That NVA equipment is probably now displayed in an ex-Supply Clerk's family room, to illustrate fanciful tales about his combat experiences in Vietnam.

    Our final several days in the mountains were spent waiting out a driving rainstorm. We completely ran out of food because the RS bird couldn't fly, but I didn't run out of cigarettes, because I had them squirreled away in every nook and cranny of my rucksack. We set up two-man poncho shelters, clustered around a clump of small trees on the side of a mountain slope. 2nd Platoon just remained in a tight defensive posture, not sending out any patrols. It was the only time I ever stayed in the same location for several days, but visibility was severely curtailed and I didn't think the dinks would be out walking around in the downpour trying to find us. The lightning was so bad that it blew out a radio and set off some claymores. Water was running through the poncho hootches, as if we were camped in the middle of a stream. Some lucky men had air mattresses, but everything soon became soaking wet. Everyone was drenched to the bone, shivering and miserable. The 2nd Platoon guys shared their last remnants of food, coffee and hot chocolate, so it was a bonding experience, despite the misery. Lightning blasted a nearby tree, knocking all the limbs off of it, and some soldiers said they could feel the electricity running through the water. When the torrential rain finally lifted, 2nd Platoon also ran out of smoke grenades, because we used up all of them on a resupply pilot who didn't know

The Mad Fragger and Me

how to read a map. I finally brought him in with flashes from my emergency signal mirror, which I carried for shaving. When I ran out into the LZ to help bring in the supplies, I became lightheaded and almost fainted from the exertion, probably because I had not eaten anything for several days.

On the last day, March 26th, we humped down into the Dragon Valley and rendezvoused with rest of B Company in a combined day laager. I met CPT Guill and LT Cox there for the first time. Incoming Captain Randy Guill had just been assigned to Bravo Company, to replace LT Frank Korona, who was reassigned as the Battalion Recon Platoon Leader. Our new CO was an OCS graduate and the same age as me, but far more experienced, already on his second Vietnam tour. Lieutenant Dave Cox, also a graduate of Benning's School for Boys, joined the company at the same time and he took over 3rd Platoon. With Doug Knight also aboard in 1st Platoon, all line officers in B Company were now Fort Benning OCS graduates. B Company was airlifted back to LZ Liz for perimeter duty.

On March 27th, 2nd Platoon was the firebase duty platoon and was tasked with sending an overnight "snake" (night ambush) out on the LZ Liz Access Road. This was being done regularly to keep the road open, because several trucks had been blown up there by VC mines, despite mine sweeps by Combat Engineers every morning. I put SSG Warrior in charge of the snake, because he was overdue for a crappy detail. The next morning, after the night ambush detail came back in, SSG Earl Willard, the Four Deuce Chief of Smoke, came and found me on the bunker line. He had an angry look in his eyes. I asked him what was wrong, and he said, "One of the soldiers in B Company shot your dog". Dink was not dead, but he didn't know how badly she was hurt because she had crawled under Willard's bed and wouldn't come out. I went to Sergeant Willard's hootch, got on my knees and called her. Dink immediately came out and crawled into my arms, shaking and whimpering. She was shot through the ham in a hind leg and we awkwardly bandaged it to stop the bleeding. SSG Willard borrowed a jeep and drove to FSB

Bronco, with me holding Dink in my lap. She trembled during the entire trip and cried whenever we hit a rut. We found the 59th Infantry/Scout Dog Platoon at LZ Bronco, but they told us that their veterinarian was away on R&R in Hawaii. We drove back to LZ Liz and I took Dink to the Battalion Surgeon. He said he didn't know much about dog anatomy, but he agreed to do the best he could. I told him that Dink was vicious and we might have to muzzle her, but I held her against my chest and she was stoic as he probed the wound. She seemed to know that the Doc was trying to help her and she did not try to bite him. The Doctor did not think the bullet hit bone. He cleaned and dressed the wound, giving Dink a shot of antibiotics. (Army physicians in Vietnam were *truly* full-service medical practitioners!) We took Dink back to the Four Deuce area and fixed a convalescent bed for her in SSG Willard's bunker.

SSG Willard told me Dink had gone down to an open area outside the perimeter wire, below the Four Deuce area just after first light that morning, where she always went for her morning poop. After taking care of business, she was running around and playing. As the B Company snake detail was coming back from the Access Road, one of the soldiers saw her and shot her, apparently just taking target practice. She was hit, but ran for it on three legs through a barrage of automatic rifle fire and made it back to Willard's hootch.

I went back to the 2nd Platoon and started questioning the guys who had been on the ambush detail, deliberately skipping SSG Warrior, because I didn't trust him. I picked Gary "The Mad Fragger" Smith, to start with, because I thought he was most likely to tell me the truth. He didn't want to tell me who did it, but I got totally evil with him and he finally said "Sergeant Warrior shot the dog". I asked him why, but he didn't know. They were coming back from the snake detail and they saw the dog playing around at the bottom of the hill. Warrior shot her and then laughed when she ran away bawling.

The Mad Fragger and Me

I immediately confronted SSG Warrior. He wasn't laughing any more. I'd had plenty of time to stew about the casual cruelty of the dog-shooting and I also had lots of accumulated anger about Warrior's lousy attitude and toxic behavior. It had been only 6 weeks since I joined B Company and Warrior may have recognized Dink as the dog which had followed me then, out the LZ Liz Access Road to QL1. I really wanted to shoot SSG Warrior through one cheek of his ass and ask him how it felt. I'm sure that flames were shooting out of my eyes, but I simply leaned forward at him and asked, "Why did you shoot my dog?" through clenched teeth. He said, "I didn't shoot your dog, El Tee", but he was unable to maintain any eye contact as he said it, looking at the ground. I instinctively knew that Warrior was finished in the 2nd Platoon when he lied to me about this, because I would never again be able to put even the slightest trust in him. I told Warrior that he was a lying son of a bitch and that I detested liars. I said I knew he had been continually undermining me and that he was a sorry excuse for a noncommissioned officer. I cussed Sergeant Warrior until he stunk so bad that a fly wouldn't land on him, but he kept his eyes averted and there was no backtalk. I told him to pack his gear and get out, because he was finished in 2nd Platoon. I left the bunker and went to see my new CO. I told CPT Randy Guill what had happened and he immediately understood that the problem wasn't just about the dog being shot. CPT Guill confirmed that Sergeant Warrior was fired, but he said he didn't have a replacement platoon sergeant to assign me. I told him it didn't matter because SSG Warrior was worse than worthless and I'd rather do without a platoon sergeant. I went back to the 2nd Platoon and told SP/4 Keith Moore that he was Acting Platoon Sergeant. Moore was already wearing Acting-Jack buck sergeant stripes as a squad leader. This arrangement lasted only a very short period of time, because SSG Donald R. Bland unexpectedly joined the unit as an in-country transfer from the First Cavalry Division and he was assigned to 2nd Platoon before we went out again. SSG Bland was professional, positive, reliable, and he always backed me in everything. The troops immediately respected and admired him. Things were starting to look up.

On the night of 28 March 1971, the same date that Dink was shot, Fire Support Base Mary Ann was overrun by NVA Sappers, resulting in 30 GIs killed and 82 wounded. This was one of the most disastrous battle losses ever experienced by the Americal Division and it was the deadliest U.S. combat action of 1971. LZ Mary Ann was the home firebase of the 1st Battalion, 46th Infantry Regiment, 196th Infantry Brigade, which was located in Quang Tin Province, not far northwest of our battalion's Area of Operations. There was a big flap over this, which resulted in both the Americal Division Commanding General and the 196th Brigade Commander being relieved of their commands, thus ending their careers. The disaster was caused by a general lack of alertness, based upon an assumption that the enemy would not bother launching major attacks, with the war winding down and the U.S. withdrawing its troops. It could just as easily have occurred at FSB Liz for the same reason. The FSB Mary Ann debacle did prompt a sudden sense of urgency within our battalion about regularly checking the defensive perimeter during the night, as reflected in our unit's subsequent S2/S3 journal entries. Predictably, this nocturnal checking was usually delegated to line company officers or platoon sergeants and was seldom done by the underworked battalion staff. I was already in the habit of walking my platoon's sector of the LZ Liz bunker line to ensure that my guys were awake and alert, after I finished my turn on guard duty each night, just as I checked my perimeter in the bush. I'm sure that Doug Knight and Dave Cox did the same thing. But after LZ Mary Ann was overrun, Battalion HQ ordered that designated officers or senior NCOs conduct random unannounced tours of LZ Liz guard positions during hours of darkness and formally report our nightly inspection results to the TOC each morning. If the written report was submitted late, or the inspection checklist was not completed satisfactorily, there was a lot of fussing about it from the TOC. On the rare occasion when a battalion staff officer checked the bunker line, the grunts sometimes amused themselves by having him jump through a few hoops. One staff officer entry in the S2/S3 log recorded: "At 2230 hours, Bunker #9 challenged and the inspector responded with the correct password. The inspector was told to advance 10 paces, place his ID card on the ground and back up. He was also told that he was covered with a buckshot round. The senior man on the bunker then took charge and the inspector was allowed to advance. The inspector believes the bunker had prior knowledge of the inspection and one individual decided to clown around." No doubt, probably because the "individual" thought the password requirement was silly. Grunts in the bush never used a challenge and password, which was an archaic rear-area folderol. Out in the boonies, talking about anything at night would get you killed, so we literally shot first and asked questions later.

It is noteworthy that my name was never mentioned in the operations journal entries, except in connection with the nightly perimeter inspections on LZ Liz. The S2/S3 staff apparently thought that "At 0130 hours LT Dolan inspected LZ Liz bunkers #1, 2, 3 and all were satisfactory" had more historical and operational significance than anything else I ever did. This is a nice indicator of the CYA mentality at Battalion Headquarters and the staff's tendency to focus on trivial activities at LZ Liz.

Chapter 6:

THE EASTER SUNDAY MASSACRE

Two days after FSB Mary Ann was overrun by NVA sappers in Quang Tin Province, Bravo Company Combat-Assaulted by helicopters into the mountains north and east of the Song Ve River Valley. That was also my 25th birthday, 30 March 71. The Easter Sunday massacre occurred 12 days later, on April 11th.

B Company encountered numerous indicators of increased NVA activity in those mountains. Our platoons moved around independently between various night defensive positions and day laagers on the fairly open mountaintops and ridgelines on the Nui Duong and Nui Nhan mountains, running daytime patrols down into the ravines and the dense jungle below us. Signs of enemy presence were discovered gradually, but we soon realized that the area was crawling with NVA soldiers. Our three rifle platoons were below authorized strength, consisting of about 25 to 30 soldiers each. The Company CP group, 1st Platoon and the 3rd Platoon occupied the grassy mountaintops southeast of the mountain ridgeline on which my 2nd Platoon was operating. They had especially good views into some of the ravines below them. There were a number of enemy sightings, prompting many artillery and air strikes, directed by lieutenants Knight and Cox. LT Dave "Stalking Moon" Cox called in multiple strikes from a cluster of mountainside boulders he dubbed "OP Scunnion". (OP is the acronym for "observation post" and scunnion was GI slang, meaning any action to inflict maximum violence on the enemy.) Based upon visual observation of the strikes and the blood trails found by B Company patrols, it was believed that the artillery and tac air badly hurt the enemy. Dave Cox told us he was part Blackfoot Sioux, which I thought might be true because of his hawkish face, dark hair and warrior spirit. He also claimed that "Stalking Moon" was his Indian name, but I had already seen that 1968 Gregory Peck movie.

On 4 April 71, my platoon killed an NVA "regular" with a Mechanical Ambush (MA) we left on a trail through a mountain pass. "Mechanical Ambush" was an Army euphemism for a booby trap, using a modified Claymore mine as its main component, but most our battalion's casualties were from VC/NVA booby traps, so I didn't have any qualms about using them. We had found the path, which was being heavily used, early that morning on a recon patrol. After some rumination, I decided to put out an MA on the trail, so we returned later in the day with the needed materials and set it up. After camouflaging the device with assistance from Kit Carson Scout Huynh The Hy, the MA was invisible. We returned to our patrol base and waited. The Mechanical Ambush went bang late that same afternoon. We then had to hustle to get from our patrol base all the way back to the MA site before dark. A new and very young replacement, Alexander "Sweetpea" Walton, who was probably leery of both the situation and the encroaching darkness, apparently had his M16 selector switch on auto-get-'em and his finger on the trigger. As we were creeping along on the final approach to the MA location, he stumbled and let loose with a lengthy (10 rounds or more) accidental burst from the middle of the file, which created some unnecessary extra excitement. This resulted in a whispered but harsh dressing-down of Sweetpea by his squad leader and the other patrol members. (The point man could carry his rifle unlocked, on either "semi" or "auto" if he chose to do so, but all other weapons were supposed to be locked on "safe" until a firefight started.) We found one dead NVA soldier, who was carrying an AK47 with a basic load of ammo. His face and all other exposed skin surfaces were blackened. I have a dim photo of the corpse, but it was nearly dark when I snapped the picture. A large piece of white cloth, apparently bandage material, was next to the body. This suggests that there were others in the NVA party, who probably took off because they thought we were shooting at them

The Mad Fragger and Me

when Sweetpea accidentally fired his weapon. After analyzing this incident, I always plotted an artillery barrage on every MA site and called for it as soon as our Claymore(s) exploded, to finish off or scare away any survivors. (This is what really happened, but it is interesting to compare it to the garbled account in the S2/S3 journal, which also contains incorrect grid coordinates; see A Daily Recap of Operations, B Company, on the www.1-20infantry.org website, for 4 April 71.)

A couple of days later while on patrol, we discovered a tunnel in which we could walk nearly upright, next to a wide streambed. Most NVA tunnels had to be negotiated on hands and knees, so one that large was very unusual. The tunnel led to a large underground room, where we found some evidence of recent occupancy. It may have been used as an Aid Station or hospital. The tunnel entrance had been cleverly concealed, but our point man somehow spotted it.

The 1st and 3rd Platoons were in fairly close proximity and they may have been operating together for some of the time. Dave Cox and Doug Knight now have different recollections about exactly what occurred on April 6th. On that date, a B Company patrol was ambushed by an estimated 15 NVA while on a reconnaissance mission into a mountainside ravine with a dry streambed, where a lot of enemy activity had been observed. SGT Joe Johnson, from the 1st Platoon, was killed and another soldier was slightly wounded. SGT Johnson was walking "point" and he took a direct hit from a Rocket Propelled Grenade, the shot which initiated the ambush. The antitank rocket blew him apart, horrifying his buddies. The patrol became engaged in a fierce firefight, until the NVA withdrew, allowing SGT Johnson's remains to be recovered.

On 8 April 1971, my 2nd Platoon was sent on another probe down into the same jungle area via a different route, initially moving west, then doglegging south. We were reinforced by a squad from another platoon, although I don't remember which one. Platoon leaders usually planned our own operations subject to the company commander's approval, but the order for this reconnaissance patrol trickled down from Battalion HQ. When I gave the patrol briefing, using my map to lay out the route, Kit Carson Scout Hy strongly argued against going into that area. He said, "No go there, El Tee, beaucoup VC." I responded, "No sweat, we crocodile beaucoup VC". Hy said, "*BEAUCOUP* sweat! *BEAUCOUP* VC! No go!" We had our orders, so I shrugged and said, "We go". So we went, with Hy walking "point", but in a way that I had never before seen him do it. He squatted and duck-walked for much of the time. Sometimes Hy stood upright when the vegetation allowed it, but at all times he eased slowly through the jungle, making no noise whatever. Hy was a hardened combat soldier, so his statements and behavior were unsettling. We all tried to imitate Hy's stealth, with varying degrees of success, but we were certainly a lot quieter than normal. It was a difficult movement through heavy jungle, our progress slowed by numerous "wait-a-minute vines" and the need to avoid detection, which prevented the use of noisy machetes. At 1302 hours, we found three bunkers, tunnels and several fighting positions which had been recently destroyed by artillery, at grid coordinates 634538.

Continuing on through the rugged terrain, about a klick away and two hours later, we found a faint NVA trail. The path led us to an NVA base camp, at about grid 634528. I could actually smell the enemy before I saw anything. The odor was pungent, sort of fishy and hard to describe, but I instinctively knew it meant the enemy was near. It was extremely hot and humid. I remember the sweat was pouring off of me so that it was almost impossible to keep my spectacles clear enough to see adequately, and my jungle fatigues were soaked and sour from sweat. The steamy jungle opened up slightly as we eased into the base camp. We fragged the first tunnel we found and I crawled into it with a flashlight and my .45 pistol. The tunnel was about 4 feet in diameter. It went steeply down about 5 feet, then zigged 90 degrees to the left, sloping deeper for about 30 feet, then it zagged 90 degrees to the right, forming two right-angle blast walls to absorb shrapnel from grenades. After about another 30 feet, the tunnel dead-ended in an underground room. This simple but ingenious design was typical of NVA tunnels used as air raid/bomb shelters. The proper search technique was to stick the flashlight around each corner, to see if the light drew any fire, before looking and then crawling around the corner. I found one old NVA pistol belt, but nothing else. Crawling underground, alone on hands and knees, into a black tunnel, which might contain enemy soldiers or booby traps, is an unnerving and claustrophobic experience, to put it mildly. I was both relieved and elated when I crawled back out into the daylight, my heart beating wildly. (The Tunnel Rats' motto was *Non gratum anus rodentum,* probably a comment about their job descriptions.)

A few minutes later, while one of my soldiers was searching another tunnel, I told the "attached" squad leader to follow me with his squad. They had been lollygagging along and hanging back, obviously trying to do as little as possible. I started moving cautiously down an adjacent trail which had not yet been checked, intending to clear it and post security for the search element. After creeping along the trail for 50 to 75 meters, I turned and discovered that nobody was behind me. I was astonished and pissed off, because 2nd Platoon troops would not have let me go on alone, no matter how spooky the situation. I walked back and found that my platoon sergeant was in a rage because he had somehow discovered what had happened. SSG Donald Bland had pinned the squad leader, a stocky buck-sergeant, against a tree. SSG Bland's face was contorted and frightening to behold. His nose was a fraction of an inch from the other sergeant's nose and he was snarling terrible threats through clenched teeth. Two or three 2nd Platoon soldiers were present, standing silently but with grim expressions and weapons ready, clearly backing up Bland. The other members of the attached squad were nearby, all looking at the ground. (Don Bland was a soft-spoken 21 year old Arkansas draftee who had graduated from the Fort Benning NCO Academy. He always maintained a calm demeanor, he was extremely competent and a nice guy. He therefore gained immediate acceptance by the troops, who looked to him for approval as much as they did for guidance. But on this occasion our brotherly platoon sergeant suddenly transformed into a werewolf. I've sometimes wondered if this was just a terrific performance delivered at the right moment, but it did not appear to be an act.) I was anxious to get rid of the worthless squad, but their craven behavior did not corrupt my 2nd Platoon troops, God bless 'em.

We could not determine exactly how large the base camp was, because the bunkers were widely disbursed and heavily camouflaged. There was no defined perimeter or recognizable shape to the camp. We searched carefully within the framework of available time, but the base camp sprawled out through the jungle and I was certain that we did not find all of it. There was one large bamboo-framed building with a thatched roof and open sides, containing cooking equipment. The large structure was obviously a mess hall, probably also used for classes and meetings. The NVA had woven and tied together the jungle foliage above the building's roof, so the trees grew into a permanently green overhead screen. We also found spider holes, latrines, tunnels and large bunkers with connecting trails which were similarly camouflaged overhead, to make the base camp invisible from the air. The occupants had not cleared out any ground foliage to establish fields of fire, so we were almost on top of each bunker or tunnel entrance before we saw it. Fire pits were still warm and small items had been dropped in haste, signs of sudden evacuation. The place obviously had been built as a jungle hideout, not as a defensive position, which may explain why the NVA deserted it without a fight when we approached. Everything looked heavily used, but clean and well maintained. This base camp had been occupied by a much larger force than my platoon. I knew there were no friendly units close enough to help us if we got into a serious fight. The use of artillery and tactical air support would have been difficult because of the rough terrain and heavy jungle canopy.

The situation was very spooky. The aggressive ambush of SGT Johnson's patrol by a relatively large NVA force two days earlier, Hy's wariness about the area, and the eerie silence of the expansive enemy base camp, made me realize that this operation was not a good idea. A much larger American force should have been sent in, not a single platoon. Similar doubts were probably entertained by my men too, although not openly expressed.

We became pressed for time, because it was fairly late in the afternoon when we found the base camp and it took time to explore it. We finally had to abandon the search, because I knew we would run out of daylight if we did not pull out. We found about a dozen large bunkers, but it did not appear that we had found all of them. It was impossible to destroy the hootches, bunkers and tunnels with what we were carrying, so we just searched them, without results except for some souvenir NVA equipment. It had taken us all day on 8 April 71 to find the camp, partially search it and withdraw to an NDP on the high ground. Everyone was exhausted that night, from the physical effort and the adrenaline overload.

The terse tone and specificity of the instructions from the S3 (Battalion Operations Officer) to the Bravo Company CO, as recorded in the operations log for 8 April 1971, were most unusual: "1. Dig in NOW. 2. Move patrol base north at first light. 3. Do not use the same trails/same areas as today's patrols. 4. Keep eyes open for enemy activity against you." The implied sense of urgency in this message suggests that the S3 understood the significance of our discovery and had a related concern that B Company's situation was precarious.

I clearly remember directing a high altitude bomber strike* on the NVA base camp in an attempt to destroy it, from a nearby mountaintop. This air strike was not recorded in the S3 log, but I'm sure it occurred the next day, 9 April 1971. An Australian pilot ("G'd-eye ould buddy, I'm shooting for you t'd-eye") led this effort in an OV10 Bronco. He dove his small plane on the jungle and marked the target with smoke rockets at the location where I thought the camp was located, then a bomber followed up. The bomber was very high in the air, but the crew dropped their massive bomb pattern exactly on the area marked by the smoke. It was an impressive demonstration of precision high altitude bombing, but the weak link in the effort was the Forward Observer (FO), i.e., me. I wasn't sure of the exact base camp location, because of the rugged terrain, the dense jungle and the different perspective from which I was coordinating the air strike. But I plotted the target and adjusted the smoke carefully, hoping that the bombs hit the right location. We would have had to go back in there on foot to confirm destruction of the base camp, which we did not do**. We humped down into the Song Ve Valley the next day, 10 April 71, where B Company was extracted by airlift for rotation to LZ Liz, for perimeter security duty. Delta Company 1/20 Infantry was simultaneously inserted by helicopter into the same Song Ve landing zone, to replace B Company as an operating force in the area.

*[*2nd Platoon soldier Terrance "Curly" Schilling captured this entire air strike on Super 8 movie film. Curly reclined on his back to steady the camera, while he zoomed in on the aircraft dropping bombs from high altitude. The image of the bomber is fuzzy, because it was flying so high, beyond the resolution ability of Curly's camera lens. The falling bombs and their impact on the jungle base camp area are shown in sharp focus, however. Curly's amazing combat footage was stored away and forgotten for many years, but this film survived and has now been preserved on DVD.]*

*[** 40+ years after the events described, I noticed a records anomaly which prompted me to review the Daily Recap of Operations feature on the www.1-20infantry.org website, for 14 April 1971. I was surprised to learn that Delta Company had been sent into the area of the bomber attack on that date, five days after the strike. No one advised us of this at the time. D Company*

The Mad Fragger and Me

reported that they found a large NVA base camp at grid 634526. This is only a 200 meter variance from the base camp coordinates I reported on April 8th, so it was undoubtedly the same place. It is clear that my platoon walked into one sector of the sprawling base camp and searched a portion of it, before we withdrew and bombed the crap out of it. On April 14th, Delta Company found seven recent enemy KIAs there in graves, two estimated to be 2-4 days old and the other five estimated at 1-2 weeks old. Delta Company reported finding 25 major bunkers, 50 fighting positions and 10-15 hootches in the base camp, most of them demolished. A CHICOM 82mm mortar tube was found, already destroyed. D Company also recovered other munitions and pieces of equipment, plus a large number of documents and letters. The Operation Finney Hill <u>After Action Report</u> states that the base camp was destroyed by an air strike, thus verifying that it had been wrecked by the April 9th bomber attack. The base camp may have been the headquarters of the 40th NVA Sapper Battalion, which was known to be located somewhere in that general area. Regarding the five "older" NVA casualties, either the NVA moved back into the camp in time for the bomber strike to hit them on 9 April 1971, or Dave Cox and Doug Knight killed them several days prior with their art'y and tac air attacks. Either way, using U.S. air assets, B Company platoon leaders gave the NVA a vicious pounding. It is possible that enemy dead from the Easter Sunday battle on 11 April 1971 were carried the short distance from that location and buried, which would explain the two fresher graves.]

    B Company was occupying the perimeter on LZ Liz on Easter Sunday, 11 April 71. In late afternoon, an urgent message came down to us from the TOC. A platoon from Alpha Company had been overrun, in the mountains east of the Song Ve, the general area we had just vacated the day before. Bravo Company was ordered to immediately Combat Assault a reaction force to rescue the survivors and to help evacuate their dead and wounded. The record shows that 1st Platoon B Company made the CA, but that is not quite correct. Doug Knight's 1st Platoon was the firebase Duty Platoon on that date, but for some reason he could muster only fifteen soldiers, about half of his men. CPT Guill asked me to assemble a detail of ten men from 2nd Platoon, to bring 1st Platoon up to strength. Everyone in 2nd Platoon was willing to go and I decided to go with the group, because I was reluctant to send my soldiers into combat under another lieutenant's command. SSG Don Bland announced that he was going too, so we picked eight of our toughest and most reliable soldiers to accompany us. Among them were Bob Swanson, Curly Schilling, Paul Malonson, Pancho Ramirez and Randy Robinson. I think that Harold Weidner and Keith Moore also went on the mission. I don't remember who our eighth soldier was. We were rushed and the mission order was sketchy so we just took all the ammo and hand frags we could carry, but nothing else except canteens and a radio. I later discovered that Jim-Jim, our 14 year old Vietnamese "Speakeasy", also hopped on one of the choppers at the last minute, armed with his M16A1 rifle, .38 Special Smith & Wesson revolver and hand grenades. He came with us as an extra rifleman, not as an interpreter. There were 26 grunts in our group from B Company, eleven of us from the 2nd Platoon.

    I knew it was going to be bad, but I still wasn't mentally prepared for the situation on the ground. I was sitting on the floor in the starboard doorway, as the aircraft approached the small landing zone on the side of a mountain. The door gunner on that side leaned toward me and shouted, "IT'S A <u>HOT</u> LZ!!" I suddenly had an overwhelming desire to get off that chopper. I slid out the door and stood outside on the skid, holding on to the door frame and straining to see what was going on below. When the door gunner started firing his M60, the muzzle blast was close to my ears, which were already popping from the very rapid descent from about 2,000 feet, making me cringe from extreme inner ear pain. There was a lot of smoke in the LZ and green tracers were coming up at us from the surrounding jungle. There was room to bring in only one ship at a time, but the pilots did not land, probably

The Mad Fragger and Me

because of ground debris and limited visibility. As each helicopter neared the ground, the smoke parted from the prop wash and we jumped from the choppers while they were still 6 or 8 feet off the ground. As soon as we hit the ground and the prop wash cleared, we were assailed by the horrible stench of burnt flesh and aviation fuel, mixed with the odor of death. Alpha Company survivors were still engaged in a sharp firefight, which we joined. The oval landing zone was a small rocky clearing on the side of the mountain, perhaps about 40 meters by 70 meters. The Battalion resupply chopper had been shot down in the LZ. The LZ was littered with debris and GI corpses, and a large section of the ground was scorched and smoking. The main rotor hub of the resupply helicopter was recognizable, but most of the chopper had totally burned up. When the bird went down, its rotor blades had decapitated or dismembered some of the troops, so the place looked like the scene of the most graphic imaginable massacre. It was ultimately determined that there were a total of eleven dead GIs, and body parts from them, scattered around the LZ, some of them burnt and charred. The malevolent look of the LZ and the rank brimstone odor made me feel like I had just descended into hell. Most of the Alpha Company guys who had survived the initial attack seemed to be in a state of shock and the amount of carnage in the LZ was in itself shocking. As if to accentuate the horror through irony, one young G.I. was laying dead on his back in the middle of the LZ, shirtless, but without a mark on his body. Our medic examined the dead soldier, but could not find any injury or determine the cause of his death.

When our B Company element got on the ground, it was chaotic until we got organized. My friend 1LT Dennis Ransdell, the A Company Executive Officer, had assumed command before we arrived. We did not have an Artillery Forward Observer with us, but Infantry lieutenants routinely performed the same function. Dennis, Doug Knight and I took turns adjusting artillery and air attacks.

Tom Dolan

Huey C Model helicopter gunships ("Sharks" from 174th Assault Helicopter Company) came in so low on their gun runs that I saw their skids hitting the treetops, and they broke station to reload several times. Those gunship crews were wildly daring and they always charged to our rescue whenever we found ourselves in trouble. We looked upon Sharks as "our" gunships and their presence was always reassuring, more so than the other gunship support we sometimes got from aviation units outside of the 11th Brigade. The shot-down resupply ship, call-sign "Dolphin 21", was also from the 174th AHC.

Two USAF F4 Phantom fighter-bombers were on station and they launched an attack shortly after we landed. The F4s screamed in so close that we could see the pilots' faces as they released their napalm and bombs. The concussion and deafening noise from the 500 pound bombs and the fierce heat from the napalm were physically painful, bringing new meaning to the words "danger close". Even though our ears were ringing from the thunderous blasts, we could hear obviously large chunks of shrapnel whizzing through the air overhead. We hugged the ground, which shook under us exactly like an earthquake. The level of violence unleashed by this air strike is impossible to describe and it scared the hell out of me. I remember having a confused thought that we had brought in the tac air too close, but there was nothing we could do about it except ride it out. We actually didn't have any control over the proximity of the air strike, because the fast-movers were just dropping their ordinance as close as possible to the smoke grenades which we tossed out to mark our perimeter. The skill of those fighter jocks was wonderful and we were also lucky, because the bombing was extremely close but we didn't take any casualties. Whenever gunship runs or air strike sorties were interrupted, we called for more artillery. We used every available means to inflict overwhelming violence on our opponents, which is the basic technique for winning any brawl.

The Mad Fragger and Me

The S2/S3 journal states that Dolphin 21 had brought hot chow and Methodist Chaplain Merle Brown to provide Easter Sunday services on its first resupply run. The attack came around 1600 hours (4 PM), when Dolphin 21 returned for backhaul and to pick up Chaplain Brown. 3rd Platoon A Company survivors told us that they had one small observation post (OP) out, to the north of the LZ. The NVA had suddenly emerged from the jungle and launched a highly coordinated assault, killing everyone on the OP and simultaneously shooting down Dolphin 21, just as it was lifting off, with a rocket propelled grenade. (The S2/S3 journal states that the ship took hits from two U.S. 40mm grenade rounds, but this is not correct.) NVA sappers then ran through the LZ throwing satchel charges, and they were followed by a firestorm of enemy B40 rockets, grenades and small arms fire. One sapper paused to pick up a C ration can of spaghetti and took a direct hit from an A Company 40mm blooper, which blew off the side of his head. The A Company soldiers gamely tried to fight back, but they were stunned and overwhelmed by the sudden violent attack. No one knows the size of the attacking force, but based upon the impressive size of the nearby NVA base camp, it was very much larger than the American platoon. The carnage I saw and the statements of the survivors indicated that the initial assault was savage and horrible.

The landing zone was a small rocky clearing, relatively flat, like a slightly tilted shelf on the somewhat steep mountainside. The clearing was the only location in the immediate area where helicopter resupply could have been received with convenience and ease. One fighting position had been scratched out of the rocky ground in the CP Group's section of the LZ, but there was no other evidence that anyone else tried to dig in or clear fields of fire. The perimeter was completely unprepared, the jungle encroached closely on the clearing and overall it was just a miserable location to try to defend. The coordinated and precisely timed attack by sappers was an indicator that 3rd Platoon A Company had been under close observation by the NVA for a considerable period of time. NVA sappers were highly trained elite soldiers who operated like commandos, but they were not suicidal. Sappers always relied on detailed reconnaissance and meticulous planning to achieve surprise and shock in their attacks.

A Company had made a CA from LZ Dragon to the top of the mountain on April 2nd. SP/4 Frank Schurich was the surviving Platoon Radio-Telephone Operator/RTO. He said 3rd Platoon had humped down from the top of the mountain, crossing a high speed NVA trail on the way. There was a lot of "sign" everywhere, making it obvious that a large number of enemy were in the area. Arriving at the new LZ, the 3rd Platoon cut down trees to fully clear a landing area. SP/4 Schurich dug a fighting hole, but he was the only person who did so. The troops did not dig in because no one told them to do it. Their lieutenant was indifferent to his leadership responsibilities and he avoided decision-making. The 3rd platoon also had many newbies and few NCOs. The platoon was ordered by Battalion HQ to stay in the same place for a number of consecutive days. SP/4 Schurich said he had argued against remaining in this static location, but the 3rd Platoon leader and the A Company Commander would not move the platoon. Frank Schurich became so concerned that he anonymously radioed the Battalion TOC and complained about staying in the same location for so long. The TOC spokesman told Schurich that he would be brought up on disciplinary charges for violating the chain of command, if they ever found out who he was. So the 3rd Platoon remained in place. (B Company Commander Randy Guill later said that he also warned the Battalion Commander that the unit was going to get whacked by the NVA, because he had seen them taking resupply in the same location, four days in a row. The CO told CPT Guill to mind his own business... the A Company Commander knew what he was doing.)

As Dolphin 21 was trying to land for backhaul on April 11th, SP/4 Frank Schurich saw an NVA soldier stand up in the jungle and fire an RPG rocket at the resupply bird. The RPG round hit the ship and it began to crash, so Schurich dived into his hole to escape the thrashing chopper blades. Dolphin 21 went down on top of a small depression, where the platoon had cached all their M72 LAWs and they cooked off, adding to the bedlam and carnage. Frank Schurich's PRC25 radio had been shot to pieces, so he ran out into the maelstrom and grabbed another radio. When he got it back to his hole, he discovered that the handset was packed with the brains of its former operator, who had been decapitated by helicopter blades. After he cleaned the handset as best he could, he found that the radio still worked and he used it to call for help. He assumed responsibility for coordinating response to the attack, because his platoon leader was nowhere to be seen. SP/4 Schurich called for help from the CP, requesting artillery, gunships and a MEDEVAC. When the Dust-Off ship made its first approach to come in, Schurich told the pilot that the LZ was too hot to attempt a landing. The pilot tried to land anyway, but he then had to abort because of the fierce ground fire. The MEDEVAC was able to land on a later second attempt. 1LT Ransdell arrived on the MEDEVAC chopper and took over the platoon's defense, while Schurich continued to operate the platoon radio. Frank Schurich was surprisingly calm, at least by the time I talked to him. His actions and his attitude indicated that he was tough-minded and capable, the kind of guy you'd want to have next to you in a foxhole when a situation went to hell.

  The 3rd Platoon Leader had survived the attack and he was not wounded. When I attempted to speak with him on Easter Sunday, he was obviously dysfunctional. He repeatedly babbled, "I couldn't do much because I was pinned down… I was pinned down… I was pinned down", but his manner was furtive and he couldn't maintain eye contact. A surviving soldier said that the lieutenant disappeared when the attack started. He was later found crying, curled up in a fetal position under some jungle foliage. The soldier also commented, "I understand that everyone has a breaking point, but he was supposed to be in charge and he ran away".

  1LT Dennis Ransdell, the A Company XO, had come out from the rear area to visit the Company Commander at the CP, on top of the mountain. When the shooting erupted and the call for help came from SP/4 Schurich, Ransdell recruited a reaction force consisting of five enlisted men. They faced an initial problem of how to get into the 3rd Platoon's LZ, because there was a raging firefight going on there. No slicks were immediately available, but the group was picked up and inserted by a MEDEVAC chopper. The actions of Ransdell's tiny force demonstrated remarkable courage because there were only a few of them, but they still went boldly into a desperate situation to save their comrades. 1LT Ransdell and the five other soldiers in the initial reaction force should have been decorated for valor, but I doubt that it happened. In the usual course of events, the brass hats routinely awarded each other significant medals with flimsy justifications, but the grunts in the lower ranks typically just received standard "I was there" medals. My impression at the time was that decisive action by two soldiers in particular, SP/4 Frank Schurich and 1LT Dennis Ransdell, prevented the situation from becoming far worse than it was.

Somehow, three crewmen from the resupply helicopter had gotten out of the bird unscathed when it was shot down, but Chaplain Merle Brown and Crew Chief Wayne Baggett, were killed. Our battalion's Resupply Sergeant was wounded. The surviving helicopter crew looked oddly out of place on the ground in their Nomex flight suits, unarmed or carrying only sidearms. It was amazing that anyone had been able to get out of that chopper alive, but they were fairly composed, considering what they had just been through. Their buddies from the aviation unit extracted them pretty quickly. Many years later, I corresponded with Warrant Officer Bob Chipley, the pilot of Dolphin 21. He expressed remorse about the carnage inflicted on A Company troops by his chopper's rotor blades, but I know he was entirely blameless. Dolphin 21 was shot down because Mr. Chipley was trying to resupply a unit which had remained for far too long in a static and unprepared position. All responsibility for the disaster rests with the 3rd Platoon Leader, the

The Mad Fragger and Me

A Company Commander and the 1/20th Infantry Battalion Commander.

Warrant Officer 1 David Wyatt and his MEDEVAC crew were the other unsung heroes of the day. Mr. Wyatt's call sign was Dust-Off 54 and his ship was called *Zig Zag Man*, with that name and an appropriate cartoon logo painted on its fuselage. (On Easter Sunday morning, the Doctor at LZ Bronco's Aid Station had asked David Wyatt to assist him with a pregnant Vietnamese girl, who was in labor and having a difficult delivery... I say again, Army physicians *were* full-service medical practitioners! Mr. Wyatt performed nursing duties during the baby's deliver, demonstrating that MEDEVAC pilots *also* provided any required ancillary services, under all conditions!) Late in the afternoon, Dust-Off 54 was assigned to evacuate the wounded from the 3rd Platoon's LZ and *Zig Zag Man* flew out to the battle from the Duc Pho airfield. Shark gunships were already on station when Dust-Off 54 arrived at the fierce firefight. The person in charge on the ground (SP/4 Schurich) told him not to try to land, but Mr. Wyatt made an attempt anyway, with the Shark gunships flying cover. Dust-Off 54 had to break off because of the intensity of the ground fire. SP/4 Schurich also told WO Wyatt that they didn't have enough uninjured personnel to load the wounded. Someone (1LT Ransdell?) asked Mr. Wyatt to ferry the initial reaction force into the besieged landing zone. MEDEVAC regulations strictly prohibited the transportation of armed combat soldiers, under any circumstances. (The Army hierarchy was concerned about preserving the noncombatant status of the unarmed air ambulances, but the enemy always tried to shoot them down anyway.) Mr. Wyatt severely bent these Standing Orders when he picked up the Ransdell group, reasoning that they were "patient protectors" who were needed to accomplish his medical mission. His gutsy decision may have saved the 3rd Platoon from total annihilation. During David Wyatt's second landing attempt, Shark gunships were all around *Zig Zag Man*. On the final approach, he could see Shark rockets and tracers going past both sides of his ship. The suppressive gunfire was so fierce and so close that Mr. Wyatt's crew told him not to turn or flare, just go straight in. He did that and they landed without any holes in them or the chopper. Dust-Off 54 evacuated the most grievously wounded and the second-up MEDEVAC ship was able to pick up the rest. (David Wyatt was shot down and seriously wounded eight days later, on 19 April 1971. He was then evacuated to the United States for extended treatment and rehabilitation, but he was later able to return to flying. Mr. Wyatt retired from the Army as a Chief Warrant Officer 4 in 1983.)

The "urgent" wounded had been dusted off before our B Company element arrived, but some lightly wounded soldiers were evacuated later. We pushed wounded soldiers and surviving Dolphin 21 crew onto the final evacuation ship, to the point that it appeared to be overloaded. At the last second, two A Company soldiers who did not appear to be wounded suddenly bolted for the helicopter. They jumped on board just as it was lifting off, before anyone could intervene. The chopper struggled to get off the ground and I held my breath because thought it would crash. But the pilot somehow got it in the air, the ship banked just above the trees and swooped down the mountain until it caught an updraft.

We called for body bags, but none came. Helicopters were sent out late in the afternoon to evacuate the dead, so the corpses and body parts were just piled on the choppers, a gruesome business. I started gagging from the stench and the visual horrors and I couldn't bring myself to help SSG Bland and some of my other soldiers with this ghastly job, a personal failing that still haunts me. While the human remains were being loaded on the aircraft, one of my men handed me Merle Brown's Zippo lighter. CPT Brown was a pipe smoker and some lieutenants from our battalion had presented the Zippo to him. The lighter was engraved with his name, rank and the motto, "If You Ain't a Chaplain, You Ain't Shit", which was a knock-off of the frequently encountered maxim, "If You Ain't Infantry, You Ain't Shit". It was back-hauled with the other

The Mad Fragger and Me

personal items, weapons and equipment belonging to the casualties. I hope that the Zippo made it all the way back to his family and that they recognized it as a slightly vulgar symbol of the high regard the junior officers had for Chaplain Merle Brown.

Soon after we landed, we were ordered by radio to "run an infantry sweep" of the jungle around the LZ, which sounded very tactical and all. The Officer Candidate School at Fort Benning didn't teach Infantry Sweeping 101 as far as I can remember, but maybe I slept through that class. I think 11 April 71 was the first time I'd heard this phrase. I wasn't exactly sure what an infantry sweep was, but it sounded like it was probably similar to a cantonment area "police call", where everyone walked on line through an area to pick up trash. The order to sweep the area reflected ignorance of the battle situation, because we were still receiving incoming fire. We attempted to communicate this to Battalion HQ, although in somewhat more diplomatic language. The "sweep" order was then reiterated more loudly and forcefully by the Battalion Commander, who was probably starting to get spooked by the disaster he had on his hands. It was futile to argue about it, so we just continued with what we were already doing. The S2/S3 journal, completed miles away from the action, erroneously recorded for posterity that we were sweeping the area. (I learned later that Battalion Commanders were very fond of ordering infantry sweeps after violent engagements, even at night. B Company platoon leaders would always reconnoiter the area after an engagement to determine results, without being told to do so. We would automatically do this as long as we thought that we probably had the upper hand and would not be needlessly risking the lives of our troops. But we also knew that the enemy often tried to lure American units into booby-trapped areas with sniper fire or other enticements. If we thought the situation was a set-up, or too hazardous to immediately go charging in, we would then do something different, such as walk in artillery to detonate suspected booby traps. It was therefore <u>never</u> necessary to order a sweep. Some battalion commanders could not resist flexing their authority with platoon leaders on the ground, even though they were safely sitting on their butts in the brightly lit TOC, far away from the action. Perhaps they wanted to demonstrate that "Battalion Commander" was more than just a ceremonial title. The company commander was bypassed whenever a battalion commander decided to micromanage a platoon leader, grievously violating the chain of command. During another incident which occurred after the Easter Sunday fight, another battalion commander ordered 1LT David Cox to conduct a night river crossing, to "sweep" for KIAs in the dark, after Dave reported hearing his mechanical ambush detonate. He denied approval of Lieutenant Cox's counter-recommendation to fire in artillery and to check the area at first light. Stalking Moon then famously responded, "I need *YOU* to come out here from the rear area and *SHOW ME* how to do that". After a significant pause, the battalion CO told Dave to keep him posted.)

    Late in the afternoon on 11 April 1971, too late to exercise any other options, we were told that we would be remaining in the same location overnight. This seemed like a dreary idea. We knew by then that 3rd Platoon A Company had been overrun because they had stayed in the same location far too long. The Battalion Commander had ordered 3rd Platoon to remain in the same NDP/PB for more than a week, as a platoon-size "Observation Position", according to survivors (and S2/S3 log entries). But the little clearing was surrounded by rugged terrain and dense jungle, which prevented any significant observation of NVA activity in the area. The A Company Commander and the 3rd Platoon Leader inexplicably complied with this order. It was Standard Operating Procedure for rifle platoons to continuously move around into new NDPs and day laagers, just as we constantly changed patrol routes and ambush sites, to prevent being patterned and exploited by the enemy. All seasoned grunts knew this, but apparently the Battalion CO did not. (Grid coordinates in the S2/S3 journal indicate that 3rd Platoon had

The Mad Fragger and Me

been mucking around in that same location since April 3rd, *nine days!*)

When it became evident that an overnight stay on 11 April 1971 was not avoidable, we requested food, water, emergency ammo resupply, entrenching tools, Claymore mines, trip flares, bug dope and hand frags. Just before dark a chopper dropped off a case of hand grenades, but none of the other items. Fragmentary grenades aren't very useful at night in the jungle, because they can't be thrown in the dark without the risk of unseen bounce-back off of trees. We were not desperately short of small arms ammunition because we had carried in so much with us and platoon sergeants redistributed what was still available. But we had nothing with which to prepare an adequate Night Defensive Position and battalion headquarters apparently had no concern about that.

We were provided with two strobe lights, which Doug Knight placed at either end of the LZ just before dark, to mark our position for aircraft. The strobes were turned on and left until the batteries died late that night. After dark, we moved a short way into the jungle, in groups of three or four, to form a loose perimeter around the LZ. We had to just hunker down, because we had no entrenching tools with which to dig in. A light rain started, but that was the least of our problems. The enemy had been beaten back by U.S. firepower, but they apparently moved in closer to our perimeter after dark, because we could occasionally hear movement around us in the jungle. I was not sure what they were doing, but I initially thought they were preparing to attack again and I knew we were vulnerable. I also knew there was a very large NVA unit in the area, because we had walked into their nearby base camp a few days earlier. I remember thinking that I probably would not live to see the sun come up the next morning. It turned out that the NVA did not assault or actively probe our perimeter that night, so they may have been trying to retrieve their dead and wounded. Artillery Delta Tangos were "registered" and were requested intermittently throughout the night. An Air Force AC-130 Spectre gunship (a converted cargo plane, called "Puff the Magic Dragon" by grunts) was on station until late that night. From the ground, Puff's side-firing electronic Gatling gun sounded like a loud chain saw and it looked like a dragon spewing out a stream of red tracers into the dark, a very intimidating demonstration of firepower. The presence of the Spectre gunship and the intermittent art'y probably kept the NVA off our backs. Flares dropped by the Puff crew also provided regular but eerie illumination until late at night. Nobody on our perimeter fired his individual weapon, due to an absence of specific targets and because we knew that muzzle flashes would pinpoint our positions. Occasionally someone risked tossing a grenade at sounds of movement in the dark, but we were lucky in taking no casualties from bounce-backs.

After my initial enthusiasm for rescuing A Company abated, my mood started to change. From the minute we arrived, it had been clear that the best option was to evacuate the survivors and KIAs, then withdraw and take revenge at some later date when we were able to dominate the situation. Success or failure in Vietnam combat was always measured by body counts and the little LZ had no tactical or strategic value. It made no sense to leave us there overnight, except as bait. As I sat in the drizzle on the side of that dark mountain, listening to the enemy making noises in the jungle, I began to obsess about the situation, the way I sometimes do when I wake up in the middle of the night thinking about mundane things which I just can't get off my mind. I realized that I was doing this and that it was not healthy or productive, but I couldn't stop replaying the horrors of the day in my mind. Finally, it occurred to me that I previously had been even more anxious, in fact sick to the depths of my soul with gut-wrenching fear, while sitting in Father Richard Colgan's freshman homeroom class at Loyola High School ten years earlier, knowing that I had not done my Latin homework. On a daily basis, Jesuit priest Colgan had applied loud, shocking, sometimes violent, and always terrifying classroom interventions with delinquent teenage scholars like me. From that point on that

The Mad Fragger and Me

night I was okay. (Some years later, I saw Dick Cavett interview Alfred Hitchcock on TV. During the interview, Hitchcock intoned in his imperious voice, "I was educated by *Jesuits*...and *that* was how I learned about FEAR". Me too.)

After the adrenalin wore off, fatigue hit us like a freight train. By around midnight we were all so desperately weary that we didn't give a damn about the NVA, or the hordes of mosquitoes which were also attacking us. Staying awake all night was impossible and we took turns sleeping. Sounds of enemy activity tapered off as the night wore on. They were no doubt exhausted too.

Resupply came the next morning, including the heavily rubberized black body bags which we no longer needed. We also received C rations and water.

The NVA sapper who took the 40mm direct hit while picking up the can of spaghetti, was wearing only a pair of black gym shorts and Ho Chi Minh sandals. His entire body was blackened with charcoal, reminding me of the NVA soldier we had killed a week earlier. The sapper died in a contorted position, with the C ration can still in his hand. SP/4 "Robby" Robinson had a macabre sense of humor which often surfaced during periods of high tension. Robby discovered that rigor mortis had stiffened the body into a twisted caricature of a ballet pose. SP/4 Robinson made a show of having an outrageous dialogue with the dead sapper, while he leaned the rigid corpse up against a tree and shoved the can of spaghetti into the hole in his head. He then sat down in front of the sapper to eat his breakfast. At about that time on 12 April 71, our Battalion CO's boss, the Brigade Commander, flew in. The bird colonel was scowling as he got off his helicopter. He didn't say anything about the horrible sapper leaning against the tree, but he had other questions. I no longer remember exactly what he asked or how we responded. I was (and I still am) angry that so many GIs had been killed and wounded because of abject stupidity and leadership failure. We were not happy about being staked out all night as bait, especially because our request for emergency resupply had been mostly ignored. Our comments to the BDE CO may have reflected this. I clearly recall the Brigade Commander's dour facial expression and his angry body language. I think he knew exactly what had happened, and why, without being told. None of the TOC Commandos ever came out to the massacre site from our battalion headquarters.

Only two surviving enlisted soldiers from 3rd Platoon A Company remained with us overnight, one of whom was Frank Schurich. The 3rd Platoon Leader was nowhere to be seen on Monday morning. I believe that he was one of the two unwounded soldiers who jumped on the final evacuation bird with the lightly wounded on April 11th.

An A Company patrol came down from the mountain top on April 12th, led by SGT Mike Dosser, a friend of SSG Don Bland's from AIT and the NCO Academy. SGT Dosser took advantage of this opportunity to collect $10 from Don Bland, an overdue wager from the 1969 Arkansas/Texas football game. I think that SGT Dosser's patrol came to escort LT Ransdell and his reaction force back to the A Company Command Post. Our B Company party was extracted by helicopters later that morning and we returned to LZ Liz.

It was interesting, many years later, to see Battalion's responses to the "Brigade Commander's questions", apparently transmitted at 1351 hours, 12 April 71. The Brigade Commander had already come out personally to the killing ground, so he knew that "Perimeter 100 meters by 60 meters w/individual dug fighting positions" was baloney. This may have contributed to his decision to immediately relieve the 1/20th Battalion Commander. Our Battalion Commander might not have been aware that the 3rd Platoon A Company had not dug in, or cleared fields of fire, but it was his job to know. He ordered the platoon to stay in the same location for nine days, causing them to be overrun. I didn't previously have anything against him because he was a likeable man, but in this case he placed his troops in jeopardy for no discernible reason. He also ignored the explicit warnings from SP/4 Schurich and CPT Guill. The slaughter on Easter Sunday was primarily his fault, but the A Company Commander and the 3rd Platoon Leader were also culpable. The 3rd Platoon Leader was subsequently reassigned as OIC of the Access Road Guard at LZ Liz, a newly formed detail comprised of druggies and other misfits. As far as I know, the A Company CO was not relieved of his command or otherwise punished. I have never understood why a piecemeal platoon from B Company was sent into the fracas. The A Company Commander should have insisted upon rescuing his own troops with his other two rifle platoons, which were already in the immediate area, but he remained completely out of the action.

    I did not see the second NVA/KIA, or the AK47 which was allegedly captured, according to the S2/S3 log. Battalion HQ was desperate for anything to offset the debacle, so the second KIA may have been imaginary. The AK 47 was probably a throw-down piece, left over from a prior action. It is possible that other enemy soldiers were killed and dragged off however, because the enemy always tried to evacuate their dead, to deny us the satisfaction of a body-count. On the other side of the ledger, 11 GIs were killed and 10 were wounded. The 3rd Platoon, A Company, 1st Battalion 20th Infantry took 19 of those 21 casualties and it was decimated as a fighting force on 11 April 1971.

    Participating in this action was like riding an emotional roller coaster and it was stressful. The initial assault to save our comrades was thrilling, but this was quickly followed by gut-wrenching horror at the carnage in the LZ, outrage at the leadership incompetence which caused the debacle, shocked disbelief that we were going to be kept there *again* overnight, raw fear when the adrenalin wore off, and extreme frustration afterward that our side got so badly mauled in this fight. When my emotions subsided and I was able to analyze my feelings more objectively, my distain for poor U.S. leadership was matched by grudging admiration for the North Vietnamese Army. Bravo Company had given them a vicious pounding in the two weeks prior to Easter Sunday. We had also walked right into Charlie's house and challenged him, perhaps stirring up the hornet's nest that stung A Company. The NVA courageously fought back at U.S. forces, using the limited resources available to them. They were very tough, dedicated and determined soldiers, truly worthy opponents.

Stalwart soldier Frank Schurich became *persona non grata* at Battalion HQ. He decided to shoot the Battalion Commander upon his return to LZ Liz, but the colonel's driver grabbed Schurich's rifle when he went to the TOC to act on this idea. He was then transferred to a rear job in another unit at Da Nang, but he got into some other trouble, so Schurich was locked up there by the MPs. Alpha Company's XO Dennis Ransdell found out about Frank's detention, picked him up in Da Nang and brought him back to Chu Lai. Frank Schurich had been placed under disciplinary charges, but 1LT Ransdell tore up the Field-Grade Article 15 paperwork when Schurich reached his DEROS date. SP/4 Schurich was told that he had been put in for a Silver Star for his actions on 11 April 1971 (which he undoubtedly deserved). He was later awarded only an ARCOM, again proving that no good deed shall go unpunished in the Army. SP/4 Schurich's actions on Easter Sunday 1971 nevertheless provide a shining example of what can be accomplished by a single determined soldier, when he is thrown into dire circumstances.

The location of the Easter Sunday fight was correctly recorded in the S3 log at grid 628523. That location is only 500 meters (about 3/10 of a mile) from the NVA base camp my platoon discovered on 8 April 1971. A look at the proximity of those two locations on the map makes me wonder how Alpha Company's 3rd Platoon could have missed discovering the NVA sanctuary, if they conducted any serious patrols during the nine days they spent in that area.

According to an article in *VFW Magazine*, the Easter Sunday battle was the fourth deadliest single firefight for U.S. troops in Vietnam during 1971.

Chapter 7:

ROLLING UP THE BODY COUNT

When I first went to the bush, I experienced fear. Not so much about getting killed, because I was still young enough to feel invincible, logic and the nonstop violence around me notwithstanding. I had a vague notion that it would be better to get killed than maimed, but I was not really worried about that possibility either. Nevertheless, I was scared and not able to eat very much during my first six weeks in the bush and I quickly lost a lot of weight, about 30 pounds. After I thinned down to my fighting weight of around 160 pounds, I went to LZ Bronco for some reason and I stopped at the E Company Orderly Room to say hello to "Top" Moore. First Sergeant Moore did not recognize me when I first walked in, because I had lost so much weight. Mai recognized me though, when I wiggled my eyebrows and asked if she wanted to go to the bunker.

What caused my anxiety and loss of appetite was the possibility that I would screw up and get somebody else killed. This was a very real possibility and it is difficult to adequately explain how the frequency and weight of the decisions continually made by a rifle platoon leader potentially affected the safety of all his troops, all the time. For about the first six weeks I was in the bush in Vietnam, I mainly felt the oppressive responsibility I had for the 30-or-so young guys under my command. After that initial period, I did gain confidence and learn to relax somewhat. I nevertheless remained acutely aware of how dangerous our daily activities were and I tried to stay alert and focused.

There were no tactical objectives in Vietnam combat operations, such as to "take that hill" or "hold this ground". There were just murderous gangs on two opposing sides, roving around in the mountains and in the paddies, trying to kill each other. I soon came to realize that my primary mission was to kill as many VC and NVA as possible. They were doing a credible job of trying to do that to us, so other than the dink we wasted in front of his son, I never felt the slightest remorse about killing the enemy. For this reason, I'm somewhat skeptical about the need for professional counseling after someone commits an act of violence, or PTSD disability claims based on the same issue, but I don't know what goes on in someone else's head. I don't like to admit this because I know how it sounds, but I'm trying to be honest here, it quickly became fun to hunt down and kill the enemy. This game was much more competitive and satisfying than finding rice caches and enemy bunkers, or the other things we were expected to do. It probably doesn't make sense, but I also took it personally that the NVA were trying to kill me and my troops. So I became callous, ruthless and bloodthirsty. I soon spent most of my time trying to figure out ways to kill the enemy. We did kill a fairly large number of them and I used this fact to keep my troops motivated. I thought that the platoon would be more formidable if we were cohesive, aggressive and remorseless. I tried to *lead* my soldiers as I had seen Shane Pinkston do it, rather than just supervising platoon operations and issuing orders. After I gained their confidence, my men began to respond to these efforts. The 2nd Platoon B Company soon became the most cohesive and successful rifle platoon within the 1st Battalion, 20th Infantry Regiment. Yeah, I know, that sounds like a wild flight of fantasy by a young officer who was too full of himself, but any of my soldiers from 1971 will verify the truthfulness of that statement.

    As a matter of leadership principle, I would never tell my troops to do anything that I would not do myself. Over a period of time, they probably realized this. I was often the first to crawl into bunkers or tunnels we found, and I occasionally walked "point" at night, just to demonstrate "leadership by example". I would not take my troops into an attack unless I was pretty sure we already had the upper hand, preferring to use maximum fire support instead. I knew it was better to pick our fights and to take down

The Mad Fragger and Me

Charlie Cong on our terms rather than his. I decided that I would do my best to send all of my soldiers back to their mothers intact, and I was able to do that. I had a total of 7 guys wounded in three different incidents. Some of these injuries were painful, but none of the wounds were really serious or permanently disabling. Nobody from 2nd Platoon was killed, crippled or maimed during the six and one-half months I led the platoon. This was probably somewhat attributable to Dumb Irish Luck, but the absence of serious casualties was also largely due to the skills of our point men and partly due to my caution.

Captain John Pinkston had convinced me that the mission must always come first and that mission accomplishment cannot be compromised for the welfare of the troops. But by 1971 we were fighting a war from which the U.S. was already withdrawing, somewhat blurring the significance of mission accomplishment. My primary mission was to send Charlie on final cruises across *The River Styx*, but that did not necessarily require American boys to be killed in the process. And a good Infantry officer always takes care of his me. Because of the dilemma created by forfeiture of the war and anxiety for the safety of my troops, I became very cautious about how to persecute Charlie Cong. I never developed much enthusiasm for taking unnecessary chances, nor did I wish for my troops to take needless risks. Whenever we got into a firefight, I always used plenty of artillery or gunship assets to put the whammy on Charlie, rather than risking my life or the lives my troops. I was frugal in my personal spending habits, but I did not hesitate to spend thousands of taxpayer dollars on artillery and tactical air support to punish our opponents. I occasionally had difficulty getting supporting fire clearance for safety reasons, but the Artillery Liaison Officer would usually fire the mission if I told him to put my initials on the clearance document, thus accepting responsibility for any mishap. But no one ever questioned, or tried to downsize, my requests for massive artillery barrages, or multiple gunship sorties. It is amazing that nobody ever second-guessed me on these things, considering how frequently the TOC Commandos tried to micromanage other "contact" decisions.

Other than my initial apprehension about making a mistake and getting someone killed, I was seldom really scared in combat. I sometimes experienced fear if the enemy surprised us, or when things were going badly, but whenever that happened, I tried to stay calm and look like I knew what I was doing. On the other hand, if we were in a firefight and bringing a shit storm down upon the enemy, I always felt a rush of adrenalin and a sense of euphoria. The continual possibility of tripping a booby trap worked on my head somewhat, but dink mines were just another fact of life which had to be coped with. I was not really afraid of Charlie Cong, rather I thought he ought to be afraid of us. Most of my troops had the same attitude. We owned the jungle, the paddies, the hamlets, or wherever we happened to be, and if Charlie had any sense he'd steer clear of us, because we were *The* Second Platoon. Many other rifle platoons tried to avoid contact during that period in the Vietnam War, but 2nd Platoon B Company actively sought out the VC/NVA and we really tried to kick their butts when we found them. Success in our effort to dominate the enemy was measured by *body count*.

Salesmanship is a key component of all military leadership, from Squad Leader to Division Commander. An infantry leader can motivate and inspire his men if he sells them on the idea that there is intrinsic value in belonging to their team, because belonging to an effective unit instills pride and self-respect. This works only if the unit is really good, because soldiers quickly know if they are being subjected to a snow job. It helps if a leader is somewhat intuitive, or better yet prescient, about exploiting tactical opportunities. Effective combat leaders at all levels have the ability to quickly adapt to changing circumstances and to improvise as situations require. I had not yet heard of "situation analysis" or "managing for outcomes" as management tools, but I intuitively used those techniques in 1971. I was forced by circumstances (and by my survival instincts) to become totally immersed in the combat environment. When I was fully oriented to what was going on around me, I began to deliberately look for methods and opportunities to dominate the enemy. This boiled down to being alert to strengths, weaknesses, opportunities, threats… and to acting accordingly. I was certainly not the only platoon leader who did this, but I able to work out a probably unique method of maximizing the 2nd Platoon's success, without putting the lives of my soldiers in too much jeopardy.

Battalion HQ wanted line companies to put out maximum night ambushes, when I first went to the field with B Company. I found these to be a wasted effort. I had difficulty keeping enough of the troops awake and sufficiently alert throughout the night and it was not possible for me to stay awake all night myself. Taking a squad out on a night ambush depleted the people available for Night Defensive Position (NDP) security and we only had about 30 troops in the platoon, total. It was difficult to patrol in daytime and go out on ambushes at night, plus 'bushes were generally not productive. The Battalion CO and his staff were not fully aware of these problems, because they were never in the field with us. They were sitting in the brightly lit TOC at LZ Liz each night, kibitzing and sticking pins in the situation map to mark "their" night ambushes. Most platoons moved into NDPs at twilight and prepared their defensive positions. Instead of doing that and later going out with a team on night ambush, I began to routinely wait until it was fully dark to move the entire platoon several hundred meters into a Night Defensive Position. We would therefore have a platoon-sized ambush each night. That was the tactic I had seen Frank Korona use so effectively in the 515 Valley on 28 February 1971. Frank may have been already doing this fairly regularly, but I think I probably made it the SOP in 2nd Platoon. In any case, I never hesitated to steal someone else's good idea and I got this one from Frank Korona. We tried to maintain maximum stealth, noise and light discipline in doing this, so we seldom dug in when we got to the NDP, if there was other cover available. In the lowlands, I tried to pick old rice paddies or small clumps of woods as NDP locations, so we could use the dikes and trees for cover. In the mountains, I looked for NDP sites with large rocks, or ground depressions, for the same reason. Sometimes we spent the night in cemeteries, on the theory that the Viet Cong would not desecrate their ancestors by attacking us there. Or, although in this case we moved in during daylight, we occupied hamlets and kept some villagers with us overnight. If none of these strategies were feasible, such as in the jungle, then we'd dig in to some extent, but we tried to do it quietly. The troops were not crazy about the practice of moving into NDPs after full darkness, because of the possibility of walking into Charlie in the dark, but that only happened to us once. I believed that the VC and NVA were always monitoring our activities, so it was to our advantage if they did not know exactly where we were located after nightfall. It appeared, after awhile, that Charlie gave us a wide berth at night, perhaps because he didn't know exactly where we were located. That was not the original intent of this tactic, but I think it provided us with an extra measure of nighttime security. Battalion HQ dropped their night ambush fixation not long after I went to the bush, but 2nd Platoon continued to move into most NDPs under cover of darkness.

    M18 Claymores are "command detonated" antipersonnel mines, meaning that they were designed to be deliberately fired by a soldier. They consist of a heavy olive-drab plastic outer body, 8 ½" long X 4" tall X 1 ½" thick, the bottom of which stands about 4 inches from the ground when the four scissor legs are folded out. The body is slightly curved with "FRONT-TOWARD ENEMY" molded in raised letters on the convex front side. There are two blasting cap wells with screw-in retention plugs on either side on the top, with a crude aiming aperture molded into the top center between the two cap wells. (Even though the aiming device was primitive, it was needed to properly orient the mine. A soldier in another company told me he learned this, when a trip flare went off outside an NDP

The Mad Fragger and Me

and he blew a carelessly aimed Claymore which had been set up to cover the flare. He and his buddy fired up the area with their M16s, but when nobody shot back, they ceased firing. Twenty seconds later, they collapsed in laughter when a mongrel dog wandered into the NDP, wagging his tail and looking for a handout.) Inside the plastic casing of a Claymore, the concave back section is packed with C4 plastic explosive. In front of the explosive, a plastic matrix holds about five hundred ¼ inch steel ball bearings, which blast out in a fan pattern when the device is exploded. They were designed to be used in a defensive role. At close range, they are a truly devastating weapon.

In the normal mode of operation, the mine was set up close to the ground and aimed. Then an electrical blasting cap, attached to a two-wire firing cord, which looked exactly like brown lamp cord, was screwed into one of the cap wells with a retention plug. The firing cord was unwrapped from a flattened plastic spool back to the soldier's defensive position, where the other end was plugged into a "Firing Device, Electrical, M57". Grunts called the firing device a "clacker" after the KLAK sound it made when dry-fired. When the safety bail was rotated out of the way and the handle squeezed, the clacker would generate an electrical charge through the circuit made by the firing cord and blasting cap, to explode the mine. It takes approximately 1½ volts to explode an electrical blasting cap, which is the same amount generated by one D-cell battery. A separate plug-in testing device would verify that the clacker was generating electricity, without exploding a cap.

At the Americal Division's Combat School in Chu Lai, they taught us how to modify a Claymore mine for trip-detonation, so it would fire automatically when a victim triggered it with a trip wire. This involved cutting the clacker plug off the rear end of the firing cord, so the two wires could be bared for later attaching them to a battery. Close to the other end, near the blasting cap, the cord's electrical wires were separated and one of them was cut, to interrupt the electrical circuit. A triggering device was spliced into the cut wire, so that the electrical circuit would be restored when it closed contact gap. The trigger was activated by a trip wire. If the device was connected to a battery, restoration of the circuit would cause the blasting cap and mine to explode. In setting up a trip-detonated Claymore, the main thing to remember was that you ALWAYS connected the battery to the firing cord LAST, and from a safe distance away. It was never clear to me whether a Claymore thus modified for trip-detonation was a mine, or a booby trap. Booby traps were supposedly prohibited by the Geneva Accords, but the Army gave trip-detonated Claymores the cosmetic label of "Mechanical Ambush" (or MA). They were sometimes called an "Automatic Ambush" (AA). The Americal Combat School taught us to use Mechanical Ambushes only for defensive purposes, such as to cover a trail approaching a unit's NDP. The tactical doctrine may have been somewhat ambiguous, but it was clear that the damned things were really lethal.

It occurred to me early that the enemy was booby-trapping us, so why not do it to him? NVA booby traps were an unpleasant fact of everyday life and there was a nasty but effective psychology behind the enemy's use of these devices. Our battalion was constantly taking casualties from booby traps, so we knew that we might blow ourselves to smithereens with every step we took. I knew that if their booby traps worried us, it would also worry the enemy if we began blasting them to kibbles & bits at every opportunity. The expanded use of Mechanical Ambushes allowed me to maximize our body count, without putting my soldiers at too much risk. Close collaboration with my Kit Carson Scout (KCS) helped me to develop *slightly* different techniques and tactics than those taught in the Combat School, which produced a huge improvement in outcomes. This did not come as a sudden epiphany, rather bits and pieces of information gradually melded into the 2nd Platoon's SOP for employing Mechanical Ambushes. Our techniques transformed MAs from defensive implements into offensive

The Mad Fragger and Me

weapons. I also got perverse satisfaction from using the VC/NVA's most shocking and barbarous tactic against them.

The trigger devices they recommended at the Combat School were either a spring-type clothespin, or a mousetrap. I had several of both mailed to me from home and experimented with them. With a mousetrap trigger, one end of the cut electrical wire was bared and wrapped around the edge of the wooden mousetrap base, through a small hole drilled near the edge, so that the bail made contact with the stripped wire when the bail snapped shut. The other end of the cut electrical wire was attached to the bail. The trip wire was attached to the mousetrap's bait holder. These proved to be too touchy and hair-triggered, so I quickly abandoned mousetraps as triggering devices. Spring-type clothespins were much better, but not perfect. With a clothespin trigger, the stripped ends of the cut electrical wire were wrapped around each gripping jaw and the clothespin was fastened to a sapling or stake. A piece of a plastic C-ration spoon handle was placed between the clothespin jaws, to hold the naked wire ends apart and interrupt the electric circuit. A trip wire was attached to the spoon handle and the other end of the trip wire was fastened to an anchor point across the trail. The plastic spoon handle was pulled out to complete the electrical circuit when the victim's lower leg hit the trip wire. But the clothespin spring sometimes put too much tension on the spoon handle, so the victim might feel the wire on his leg before it tripped. My Kit Carson Scout, Huynh The Hy, saw me experimenting with these things and he was very interested. He showed me how to carve dried bamboo into a flattened piece, about 1 ½ X 4 inches, leaving a bamboo segment node on one end. The flattened bamboo section was partially split with a knife blade, but the node joint stopped it from splitting completely through. The resulting bamboo device functioned exactly like a spring clothespin trigger. A spoon handle was slipped into the knife split to separate the bared electrical wires which were attached to the ends of the bamboo piece. The spoon handle was held firmly by the dried bamboo, but it would slide out easily to complete the circuit. This was much better than a clothespin, providing exactly the right amount of tension on the trip wire.

    I'd also had some ultra-light monofilament fishing line sent to me from home, because I thought it would be harder for the enemy to spot than the olive drab trip wire. KCS Hy showed distain for this idea. Instead, he demonstrated how to use a vine, a low tree branch, or a stem of elephant grass in lieu of a trip wire. The genius of this simple concept was immediately obvious to me. Why use trip wire or monofilament, when something natural, already growing there, would also work and could not be detected by the enemy? A short piece of trip wire was used, but only to attach the C ration spoon handle to the loose end of the vine, tree branch or grass stem. On one occasion, Hy showed me how to slit open a long blade of grass with a razor blade to run a GI trip wire inside it, tying the stem back together with tiny trip wire twist-ties. Charlie never saw our trip wires, because there weren't any trip wires, or they were concealed inside of foliage stems. We took pains to carefully camouflage everything else on the trap too, for example the white spoon handles were always darkened with a black grease pencil. The use of natural materials in lieu of trip wires heavily influenced the choice of MA locations. (Hy was impressively resourceful in all matters, using whatever was available to "make do". At one point, my battered Timex divers' watch became almost useless because GI insect repellant had melted the plastic crystal, making it opaque and almost unreadable. Hy noticed the cloudy lens and he gestured for me to give the watch to him. He brought it back about an hour later, looking like a crisp new crystal had been installed. He had polished out the cloudiness, using toothpaste and a cotton handkerchief. Who'd-a-thunk of that?)

    Some 3rd Platoon soldiers became interested in using mechanical ambushes, probably because 2nd Platoon was having success with them. They also experimented with different field expedient triggering devices, such as pressure triggers and pressure-

The Mad Fragger and Me

release devices, using rubber bands, springs, trip flare end-caps and other junk. I have no idea how these triggers worked, but the 3rd Platoon did get some kills with them. 1LT David Cox bragged that 3rd Platoon got one MA-KIA who "still had his scissors in his hand" when they found the body. I thought I was probably being set up for one of Dave's jokes, but curiosity got the best of me. Against my better judgment, I took a chance and asked why the NVA soldier was carrying scissors. Stalking Moon said 3rd Platoon discovered the dinks had been cutting their trip wires. His men then rigged an MA with a pressure-release trigger, so it would go off when the trip wire was cut. But Hy's invisible trip wires were a better solution to that problem, so I stuck with them and bamboo/spoon handle trigger devices, following the KISS principle (Keep It Simple, Stupid).

I sometimes daisy-chained two or three Claymores together to increase the kill zone, which was easily done using lengths of olive drab demolition ("det") cord, inserted in the blasting cap wells. Det cord was about 3/8 inch in diameter and looked like plastic-covered 1950s vintage clothesline. It was either white or olive drab in color, but the latter type was always issued to grunts. Det cord contained an explosive compound and it was commonly used to cut down trees, as well as to link explosive charges. Nonelectrical blasting caps were always crimped (with my teeth) on both ends of a length of det cord, to ensure that it exploded all the Claymores.

As recommended by the Americal Combat School, I used 6 volt lantern batteries to power the MAs, because they were easy to get, generated plenty of juice and had good attachment points for the firing wires. A new Claymore firing cord came with an electrical blasting cap already attached, which was stored through a hole in the end of the flattened plastic spool, with all the firing cord wrapped around it, a well-designed and safe arrangement. After an MA exploded, the battery, firing cord and carved bamboo trigger device were always picked up and used again. Replacement electrical blasting caps were individually packed in heavy cardboard tubes with shunts on the wires, which made them fairly safe to carry. But the nonelectrical caps used on det cord (and with time fuse) came loosely packaged in a flimsy cardboard box with cardboard spacers. I made a safer carrying case for nonelectrical caps from a plastic cigarette case and a small Styrofoam block with holes drilled in it for the caps. I still cringed a little whenever I threw my rucksack ahead of me out of a landing helicopter during a CA, because of all the explosives and blasting caps it always contained.

The strategies I worked out for employing MAs were at least as important as the mechanics of them. The primary innovation was to use the devices as long term booby-traps, instead of limiting them to overnight defensive use on trails approaching our NDPs, as taught by the Combat School. Enemy soldiers did many of the same dumb things we did, for example they almost always walked on trails, so this could be exploited. The main question was how to place the devices so that they would not endanger any civilians. As I became familiar with our environment, it became evident that this was not a problem as long as we stuck to the mountains. There were no Montagnards or Hmong in our AO. Lowland civilians never went into the mountains, unless they were part-time VC. The only people who ever went into the mountains were soldiers, either friendly or enemy. Because we operated as independent platoons, I always had an Area of Operation assigned to me and I owned it for the duration of that mission. All MA locations were shackled, called in and passed up through channels, so they never endangered other Americans or ARVNs. The mountains within my AO, or mountains immediately adjacent to the AO, became my trapping grounds. We were more limited in our options than the VC/NVA, who sometimes employed booby traps near populated villes, especially in the Song Ve Valley. The Song Ve villagers knew where the enemy mines were located, but they were sympathetic to Charlie and never warned GIs about the booby traps.

I did not put out the MAs willy-nilly. Kit Carson Scout Hy, who was ranked as an ARVN sergeant, had been a VC company commander (Ti Hui, or 2LT) before he Chieu Hoi-ed and came over to our side. I picked Hy's brain through Jim-Jim our "Speakeasy" (interpreter) and learned as much as possible about how the VC/NVA operated. Hy told me that if a VC/NVA trail was not used within 6 days, it probably wasn't being used at all. Hy also taught me that whenever a dink had to cross an open area on top of a mountain, he first always cut some leafy bushes. If a helicopter flew over and caught him in the open, Charlie would squat down and hold the foliage over his head to hide from the chopper. After he crossed the open area, he would discard the foliage. We started looking for cut foliage tossed off to the sides of a trail through an open area, because it would tell us if the trail was being used by the enemy, about how long ago, and the direction of travel. Most U.S. units were wary of the mountains, but I began running recon patrols into them, just looking for potential MA sites and this became the primary focus of all patrol planning. I always carried at least one complete MA on all patrols. Our point man/slack man teams knew what was going on and what to look for. We tried to find discarded leafy bushes, Ho Chi Minh sandal tracks, broken branches, foliage tied together overhead to form tunnels through the jungle and other "sign". If we did not find evidence of recent use on a trail, we'd continue to look elsewhere for a good spot. When we found a good location, an MA would be set up but it would be left out for no longer than 6 days. If it did not go off within 6 days, it was picked up and reset in another location. We were deceptive and sneaky in setting up MAs, so that Charlie was unlikely to see us doing it. One time, in Dragon Valley, we noticed in moving through a prior day-laager site, that the dinks had searched the fire pit where we burned our trash. An MA was left behind in that patrol base site, directly wired to a C Ration can of *Beef w/ Potato Slices in Gravy*. (Grunts always called that meal "Beef and Shrapnel" because the potato slices were undercooked and extremely hard.) There was a big explosion that night, I fired in some art'y and the body was still there at first light. Beef and Shrapnel was indeed lethal, especially when garnished with 500 steel ball bearings.

I put out each MA a klick or more from where we were operating and stayed completely away from the area until it went off, or until we picked it up. I never allowed MAs to be placed near 2nd Platoon NDPs or day laagers for safety reasons, because there had been too many accidents in other units from using them that way. The devices were somewhat tricky, especially with our unconventional trip wires. I always set them up and took them down myself, but only in full daylight so I could see what I was doing. This also allowed refinement of the trap's camouflage. There was only one occasion when we had set out an MA and Battalion HQ unexpectedly decided to extract B Company for movement to another location; I had to rush out with a patrol at first light to pick up the MA we'd set several days earlier, before the chopper pick-up.

Our very first MA kill occurred on 4 April 1971 as described in the prior Chapter, but I was just starting to work out my Mechanical Ambush tactical strategy at that point. We started racking up regular kills with MAs after that and word soon got around. Dave Cox tried to emulate our success with MAs and his platoon got several kills but they were never able to catch up to us. Dave and I were highly competitive with each other, so he would not ask me how I was doing it and I wouldn't tell him unless he asked. He kept a running tally in his field notebook showing the numbers of kills 2nd and 3rd Platoons had. Lieutenant Cox's troops always knew when 2nd Platoon scored another KIA, because Dave would start cussing as soon as he heard me on the radio calling it in.

I sometimes left notes on the bodies of NVA killed by our MAs: "Retired from military service by 2nd Platoon, B Company"... or, "No longer an active Party Member, courtesy of 2nd Platoon, Bravo Company". This was a counterpoint to the defeatist rhetoric which was prominent among American troops in 1971: "The night belongs to Charlie"... and "I don't want to be the last soldier to die in Vietnam". It was a security violation to disclose the identity of our unit to the enemy, but I decided that I didn't care if they knew who was killing them. The usual sentiment among U.S. troops was "Maybe if we leave Charlie alone, he'll leave us alone", but that was wishful thinking. Vince Lombardi's doctrine ("The best *defense* is a good *offense*") was a lot more compelling. If we preyed upon Charlie Cong, made him afraid to travel in his own territory because of our Mechanical Ambushes and let him know who was kicking his butt, then maybe he would fear us and leave us alone. This strategy was certainly better for our morale than skulking around like jackals, trying to avoid contact. Word did get around within VC/NVA circles about what The Famous 2nd Platoon was doing to them. Jim-Jim, our Vietnamese interpreter, came back from a periodic visit to his family and told us that the VC Infrastructure in Quang Ngai and Mo Duc Provinces had a bounty on the head of every soldier in 2nd Platoon B Company. *Wanted, Dead or Alive.*

When 2nd Platoon started rolling up our body count, we were only capturing weapons intermittently, because the KIAs were carrying only rice, or Chi-Com frags, which were always blown and never backhauled. Battalion at first ordered us to strip the bodies and send in the bloody uniforms whenever we did not get weapons. This seemed strange, until I realized they probably did not believe we were really getting the kills. Success in Vietnam was always measured by body counts and it was common practice to inflate the number of enemy KIAs. I never did that. I did not call in a kill unless we actually found a body, even though we sometimes found drag marks, brain/ lung tissue or blood trails, indicating additional enemy casualties. Bravo Company nevertheless led the Americal Division's monthly statistics on enemy body counts at least once and 2nd Platoon got most of them. Someone higher up apparently noticed this, and also that we were not taking friendly casualties. A bird colonel flew out from Americal Division Headquarters to interview me in the bush one day, to find out what we were doing differently. I spent an hour or more with him and explained the tactics/methods narrated above. I never saw or heard anything to suggest that he disseminated this information, but maybe it was added to the

Americal Combat School's MA doctrine. The interview was sort of funny, because I was filthy and I had several days' growth of whiskers. I did not know a VIP was coming and I did not have time to get cleaned up before he arrived. I asked one of the guys take a close-up photo of me right after the colonel left and I look like a hobo pretending to be an Army officer. (See the back cover.)

After I went home, 2nd Platoon's SGT Bob Swanson got B Company's last two confirmed kills (prior to the unit permanently standing down) with a Mechanical Ambush. While I was still there, I always set them up, because I trusted my own ability to select MA locations and to camouflage the traps. It was truly a platoon effort because I certainly did not operate alone, but I can probably take primary credit for the results of our MA campaign. I got 7 confirmed kills from Mechanical Ambushes, plus 3 or 4 more which were unconfirmed … strong evidence of additional KIAs, but the bodies not actually found. To give the reader an idea of the intensity of this effort, these 10 or 11 MA kills all occurred in the three months between April 4th and July 9th, despite the fact that I was away on R&R/leave for 2 ½ -3 weeks during that period. The 2nd Platoon also killed and wounded more NVA/VC in various firefights. There were no doubt additional enemy casualties inflicted by artillery and air strikes we initiated, but I will not try to guess at how many that might have been. Not counting KIAs from air and artillery attacks, there was persuasive physical evidence that the 2nd Platoon got at least two dozen kills (plus an unknown number of enemy WIAs) without losing any of our men, during my 6 ½ months as platoon leader. That is an accurate estimate, not an inflated statistic like the military bureaucracy habitually put out. Twenty-four kills doesn't sound like many, but that was a lot more than other rifle platoons in our battalion racked up during that period. And 2nd Platoon's body count "ratio" was surely higher than any other unit's because of the complete absence of friendly KIAs.

I certainly bear more moral responsibility for enemy deaths than any of my soldiers do, because so many killings would not have occurred except for my very deliberate persecution of the VC/NVA. I had few misgivings at the time, despite the fact that these deaths didn't affect the outcome of the war and were a waste of human life from that perspective. And I won't try to talk myself into feeling any remorse now, because I know that my aggressiveness saved an unknown number of GI lives. Killing VC/NVA was an essential job function, for which I will cheerfully accept full responsibility on Judgment Day.

If the reader takes the time and trouble to carefully review the S2/S3 log summaries, it will be noted that 1st Battalion, 20th Infantry units began putting out MAs all over the place, all the time. But nobody had very much success, except 2nd Platoon B Company, and to a somewhat lesser extent, our 3rd Platoon. *Neca eos omnes. Deus suos agnoscet.*

LZ Liz Helipad sign

Tom Dolan and Pete Zierden on Nui Vong

Dink and Me

Lei and Mai

Catholic Church on QL1, near Duc Pho

South OP, viewed from LZ Liz bunker line

Skippy, Four Deuce Mascot

Nui Vong, 2/22/71: L-R, top: "Curly" Schilling, "Big Al" Danis, Bruce Goins, "Robby" Robinson, "Swanee" Swanson, Gary Lane, Joe Stephens. Kneeling: Doug "Coon Ass" Landry, "Pancho" Ramirez

Dolphin resupply inbound

SGT Keith Moore, bringing in extraction bird

The Mad Fragger,
Pancho Ramirez, (unknown)

Richard "Bigfoot" Smith

Bunker #21, LZ Liz: L-R, Don Braziel, Bob Swanson, Huynh The Hy, Keith Moore, Paul Malonson, Pancho Ramirez

Tom Dolan, Keith Moore, 4/5/71

Jim-Jim and Hy on LZ Dragon

515 Valley, 5/23/71. L-R, from top, Tom Dolan, Wooly Jones, Doc Wright, Paul Malonson, Sweetpea Walton, Jim Morgan, The Mad Fragger, Soong, (unk.). Front: Gary Lane, Rufus Hill (w/M2 carbine) Wayne Wilson (w/ AK47) Craig Valashek (59th Scout Dog Platoon) and Blitz.

Doc Wright, Kit Carson Scout Hy, Don Braziel

Don Braziel, Bob Swanson, Harold Weidner, Keith Moore and
The Mad Fragger (Gary Smith) with captured Soviet (?!) flag

T`he, Thom

Soong

1LT Frank Korona

CPT Randy Guill
(photo courtesy of Doug Knight)

Jim-Jim, Wendy

Curly Schilling, Mike Jones
(Note movie camera & Bowie knife)

Doug Knight, kneeling left, fantasizing that he is me (posing with 2nd Platoon guys, The Mad Fragger, center) July 1971 (US Army Photo)

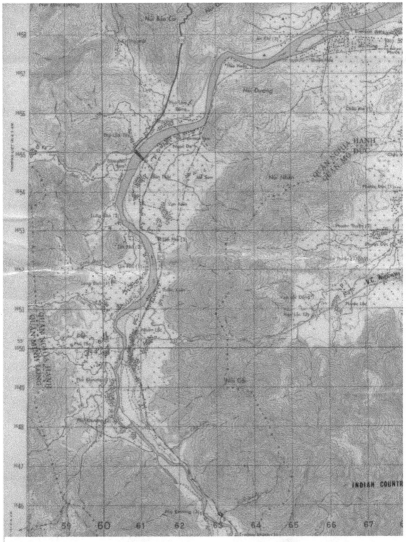

U.S. military map, showing the upper Song Ve River Valley (West) and part of Dragon Valley (East)

Chapter 8:

MORE ADVENTURES IN THE BUSH

Shortly after the Easter Sunday debacle, SSG Bland went home because his 12 month tour was over. SP/4 Keith Moore was again appointed as interim Platoon Sergeant. Acting Sergeant Moore did a good and conscientious job, despite his lack of rank or formal leadership training. I was happy that Don Bland was able to go home in one piece, but I was certain I'd never get another platoon sergeant as good as he was. I was wrong about that, because Staff Sergeant Wayne P. Wilson was soon assigned to 2nd Platoon and he turned out to be terrific. I don't know exactly when SSG Wilson joined us, but it must have been sometime in May. Sergeant Wilson was 28 years old and on his second tour in Vietnam, also having done the first one in the Americal Division, as a helicopter Crew Chief. At that point, he intended to stay in the Army for a career and it was somewhat unusual for an NCO careerist (aka, a "lifer") to go into the bush as a grunt. Many of them were riding medical profiles in the rear area somewhere, or they had finagled rear jobs running NCO clubs, or something similar. The combat leadership in 1970-1971 was primarily provided by soldiers who had moved up in rank to the E5 level, Shake 'n Bake NCOs and Infantry lieutenants. For this reason, I immediately started calling SSG Wilson "Lifer" and soon everyone in B Company was doing it. For me, it was originally just a joke but it eventually became a term of affection. SSG Wilson wore it like a badge of honor.

After the Easter Sunday disaster, we returned to LZ Liz for three days of perimeter duty and then Bravo Company was sent to the Stand Down Compound at LZ Bronco/ Duc Pho for three days of partying. Everyone got roaring drunk the last night on stand-down. We expected to go out by helicopter the next day, to take it easy and nurse our hangovers in a day laager somewhere. Instead, they took us a short distance up QL 1 on trucks and dropped us off. We then had to hump about 7 klicks cross-country to the 515 Valley for our next mission. I had to stop twice and go back for hung over and dehydrated guys who fell out along the route.

Several days later, on April 25th, one of our Mechanical Ambushes went off. As we approached, I shot some preplanned artillery into the area. I then led the way into the MA site because I had set it up. I had daisy-chained two claymores and they shredded the underbrush, making a large clearing where there had been thick foliage. We found that we had 'bushed a rice carrying party and we had one immediate KIA, a VC female carrying a heavy pack which was full of rice. She was in the middle of the new clearing, bent over on her knees. As I came up next to her, she let out a horrible last gasp and I almost jumped out of my skin. Hy was right behind me and he immediately administered a savage vertical butt-stroke to her head, knocking her over on her back. Hy chuckled and said, "No sweat, El Tee". The jungle looked like a crime scene, with blood everywhere. It appeared that two more bodies probably had been dragged off up the mountain, but when we followed we received several bursts of small arms fire from survivors. As was often the case in such situations, I did not see the enemy, but I heard the rounds cracking past in close proximity to my ears. I pulled the patrol back a little and threw some more artillery at them. We went up the trail again, but did not find the other bodies. I pulled out after going about 100 meters, because the vegetation was getting heavier and I didn't want to risk leading my troops into a hasty ambush on the trail. It wasn't worth getting GIs hurt or killed, just to chalk up a couple of more KIAs on the scoreboard. I had some initial qualms about killing a woman, but I quickly got over it. She was playing with the boys and sometimes the boys play rough. *Xin loi, Sally Cong.*

The next night, April 26th, 1LT Dave Cox fell into an abandoned well in his NDP and badly injured his knee. He suffered through the night and was dusted off at first light the next morning. (He was

The Mad Fragger and Me

sent to the 91st Evac Hospital, but when he was released, he returned to LZ Liz, on crutches and with his leg in a cast. While Dave was still *hors de combat*, the new acting Battalion Commander saw him hobbling along on his crutches and asked, perhaps facetiously, when he would be ready to go back on the line. Stalking Moon answered, "Well, if I get to do what you do, I'm ready now. But if I go back to being a rifle platoon leader, it may take a little longer.") He did come back out to 3rd Platoon after a few weeks. Of course, I could not pass up an opportunity to accuse him of malingering and faking the injury to get out of the field. He had really messed up his knee however, and CPT Guill eventually reassigned him as the B Company XO, after Greg Studdard left that slot. I don't recall when that occurred, though.

After another four day sojourn on the bunker line at LZ Liz, we went back to VC Highway/ Dragon Valley for our next mission. The 3rd Platoon got a KIA there on May 6th, by leaving behind a Mechanical Ambush in a day laager.

May 10th was a busy and ugly day for B Company. At 6:15 am, 3rd Platoon thought they heard another of their MAs detonate and a patrol went out to check. They shot in some art'y and then they hit a booby trap at 7:15 AM. Five guys had walked past the device before it detonated, so it was probably an M26 frag with the pull-pin straightened, or placed inside of a C ration can to hold the safety spoon down. SP/4 Alexander Quiroz was killed and SP/4 Larry Rowe had multiple frag wounds to his legs. The 3rd Platoon got nothing from their MA. 1LT Dave Cox was still in the rear recovering from his knee injury and he met the MEDEVAC chopper carrying SP/4 Quiroz's body at the helipad, a heartbreaking task.

That evening at 7:15 pm, we heard an explosion and I was pretty sure our Mechanical Ambush had detonated. I took a patrol out to check and I shot in some illumination, but the MA site was in heavy foliage and I could not see whether the trap was intact or not. It was not a good idea to risk walking into our own MA, so I decided to withdraw, go to our NDP and check again in the morning. Art'y was shot on the MA site intermittently throughout the night to discourage evacuation of any KIAs or WIAs.

I took another patrol out at first light on May 11th and found that our MA had detonated. 2nd Platoon had another NVA KIA and another captured AK47 assault rifle. The KIA was carrying a heavy rucksack with a large number of documents, several hundred dollars worth of piastres in cash, dozens of really interesting black and white photos of NVA soldiers in training camps and in the jungle, plus a nice portrait of his sweetheart in North Vietnam. He also had a copy of *Mad Magazine* in his pack, but I did not appreciate the irony of that at the time. I gave the cash to Hy and I kept a stainless steel Seiko watch I took off the corpse. (The watch was badly shocked and eventually stopped working.) Doc Wright took and used a heavily rubberized NVA medical aide bag the guy was carrying, but Doc gave Hy the quinine and other medicines which were inside the bag. I really wanted to keep the photos as souvenirs, but I knew they might have some intelligence value, especially in conjunction with all the NVA documents. I also knew that the REMFs would probably steal the pictures if I sent them to the rear. I finally sent the photo collection back to the rear area for intelligence analysis, with a note requesting that they be returned to me after they were evaluated. I never saw them again. The pictures are probably now in a REMF Intelligence officer's scrapbook, to illustrate his combat experiences in Vietnam.

A couple of weeks later, I caught hell from the S2 (Battalion Intelligence Officer) about that incident. I didn't care, because The Lifer had been telling me, "What are they going to do to us El Tee, put us in the Infantry and send us to the bush?" every time the brass gave us a hard time about something. The S2 wanted to know what I had done with all the money, apparently not appreciating the "spoils of war" concept. I was surprised that they knew about the money because I had not reported it, but I told him it was already spent on a big platoon party, xin loi. They knew <u>exactly</u> how much cash we bagged, from analysis of the documents. The S2 said evaluation of the documents by MACV revealed that our KIA was the chief NVA purchasing officer for Quang Ngai Province. He was returning to his unit from a major buying trip into Quang Ngai City when we killed him. We would have gotten several THOUSAND dollars if we had greased him on his way out of the mountains, before he made the purchases. The documents we captured had named names. The S2 said that *several dozen* VC/NVA sympathizers, i.e., civilians who were doing business with them, were arrested on the strength of the purchasing records.

We generally ran three daylight patrols each day when 2nd Platoon had three squads, then two patrols when we reorganized into two squads, so each man usually went on one patrol per day. It was my practice to personally go on all patrols sent out by 2nd Platoon, whether it was three or two daily. May 13th was an exception, because I developed a blinding migraine headache, which also made me sick to my stomach. I decided to stay in the patrol base and try to get rid of the headache, instead of going on that day's patrols. I took a near-overdose of APCs (all purpose capsules, otherwise known as aspirin) and strung my hammock across a little stream in a shady ravine just outside the patrol base. I was reclining in the hammock with my eyes closed and I heard a loud splashing noise, like someone running through the water upstream. Thinking that Charlie was coming, I sat up and grabbed my M16. I saw a big green lizard about 15 inches tall, running down the steam on its hind legs. It looked like a miniature Tyrannosaurus, with atrophied front legs, and it ran right under my hammock. It was one of the strangest things I ever saw.

A short time later, I heard a lot of distant shooting, apparently coming from 2nd Platoon's patrol. I ran to the PB, grabbed my gear and went in the direction of the shooting with most of the rest of the platoon. The squad leader was on the radio and he said they were in a firefight with 6 to 8 NVA. He thought they had hit at least one NVA soldier, because they saw a guy go down in the first volley. When I arrived at the fight, the dinks were still shooting back, from a large clump of woods across an abandoned rice paddy. I got on the radio and requested both artillery and helicopter gunships. The art'y battery had just called "Shot, over" when an Air Force FAC (Forward Air Controller) in a small fixed wing plane showed up on the scene. The first round of 155mm HE (High Explosive) came in and landed in the old rice paddy between us and the enemy, about 90 meters short of the wood line. The FAC wanted to get in on the action and relay the artillery adjustments, so I gave him "direction" and "proximity", then told him to "add one hundred and fire for effect " to bring the volley just inside the woods. [The artillery was coming from the battery on FSB Snoopy and we were almost directly on the "gun-target line", with the enemy between us and the gun battery. Forward Air Controllers always adjusted their fire from the perspective of *howitzers toward target*. Artillery observers on the ground always adjusted fire from the perspective of *forward observer toward target*, providing the azimuth in mils, which allowed gun battery computers to perform calculations to compensate for the angle of observation. Apparently because he didn't usually do it that way, the FAC did not relay the azimuth (direction) I gave him. Because we were on the far side of the target from the guns, this reversed my adjustment by 180 degrees. My instruction to *add 100* which would have moved the impact another 100 meters away, therefore became *drop 100*. I had requested "Platoon One in adjustment, Battery Four in effect", so 24 rounds of 155mm HE landed right on top of 2nd Platoon.] We were already on the ground behind an old paddy dike and we heard the artillery coming in on us, so we tried to get even lower. After the rounds impacted, I heard the FAC say "Oh! My! God!" into the radio. Miraculously, no one was hurt. I immediately knew what had happened, but by this time my ripping headache was leaking out of my ears. I radioed a good cussing at the FAC and told him to get lost. After the art'y got straightened out and was lifted, a Shark gunship came on station. The pilot shot up the woods with rockets and miniguns and he reported lighting up two hostiles as they ran into a bunker. I got the platoon in a skirmish line and we made a frontal assault on the wood line, weapons blazing, with the Shark crew flying cover and cheering us on. I would not normally have done that, but I was pretty certain that Charlie had already pulled back, everyone's blood was up and a gunship was covering us. We also had an audience, so it was an opportunity to add to *The Legend of the Famous 2nd Platoon*. The Shark pilot was just freaking out over our little performance, incredulous that he was watching a rifle platoon make a frontal assault across open ground. He described it to everyone listening on the Command Net, and he stuck to us like a tick. We found about 15 small bunkers in the woods and 25 to 30 fighting positions, so the enemy unit was probably larger than the 8 man group my guys engaged. The art'y and gunship rockets had destroyed most of the bunkers, but we did not find any bodies, blood trails or the two enemy soldiers the gunship had fired upon. (According to the S2/S3 journal, B Company's 3rd Platoon and an ARVN element from MACV/OP Pax were being maneuvered into positions as "blocking forces" during this skirmish, even though interception of the fleeing enemy was highly unlikely because of area terrain and vegetation.)

We went back to Liz again for firebase security in mid-May. Stalking Moon was back by then and we always gave each other a lot of flack about the relative merits of our platoons. I told him that I would buy a case of beer for 3rd Platoon if they ever got as many kills as 2nd Platoon did on a mission, predicting that would never happen.

We went back out to the 515 Valley on the next mission and Doug Knight's 1st Platoon reported killing one uniformed NVA with small arms fire on 20 May 71, but they said his companion escaped with the KIA's pack and weapon.

On May 21st, an urgent MEDEVAC was called for Shake 'N Bake Sergeant David Polise, who was severely injured by one of the 3rd Platoon's Claymores, while they were setting up the night's defenses. As he was being dusted off, SGT Polise repeatedly shouted, "WHO squeezed the CLACKER?!", so he obviously believed that someone deliberately fired the Claymore. (That day, SGT Polise had ordered several soldiers to stop harassing and manhandling a pregnant Vietnamese girl. He did not think they were molesting her, but there was also no need for them to place their hands on her. The soldiers ignored him, until he reiterated the order more loudly and at gunpoint. SGT Polise believed that one of them blew the Claymore in reprisal.) It was never determined how the explosion occurred. It may have been an accident, caused by static electricity, or by carelessness. Another possibility is that the Claymore was rigged for trip detonation and Polise wasn't told about it, either deliberately or through an oversight. David Polise lost one of his legs in the service of his country, but because the incident was either a fragging or an accident, he was not awarded a Purple Heart. Regardless of cause, this was another B Company tragedy.

2nd Platoon got two more NVA KIAs on May 23rd, with a daisy-chain MA, on a trail into the mountains to the west of the 515 Valley. We also captured an AK47 and a U.S. M2 carbine (full automatic version of the M1 carbine) and about a pound of documents. When the Mechanical Ambush went off, I called in art'y, to give us time to get there and to finish or chase off any survivors. Dog handler Craig Valashek and his K9 partner Blitz were with us. (See the photo of them posing with us after we returned to the patrol base.) Blitz was a young German Shepherd Scout Dog, but he had never seen dead bodies before. When SP/4 Rufus Hill, SP/4 Valashek and I sneaked in on the MA site, Blitz became so interested in smelling the two bodies that he wouldn't "work"... he was there to alert us to any stay-behind survivors waiting in ambush. Craig disciplined him a little and then Blitz got back with the program. We again found signs that another NVA casualty or two may have been dragged off, but Blitz was a Scout Dog, not a Tracker. We did not find the additional bodies. Dave Cox surely heard me call in the two kills and I knew that he was taking gas.

The Mad Fragger and Me

On May 27th, 3rd Platoon called in two NVA KIAs by mechanical ambush, reporting two AK50s captured, one of which was destroyed by the Claymore. Now I was the one who was taking gas.

2nd Platoon bragged to the Coke kids and villagers in The 515 Valley that B Company was kicking Charlie's butt, so he was afraid to come out of hiding to fight with us. We told them, "VC beaucoup chickenshit, VC no fight with GI". This propaganda effort produced unexpected results. On May 29th, just before dark, it started to rain. 2nd Platoon was preparing to move from our PB to our NDP, when all hell broke loose. Some dinks sneaked in pretty close and fired us up with at least one automatic weapon. I thought it was probably a crew served PK machine gun and called it in that way. The attack caught us completely off guard and created a lot of confusion. Doc Wright provided comic relief by running around in all directions amid the flying bullets, flapping his arms and shouting "Where's my GUN?! Where's my GUN?!" Harold Weidner tackled Doc and jumped on top of him, covering him with his body. Harold also grabbed one of our M60 machine guns and he started firing, but some of the hot shell casings fell inside Doc's shirt, resulting in history's first demonstration of freestyle break-dancing. (Harold was the 2nd Platoon's "Quiet Man", always steady and reliable, but never saying much.) Everyone else was snatching up weapons and returning fire too. I'd left my rifle leaning against my rucksack in the middle of a clearing, with my .45 in one of the ruck's pockets, another Dumb Irish Trick. I said something about not having a weapon and RTO Richard "Bigfoot" Smith, immediately ran out under fire and grabbed my rifle, then ran back and slid into the shallow ditch we had taken cover in. I gave him hell for doing that, but the truth is that I became anxious if I didn't have my M16 next to me when bullets were cracking around. I went up on the command net and asked the Battalion TOC for gunships. The TOC answered a short time later and said there was a new Americal Division Standard Operating Procedure: You could not get gunships unless you first fired artillery. I said okay, give me the artillery. The

TOC came back after another minute or two and said the battalion's Art'y Liaison Officer would not give his clearance, "because of proximity of a friendly ville and troops on the gun-target line". (The dinks were between 2nd Platoon and a nearby ville, all three entities on a direct line from LZ Liz, dangerous in the event of either a long round or a short round.) I said, okay, then send the gunships. They said no gunships unless you first fired artillery. (Uh-oh, *Catch 22*.) I told them to "Initial the artillery clearance Tango Delta (for Thomas Dolan) and shoot the mission". After another delay, they refused to do that too. (I swear I'm <u>not</u> making this up.) By that time it was raining hard and it was fully dark. We were within range of the 4.2 inch mortars at LZ Liz, so I requested Four Deuce illumination and they did give a clearance for that. The illumination, descending by parachutes, didn't do much good. We were laagered in a wooded area and the illumination, with the heavy wind/rain, just produced many continually moving shadows. One of the empty (and heavy) 4.2 inch illumination canisters came crashing down inside our perimeter. I heard it come down and knew what it was, so I check-fired Four Deuce. (The empty canister almost hit Bob Swanson, who was prone on the ground. Swanee later said he could not see the object which had landed heavily between his feet and he thought it was a satchel charge or a mortar round, so he drew his knees together and closed his eyes, waiting for the explosion.) In the meantime, 2nd Platoon had really blasted them with small arms and 40mm grenade fire, so the dink machine gun stopped firing and it appeared that they had probably withdrawn. I called that in and our new acting Battalion Commander, Major William Saltz (not his real name) came on the horn and he told me to "Run an Infantry sweep" of the area. We could not see anything at all in the dark, with the torrential rain. I smelled a set-up anyway and thought that the dinks were probably trying to sucker us into a booby trap. So I said visibility was zilch, but we would check the area at first light. Major Saltz again told me to "sweep". I stalled, by telling him we needed an emergency ammo resupply, which I knew they couldn't send

The Mad Fragger and Me

because the now driving rain would ground the helicopters. Sure enough, they promptly denied the emergency ammo resupply because they couldn't get a chopper up, but this also meant that MEDEVAC would be grounded if we needed it. Saltz started insisting on a "sweep", which was pure lunacy, but I didn't want to openly refuse a direct order. I started telling him, "Say again your last transmission, I am receiving you broken and distorted", over and over, clicking the push-to-talk switch, tapping on the mouthpiece and muffling my voice to befuddle the transmission. Major Saltz knew that I was giving him the business and he really got pissed off. I finally said, "I have a negative copy on your last transmission and I am moving out to my NDP at this time... negative further, OUT". By then Major Saltz was having a conniption fit, shouting threats into the radio about what he was going to do to me for disobeying his order. (This was not as funny *then* as it is now.) We gathered up our gear in the dark and moved to a hastily selected alternative NDP, around a small clump of foliage on the far side of the 515 Road. SSG Wilson redistributed available ammo at the NDP. All of us were soaked and we spent a miserable night in the rain, in a tight defensive perimeter with 50% alert. I had two Budweiser beers on ice in the canvas "cooler" on top of my ruck and I drank them while I took my turn on guard duty that night. Early the next morning, the rain stopped. I shot an artillery barrage into the area of the action, in case it was booby trapped, from an observation position off to the side of the G-T Line. It sounded like we might have gotten a smaller "secondary" explosion from a booby trap, but I wasn't sure. We then checked the area and found nothing.

    Only a few of the Coke Kids who had been hanging around our day laagers came back that day. One of the older ones made some smart-alecky comments about the VC attacking us the night before, with a knowing and insolent look on his face. I considered detaining and back-hauling the little cretin as a suspected VC sympathizer, but I finally decided not to do that. The ARVN interrogators in Quang Ngai would have definitely wiped the smirk off his face, but the hell with it. I didn't want to make war on dumb 14 year old kids, even if they were VC collaborators. But I didn't like the looks of some other new spectators who showed up that day, so I chased all of the civilians out of our patrol base, firing my rifle over their heads. Curly Schilling captured this tantrum for posterity on Super 8 movie film.

A few days later, we went to LZ Liz again. The Mad Fragger told me he'd heard something, from someone in 3rd Platoon, which suggested that they probably faked their second KIA on the last mission. They had supposedly walked past the same body twice and counted it again, or something like that. So I brushed off Dave Cox when he asked for his platoon's beer, claiming that I'd said they had to get MORE kills than 2nd Platoon, in order to collect on our wager. I later felt guilty about this, because when I really thought about it, I knew Stalking Moon would BS and joke around all day long, but he would never cheat.

CPT Guill told me that the Battalion Commander wanted to talk to me ASAP about my radio problem, grinning, shaking his head and implying that I was going to get a royal butt-chewing. Randy Guill had monitored the whole conversation on his PRC25, so he knew exactly what had happened. He said he'd told Major Saltz that I was reliable and he needed to put more trust in the judgment of the guy who was in charge on the ground. With that foundation laid by CPT Guill, I went to see the Battalion CO for a private interview in his quarters, but I was not feeling very repentant. Major Saltz's order to "sweep" had been completely whacko. I knew I had done the right thing and getting an ass-chewing for it was not a big deal. By the time I reported to Saltz in his quarters he'd had time to calm down and he didn't try very hard to reprimand me. He just said that he had to be able to expect junior officers to do what he told them to do. (*Yes Sir, Yes Sir, three bags full. What are you going to do to me, Sir? Put me in the Infantry and send me to Vietnam?*) After I left his quarters, it occurred to me that I could probably get away with almost anything, as long as my success in the bush continued.

The Mad Fragger and Me

I couldn't say anything to the men in my platoon about my conflict with the acting Battalion CO, because that would have been improper from a leadership perspective, but the guys who were close enough to hear my end of the radio conversation may have guessed that I pretended not to hear his order. Everyone who was on duty in the Battalion TOC on May 29th had heard the entire dust-up between Major Saltz and me, because the TOC radios were hooked up to speakers. My OCS classmate, 1LT Sidney Hopfer, was by then the permanent night time TOC Duty Officer, so he had heard the whole radio conversation. It was not unusual for lieutenants to bitch among ourselves about the foibles of our superiors. So Sid described how purple-faced Saltz had become when I wouldn't go blundering around in total darkness and we had a good laugh about it. Sid wanted to know how I could tell the dinks used a PK machine gun to fire us up and not an AK, sounding skeptical. I said the firing rhythm didn't sound like a Kalashnikov and I had heard the PK used different ammo. I also thought they used some kind of belt fed weapon, because the dinks had really hosed us down and nobody could change magazines that fast. Sid said he thought they could, if a whole rifle platoon was shooting back at them.

The 3rd Platoon killed a big cat with an MA on June 7th, which the S2/S3 log incorrectly recorded as a "tiger". I saw photos taken by a 3rd Platoon soldier and I remember that it was a huge spotted leopard. The 3rd Platoon had been moving to an NDP and the drag man reported that he thought they were being followed. An MA was quickly set up and the platoon moved out, but after it exploded, they went back and found a very large dead leopard instead of an NVA/KIA. The cat had bled from its eyes, nose and ears, but it had no marks on it. They deduced that it had instinctively leaped into the air when it felt the trip wire release the trigger and was killed by concussion from the Claymore. We knew that tigers were lurking in the jungle, because one was spotted occasionally. Now we had unexpected evidence that there were leopards around too. In fact, this one had deliberately followed a platoon. Maybe the leopard was just curious and curiosity killed the cat. Or maybe he was hungry. I never heard or read (except in a novel) about a GI being killed by a big cat in Vietnam, but I think it could have happened.

Later in June, 3rd Platoon called an "urgent" dust-off for two guys struck by lightning. CPT Guill was struck by several steel pellets from a Claymore which was set off by a lightning strike in the same storm, but he was patched up by the platoon's medic and he remained in the bush.

In late June we were sent to LZ Bronco at Duc Pho, to secure the perimeter during preparation of that base for turn over to the ARVNs. Our "rear area" had already been moved from Duc Pho to Chu Lai, in anticipation of this change. I missed most of the LZ Bronco security mission, because I went on R&R with my wife in Hawaii, but I was there for the first day or two. We did not really have enough troops to man our assigned segment of the perimeter. We were spread thin with only two or three guys per bunker, for 24 hour guard duty. We also had no way to get food, ammo and other supplies delivered to the troops, because the bunkers were widely separated and B Company did not possess even one vehicle, either at Chu Lai or Duc Pho. There was no shortage of vehicles among REMFs, however. Whenever I went to rear areas, I'd see soldiers driving everywhere in vehicles, often alone. I departed for Hawaii, leaving SSG Wayne Wilson in charge of 2nd Platoon. My one week vacation in Hawaii was surreal and somewhat jarring, because of the abrupt transition from a primeval existence into the lap of luxury. When I returned, I heard stories about what went on during my absence.

The Lifer was always impressively resourceful. He had spotted a derelict quarter-ton jeep, apparently abandoned on the tarmac at the LZ Bronco Airport. He made inquiries about it and was told that it was dead-lined. SSG Wilson asked if he could use it, if he could get it running. He was assured that resurrecting it was not possible, because the jeep had to go up the line for Depot Maintenance (one stop short of back to the manufacturer) in order to be repaired, but he was welcome to try. He sent SGT Paul Malonson and SP/5 Thomas "Doc" Wright to the airport to fix it. Paul, one of our Squad Leaders, had been an automobile mechanic in civilian life and Doc was a diesel mechanic before joining the Army. This was a nice but underappreciated consequence of the draft. You could always find people with all sorts of civilian skills in military service. Somehow our two mechanics fixed the jeep.

CPT Guill needed to go north to Chu Lai to see the B Company First Sergeant in the battered jeep and he asked SSG Wayne Wilson to go with him. That was a fairly long trip, more than 20 miles each way. They had found a ¼ ton trailer unattended somewhere on LZ Bronco and "borrowed" it. Doc Wright wanted some medical stuff, plus there were other supply items the company needed, so they took a shopping list with them. They got what they needed in Chu Lai and headed back for Duc Pho in the jalopy, looking like *Sanford & Son* with all their goods piled up in the back seat and in the trailer. The Lifer was driving and he was going pretty fast as they approached the outskirts of Quang Ngai City, in the Province of the same name. They heard some rounds cracking over their heads, but it was not unusual to get sniped at along QL 1, so SSG Wilson started driving even faster. The bullets kept cracking over their heads, so they finally looked back to see two Military Policemen chasing them in a jeep. The jeep had a flashing red light but no siren, so the MPs fired over their heads to attract attention. SSG Wilson pulled over and the MPs told him they were going to cite him for speeding through the villes along QL 1. (We detested MPs because they were officious and they always hassled our troops about haircuts and trivial uniform violations.) The Lifer started telling the two MPs what grunts thought of them, their mothers, all their ancestors and their progeny. They were not receptive to this litany of abuse and they started writing him multiple DRs (Delinquency Reports). The unit designations and bumper numbers of the jeep and the stolen trailer did not match. There was no log book in the jeep, which is the military equivalent of a vehicle registration. Wayne gave them a faded, illegible and dog-eared military driver's license from Fort Rucker, Alabama, which was not valid in Vietnam. They wrote DRs for those violations, for speeding, for fleeing and eluding and everything else they could think of. They handed SSG Wilson a wad of DR copies and told him the originals would come down through channels to his CO, who would determine his punishment. Wayne handed the DRs to CPT Guill and commented, "This is my CO and he doesn't like @#$%& MPs any more than I do". Randy Guill, who was impatient with the delay, tore up the DRs, threw them over his shoulder and said, "Let's go". The MPs probably had never encountered that level of defiance before. They told SSG Wilson and CPT Guill that they were going to escort them through Quang Ngai and out of their sector, so they should follow the MP jeep. There was a MACV Compound in the town of Quang Ngai, which had an Officer/NCO Club. SSG Wilson asked CPT Guill if he felt like getting something to eat, as he suddenly made a hard left into the MACV Compound. The Military Police continued driving south, unaware that they were no longer being followed by The Lifer and CPT Guill. The MPs eventually doubled back and found them sitting in the Officer/NCO Club, drinking beer and eating cheeseburgers. When Wayne later told me this story, his eyes took on a serene glow as he described the outrage of the two Military Policemen.

    After the Wilson & Guill trip to Chu Lai, the games continued. There was a LTC who was in charge of the turn-over of LZ Bronco to the ARVN and he held a daily briefing in the old Brigade HQ building. As acting platoon leader, SSG Wayne Wilson usually went to this meeting and he noticed a ¾ ton truck parked there, which didn't seem to be getting much use. 2nd Platoon representatives went back and "borrowed" the truck in the middle of the night, but "forgot" to take it back. They moved the truck around and hid it during daylight hours, but they had a vehicle to haul chow and ammo to the

The Mad Fragger and Me

perimeter bunkers. CPT Guill therefore had full use of the clunker jeep.

LZ Bronco was surrounded by a barbed wire entanglement. An area for about 100 meters beyond the barbed wire was cleared, around which a huge ville sprawled, partially around the base. Just inside the wire, there was a wide cleared space with a perimeter road in the middle that went completely around LZ Bronco. The front gate, which gave access to QL 1, was manned around the clock by MPs. The guard bunkers that B Company was occupying stood just inside the perimeter road. The bunkers were well constructed and built to about the same dimensions, suggesting they had probably been built by the Seabees when LZ Bronco was a Marine base. They were two stories high, like guard towers. The top levels were roofed and sandbagged to waist level, but open on the sides above that to maximize visibility. The first floor consisted of an enclosed sleeping bunker for soldiers who were not actually on guard duty. The guys in 2nd Platoon cleared a pathway through the wire from the ville, so that Madam Ks could be brought in after dark. (Madam Ks, or Boom-Boom Girls were Vietnamese prostitutes, who seemed to be everywhere along QL 1. We had previously learned that trying to keep the boys and the girls separated was a hopeless task.) One night the Lieutenant Colonel in charge of the LZ Bronco turn-over pulled up to the 2nd Platoon CP bunker in his jeep. He spotted the ¾ ton truck parked behind the bunker and started yelling, "That's MY truck! You STOLE my truck!" Wayne told me that panic and chaos ensued, with naked girls and GIs emerging from the bunker and running off in different directions into the dark. Everyone played dumb about the truck, nobody saw who parked it there, nobody knew nuthin'.

Somebody in 2nd Platoon found the LZ Bronco dump and reported to SSG Wayne Wilson that weapons parts, commo equipment and ammo had been discarded there. SSG Wilson sent a work detail to the dump, to see what they could recover. The detail returned with a Starlight Scope, a working PRC25 radio, field phones, weapons and other equipment. From found parts, they put together an M79 grenade launcher and an M60 machine gun. They also recovered ammunition and additional weapons' parts. The LZ Bronco REMFs had field-stripped various weapons and thrown the parts into the dump, with other serial-numbered items, ammunition and supplies. This was done to get rid of equipment which was not on their property books, because the rear area supply and arms rooms at LZ Bronco were being closed down. It was much easier for them to toss the ammo and other supplies, instead of hauling them to Chu Lai. The enemy could have found this stuff just as easily as 2nd Platoon had. The REMFs were not out in the bush fighting and dying, so they didn't give a damn.

When I came back from Hawaii, Bravo Company returned to the field.

We had a one day cease fire at the request of the North Vietnamese, to celebrate one of their traditional holidays. Battalion units were told to pull in all MAs and refrain from any other aggressive actions. We were allowed only to run defensive clearing patrols around our day laager locations. B Company was in Dragon Valley and all three platoons linked up in a single patrol base. We had seen some deer nearby, so we decided to go deer hunting, by putting on a drive through a clump of woods about 100 meters from the day laager. An M60 was placed on an old paddy dyke to shoot the flushing deer and our drivers swept through the woods. We didn't jump up any deer. We did flush a herd of wild boar, but they did not understand the hunting rules and ran at us instead of away from us. A big sow, surrounded by her litter of squealing shoats, came charging down a trail at Richard "Bigfoot" Smith, who dropped her with his M16, a lucky shot to the spine. Some of our country boys butchered the pig and we spent the rest of the day roasting and feasting on wild pork. The meat was tough, stringy and strong tasting, barely edible even with lots of field-expedient barbeque sauce. But the pig feast was festive and something different to do. Somehow, nobody got trichinosis.

The Mad Fragger and Me

Sometime during the May-June period, Bigfoot Smith asked if he could speak with me. He was my RTO, so we spent a lot of time together and we talked to each other all day long. I was curious about what was coming next, because of his formality. Smitty said that the other African-American guys in Bravo Company had decided to ask that they be put together, in 2nd Platoon. There really weren't very many black troopers in the company, probably seven or eight guys. As the spokesman for the group, SP/4 Smith had already approached Randy Guill with this request. Predictably, CPT Guill at first said that the Army had been desegregated for 20 years and now the black troops were asking him to reverse that policy. Smitty had anticipated this and he had his arguments ready, assuring the CO that this change would really promote operational efficiency and racial harmony within the unit. He said Guill had finally agreed to it. I did not know about this proposal and I was miffed that CPT Guill had not discussed it with me before approving it, but I just said to Smitty that it was okay with me, with one caveat: I absolutely would not take "Brother Sparks" into the 2nd Platoon. The 1st Platoon's PVT Delbert Sparks (not his real name) was a notoriously angry and militant Black Power agitator, who acted like he hated every white man who ever lived, but especially officers or others in positions of authority. He had given 1LT Doug Knight a really hard time, even though Doug was half Asian in ancestry and fair to all his soldiers. Sparks had already been busted in rank for insubordination and he was under additional court martial charges for more of the same behavior. I therefore said that we did not need Sparks or his disruptive influence in 2nd Platoon. Smitty told me he knew I'd say that and he had already discussed it with Sparks and the other black guys. He guaranteed that they would keep Sparks in line and I would have absolutely no trouble from him. I was skeptical and we discussed it at length, but I ultimately agreed to take Sparks too, mostly because of Smitty's credibility. What Bigfoot told me turned out to be completely true and I never had any problem at all with Bro Sparks. The black guys blended right in to 2nd Platoon and working/living together did seem to boost their morale. Richard Smith's intelligence and strong personality made him a leader among the black troops and he was also respected by nearly everyone else. His positive influence did in fact increase harmony within the unit, despite the widespread racial animosity which existed within society and the Army at that time. Some conflicts still surfaced periodically, and whenever a clash occurred between a white soldier and a black soldier, it was usually assumed to be racial in nature. But racial hatred was not a continuously open sore within B Company while I was there, as it was in other units.

After celebrating Independence Day on LZ Liz with a "Mad Minute", we went back again to Dragon Valley. On July 9th, one of our patrols went through a day laager we had used a few days before and we noticed signs that Charlie had been going through our trash in the burn pit. The patrol took a long break there. The guys milled around and played grab-ass to create a diversion, in case we were under observation, while I set up a rigged can of Beef and Shrapnel as a surprise for the NVA. The C-Rat can was left lying out in the open, but near a tree line, as if a GI had dropped it inadvertently. It was wired to blow a single Claymore suspended in a tree.

That night we were moving into our NDP after dark and we walked into what was probably a hasty ambush. The dinks fired us up prematurely, before we walked into an actual kill zone*. Bob Swanson was walking point. SP/4 Gary Smith, aka The Mad Fragger, was the slack man and he was temporarily carrying one of our two M60 machine guns, because the squad's regular gunner was on an in-country R&R. I was the third or fourth guy from the front of the file. The silent and dark night suddenly erupted with the loud roar of full-automatic fire and bright muzzle flashes, several long bursts, probably from at least two AK47s. Everyone towards the front of our file immediately spread out and hit the dirt, returning fire while enemy rounds cracked around us. The abrupt and shocking ambush, from just ahead of us in the dark, apparently scared the crap out of

The Mad Fragger and Me

The Mad Fragger. But instead of cowering, he lost his temper and did a credible *Sergeant Stryker/Sands of Iwo Jima* reenactment. He screamed curses and challenges at the VC/NVA, firing the M60 from the hip, standing up the whole time and advancing. He had The Pig on a long sling over his shoulder and at least two belts of ammo linked together. He was raising all kinds of hell, and if I had been Charlie Cong, hearing him roaring/blasting and seeing the muzzle flashes moving towards me, I would have run for my life, which they apparently did. We were all yelling at The Fragger to get down and he finally got down, but he had broken up the ambush with his one-man assault. I called for artillery on the finger above the dinks, intending to walk it down behind their probable route of retreat. One of my guys thought he was shot, but it turned out that a bullet had hit a can of peaches in his rucksack and the warm sticky juice was running down his back... he thought it was blood. Then The Mad Fragger realized that he really *was* shot and he started carrying on about it. Doc Wright threw a poncho over The Mad Fragger and we both got under it with a flashlight to examine the wound. The flashlight batteries immediately died, so Doc completed his examination and treatment by the light of a Zippo cigarette lighter. It appeared that a bullet had raked The Mad Fragger across the ribs and opened him up a little. There was a lot of blood, but the wound did not look too bad. It was hard to tell though, because The Fragger was thrashing around and yelling that he'd been shot. He began to calm down because Doc Wright told him it was a minor wound but we'd dust him off anyway, and I said he was going to get a Purple Heart and also another medal. We discovered that one of the bipod legs had been shot off of his machine gun, perhaps deflecting the round that creased him. I check-fired the art'y and called for a "priority" MEDEVAC. Strobe lights and the special batteries they used were items we were supposed to be able to get through supply channels, but couldn't. So SSG Wayne Wilson walked out alone into an abandoned rice paddy with another flashlight to bring in the Dust-Off chopper, an act of casual courage which did not surprise me. Wayne's action was not the kind of thing for which I could recommend a medal, but doing it 100 meters from the site of the sudden firefight nevertheless took a lot of guts. I lied to the MEDEVAC pilot, assuring him that the LZ was secured, even though I didn't have a clue about that. This was a relatively minor action, but it was chaotic because Charlie Cong caught us by surprise. I recommended Gary Smith for a Bronze Star for Valor, for suppressing the enemy ambush with his one-man machine gun assault. The awards clerks downgraded it by one level. He got an Army Commendation Medal with "V" device for valor, and his Purple Heart. (I would have loved to have been there to see The Mad Fragger strut off his Freedom Bird in the U.S., wearing his Combat Infantryman's Badge and all his ribbons and bows, especially if any long-haired war protesters were around. He'd have surely given them as much hell as he gave the NVA when they bushwhacked us that night.)

[*Bob Swanson, who was walking point, later said that he had arrived at our NDP destination and he was pointing out 2nd Squad's sector of the perimeter to The Mad Fragger. The Fragger looked in that direction and started growling, softly but audibly, like he was imitating a tiger. Swanee wasn't sure whether he was just fooling around, or if he had heard something and was deliberately issuing a challenge. The night immediately erupted with AK flashes and muzzle blasts. The Mad Fragger's challenging growl probably saved us from walking into a full ambush.

I was angry that Gary Smith was hurt and I told the platoon that we would not rest until we had gotten revenge on the VC/NVA for wounding him. This occurred sooner than expected. We withdrew down the finger and into an alternative NDP, which I hastily picked. Later that night, I heard a loud "BOOM" and knew that Charlie had caught hell from our Beef & Shrapnel Blue Plate Special. I called for the Delta Tango plotted on the MA site and we went out at first light to confirm one more kill. The KIA was in uniform, but his comrades must have recovered his weapon before

The Mad Fragger and Me

the art'y came in on them. The S2/S3 log description erroneously attributed the kill to our 1st Platoon.

Sometime prior to the above incident, in May or June, we got another MA kill, but I could not find it in the S2/S3 log summaries to establish the date. It is worth describing, if only to convince the reader that I am telling the unvarnished truth in this narrative. We had gone on a long and exhausting recon patrol from the 515 Valley into the mountains. We discovered a wide and idyllic mountain stream with a lot of large rocks, running down between two mountains and around the base of one of them. As we were returning down the broad stream bed, the point man spotted a trail coming out of the jungle to the water, even though the trail entrance was not easy to see. We went up the trail a short distance and it had all the signs of heavy and recent use, including Ho Chi Minh sandal tracks. The trail was like a tunnel through the jungle, completely clean and clear, but totally enveloped by heavy vegetation on both sides and overhead. It was an ideal MA site. I set up two Claymores, daisy-chained together, using a low foliage branch as a trip device. The next day, we were goofing off in our day laager between patrols and heard a loud KABOOM come from the MA site. (As a point of literary style, one Claymore went BOOM and two went KABOOM). Artillery Delta Tangos were plotted on and around the MA site and I called for them while the guys got geared up. They were excited about the prospects for several possible kills, so two soldiers who did not usually walk point/slack wanted to do it and I let them. The approach to the stream bed required us to move on a trail through some heavy vegetation. I was about the 4th or 5th man from the front and I crouched on the trail while the point team, including KCS Hy, went ahead to reconnoiter the stream bed. All hell broke loose up ahead, a high volume of automatic weapons fire, M16 (brrrrup... brrrrup...brrrrup) and AK47 (kak-kak-kak-kak) plus a lot of yelling in Vietnamese. The shooting stopped and the point man came running back down the trail with the slack man close behind him. The point man's eyes were wide with fear and he yelled, "Di di mau! Get the hell out of here El Tee!" so we all turned and ran. We ran about 30 meters and stopped when we heard some more shooting back in the stream bed, obviously an M16 on rock 'n roll. I looked around and said, "Where is Hy?" Then I started running back in the other direction, followed by the entire patrol. I found Hy still in the stream bed, looking upstream with several empty magazines on the ground next to him. He said, "GI Number Ten, El Tee" with contempt in his voice. I didn't blame him and I'm sure my face turned red. I tried to get Randy Guill on the radio to request more artillery, but he was inexplicably yammering with Dave Cox on the company command net. Despite all the shooting, I couldn't break in to their radio conversation, so I led the patrol back up to the MA site without an artillery prep. As I crept in the final few meters, I spotted a shock of black hair up ahead. I was carrying an M203 and I put a 5.56mm round through the head, to make sure the guy was dead. I also shot several 40mm HE grenades into the jungle beyond the body. There was only one body and no drag marks, so if there were any additional NVA casualties, they were carried off. The soldier's AK47 was still with the body. The two Claymores had totally devastated that section of jungle. We should have gotten more than one kill, unless the NVA had been really widely dispersed on the trail, so I guess they were. It was not clear why the other NVA soldiers were 100 meters downhill in the streambed when we got there, or why they had not recovered the weapon. They may have run in the opposite direction in confusion, when the shocking Mechanical Ambush blew up their point man. The almost immediate Delta Tango barrage probably added to their panic and bewilderment.

In later talking with Hy through our Speakeasy, I learned that our point team had spotted a group of NVA soldiers as they entered the streambed. Hy took them under fire and hit one in the leg, yelling at them in Vietnamese to surrender. The Gomers returned Hy's fire. Instead of joining the fracas, the other two soldiers in the point team turned and ran. Hy stayed there alone and continued to

The Mad Fragger and Me

fight the NVA as they evacuated their wounded comrade. I was really upset by this incident because I should not have allowed two shaky guys to walk point when contact was imminent, because of the possibility that they might fold under pressure. Even worse, I turned and ran with them when they retreated down the trail. I didn't even try to explain to Hy that I thought he was falling back too, when the point man told us to sky-up. There was just no excuse for what occurred. The two guys who ran away were not mentally prepared for the abrupt confrontation with the NVA and they panicked. But they also followed me and their squad leader back into the streambed, when they realized that Hy had been left behind. I therefore think that sudden fright temporarily overwhelmed good judgment. It was not our finest hour, to be sure.

I recommended Hy for a Silver Star, knowing that the rear area awards clerks would probably downgrade it to a Bronze Star with "V" device, which was probably the right level of award for what he did. This illustrates the usual outcome of that automatic-downgrade policy... when we became aware of it, we usually inflated our award recommendations to compensate. I guess you'd have to recommend Sainthood, if you ever ran into a Medal of Honor situation. Another inequity was that there was a policy (perhaps unwritten) which prohibited awarding anything higher than a Bronze Star to a Vietnamese national. That made no sense, but at least I have the satisfaction of knowing that Hy got the highest U.S. combat award he was able to get. He earned it many times over while he was with 2nd Platoon, through his courage and his always sage advice. Hy ranked and was paid as an ARVN Sergeant, but SSG Wilson and I were shocked when we somehow discovered how small his monthly paycheck was. He had a wife and child to support too. Wayne and I discussed it and we decided to supplement Hy's pay out of our own pockets. It wasn't much, $20 or $30 per month I think, but I'm sure it made a big difference to him.

Another organizational change occurred in June or early July 1971, but this one was harmful. We had not been getting many replacements because the Battalion was supposed to Stand Down permanently and B Company was also short one platoon leader. For these reasons, CPT Guill decided to collapse three platoons into two, by breaking up the 3rd Platoon and reassigning those soldiers. This created a problem in 2nd Platoon, because we received SGT Jethro Dingleberry (an alias) with the other 3rd Platoon transfers. Dingleberry was reputed to be a warrior and he looked the part. He was tall, strongly built and rugged in appearance, but SSG Wilson and I soon discovered that his reputation was wildly inflated. The 3rd Platoon troops had been battle-shocked by their prior casualties and they had been without effective leadership after El Tee Cox was reassigned. As individual entities, the 3rd Platoon soldiers were not different than any other soldiers. They would have assimilated easily into 2nd Platoon, if they had been divided up between Sergeants Moore and Malonson, but I made the huge mistake of leaving them together as the nucleus of our resurrected Third Squad under Dingleberry. The first peculiar thing I noticed was that SGT Dingleberry tried to discourage me from accompanying his squad on all its patrols. This was later explained when one of his men disclosed that they had been in the habit of going out a short distance from day laagers, then sitting down and calling in bogus SITREPS, but my presence brought this practice to a screeching halt. It soon became obvious that Dingleberry was afraid to do routine things our "old" 2nd Platoon guys took in stride, but he tried to hide this with bluster. SGT Dingleberry was a swaggering blowhard whose apprehensive demeanor showed that he was afraid of combat, an incongruous contradiction which was almost comical. He also resented authority, so my indifference to his boasting and posturing probably increased that resentment. The 2nd Platoon had been a group of about 30 very diverse young men who somehow got along together, compensated for each others' weaknesses and depended upon one another in matters involving life or death. There was occasional bickering, just as with any brothers, but the 2nd Platoon had basically functioned as a large and cohesive family,

The Mad Fragger and Me

which was an unforgettable experience for all of us. This karma was disrupted when the 3rd Platoon soldiers joined us, because of their timid mindset. During our Stand-Down break in July, it became evident that Dingleberry could not handle alcohol and he went completely whackodoodle whenever he got liquored up. He was a rotten apple and he began to spoil the barrel.

Bravo Company went to Chu Lai for Stand-Down from July 14 through 17th. I also went to Bangkok, Thailand for one week on leave in July or August, but I don't know the exact dates, for reasons I will explain later.

My last mission in Vietnam was pulling perimeter security on Nui Vong, also called Hill 103 on American maps, from August 7th through the 15th. Randy Guill said he assigned that job to 2nd Platoon because I was "short" and he didn't want to write to my family to tell them I was killed on my last day in-country. Even though it was supposed to be an easy mission, some interesting events occurred during the nine days we were on Hill 103. The permanent party troops on Nui Vong were designated as "Q Company", which was comprised of soldiers on light duty medical profiles. Nui Vong had been a French Foreign Legion outpost during the Viet Minh War prior to 1954 and it overlooked a large piece of lowland terrain adjacent to the Song Ve River. The French Legionnaires had dug a deep (approximately 10') and wide (about 12') trench partially around the hilltop, forming a "C" shape. The trench looked like a dry moat. Because it was not located along or below the military crest, the trench was not a defensive obstacle, nor could soldiers fight from it and its tactical purpose was mysterious. The 1/20 Infantry perimeter defenses included a dug-in M48 medium tank. There was also a 106mm recoilless rifle, which had been surveyed-in by Army Engineers to operate in tandem with a "Pipsi Five" ground surveillance radar set. The 106mm antitank rifle was fired at night on human targets in the lowland area which were identified by the radar, using "beehive" rounds with delay fuses. The battalion Four Deuce Platoon still had a "jump" 81mm mortar team assigned to Hill

103, which also got most of its targets from the ground surveillance radar detachment. These arrangements made it quite dangerous for enemy soldiers to move around in the lowland area west of Hill 103 at night. The Nui Vong outpost had a four-hole latrine and a single shower, but no mess hall or other facilities. There were no full size bunkers or sleeping quarters for the troops on the perimeter, just scant fighting positions.

Following his long stint as the Battalion Recon Platoon Leader, 1LT Frank Korona had been the Q Company Commander for a short time, but he was unfairly relieved of this command just prior to his DEROS date. This occurred as a result of an unannounced inspection by the Americal Division's Commanding General, who found that the Nui Vong outpost was seriously deficient in its defenses. This created a panic in the TOC, because they knew the outpost's problems were actually the result of command neglect by Battalion Headquarters. But Frank Korona was a convenient scapegoat. LTC James Whitley was by then the 1/20th Infantry Battalion Commander. There were various rumors going around about LTC Whitley, including scuttlebutt of a personal vendetta by the 11th LIB Commander, which had placed Whitley's career prospects in jeopardy. Somebody's head had to roll, so Korona was sacrificed to save Whitley. (1LT Frank Korona was commissioned through ROTC, so he was not a member of the West Point Protective Association. He also had a known enemy at Battalion HQ, a certain WPPA major, who had been oddly hypercritical of 1LT Korona's performance as the Recon Platoon Leader. Frank's status as the most decorated soldier in the battalion, with four combat awards for valor, may have been a source of petty jealousy.) It was no secret within the unit that Lieutenant Korona had been relieved of the Nui Vong command, but LTC Whitley and his TOC Toadies did not have the moral courage to inform *him* of this. They instead told 1LT Korona that he was being sent to Chu Lai for some time off, prior to going home. Frank Korona was replaced as the Q Company Commander by 1LT Tom Pribil, formerly a rifle platoon leader in another

The Mad Fragger and Me

company. I did not know Pribil before we went there on August 7th, but he seemed like a nice guy. He knew that his predecessor had been relieved and that the Commanding General was coming back for a follow-up inspection of Nui Vong's defenses. 1LT Pribil didn't want to be relieved too, so he initially came on strongly with SSG Wilson and me. He complained that the rifle platoon we replaced on Nui Vong was lazy and he'd had all sorts of problems with them. We assured him that would not happen again and we would get the outpost squared away.

When Wayne Wilson and I inspected the defenses with LT Pribil, we could see that there was indeed considerable room for improvement. When I had been on Nui Vong during my first B Company mission in February, our battalion was in the process of abandoning it. B Company had helped Combat Engineers destroy Nui Vong's defenses, using Bangalore Torpedoes to blow up the barbed wire and concertina, the only time I saw or used those WWII contraptions. Some of the defensive wire had since been replaced and the fighting positions were partially rebuilt, but more barbed wire and sandbags were clearly needed. Because of all the heat that came down after the failed inspection, Battalion HQ brought in a large supply of engineer stakes, sandbags, barbed wire and concertina. SSG Wilson organized our work details for maximum efficiency. He set it up so that a crew would be constantly working during daylight hours, but in rotating two hour shifts, so that nobody killed themselves working in the sun. He explained the situation to the troops and told them it was important that they be seen working, productively, if we got an unannounced inspection. SSG Wilson's plan ticked along perfectly and our guys worked diligently. We quickly depleted all the construction supplies and ordered more. In the absence of engineer materials, we started working on eyewash stuff that would impress the lifers, such as grenade sumps, secondary foxholes, night aiming stakes, traversing bars and range cards. An old field notebook I have from that period lists these tasks: *Trash detail. Police call. Burn out latrine. Sandbag caps & retrieve claymores daily. Sandbag E8 CS launchers. Work on parapets & fighting positions. Order ammo & claymores. Build blast walls. Range cards. Aiming stakes. Bury commo wires. Raise phones in F.P.* (Now I don't remember what the heck an "F.P." was, or what "raise phones" meant.) My ammo resupply list shows: *2 cases M-16, 1 case 7.62, 1 case 40mm, 6 claymores, 4 LAWs.*

The day we arrived on Nui Vong, we were asked to provide an Infantry escort for the M48 tank which was being sent to LZ Snoopy to tow back a "water buffalo" trailer. SSG Wilson decided to go with this detail, but the tank hit a booby-trapped 155mm artillery round and blew up. A track and a couple of road wheels were blown off the tank. Five of my guys were wounded, but SP/4 John "Slue-Foot" Schmidt was the only casualty who had a visible wound, a hole in his leg from a piece of shrapnel. The others, SSG Wayne Wilson, SP/4 Harold Phillips, SP/4 Salvador Sanchez ("Eek") and SP/4 Arthur Telamentes ("Meek"), had broken eardrums and/or possible concussions. Wayne Wilson was back the next day and he said the S1 had tried to persuade them to sign statements indicating they had not been injured as a result of enemy action. SSG Wilson told the guys not to sign, so they would remain eligible to receive Purple Hearts. I was pretty upset with SSG Wilson when I found out he'd allowed our grunts to ride on top of the tank instead of walking, but that was the only mistake I ever knew him to make. There was a big brouhaha about who authorized the tank to go to LZ Snoopy in the first place. There is a lengthy write-up in the S2/S3 log for August 8th, describing the petty nonsense the TOC Commandos thought was important; the wounded grunts are barely mentioned. Slue-Foot Schmidt came back to us a few days later, limping, but still cheerful and smiling as usual.

For some reason, they thought the booby trapped 155mm was command detonated and two female detainees were caught running away from the explosion, which is what civilians usually did when something like that happened. I doubted that they were involved and I would not have detained them. But they were blindfolded, their hands were tied behind them and they were brought to Nui Vong, for evacuation and questioning by Vietnamese authorities. One was a middle aged Mamma-san and the other was a girl about 14 or 15 years old. One of my guys came to me and said he thought I should go and check on the girl, because he didn't like the looks of a strange GI who was hanging around her, and he was suspicious about what he might be doing. I didn't like the looks of him either and he didn't have a satisfactory answer when I asked him what he was doing there. The teenager was bawling hysterically and I really think the SOB had been molesting her. I broke bad on the guy and ran him off, but there wasn't much else I could do. She did not speak English and we had no one available who could translate Vietnamese.

During our stay on Nui Vong, I had a minor run-in with the new Recon Platoon Leader, who had replaced Frank Korona in that slot. I had previously been offered the Recon job, but I turned it down and another lieutenant was appointed instead. The small Recon Platoon sometimes did reconnaissance missions, but it was also used as a Battalion immediate reaction force. They were all volunteers and they wore camouflaged jungle fatigues instead of plain OD uniforms. The Recon Platoon was a gung-ho and aggressive combat unit, but it was considered to be "elite" and some of its members were predictably a little full of themselves. The Recon Platoon had been hanging out at Nui Vong, but they weren't really doing much. They had dug in around the disabled M48 tank and secured it the night of August 7th, until an M88 Tank Retriever vehicle could be brought in. My 2nd Platoon was spread very thinly on the perimeter, with only two soldiers, or occasionally three, for all night guard duty on each fighting position. I told the new platoon leader that the Recon Platoon was going to have to cover some of the perimeter positions. He informed me that Recon was a special unit and they did not pull guard duty on firebase perimeters like common grunts. By that time in my tour, I was probably The Senior First Lieutenant of the World, so I was not sympathetic and I immediately got my butt on my shoulders. I told him he could either take over a few of the guard positions, or he could get his ass off Nui Vong and set up an ambush outside the perimeter each night. The 2nd Platoon was not going to pull extra hours on guard duty so he and his prima donnas could get more sleep. Surprising me, he was very gracious about this, despite my bumptious reaction. He did not argue about it at all and Recon took over some perimeter defensive positions.

I was in the 2nd Platoon CP bunker on Nui Vong one day and Brother Sparks came in, dragging a uniformed Vietnamese soldier by the collar, with his M16 pointed at the guy's head. PVT Sparks stated that the man was a Kit Carson Scout from another unit and he had caught him stealing a cassette tape player from the rucksack of one of our soldiers. Our Speakeasy was home on leave, so I tried to question the KCS in piggin English and the little bit of Vietnamese I could muster, but he kept saying "No bic"... "No bic" (I don't understand) to everything I asked. Meanwhile, Bro Sparks was still holding him by the collar, looking bored, impatient and sullen. He finally asked, "What do you want me to do with him, El Tee?" Frustrated, I said, "Take him outside the wire and crocodile him, then get rid of the body." Sparks answered "Okay" and started dragging the dude away, no doubt to kill him and dispose of the corpse. The Vietnamese guy started whimpering and babbling, "Me bic number one, El Tee! Me no steal from GI again! Me go now! Me no come back!" We did let him go. It was too much work to dig a grave. So Delbert Sparks, his surly 'tude and his reputation for remorseless violence served me well in the end. I hope that PVT Sparks later lost the demons which possessed him as a young man, because it must have been terrible to drag around so much rage and hostility all the time. Despite his prior acts of insubordination, while he was in 2nd Platoon I never had any reason to complain about his soldiering.

I was in the Nui Vong Command Post and a radio call came in that visitors were inbound by chopper. The Hill Commander was busy with something, so I went to the helipad to meet them. Three

The Mad Fragger and Me

First Lieutenants from Company G, 75th Infantry Regiment (Ranger) got off the bird, resplendent in custom tailored, heavily starched jungle fatigues. Their uniform shirts had conventional Ranger tabs and Americal patches, but their names, US Army, jump wings, CIBs, crossed rifle infantry insignia and lieutenants' bars were custom embroidered directly on the material. Their bush hats were heavily starched and carefully shaped, also directly embroidered with lieutenants' bars on the fronts and their names on the backs. They all carried CAR15s and wore wire-rimmed aviator sunglasses. They also carried .45s and their black G.I. flap holsters were highly spit shined, as were the leather sections of their jungle boots. They only needed ascots and swagger sticks, to complete their Hollywood Hero costumes. We went to the CP Bunker and they explained that they were there to coordinate with us about an operation the Rangers were going to run in the lowland area between Hill 103 and the Song Ve Valley, which Nui Vong overlooked with its AN/PPS 5 Ground Surveillance Radar. Rifle companies from our Battalion operated in that area all the time. We also operated further west into the Song Ve Valley which was *really* dangerous, but the Rangers acted like their mission near Hill 103 was a very big deal. I have no idea why it took three heavily starched and spit-shined First Lieutenants, probably all West-Pointers, to coordinate this.

When the 75th Ranger group went into the lowland area, they got in contact the first night and we could see tracers going back and forth from our perch on Nui Vong. I went into the Nui Vong TOC to listen to their transmissions, because Tom Pribil had a radio on their "push". They did the usual things at first, calling for illumination, artillery and gunships, but then they began to demand extraction. I commented to Pribil, "What the hell do they think they're out there for? They are supposed to find and kill the enemy." I decided that I was underwhelmed by G Company, 75th Rangers.

The Four Deuce Platoon's 81mm contingent on Hill 103 had expanded and their facilities were greatly improved since my days with them. They had built a huge underground bunker, which was heavily sandbagged across the top, so the roof was about 2 feet above ground level. A soldier had driven a steel stake into the center of the roof and attached a very long dog chain to it, with the other end attached to the collar on his pet monkey. One of the other guys, SP/4 Bob Bunch, would come by every day and tease the monkey. You could see that the monkey hated Bunch, because it had facial expressions just like a human's, but much more exaggerated. SP/4 Bunch would walk up, taunt the monkey by yelling "Hey, monkey! Mon-Keeee!"... and run away. The monkey would stop whatever it was doing and chase Bunch at full speed, fangs bared and shrieking at him. Bunch would stop just past the length of the 100 foot chain and turn around, arms folded, watching the monkey. As the monkey got close to Bunch, it would get up on its hind legs and continue running, with its arms and paws extended, like a movie monster bent on tearing him apart. Then the monkey, still going full speed, would reach the end of the chain and be jerked violently back, head over heels. This performance never varied day after day, because the monkey never learned what was going to happen when he reached the end of the chain. I was watching this one day, and as the monkey started to chase after Bunch, another guy ran out and took the end of the chain off the stake. Bunch turned as usual and folded his arms. Then he suddenly realized the monkey was still coming. The outraged monkey chased him all over the outpost, shrieking and screaming the whole way, and it was hilarious. Nobody tried to grab the end of the chain, or to help Bob Bunch in any way. I saw guys lying on the ground, crying, they were laughing so hard. *Sic semper tyrannus.*

    The Commanding General of the Americal Division did return to Hill 103 to re-inspect its defenses. He came unannounced, with an entourage of bootlickers. The inspection did not start well for us. The CG wanted to know why no work details were busy filling sandbags or stringing wire. LT Pribil and I told him that we had used up all the sandbags, wire and engineer stakes, but more had been

The Mad Fragger and Me

on order for several days. We pointed out the results of our labors since his last visit. A group of higher ranking officers from Battalion HQ soon arrived by chopper, which relieved me of touring around with him and listening to his pontifications. The Major General had his Enlisted Aide with him, a SP/6. SSG Wayne Wilson buttonholed him, complaining about how we grunts were fighting the war, but were being treated like bastard stepchildren by everyone in the rear. Wayne Wilson told him about all the essential things we could not get through supply channels, such as BA30 flashlight batteries, foot powder and strobe lights. The most critical supply item on SSG Wilson's complaint list was LSA (Lubricant, Small Arms), which was high viscosity synthetic oil we needed to keep our M60 machine guns running. (When the LSA supply dried up, we tried to get by with some WD 40-type spray oil we received in a CARE package from a ladies' church group Back in The World. It worked fairly well on M16s, but the stuff was too thin to work on an M60 when it got hot. The spray oil just burned off after fifty rounds or so and the gun would lock up. We carefully hoarded all the LSA we could get, for use on the M60s. We had ordered LSA over and over and over again, but it was never available according to our supply people.) SSG Wilson was not exactly shy about raising hell when we weren't getting what we needed. He really unloaded on the CG's dog robber, telling him that the REMFs were too preoccupied with getting their tennis courts resurfaced to be bothered about getting LSA for us lowly grunts. The SP/6 listened to him and passed the word, because the next day we received a delivery of all the things we needed but had not been able to get, including a full case of plastic LSA bottles. We suddenly had so much LSA we didn't know how we were going to carry it all. The other thing I remember about this issue was that Battalion HQ was really miffed at us, because they got reamed out about our nonresponsive supply system. But what were they going to do? Put us in the Infantry and send us to Vietnam? Xin loi, Battalion Headquarters.

Tom Dolan

Two nights before I was scheduled to DEROS, somebody started shooting into the gathering darkness off of one of the positions on the perimeter. There was a lot of hooting and yelling, so we knew that some of our troops were just fooling around. SSG Wayne Wilson and I strolled the short distance to the defensive position, to tell the guys to knock it off. We found ersatz warrior Jethro Dingleberry, completely blotto, with two or three others from the recycled 3rd Platoon, who were somewhat less inebriated. (We later learned that they had sneaked off to nearby LZ Snoopy and brought back beer in sandbags.) I told them to quit screwing around with their weapons. Dingleberry unexpectedly aimed his M16 at my chest from point-blank range and I heard the selector switch go "click, click", meaning that he had switched it to full automatic. His finger was on the trigger. His face was contorted with rage, he called me several obscene names and he said that he was going to kill me. I told him to lock the weapon and put it down, but he continued cursing me and making death threats. He was so crazed and wild-eyed that I really thought he might pull the trigger. The other members of his squad seemed unmoved by this, or more probably they were afraid of Dingleberry in his psycho mode. Either way, they proved that I could not depend upon them in a crisis. This incident would not have occurred if either SSG Wayne Wilson or I had been armed, because Dingleberry was a typical bully, always cowardly unless he had an overwhelming advantage of some kind. I told Dingleberry I was going to court-martial him. SSG Wilson and I then returned to the Platoon CP bunker. I was furious about this loutish attack and my choices of courses of corrective action were: (1.) Immediately go back with my M16 and shoot Dingleberry, or (2.) Wait until he sobered up and deal with him then. I leaned toward the first option, but SSG Wilson persuaded me that it was better to exercise the second choice.

"Insubordination" is simply the refusal to assume a subordinate role in an interaction with someone of higher rank. This is most commonly manifested, in a military context, by failure to carry out a lawful order from someone of higher rank. It almost never includes overt defiance, deliberate denigration of the superior officer, or physical threats against him. The abusive language Dingleberry used and his death threats while brandishing a deadly means to carry them out, in the presence of others, raised his insubordination to a much higher plateau. I had become accustomed to immediate obedience from the 2nd Platoon guys, as well as to their loyalty and respect, but I received no such allegiance from the 3rd Platoon retreads. The next morning Sergeant Wilson got the entire platoon together and he reamed out Dingleberry and his cohorts. Dingleberry was meek under Wayne's lambasting, as he always was when he was not full of liquid courage. SSG Wilson told them that the entire platoon had been disgraced by their behavior and the only man who really wanted to be there was leaving in another day. All alcohol was banned for the duration of the mission on Nui Vong.

I spent my last full day on Nui Vong writing up disciplinary charges and a detailed witness statement, charging Dingleberry with verbal assault on a commissioned officer, mutiny and insubordination. When I left the unit the next morning, I delivered the paperwork to CPT Guill, confident that he would relieve Dingleberry and file court martial charges. (SSG Wilson went home on stateside leave after I was discharged and I visited him at his home in New Jersey. During that visit, Wayne told me that disciplinary charges against Dingleberry were dropped immediately after I left the unit, on the grounds that I was not available as the primary witness. Dingleberry was not removed from his leadership role, or reduced in rank through an Article 15. Instead of court-martialing Dingleberry, they pinned an Army Commendation Medal on him during the battalion's final Stand Down ceremony. That validated my earlier decision to quit the Army because of its weak leadership. This is an example of the deterioration in discipline which was occurring in 1971, and the military establishment's reluctance to deal with it.)

Despite that final incident, I was somewhat reluctant to leave the 2nd Platoon, because it did not feel like the job was finished. I was relieved to be going home in one piece, but I did not have a sense of euphoria about it. I later regretted not writing down my soldiers' names and addresses, but at that war-weary point it seemed best to put the whole Vietnam War experience behind me. The very last thing I did before I got on the chopper for LZ Liz, was to give my off-the-books M1911A1 pistol and three magazines of .45 ammo to Kit Carson Scout Huynh The Hy, who was delighted with the gift. Hy had often borrowed my sidearm when he went home on leave and he always carried it in his waistband under his shirt. I told him not to turn the pistol in to the supply sergeant if he went to the rear and he said he understood. I hope I'm wrong, but I suspect that Hy may have died when South Vietnam was overrun by the Communists in 1975. If so, I hope he went down fighting with my .45.

The rest of B Company had rotated to LZ Liz. I checked out with CPT Guill, who said he had already done my OER (Officer's Efficiency Report) but he was not ready to show it to me. It had to be revised to tone it down, he said, "…because it sounds too much like a Medal of Honor citation". He told me I was possibly the best rifle platoon leader he had ever known, then he paused and said he had known one who was better during his first tour, "But that lieutenant was so good it got him killed". I told him I appreciated that, we shook hands and I left. I never did see that OER. That was the only time anyone told me that I had done a good job in Vietnam.

[A careful reader may have noticed some blips in this narration. Stalking Moon was briefly assigned as B Company's Executive Officer after he was injured in the field, then he was transferred to HHC as the battalion Support Platoon Leader/Assistant S4. The XO was usually a company's senior lieutenant, but Dave Cox had been an exception because of his knee injury. After Dave was moved to the battalion staff and a new

The Mad Fragger and Me

lieutenant was assigned to B Company, CPT Guill offered me the open Executive Officer job. I suggested that he give that slot to my friend Doug Knight, who was several months junior to me. I did not care about the purely nominal promotion, which I saw as just an opportunity to get out of the bush. I'd previously had a rear job in E Company and it was Doug's turn, plus I preferred to be a line officer. Doug Knight was appointed as the B Company XO in mid-June.]

This concludes my recollection of incidents which are tied to incidents recorded in the S2/S3 journal, but everything that happened was not written down in that log. I still have lots of other memories which are not date-specific. The readers of this memoir are therefore going to have to suffer through a few more chapters.

Chapter 9:

REAR AREA FOLLIES

Although we did not spend much time in the rear areas at LZ Bronco (Duc Pho) and Chu Lai, interesting things happened when we did get there. I have already written about Duc Pho and don't have much to add, except that Mai and Lei lost their jobs with E Company and they were left behind when the Battalion rear area was moved to the sprawling Americal Division base at Chu Lai. For us, Chu Lai was mainly a recreational area. It was located along the South China Sea and the $1/20^{th}$'s cantonment area was at the opposite end of the base from the Division Headquarters' facilities. The base was relatively narrow, perhaps one mile across, but six or seven miles long, wider at the southern end where the airport was located. There was a hardball road running through the center of it, roughly north and south, with smaller unpaved finger roads going off of both sides. The $1/20^{th}$ area was not far from the airport, seaside of the main road, adjacent to a beautiful beach with white sand. There was a sandy Battalion street, featuring a row of screened single story plywood buildings with peaked tin roofs along each side, which were the company orderly rooms, supply rooms and battalion offices. There were other buildings scattered around the area in a random way, a mess hall, staff sleeping quarters, a shower building and so forth, which were shaded by evergreen trees. The buildings had been constructed by Seabees during our area's previous life as a USMC compound and they were simple but well built. Our sandy little village had a rough but comfortable feel to it. Probably because there were few vehicles around, it was reminiscent of a frontier town in the western United States. At the far end of the Battalion area from the entrance road was a large Stand-Down Compound. The Compound was next to the beach and it contained about a half-dozen one story plywood barracks buildings and some other structures. It was always hot in-country, but there was usually a breeze at Chu Lai, the sea air was wonderfully fresh and it was mostly devoid of the strange odors which permeated the rest of Vietnam.

Stalking Moon had been sent to the rear because of his knee injury, initially as the B Company XO, but then he was transferred to Headquarters & Headquarters Company as the Battalion Support Platoon Leader/Assistant S4. He obtained a very comfortable building for his quarters, where he invited Doug Knight and me to stay when we were in Chu Lai. (CPT Guill had quarters in B Company's Orderly Room building.) Dave Cox's airy building was about 16'x24' and it was built on low stilts above the sand. It had screens around all sides, from the tops of the plywood half-walls to the peaked tin roof, with enough overhang of the eves to keep the rain out in a moderate wind. There were also plywood storm flaps which covered the screens during monsoons. There was a nice bar in one corner, with barstools, and a small refrigerator which Dave kept stocked with beer. He had standard G.I. bunks for the three of us, with springs, mattresses, sheets, cased pillows and blankets. There was a large oscillating floor fan. Each lieutenant also had a wall locker for his spare jungle fatigues and personal belongings. My wall locker already had a little strip of Dymo label tape on it which read KILL VC FOR MOM'S APPLE PIE.

According to the S2/S3 journal, Bravo Company was in Chu Lai only once for Stand-Down, for four days from July 14th through 17th, 1971. It is now hard to believe that so much occurred during just a four day period of time. I went through Chu Lai on several other occasions, going to and from R&R to Hawaii, and on leave to Bangkok, but I was traveling alone at those times. The normal Stand-Down interval for rifle companies was once every three months, confirming that there was just one four day visit there with B Company.

A Stand-Down period was a short vacation, during which grunts relaxed and partied. We listened to music, gambled, played

The Mad Fragger and Me

silly word games with Donut Dollies, drank beer, attended rock 'n roll floor shows and watched Hollywood movies. The Stand-Down Compound was surrounded by a tall chain link fence topped with barbed wire, much like a prison enclosure. This was a symbolic barrier, to keep us primitive grunts separated from the more civilized members of the U.S. Army. Although we could come and go as we pleased, it was clear to us that we were not supposed to mingle too much with the REMFs. The first thing we did upon arrival for stand down was to turn in all our weapons and ammo at the supply room. I always kept my .45, which was not on the property books or officially issued to me, but I seldom carried it around in Chu Lai, because we were not supposed to enter the Officers' Clubs, the PX or other facilities with weapons. The Stand-Down Compound contained barracks, latrines, a beer hall/club, and a roofed outdoor stage building with open sides. Boxing gear, footballs, basketballs and softball equipment were available. There were Americal Division facilities we could access at the northern end of Chu Lai if we could find transportation, such as a barber shop, tailor shop, PX, NCO Clubs, Officers' Clubs, plus small Vietnamese purveyors of souvenirs, engraving and embroidering.

While we were on Stand-Down, B Company's platoon leaders and platoon sergeants stayed with the troops in the compound to keep a lid on their high jinks, so we were never completely off duty. Chief of Smoke SSG Earl Willard was in the Stand-Down Compound with about 10 guys from the Four Deuce Platoon, while B Company was there in July. The first day, I ran into him in the club and he invited me to the Four Deuce Platoon's barracks for a quiet snort of some good whiskey he had in his duffle bag. When I walked ahead of him into the building, something brown and furry with a mouthful of flashing teeth leaped at me from the top of a double bunk next to the door, shrieking and screaming. Willard grabbed the monkey's chain and jerked it across the bunk toward him, simultaneously slapping it hard across its face with his other hand, knocking it back into the corner, gruffly commenting "You damned filthy bastard." Sergeant Willard had that right, because the little beast had fouled the mattresses terribly and that corner of the barracks was as funky as a monkey. The monkey cowered in the corner, covering its head with its arms and paws, peaking out occasionally with its bright eyes to see if Sergeant Willard was still close enough to strike it. Its facial expressions clearly communicated that it feared SSG Willard, just as its grimaces expressed its hatred for the GI who teased it daily (a month later) on Nui Vong. I invited SSG Willard to move into the barracks B Company had for our lieutenants and platoon sergeants, so he did.

During the days, we played softball, went to the beach, hung out in the compound's beer hall/club, or attended traveling floor shows. At night, we usually watched movies or left the compound to go to the Chu Lai Officers' or NCO Clubs. Dave Cox now claims that he and I got up on the stage one afternoon, to dance with the showgirls in a Filipino rock 'n roll floor show, to the delight of B Company troops. I always say that I didn't go to floor shows, rather I stayed in the barracks and read my bible. He also claims to have photos, but I still haven't seen them. Dancing with the show girls to entertain our troops sounds credible, but I don't remember doing it, so I will probably continue to deny it unless I see photographic proof.

The troops were always told to turn in their weapons, ammo and explosives at the Supply Room. I didn't like to disarm my guys, but there didn't seem to be any choice. Weaponry does not mix well with alcohol, which flowed freely in the Stand-Down Compound, but it was an honor system and we did not shake them down for weapons or explosives. Grunts leaned heavily on each other all the time, which tended to form a bond of trust between officers and EM, so I could usually assume that my soldiers would follow instructions. One night SP/4 Joe Stephens got tanked up and he found a hand-popper which he had forgotten to turn in, in his rucksack. Hand-poppers were pyrotechnic signal rockets which, when fired, go up with a loud "whooossh" and then explode in a

The Mad Fragger and Me

white, red or green star cluster a couple of hundred feet in the air, like fireworks on the 4th of July. Stephens wondered what a hand-popper would do <u>inside</u> a building, so he fired it off in the 2nd Platoon's long one-room barracks. I wasn't there to see it, but it apparently created a spectacular special effect, when it ricocheted around the ceiling, floor and walls and exploded in a red star burst, setting a bed on fire. I was angry and I reamed out Stephens, but nobody was hurt, nor did the barracks burn down. That was another thing about leading 25 to 30 boisterous young soldiers. You could never predict what one of them might do next.

SSG Wayne Wilson and I had extra uniform shirts made up to simulate each other's ranks, so we could go to the Officers' Clubs and the NCO Clubs together. Wayne claims that "1LT" Wilson, 1LT Korona and 1LT Dolan were at an Officers' Club one night and we attempted to hit on some Army nurses, but we were rebuffed because they said we smelled bad. Frank Korona was in fact at the Stand-Down Compound while B Company was there in July 1971, but he doesn't remember that incident and neither do I. I will admit it's the type of memory we'd probably try to suppress. Wayne and I did go to one of the Officers' Clubs and it is highly probable that Frank or other lieutenants were with us. The Main NCO Club was more fun than the Officers' Clubs because it was much rowdier, but there can be too much of a good thing. I was in the NCO Club one night with most of the 2nd Platoon (everyone was given temporary promotions to E5, by pinning sergeant stripes on them) when "SSG" Dolan tried to pacify a giant buck sergeant, who was bent on beating the snot out of Keith Moore. SGT Moore, who was about one-third the other guy's size, had shown undue attention to the stranger's favorite Vietnamese bar girl and Keith refused to back off. The huge E-5, who could have been Shaquille O'Neal's father, grabbed me by the lapels and literally lifted me off the floor, earnestly telling me what he was going to do to me if I didn't mind my own business. The next thing I knew, Pancho Ramirez had the guy by the throat, and he was furiously saying, "Let go of him,

THAT'S MY LIEUTENANT". Pancho was a tough Mexican-American, even smaller than Keith Moore. It was a mystery how Pancho managed to reach the guy's throat, but maybe he was standing on a chair. In another second, the massive buck sergeant was surrounded by SSG Wilson and the other guys, who were all ready to fight. I was more conciliatory because I was thinking ahead, about how I would explain to the Battalion Commander why I got into a barroom brawl and busted by the MPs, while impersonating a Staff Sergeant. Anyway, the Chu Lai NCO Club was a rockin' place.

    Wayne Wilson discovered that there was a Korean Restaurant in Chu Lai and he suggested taking Hy out to dinner there, because we couldn't get away with dressing him up as an American officer or NCO. Hy was at stand-down with us and he legitimately ranked as an ARVN sergeant, but Vietnamese enlisted personnel were not allowed into any of the GI clubs outside of our Stand-Down Compound. At the Korean Restaurant I had my first exposure to kimchi, the Korean national dish. The kimchi was so incredibly hot that it brought tears to my eyes and made my nose run, but I really liked it. The fried rice with beef was excellent and the meal was served with beer and chopsticks. I thought the Asian waitress was probably Korean, but Hy rattled off something in Vietnamese, she nodded and left, coming back with a large table spoon. Hy held up the spoon and said "number one". Then he held up the chopsticks and said "number ten". We had a great time, despite Hy's limited English and Wayne's/my even more limited Vietnamese. We were completely at ease with each other and the difficulty in making ourselves understood just added to the hilarity.

    One night I was asleep with several other lieutenants and senior NCOs, including SSG Earl Willard, in the one-room officers' barracks. Around midnight, the door on the far end burst open and my squad leaders, Doc Wright and several other senior guys from 2nd Platoon staggered in, led by SSG Wayne P. Wilson, who kept shouting "Follow me, men!" They were all roaring drunk and unrecognizable, except for their voices, because they were wet and

The Mad Fragger and Me

completely covered in sand. They looked like sand statues you'd see on a beach in a resort area, except for their blinking eyes and pink mouths. They had been out on the beach, partying, and decided to go swimming in the South China Sea with their clothes on. Then they all rolled in the sand and decided to find me and wake me up, so I could join the party. (In the group was a redheaded Shake 'N Bake buck sergeant named Lenny or Lonnie-Something. Lenny/Lonnie was not a Squad Leader, rather he was designated as an assistant to SGT Malonson, but he had extended his tour to get a rear job and he was scheduled to depart the next day.) After everyone was wide awake, Wayne Wilson again shouted "Follow me, men!" and led them out the door at the other end of the building. Lenny/Lonnie remained behind to verbally abuse a newly assigned 2LT, because the lieutenant was wearing jump wings and a ranger tab. I told Lenny/Lonnie to knock it off and get out, but he turned on me, defiant and threatening. The confrontation immediately escalated into a fight, but Lenny/Lonnie was so sloppy drunk that I couldn't hurt him. We fell on my bed at one point, grappling with each other. Then I got a grip on him, dragged him to the door and physically threw him out of the building, down the outside steps. I was wearing only OD boxer shorts and by the time the scuffle was over, I was covered with sand and my bed was full of it too. I had to strip the bed and shake out the sheets, then walk all the way over to the shower building to wash off the sand. I tried to talk to Lenny/Lonnie the next morning before he left for his new job, but he was surly and hostile. Prior to this incident, Wayne Wilson and I had been puzzled about why other guys disliked him, because none of them could cite anything specific.

One afternoon after watching a floor show, I got a whuppin' from Mike "Wooly" Jones, who was a sturdy kid and strong as an ox. I think he had been a varsity wrestler in high school. Mike was feeling his oats, probably fueled by a few beers, and he challenged me to a wrestling match. An infantry platoon leader could not turn down a challenge like that, but I was badly outmatched and Mike pinned me in no time. Unlike the barracks fight with Lenny/Lonnie, the wrasslin' bout with Wooly was just rough horseplay. During that same Stand-Down, Mike Jones and Bob Swanson went partying together one night, out of the compound. They got falling-down drunk and were trying to find their way back to our barracks area, holding each other up as they staggered down a road. They came upon a cluster of buildings in the dark and the soldiers outside one of the buildings called out something to them. Swanee and Wooly didn't understand what they said, but they thought the strangers were trying to pick a fight, so they shouted insults at them and charged the building. They ran directly into an unseen barbed wire and concertina barrier, becoming badly entangled. The soldiers inside the compound came out and untangled them from the wire, then brought them into the building and patched up their razor wire cuts. They put Swanson and Jones in their own beds to sleep it off and sent them on their way the next morning. Mike and Bob had fortunately blundered into the Warlords, the Americal Division's Aero-Scout Rifle Company. They were no doubt recognized as fellow grunts in distress and taken care of for that reason.

Around midnight on July 15th, SSG Wilson and I got word that the MPs had three of our guys locked up for busting up an artillery battery's club. All three were former members of the 3rd Platoon who only recently had been reassigned to 2nd Platoon. We borrowed a jeep and went to the Chu Lai MP Station to get them out. When we pulled up outside, we could hear someone screaming and pounding on sheet metal. That proved to be Jethro Dingleberry, who was confined in "D Cell", which was a steel CONEX shipping container they used to lock up violent prisoners. We talked to the other two guys, who were not confined. One of them was SP/4 (later, SGT) Rob Thomas, who had unsuccessfully tried to contain the situation as it escalated. I don't remember who the other soldier was. They had been out drinking and they crashed an art'y battery's club, where a brawl started. The Artillery Battery's First Sergeant tried to break up the fight, but Dingleberry, always the thug, bravely beat the crap out of the much smaller man. Dingleberry also assaulted several MPs, which is why they locked him in D Cell. The whole time we were at the MP Station, Dingleberry was banging on the walls of the CONEX and shrieking obscenities, making a continuous and deafening racket.

I told the MP NCOIC, a Staff Sergeant, that the boys had been in the bush a long time and they were just being frisky. I said we would take them off his hands and our CO would come up with a suitable punishment (certain that CPT Guill would laugh it off). The sergeant said he couldn't release them on his own authority, so I told him to go get his Staff Duty Officer. He refused to do that, because the SDO was a major and he was asleep. The major would not be happy about getting up in the middle of the night to talk to a lieutenant about something the SSG should have handled. I tried telling the MP/NCOIC that the situation was obviously a fight, not an assault. If he was going to keep my guys locked up, we wanted to press countercharges against the artillery troops, because they had started it by making disparaging remarks about the Infantry and our guys were just defending their honor against those vulgar Redlegs. He said we couldn't press countercharges, but I quoted the UCMJ (Uniform Code of Military Justice) clause that says any service member subject to the UCMJ can press charges against any other service member who is subject to the UCMJ. I began demanding that the MPs go pick up the artillery people, that the sergeant go get the SDO out of bed, and everything else I could think of to demand. SSG Wayne Wilson chimed in and added to the clamor. The beleaguered sergeant then said he'd release SP/4 Thomas and the other soldier to me, but not Dingleberry. With the benefit of 20:20 hindsight, I should have left Dingleberry there to rot, but this incident was the first real indicator of a problem with him, so I said we had to have all of them. The argument went on for quite awhile, with Dingleberry going bonkers in D Cell the whole time. Finally, the sergeant said he could release Dingleberry only if the art'y battery's First Sergeant agreed to drop his charges.

Wayne Wilson and I somehow found the artillery battery and we got the First Sergeant out of bed. He was a very small fellow with bandy legs and he came out to meet us wearing white boxer shorts, a white tee shirt and shower shoes. He looked like a little white raccoon, because he had two black eyes and it was hard not to laugh when we first saw him. He was still seething mad about being assaulted in his own domain by our hooligans and we had to do a lot of apologizing and fast talking. We finally persuaded him to sign a statement that he would drop the charges.

Dingleberry was still going berserk in D Cell when we returned to the MP Station. SSG Wilson, the other two EM and I had a hard time getting him under enough control to hustle him out of the building and he was sullen on the jeep ride back to our company area. We sent the troops to bed and Wayne and I went to the B Company Orderly Room. We were in there drinking a beer and rehashing the night's adventure, when the Battalion S1/Adjutant, a 1LT, came in and started jumping all over us. By that time, it was probably 0300 or later, I was really tired and he caught me off guard. I took the abuse silently, while trying to mentally process what he was saying. He was upset about a phone call he received about our troops wrecking another unit's club and/or my behavior at the MP Station. I think he may have had other grievances about incidents in the Stand-Down Compound, or other mischief we'd done. Fortunately, SSG Wilson was present and he was his usual helpful self. He assured the lieutenant that we *really* didn't give a damn about what some staff puke thought about our behavior, the S1 was not in our chain of command so he could go to hell, and so forth. The rebuttal was over the top, even for Wayne Wilson, who was never a shrinking violet. I was giddy with fatigue and I had a good laugh at Wayne's diatribe, which did not go over well with our esteemed Adjutant. The lieutenant was an overbearing Ring-Banger and he tried to lock SSG Wilson's heels for being insubordinate. Wayne remained completely defiant and of course I didn't intervene because the S1 had tried to jack me up too. I don't

The Mad Fragger and Me

remember his name, only that he was a West Pointer, a gadfly and an idiot.

There was already some bad blood between us for reasons I no longer remember, but from that point on, that S1 and I were bitter enemies. Within a day or two of the MP Station incident, he tried to flex his muscles by involuntarily reassigning me to Brigade Headquarters as the Public Information Officer (PIO). That was actually a cushy rear job, which involved traveling around and interviewing soldiers, then writing Hometown News Releases and similar articles for publication in civilian and military newspapers. But it was a convenient way to get rid of me and the Adjutant knew I had turned down other rear jobs. CPT Guill tried to get me out of the reassignment because he knew I wouldn't want it. Randy Guill told me I wasn't going to be able to stay with B Company this time, but I went to see the S1 about it anyway. The Adjutant told me I had no choice in the matter because I had been selected for the job personally by the Brigade Commander and I was the only lieutenant in the Brigade who had a degree in English, so I had been irrevocably anointed as the new PIO. Our S1 was obviously gloating about forcing me to do something I didn't want to do, which made me even more determined not to do it. He told me to draw new jungle fatigues and boots. I was also instructed to get a haircut, spit shine the new boots and take the fatigues to the tailor shop for alteration. I was to turn in all my field gear, weapons, ammo, and report to the Brigade S1, a Captain Somebody, at a specified time the next morning. Yeah, right. What were they going to do? Put me in the Infantry and send me to Vietnam? I ignored his "orders" about getting a haircut, replacing my uniforms and turning in my gear.

The next morning, 18 July 71, I told CPT Guill I would try to rejoin B Company at the airport, before it was picked up for the planned Combat Assault. I put on my most disreputable fatigues, my old boots and bush hat. I shouldered my rucksack, picked up my rifle and hitchhiked to the 11th Brigade Headquarters. I walked into

Captain Somebody's office at the Brigade S1 Shop, wearing my bandoliers, frags and rucksack. I grounded my weapons and gear on his office floor and introduced myself. The S1 did a double-take. Hadn't I been told to turn in my field equipment and draw new uniforms? Yes I had, but I didn't want to be no stinking Public Information Officer... in a flash of inspiration, remembering the Dymo tape motto Dave Cox put on my wall locker, I said, "I just want to go back to the bush and Kill VC for Mom's Apple Pie." The Captain laughed and told me to get the hell out of his office, so he could find a sane person for the PIO job. I hitchhiked out to the airport and found Bravo Company, just before the choppers arrived. When I came humping down the road carrying all my field equipment and weapons, Captain Guill just shook his head in disbelief. I was especially gratified when I thought about the frustration our Battalion S1 would feel, when he was told to cancel the orders for my transfer to Brigade Headquarters.

All of the above incidents occurred during our unit's four day Stand-Down, 14-17 July 1971. Curiously, I hardly remember anything at all about B Company's earlier Stand-Down break at LZ Bronco/Duc Pho, which had occurred 16-18 April 1971.

Many of the young Vietnamese women were very handsome, especially the ladies from the cities, who were usually slim, well groomed and beautifully attired in traditional ao dai outfits. The French had occupied Vietnam as part of their Indochina colony for a long time and the Eurasian girls were even more striking in appearance. Whenever I went through a rear area, particularly airports, I was exposed to and appreciated this exotic female pulchritude. I rarely saw any "round eyes" and the Army nurses or Red Cross Donut Dollies sometimes suffered by comparison to the local beauties. But there is an exception to every rule. I was in a busy airport somewhere in Vietnam one time and I saw two tall and leggy American girls I can still picture in my mind's eye. One was blonde, one was brunette, both were in their twenties and they were drop-dead gorgeous. They were wearing starched OD jungle fatigues which had been cut down to fit them perfectly. I had never seen jungle fatigues which were filled out like *that*, which is why I remember them 40 years later. The girls were not in the military, because they wore no insignia and they had tall, brown leather, high-heeled "Go-Go" boots. They were nicely made up, but wore no head gear, so their tresses flowed. The overall effect was amazing and they were clearly enjoying the carnal admiration of all the GIs coming through the airport. They were probably civilian entertainers, but I bet the MPs didn't hassle them about their multiple "uniform violations".

Stalking Moon and I always played a game of "Can you top *this*?" with each other, in and out of the bush. I now concede that Dave won the game, hands down. The Famous 2nd Platoon outperformed all other battalion rifle platoons in inflicting mayhem on the enemy, but I never came close to matching Lieutenant David Cox's panache, uninhibited hell raising and inspired lunacy. Whenever Dave was confronted with a problem to solve, he operated on the old military principle of "Do *something*, even if it's wrong". If the pressure was really turned on, he'd always shoot first and perhaps think about aiming later. He got himself into a series of scrapes in the rear area, so Doug Knight and I always looked forward to finding out what kind of trouble he had been in since the last time one of us was in Chu Lai. Dave's escapades were always wacky, impulsive and entertaining. And he usually seemed to get caught with his pants down.

It was rumored that there was some sort of personal feud between our Battalion CO and the Brigade Commander. One purported outcome of this was an 11th Light Infantry Brigade inspection, which our Chu Lai mess hall failed because it did not provide a proper homelike atmosphere for the troops. Specifically the mess hall did not have curtains. This is an example of the nonsense with which the rear area brass would become preoccupied. The Battalion Executive Officer told Stalking Moon to put up curtains in the mess hall, before 11th BDE came back to inspect it again, which was soon. The XO said he didn't care how Dave did it, which was always a mistake to say to him. Mess hall curtains were not an item which could be requisitioned through supply channels, or purchased on short notice. Dave borrowed a truck and went to the 198th Light Infantry Brigade mess hall, where he introduced himself to the mess steward as "the new Division Fire Marshall". He inspected the burners on field ranges, the fire extinguishers and so forth, complimenting the sergeant on running a tight operation. As he was leaving, the "Fire Marshall" suddenly had an afterthought and he asked the mess steward if his curtains had been fireproofed. The sergeant didn't know, because the curtains were already there when he was assigned to his job. 1LT Cox told him it wouldn't hurt to have the curtains treated again with fire retardant, so he could have the KPs take them down and load them on Dave's truck. He promised to have them fireproofed and to bring them back as soon as possible (*after* the 1/20 mess hall was re-inspected of course). While the curtains were being taken down and loaded on the truck, the 198th LIB Command Sergeant Major walked in and asked what was going on. He was introduced to "Lieutenant Cox, the new Division Fire Marshall, who is taking our curtains to have them fireproofed". The CSM responded, "He is NOT the Division Fire Marshall". They thought 1LT Cox was trying to steal the curtains and they called the MPs, who placed him under arrest. But someone in the Provost Marshall's Office apparently had a sense of humor and they let Dave go, after he explained his scheme.

On another occasion, Stalking Moon closed down the entire Chu Lai airport. He had been ordered to get an emergency resupply of artillery ammo out to the firebase ASAP. He ran around like a wild man, laying-on the ammunition, borrowing a truck and hauling ammo to the airport. He had a CH47 Chinook inbound to pick up the ammunition and deliver it, but no way to load it on the chopper, because he was making up this operation as he went along. He spotted a cargo net next to an airport office and "borrowed" it. The ammo was loaded into the net and Dave was connecting it to the

The Mad Fragger and Me

Chinook's lift hook, when an irate warrant officer came running down the road yelling "Stop! You stole my cargo net!" Cargo nets were rated by ACL, or the maximum Acceptable Cargo Load, but Infantry lieutenants didn't know much about stuff like that. Dave heard the warrant officer shouting, so he signaled the CH47 Crew Chief to take off. The big chopper lifted off, but the overloaded net came apart over the main runway and hundreds of packing tubes of art'y rounds went rolling across the whole airport, shutting it down completely.

Fighting with enlisted men or NCOs was strictly prohibited by Army regulations and could result in court martial proceedings against an officer. Nevertheless, there was an unwritten rule in the Infantry branch that a lieutenant did not have even one hair on his butt, and was not fit to command troops, unless he was willing to do "close order knuckle drill" with any enlisted man, at any time. Dave Cox was responsible for the operation of the Chu Lai Stand-Down Compound, as an extra duty when he was the Support Platoon Leader/Assistant S4. While another line company was on Stand-Down, a floor show had been brought in for entertainment and the show girls were changing into their costumes in a dressing room above the stage. The dressing room was accessed by a long flight of stairs, built against the outside wall of the stage shell. The lock on the dressing room door was broken, so 1LT Cox was standing on the landing at the top of the stairs, guarding the door against intruders. Dave Cox was a pretty big guy. He had played fullback on the University of Georgia football team and he looked a little like Crazy Horse, so few sober people would tangle with him. A drunken Master Sergeant staggered up the stairs and tried to enter the dressing room. Dave stopped him and told him he couldn't go in. The MSG cursed at Dave and threw a punch at him, so Stalking Moon dropped him... down the entire flight of stairs. The poor man broke his arm. A hubbub was raised about the incident, but Dave insisted that he acted in self-defense and the matter was eventually dropped. Every time Dave told us one of these stories, he'd laugh about it, no matter how much trouble he had gotten into.

There is an old story about an Army pack mule, loaded with equipment, which fell off a cliff in France in 1918. By the time everyone got done piling on, it was estimated that the dead mule had been carrying more than a million dollars worth of equipment, all of which was dropped from property books by various Army units. That is what was euphemistically referred to as a "combat loss". The same thing occurred all the time in Vietnam. Any time a firefight, a flood, an accident or some other mishap occurred in the bush which reasonably could be blamed for an equipment loss, the unit Property Book Officer could report any previously missing serial-numbered item as a combat loss. That piece of equipment would then be permanently written off the books and a replacement could be requisitioned. The problem was that the missing equipment was usually just misplaced and it generally turned up later in another unit's supply room, or in some other nook or cranny. The property books were continuous and they got passed along through changes of command, so these anomalies accumulated over time. All units would therefore end up with a lot of extra weapons and other equipment they weren't supposed to have, but that wasn't really a problem unless there was a strict accountability inspection. Those inspections occurred only rarely and under unusual circumstances, such as when a unit permanently stood down and its colors were retired. Then the <u>current</u> unit Property Book Officer (PBO) was left holding the bag. That of course happened when 1st Battalion 20th Infantry Regiment formally closed out its Vietnam combat operations in early October 1971 and guess who the Property Book Officer was? A logistics Chief Warrant Officer usually filled that slot, but the last CWO was already gone, leaving the PBO job, by default, to 1LT David A. Cox. In preparation for the permanent unit Stand Down, all battalion equipment was inventoried and a lot of extra gear was found, including about three dozen excess M16 rifles. All of those weapons already had been dropped from the property books by prior PBOs. Dave was told that the rifles could not be turned in and that he had to get rid of them. So he reluctantly deep-sixed them in the South China Sea from a helicopter. On his way to his next assignment, Dave was also tasked with turning in the Battalion Colors in Saigon. There were around forty campaign streamers on the Battalion's flag, including 12 from Civil War battles. Dave's great-great-grandfather was killed in Pickett's Charge and he thought nobody would miss the Gettysburg battle streamer, so he took it as a souvenir. The flag inventory officer in Saigon almost immediately asked, "Where is the Gettysburg streamer?" It was too late to blame it on an Army mule falling off a cliff in 1918, so Dave admitted he had taken it, to honor his ancestor's death at Gettysburg. The indignant captain told Lieutenant Cox that stealing the battle streamer was a court-martial offense and he threatened to draw up charges. Stalking Moon had dumped thousands of dollars worth of weapons into the ocean and everyone expected him to do that, but a REMF officer in Saigon wanted to court-martial him for souveniring a four foot length of blue and grey nylon ribbon with "Gettysburg-1863" embroidered on it. (You *know* that I couldn't make up this stuff.)

There was a Class VI Resupply Yard in Chu Lai, which was a wonder to behold. "Class VI " is the Army euphemism for drinking alcohol and the Chu Lai yard was like a large retail liquor store Back in the World. They had every type and most brands of alcohol. One of the few perks I had as an officer was a Class VI ration card, which allowed me to purchase a generous amount of hard liquor each month. Ration cards were issued only to officers and to senior NCOs, pay grade E7 and higher. Each time a bottle was purchased, the cashier would punch a hole in the card, which was how they kept track of the monthly quota. The really miraculous thing about the operation was the pricing, because there were no import tariffs, taxes, profits or other markups. A quart of decent scotch, like Cutty Sark, J&B or Johnny Walker went for about three bucks MPC. Bourbon was even cheaper. I seldom drank hard liquor in Vietnam, usually sticking to beer because the climate was so hot. But I sometimes took orders from my troops and NCOs, to make liquor runs for them with my ration card.

Bravo Company had a tall, dour and physically fit First Sergeant named Heinz Ruby, who had a reputation for nastiness when he'd been drinking. He had a strong German accent and there was a rumor that Heinz had served in the Hitler Youth, as a teenager in WWII. My troops told me that during El Tee Korona's first stand-down, he was sitting in the little club at the LZ Bronco compound drinking beer with the other 2nd Platoon guys. 1SG Ruby came into the club, drunk, and announced that he was going to kick Lieutenant Korona's ass. Frank responded, "No sergeant in the <u>entire</u> U.S. Army can do that". A brawl ensued and 1LT Korona gave 1SG Ruby a thrashing, which greatly entertained the 2nd Platoon guys. (I asked Frank Korona about this incident and he gave me an evasive and ambiguous answer, commenting that you don't always clearly recall things that happened when you'd been drinking. *But* he didn't deny that it occurred.)

At a later date, First Sergeant Ruby lost his right-hand-man, the Company Clerk, due to normal troop rotation. Not long after the Clerk's departure, Ruby flew out on the resupply bird to 2nd Platoon's patrol base to see CPT Guill. I overheard 1SG Ruby complaining bitterly to the CO about not being able to get a school-trained Company Clerk as a replacement. I interrupted their conversation and told Ruby that one of my soldiers would probably make an excellent "OJT" Clerk. Angelo Onevelo (grunt-name, "Zip") was intelligent and conscientious. He had earned a bachelors' degree and he was drafted into the Army out of graduate school. Zip had mentioned to me in casual conversation that he was a pretty fast two-finger typist. Onevelo had no enemies in 2nd Platoon, because he was always friendly and considerate towards everyone. He never complained or shirked an assignment and he always tried hard. There was only one hitch in Zip's giddy-up, which was probably related to his kind and erudite nature. It normally took time for newbies to adapt to our violent and rude existence, but Zip had continued to be flummoxed by grunt life. Despite sufficient time to adjust, he remained jumpy, rigid and error-prone, making me worry that he'd get himself killed. After hearing all this, 1SG Ruby decided to try out Ange Onevelo as an apprentice Company Clerk. He did a superb job, pleasing our grumpy Top Sergeant to no end. Everyone was happy.

I went through the Chu Lai Orderly Room in June on my way to R & R in Hawaii. When I came back from Honolulu, I described to Zip Onevelo the good time I'd had and he said, "You are entitled to go on leave too, Sir... so why don't you take leave and go somewhere else?" I commented that the CO would never sign off on that and Zip answered "CPT Guill signs EVERYTHING I put in front of him, El Tee". I knew that most REMFs were taking both R&R and leave, and I had certainly paid my dues in the bush, so I told SP/4 (later, SGT) Onevelo to go ahead and cut leave orders for me. When the orders came through, I told Randy Guill I'd be leaving on such-and-such date to go on leave for 7 days. He blew his stack, saying that I had just recently come back from R&R, and now, incredibly, I expected to go on leave too? I innocently asked, "Isn't this your signature on my orders?" which was the perfect squelch.

Leave orders were not destination-specific. I wanted to go to Australia, but unlike guys going on R&R, GIs who were going on leave did not have reserved seats and they flew standby/space-available. When I got to the R&R Center in Da Nang, I bumped into three enlisted men who had worked for me in the Four Deuce Platoon. They had been waiting there several days for standby seats on a flight to one of the R&R/leave destinations. They told me there was no flight to Australia anytime soon and most of the flights to other destinations were filled, but there were seats available on a plane to Bangkok the next day. That was where they had decided to go and they invited me to hook up with them, so I did. All four of us stayed at the Parliament Hotel in Bangkok, which was one of many on the list of approved U.S. Military R&R Hotels. The briefing officer at the Bangkok R&R Center tipped us off to the merits of Tai rice beer, which is wonderful stuff, smooth, 18.5% alcohol, inexpensive and served in large (1 quart?) bottles. It took us a bit longer to discover the merits of the local cuisine, but when we did, we all but abandoned the Western-style food served in the hotel restaurant. We went on many sightseeing tours, to shows, clubs and we did a lot of partying, so the three EM quickly ran low on money. I decided to try to cash a personal check, in order to loan them $100 each, and to get a little extra cash for myself. I took a cab to the U.S. Air Force Base PX and cashed a check for $400 from my Maryland National Bank checking account. That was a very large amount of money in those days, but all I had to do was show the PX cashier my U.S Army I.D. card! (The guys promptly paid back the entire amount, after we returned to Vietnam.)

    After I'd left Chu Lai on leave, I realized that I had forgotten to sign out in the Orderly Room's Perpetual Sign-in/Sign-out Log, which worried me a little. When I got back from Thailand, I told our Company Clerk this, commenting that I needed him to fix the records. SP/4 Onevelo said OK, he would just cancel my leave orders and I should destroy my copies. I told him no, he didn't understand, the Perpetual Log had to be fixed, because I'd forgotten to sign out. Zip said, "No El Tee, *you* don't understand. You never *left* on leave. You didn't *go* to Bangkok. You were *here* the whole time. The Army will pay you for the unused leave when you are discharged." That is why I don't know when I was in Thailand... all copies of the leave orders were pulled from my 201 File and destroyed by Zip Onevelo. My non-trip to Bangkok was the most fun I never had. And when I was discharged, the Army did pay me for a week of accrued leave not used in Bangkok.

    Wayne Wilson, Dave Cox and I had a mini-reunion in Ocean City, Maryland in May 2010. Dave asked me if I remembered the night we were thrown out of the Commanding General's Officers Club, next to the Americal Division HQ in Chu Lai. I did indeed remember it and I attributed the incident to an ancient and faded

The Mad Fragger and Me

set of jungle fatigues with a "Stalking Moon" name tape, which Dave sometimes wore to confound the Lifers in the rear area. A major came up to us and told us we'd have to leave the O Club, because our attire did not meet their standards. I thought there was a third El Tee with us, but I could not remember who it was. Dave said that was generally correct, but it wasn't just his Stalking Moon outfit that got us tossed out of the club, rather it was the fact that we were grunts and we were all wearing our field jungle fatigues, which were the only uniforms we had. (Our jungle fatigues were tailored and had all the required patches and insignia sewn on, but they were faded and had been repaired in places. The uniforms were clean and had been pressed, but not starched. The black dye in the leather parts of our scuffed and scarred jungle boots was leached out from wearing them in water all the time, so the leather was almost white and boot polish did not improve them much. We were slightly shabby from the wear and tear of combat, but we didn't really look like bums. We'd had haircuts and shaves and we thought we looked presentable enough to go into a bar.) Dave said the prissy REMF major intercepted us in the Officer's Club lobby, before we even got into the bar, and told us we were not welcome there. Dave asked me if I remembered what I'd said to Major Prissy, but I did not. This is how Dave told it to Wayne: "Every time Tom got ready to stir up some shit, he'd let his eyeglasses slide down on his nose and peer at you over top of them while he was thinking. Then he'd use one finger to push his glasses back into place and say whatever he was going to say. When that major told us we'd have to leave because our attire did not meet their standards, I saw Tom's spectacles slide down to the end of his nose. He stared at the major over the top of them and I got curious about what he was going to say. Then Tom pushed the glasses back in place with his trigger finger and he said, 'You people apparently are not aware that there is a war going on out there.' "

    I do not remember saying that to the major, but Dave accurately described my habit of letting my glasses slide down on my nose prior to delivering a zinger, so his story is probably true. Wayne Wilson listened to Dave's recitation about the Officers' Club confrontation and he said it reminded him of the time he and I went to the Chu Lai Post Exchange, asking me if I remembered *that* incident. I recalled being in the PX once or twice, but that's all. Wayne said we went to the PX together, but there was a long line of rear-area soldiers waiting to get in, which wrapped around the outside of building. According to Wayne's story: "Tom said, 'Come on, we're not waiting in line with all these damned REMFs', and we went right up to the front and barged into the queue. A major, wearing Signal Corps brass, came up to us and he said, 'Excuse me lieutenant, but do you mind explaining to me why you two went to the front of the line, ahead of all these soldiers who have been waiting to get into the PX, including *me*?' The major was so angry that he was shaking, but Tom was unbelievably calm. Tom said, 'No sir, I don't mind. As you can see from the appearance of our uniforms, we are grunts and we just came in from the bush. The Commanding General put out a new directive which says that infantrymen who come in from the field do not have to wait in line at the PX and they can go right to the front.' The major looked like he was going to have apoplexy, but he did not know what to say and he just walked away." When Wayne told this yarn, I said he and Dave had been hanging around with each other too much, and they were starting to make up terrible stories about me. Wayne adamantly responded, "I swear to God, that is the absolute truth, those were your *exact* words, I remember it like it happened yesterday. You braced that major and he didn't know what to do about it."

I thought about it later and I began to remember the conversation with the Signal Corps major. He obviously hadn't believed me, and plainly Wayne Wilson hadn't either, but I think there really was a CG directive saying that grunts didn't have to wait in line at the PX, or at least someone had told me there was. The story isn't as good that way, but the incident occurred many years

The Mad Fragger and Me

ago, so I'm not sure. Anyway, if there wasn't such a directive from the Commanding General, there *should* have been one. One of the regular complaints from grunts was that all the good stuff was always sold out at the PX, because the REMFs gobbled up everything as soon as a shipment of Japanese cameras, Seiko watches or Panasonic tape decks came in. The PX shelves were usually bare whenever the infantrymen got there.

When we came to the Chu Lai base and the guys would try to go to the PX or someplace like that, they'd often come back with DRs (Delinquency Reports) for "uniform violations" written by the MPs. This was usually done because their hair was too long, or they were wearing camouflage bush hats with OD jungle fatigues, or they didn't have name tapes on their shirts, or they were sporting Peace tokens, or some equally serious rear-area crime. CPT Guill always tore up the DRs, but it was irritating for our combat soldiers to be written up by MPs who were preoccupied with trivia. The rejection of Dave and me at the Officers' Club illustrates the attitude of many rear-area officers, who didn't have a clue that a few of us were involved in a shooting war. REMFs lived in a world of their own, with a completely different set of problems and priorities: *Will the Army ship home my huge stereo system at government expense? How can I get tickets to Bob Hope's Christmas show? Will Joey Heatherton be there? Who can we get to fix the pump in the Officers' Swimming Pool?*

Pogues usually gave grunts a wide berth, especially when we were coming in from the bush. When I was going on R&R to Hawaii, I bummed a chopper ride from LZ Bronco to Chu Lai. The pilot landed at the northern end of post, at Division HQ, several miles from our company Orderly Room. I started walking south with my thumb out, carrying 100+ pounds of gear on my back, in stifling heat of 110 degrees or more. I was quickly drenched in sweat. No one would pick me up, and empty vehicle after empty vehicle, except for a REMF driver and maybe a passenger or two, passed me on the road. I'm sure it was because they saw I was a filthy grunt, staggering along under my huge rucksack like a crazed hunchback, dripping with grenades and other weaponry. Pissed off, I finally walked out in the middle of the road and stopped a deuce 'n half at gunpoint. The truck was empty, being driven by a Staff Sergeant. I showed him the black lieutenant's bar on my collar and I said, "I need a ride. Do you have any problem with that, sergeant?" He said he did not, but I would have shot out the tires on his crummy truck if he'd tried to drive around me. What could they do to me for that? Put me in the Infantry and send me to Vietnam?

I once read a Vietnam War novel in which the author, a former platoon leader, stated that all civilized people, including garrison troops and Vietnamese civilians, always reacted to an Infantry rifle platoon exactly like it was a traveling psycho ward, with all the patients armed to the teeth. That is true. It is also a fact that we grunts reveled in our fearsome reputation and played our role to the hilt whenever we were in a rear area, so it was not irrational for the REMFs to be wary of us. It is a mystery to me why the general public thinks that all Vietnam Veterans are created equal, when the vast majority of them were never really exposed to actual combat or to serious danger. It is true that rear area troops were occasionally killed by random enemy rockets or other flukes, but those incidents were rare. The general public is also not aware of the shabby treatment grunts generally got from everyone else in the Army, whose jobs actually existed only to support us. There was a saying in the Army that the Infantry is called "The Queen of Battle", because the Infantry gets screwed by everyone. *Xin loi, Crunchies.*

Chapter 10:

SOLDIERS AND DOGS

I refrained from getting too close to my troops, as did the other lieutenants I knew. Most of my Snuffies were good guys and I would have liked to have been their buddy. But that would have been contrary to basic leadership principles and untenable emotionally if one of them was killed. I was friendly with my men, but being "friendly" is not the same thing as being "friends". These strictures did not apply to other lieutenants and it was clear that Dave Cox, Doug Knight and Frank Korona were true friends, with our friendship solidified by mutual experiences. SSG Wayne Wilson also fell into this category, because I instinctively knew he would not take advantage of the situation when the normal prohibition against close friendship between an officer and an NCO was relaxed with him. In the bush, I hated to get up in the morning for "stand to". The Lifer managed this problem by fixing me a C-rat can of instant coffee every day just before first light, which was the most delicious stuff I've ever tasted. I have no idea how SSG Wilson managed to heat the coffee in the dark, or how he made it taste so good. But more significantly he acted like the older brother I never had, always taking care of me and doing everything he could to keep me straight and our platoon out of trouble. Despite our close friendship, I never addressed SSG Wilson by his first name in Vietnam, always calling him "Sergeant", "Sarge" or "Lifer", and he always addressed me as "El Tee", "Lieutenant" or "Sir". I totally trusted him and there is still no one in the world who I would rather have watching my back. I maintained a professional distance from the other enlisted men and I had only occasional contact with other platoon leaders, so life in the bush would have been lonely indeed without SSG Wayne P. Wilson.

Although it was always somewhat of a joint effort, by Infantry tradition the Platoon Leader was in charge of operations in the field and the Platoon Sergeant ran the platoon in cantonment areas. One of the PSG's continual responsibilities was equipment/supplies/logistics and I quickly learned that I could just ignore this because Wayne Wilson would take care of everything. But leaving SSG Wilson entirely to his own devices sometimes required a leap of faith. On one occasion, The Lifer decided we could use one more radio than we were authorized to have. He got a standard requisition form and filled it out to draw another AN/PRC25 radio and extra batteries. He then took the form to a SP/4 Major in our unit and had him write "OK" at the bottom, sign his first name in the signature block, then "Major", as if that was his rank instead of his last name. SSG Wilson took the requisition to the commo hootch and passed it off on an unsuspecting enlisted man, who issued him a PRC25 and two extra batteries. A couple of days later, the Battalion Signal Officer confronted SSG Wilson with the bogus requisition and congratulated him on his creativity. He also instructed Sergeant Wilson to turn in the radio and to tell SP/4 Major to stick to being a "Specialist" in the future.

My other closest friend in Vietnam was Dave Cox, although nonstop competition with him made our friendship a little edgy. Dave and I operated in the bush together for only a few months. During that period, we bickered constantly whenever CPT Guill was around, to amuse ourselves and to drive him crazy, sometimes abetted by other lieutenants. Poor Randy Guill probably felt like he was trying to herd cats. Dave Cox and I also entertained ourselves by waging a campaign of attrition against the enemy, trying to play with Charlie's head in so doing, and competing with each other in the process.

Wayne Wilson, Dave Cox and I could not have been more oddly different as individuals, but we were still brothers in arms. Wayne is a tough and gutsy Jew with unabashed liberal leanings. He was a champion of the underdog and sympathetic to the plight of

The Mad Fragger and Me

the Vietnamese. He was noticeably vigilant about protecting the interests of our black soldiers, but without coddling or favoritism. SSG Wilson also went out of his way to welcome and orient newbies, always sensitive to their feelings of alienation and fear of the unknown. Despite his "Lifer" nickname, after his second tour in Vietnam, Wayne got out of the Army. He became a pot-stirring college student, eventually graduating from that liberal bastion, Rutgers University. Dave Cox was humorously flamboyant and tried to pass himself off as a swashbuckler or a Southern Gentleman, with obviously exaggerated overtones. He is a hardnosed but soft spoken South Carolinian, self described as a "pew-jumping Baptist". He somehow graduated fourth in his OCS class, so he had a choice of any Army branch. Instead of choosing Signal Corps, Quartermaster Corps or some other safe branch, he picked the Infantry. Dave pretends to be still fighting the Civil War, which he always refers to as "The War of Northern Aggression". Like me, Dave is somewhere to the right of Vlad the Impaler, in his opinions and his politics. He somehow managed to limp through both Jump School and Ranger School after Vietnam, although crippled by his bad knee. In spite of that, or perhaps partly because of it, he was selected as the Honor Graduate in his Ranger School class. Dave was originally drafted, but he is the only one of my acquaintances who stayed in the Army long enough for a full service retirement, as a Lieutenant Colonel. During his 25 year Army career, Dave also earned a PhD in Clinical Psychology. Characteristics Dave, Wayne and I shared were a strong sense of humor, commitment to duty, honor, determination, patriotism, mule-headedness, occasional impulsiveness and pride in our brotherhood. On second thought, maybe we are more alike than we are different.

    Dave Cox says that his grandmother was a full-blooded Blackfoot Sioux, but he got his "Stalking Moon" appellation from his OCS classmates because of his love of the night ambush and his habit of roaming around the barracks at all hours of the night. Dave encountered a rebellion by some of his troops (instigated by Jethro

Tom Dolan

Dingleberry) during his first field mission in Vietnam. He crushed that insurrection, but he was never able to fully trust some of his troops, nor did he ever have a reliable platoon sergeant to watch his back. Some people in Dave's platoon were a little worried that he might be psychotic and he tried not to disabuse them of that notion, because it was to his advantage for certain individuals to fear him. I can understand why they might have thought that he was nuts, because The Stalking Moon always appeared to be wonderfully demented. One of his former troopers told me that they spotted an NVA soldier on one occasion and Dave charged after him, saying that he was going to go get some medals. He is still convinced that 1LT David Cox was loony.

Stalking Moon ignored my periodic reminders to show proper deference by always addressing me as "Kemosabe", but he customarily paid very little attention to anything that anyone said to him. David Cox had a willful and perverse personality, but it was suffused with his sense of humor. He was always inclined to openly challenge authority, without any noticeable concern about the possible consequences. He tells hilarious stories about the things he did in OCS to deliberately provoke his Tactical Officers, which he thought was great fun. That was how he earned the all-time Fort Benning record for marching 144 OCS Punishment Tours. When David Cox was commissioned as a 2LT, he was amazed to receive orders to perform his troop duty as an OCS Tactical Officer. Even more astonishing, his new Company Commander knew all about Dave's prior antics as an Officer Candidate. (During their first OCS formation, the Captain informed the 6th Platoon that he had bad news for them, because their Tactical Officer, known as The Stalking Moon, was psychologically disturbed and completely unpredictable... there was no stunt they could dream up which he had not already done.) David Cox was not intrinsically resentful of authority, rather he engaged in rebellious behavior mostly for sport. This was also his way of rocking the military boat, to keep things in perspective and on the right track. Captain Guill ruled Our Little

The Mad Fragger and Me

World like a benevolent dictator, but Stalking Moon sometimes challenged Randy Guill in the same way as he had his OCS Tactical Officers. Captain Guill was certainly aware of 1LT Cox's sometimes unruly behavior, but I doubt that he understood Dave's more esoteric motives. It is hard to appreciate the amusement in a situation, when your tail is being twisted as part of the entertainment. CPT Guill struggled to maintain discipline and good order within B Company, while 1LT Cox tried to keep him guessing about whether he was successful in that effort. The quirky relationship which developed between them was very funny to observe.

We were at LZ Liz for perimeter security on one occasion and CPT Randy Guill called Doug Knight, Dave Cox and me to the mess hall for a meeting. He immediately started chewing us out about our KPs showing up late that morning and it just went on and on. CPT Guill must have really gotten reamed out about our tardy KPs by the Battalion Commander, because the dressing-down he gave us was out of all proportion to our crime. Unlike Stalking Moon and me, Doug Knight was always easygoing and compliant, but after awhile all three of us were looking at each other, asking with our eyes, "*What is wrong with this guy?*" David Cox finally interrupted the CO's tirade by taking a genuine silver dime out of his pocket and flipping it across the table to Randy Guill, who caught it in the air and looked at it in a puzzled way. He asked, "What's this for?" Dave answered, in his full South Carolina drawl, "You can use that to call somebody who *gives* a shit". He said it in such a droll and unconcerned way that we all cracked up, including Captain Guill. (This is an example of how Dave always tried to help his superiors regain a proper perspective whenever they went off the rails. Randy Guill later commented in Dave's Officers Efficiency Report, "Lieutenant Cox is somewhat brash, but it usually does not detract from his effectiveness as an officer". *That* is an example of artful use of the English language!)

The infantry lieutenants in our battalion were friendly with each other, with a few notable exceptions, because we were all in the same fix. Most of us were, had been, or soon would be, rifle platoon leaders. The majority, who tried to lead by example, had a life expectancy which was lower than other soldiers. Some of us were in an "us against them" relationship with Army bureaucracy, leading to a certain amount of cynicism and rebelliousness. We often struggled to solve leadership problems without much help from anyone else. Some lieutenants never got their acts together, but most did. We were at the bottom of the officer corps' food chain, but we had the most difficult and dangerous jobs. Within our AO in 1970 and 1971, it was truly a "Lieutenants' War". Many lieutenants, predictably, just wanted to get by and bring their troops home in one piece. A few lieutenants became proficient in small unit jungle warfare, because of total immersion in it, autonomy of operation and the Darwinian survival principle. They eventually knew a lot more about this type of combat than did many of the line and staff officers in the upper echelons. There were only 12 rifle platoon leaders in an entire infantry battalion at any given time, but we didn't have much direct contact with each other. Whenever a group of infantry lieutenants did get together to party, it was usually a macho affair, with plenty of testosterone-fueled bragging, humorous stories and good natured insults. I have mentioned Sid Hopfer, Roger Mackintosh, Dennis Ransdell and others I knew directly. They were all friends of mine, but there were many others. I'm not going to try to recite other names, because I've forgotten too many of them. It was satisfying to be part of this brotherhood and our responsibilities were well above our O-2 pay grade. "First Lieutenant, Infantry" was the best and most prestigious rank in the United States Army, as far as I was concerned.

CPT Randy Guill was a good CO. I liked and respected him, but we did not really become personal friends while we served together, because Guill maintained a professional distance from his platoon leaders, just as I did from my EM. He had a thorough

The Mad Fragger and Me

knowledge of the capabilities of all NCOs in B Company, and he knew most of the enlisted men almost as well. He was protective of our soldiers and he was visibly distressed by our occasional friendly casualties. CPT Guill was certainly aware that we were fighting a war which was a lost cause. Guill was appropriately cautious and he did not really push the platoon leaders to engage the enemy, but he did not try to hold us back either. He typically gave broad direction to his lieutenants and trusted us to figure out how to produce the desired results. Dave Cox, Doug Knight and I loved his *laissez-faire* leadership style because it gave us maximum authority and flexibility, but a West Point graduate who was assigned to B Company in June 1971 obviously did not "get it". The cherry lieutenant clearly expected CPT Guill to solve all the leadership problems in his platoon. He constantly bitched about the shortcomings of his soldiers, instead of taking charge and *leading* them. He was also petulant, impertinent towards CPT Guill and hilariously unaware of his "Young Lieutenant" status among the other officers. Comic relief, courtesy of the U.S. Military Academy.

Although CPT Guill was competent and well liked, he was stubborn and he could be a pain in the ass at times. My platoon found an old VC grave one time out in the 515 Valley and CPT Guill ordered me to open it, hoping to get credit for another enemy KIA from a recent skirmish. I radioed back to him that it was clearly an old grave, but he insisted that we dig it up. That has to rank, pun intended, as one of the most grisly and disgusting things I've ever done. I decided then and there that I would never open another ripe grave, even if General Creighton Abrams personally ordered me to do it. CPT Guill had a known weakness for Chuckles gummy candy, especially the green ones, from the Sundry Packet cartons, and he also had a reputation in B Company as the worst Spades player in Vietnam. *[Randy Guill now claims that this was a ploy. He alleges that he and RTO Bob Scates discovered that they were a great Spades team, almost able to read each other's minds, so they had "Roop" Ruppert spread the word that they were terrible players* and easy gambling marks. I never played cards so I don't know, but Stalking Moon still swears that Randy was a really terrible Spades player.]

    Some lieutenants did not wear rank insignia on their jungle shirts or bush hats, because they thought it made them targets for the enemy. My lieutenant's bars and crossed rifle insignia could not be removed because they were embroidered directly on my shirt collars, but a black bar is hard to see from a distance and we usually wore OD tee shirts during the day anyway. More realistically, the long whip antenna on the platoon radio really *did* indicate that the person standing next to the RTO, holding the handset to his ear, was probably an officer.(Short whips were usually used on squad radios.) David Cox teased his somewhat nervous RTO, Leonard "Daffy" Davenport, by commenting extensively about how the long whip antenna on his PRC25 made Daffy a primary target of VC snipers or NVA ambushes. Daffy responded, "Oh, that's all right El Tee… they'll probably let me walk on by, and then they'll light your ass up." Daffy may have gotten even for Dave's teasing, though. 1LT Cox preferred to take the last turn on NDP guard for his CP Group, so he would be fully awake and alert at first light. Not everyone had a timepiece, so it was common practice to pass along a luminous-dial wristwatch all night, as each guy was awakened for his turn on guard duty. Early one morning, Stalking Moon was awakened and the communal wristwatch was handed to him at 0500, according to the illuminated hands. Dave pulled his guard turn, then he waited and waited, but the sun did not come up on time. He waited some more, but BMNT still did not arrive. It finally occurred to him that an earlier guard during the night had merely moved the time ahead 1 ½ hours, passed along the wristwatch to the next guy and gone back to sleep. This meant that the last person awakened, Dave, had to pull a double guard watch. Because of prior stunts which had earned him his nickname, Daffy Davenport was the suspected culprit, but Stalking Moon could not prove that he did it.

The Mad Fragger and Me

In 1971 the U.S. was beginning to pull out of Vietnam, but a few of us were still trying to win, or at least we refused to give up. Most Infantry lieutenants were fairly cautious, because we knew that our government was throwing in the towel. The troops were also well aware that we were pulling out of Vietnam and this created a leadership problem, especially for those of us near the bottom of the chain of command. Platoon leaders were often caught in a squeeze, between the Higher-Highers who sometimes ordered us to do stupid things, and our concern for our troops, who were justifiably reluctant to stick their necks out too far for a lost cause. Despite that reluctance, it was essential for maintenance of good order, military discipline and the platoon's survival that my troops instantly comply with everything I told them to do, especially when the poop was hitting the fan. I was not easy in my demands, never hesitating to push them hard or to raise hell when I thought somebody needed to be chewed out. But my troops did not seem to resent this and they appeared to understand the need for discipline. Unlike "elite" units in which members were selected through a grueling initiation process, my men were thrown together purely by luck and happenstance, but it did not diminish their combat performance. The 2nd Platoon guys were tightly knit, they depended heavily on each other and most of them had too much pride in themselves to chicken out when the going got tough. Although it was not always true in other platoons, most of my guys were dependable and conscientious. The few who were a little shaky were kept in line by peer pressure. As a group, they were the best young men I've ever known. Years later, Roger Webber, our Hillbilly Philosopher, said to me, "You know, I *really* wouldn't want to go through that experience again. But if I *had* to do it again, I'd want to be with *exactly* the same guys I was with the first time". Me too.

A very few soldiers, like Lieutenant Frank Korona and Sergeant Doug Landry, were adrenalin junkies who thought it was great fun to find the enemy and then kill him in close quarters combat. I admired their courage, but their brains and their gonads were wired differently than mine. Frank is of Polish ancestry, with that cultural predisposition for courage in battle. I can imagine him gleefully riding out on horseback with the Polish Cavalry in 1939 to counterattack Hitler's Panzers. Frank was modest and self-effacing, never talking about himself or his combat exploits. He never wore his jump wings or CIB on his jungle shirt, although he had earned those badges. He sometimes did not bother to wear rank insignia or Infantry branch crossed rifles, displaying just a "Korona" name tape and "US Army" on his uniform. Doug Landry, whose grunt moniker was "Coon Ass", was also modest and quiet. Doug seemed to be always cracking jokes and his wonderful Cajun accent added to his unique persona. Coon Ass looked like a youthful rendition of Johnnie Carson and his abiding good humor reinforced that impression. SGT Landry went home to Thibodaux, Louisiana not long after I joined 2nd Platoon, but when he left, he was legendary within Bravo Company for his courage in combat.

It was amazing how well I got to know the strengths and weaknesses of the guys in my platoon. I probably knew more about what they would or would not do under stress and pressure than their parents did, and what I didn't know, SSG Wayne Wilson did. As an NCO, SSG Wilson was in a better position to develop relationships with our soldiers, but I sometimes also got close to them in a personal way, because it was just not avoidable. One of my fine young soldiers came to me in tears because he had received a "Dear John" letter from his wife, who confessed that she had been sleeping with his best friend and was leaving him. OCS had not prepared me for that, but I did the best I could as an OJT marriage counselor. Another young trooper approached me, wracked with guilt, to confess that he had tried smoking some weed while he was in the rear area. I gave him a mild butt chewing and absolution, then sent him on his way with an admonition not to do it again. I was touched by these occasional personal encounters, because of the trust which was implied by them.

The Mad Fragger and Me

Although he was only with me a short time, youthful SSG Donald Bland was one of the most competent and professional NCOs I ever met. He had a rare ability to inspire confidence and admiration in his subordinates, with no apparent effort. He really should have been an officer. If he had stayed in the Army, he would have been an excellent candidate for OCS, or for a direct commission. I made a comment to Randy Guill one time about Staff Sergeant Bland's amazing leadership skills and he responded, "Yeah …based upon leadership ability, Don Bland *should be* our Battalion Commander".

Like SSG Bland, SGT Paul Malonson was a graduate of the NCO Academy at Fort Benning, which was patterned after the OCS program, except it was only 12 weeks long. SGT Malonson hailed from Massachusetts and he possessed a broad New England accent. He came into the unit around the same date I did. The guys in Second Squad initially gave him a hard time, disparaging him as a "Shake 'N Bake", but SGT Malonson overcame the resistance and established credibility as their Squad Leader. He was appropriately cautious, but he was also mission-oriented. He led by example in a low key but effective way. He never bitched when the going got tough and he was not afraid of combat. SGT Malonson was our platoon's taciturn Yankee, so it was very difficult to know what he was thinking. Paul's serious demeanor probably inspired Randy "Robby" Robinson, who was in Keith Moore's squad, to harass him without mercy. Robby was part Navajo, but he did not conform to the stern Native American stereotype. He was rowdy, boisterous and uninhibited, with a penchant for practical jokes. Robby had been a wrestler in high school and he regularly attacked SGT Malonson when he least expected it, jumping on him from behind, wrangling him to the ground, immobilizing him with various wrestling holds and generally driving him crazy. Robby was *Kato,* to Paul's *The Green Hornet.* SGT Malonson had been an auto mechanic in civilian life and he had an abiding interest in cars. I have no idea why the Army did not make him a Motor Sergeant, but the motor pool's loss was our gain.

I think Paul Malonson was a Squad Leader under my command longer than anyone else, except perhaps Keith Moore. SGT Moore was a dependable young man who always leaned forward in the foxhole. Keith was a superb point man and he usually assumed that role when his squad was leading the platoon. He was consistently tough and aggressive in combat, but never to the extent that he was reckless, always showing good judgment. He was promoted through the ranks to Sergeant E-5 because of these characteristics. Keith Moore was Acting Platoon Sergeant for awhile, because I thought he was the best man available. He did not disappoint me, assuming the role with confidence and always taking care of business. We had other buck sergeants who came and went, but Malonson and Moore provided continuously reliable and steady first echelon leadership. These two Squad Leaders were largely responsible for the cohesion and high morale among 2nd Platoon members. I tried not to interfere with what they were doing.

Some guys forged an extra-close friendship and working relationship with one other soldier in the platoon. We had several established point man/slack man teams which probably best illustrate these partnerships, consisting of Keith Moore/Robby Robinson, Bob (Swanee) Swanson/Huynh The Hy and Terry (Curly) Schilling/"Arthur Ambush" Bush. Although they were not a point/slack team, two soldiers (Salvador Sanchez and Arthur Telamentes) were so tightly knit that they were dubbed "Eek and Meek" by the other guys, after the comic strip mice of the 1960s. Sanchez (Eek) usually did all the talking for the pair, while Telamentes (Meek) nodded his head in agreement. It was interesting that these alliances developed without regard for social, racial or even language barriers which might have existed back in The World. Swanee could not speak Vietnamese and Hy knew very little English, but it did not matter in their relationship. Hillbilly Webber told me he was brought up to not associate with black people, so he didn't know why he and Sweetpea Walton became such close friends. Curly Schilling and "Arthur Ambush" were also a white and black pairing. "Arthur Ambush" had been raised in his old Detroit neighborhood as Moses Bush, but he took great pride in his grunt moniker and he often wore an "Ambush" name tape on his jungle shirt. These foxhole buddies were usually close friends with many other guys too, so a lot of additional bonding went on among members of the 2nd Platoon.

Most of the young men in the 2nd Platoon were nice guys. "Doc" Wright, "Bigfoot" Smith, "Swanee" Swanson, "The Mad Fragger" Smith, Harold Weidner, Don Braziel, "Redleg" Speith, "Slue-Foot" Schmidt, "Sweetpea" Walton, Jim Morgan, "Curly" Schilling, "Hillbilly" Webber, "Pancho" Ramirez, "Wooly" Jones, "Big Al" Danis, Sam Stephens, "Arthur Ambush" Bush, "Zip" Onevelo, Rob Thomas and "Krebs" Krebsbach all fit the nice guy description, but so did most of the others. As individuals, each of them was just an average young man trying to get through a difficult situation without getting killed. They came from different ethnic and socio-economic backgrounds. Some of them were smarter than others and they had widely varying personalities. Some had special skills and some did not. But there was nothing really remarkable about any one of them as an individual. Nevertheless, when put together as a combat team they were a formidable and energetic *force*. Few of them really wanted to be combat infantrymen in Vietnam, but they *would* fight to protect each other. These guys deserved a lot of credit for just being there, but they did a lot more than merely show up for the war.

Many high jinks went on in our day laagers and in the rear areas, as might be expected among a group of young men who sometimes needed to interrupt either emotional strain or monotony. In contrast to their grabasstic capers during down time, the clowns among us transformed into serious professional soldiers when it was time to go out on patrol or on some other operation. Everyone always soldiered-up with the rest of the gang whenever the situation required it, but if battle tension threatened to overwhelm us, one of the jokers would crack an absurd jest or engage in some ridiculous antic, to make everyone laugh in spite of the gravity of the situation. This team dynamic was consistent and fascinating. And 30 young men fighting as a team are much more formidable than 30 individuals doing their own thing. It was like belonging to a large and exuberant family, who stuck together despite difficult situations and occasional squabbles.

I heard that E Company's CPT Tobias Macadamia had been transferred to another battalion (no surprise because of his dreadful personality, but unique in my experience) and that he had been wounded. People who remembered his nasty behavior in Echo Company typically commented, "I bet the little SOB was shot by his own troops". On behalf of all the guys in the Four Deuce Platoon and Skippy our mascot, I want to say I hope it hurt like hell. I was in Chu Lai one time and I bumped into my friend 1LT Jerry Brown on the battalion street. Jerry, who was then the Battalion S1/Personnel Officer, told me that he was seriously concerned because Macadamia had really frosted me with the OER (Officer's Efficiency Report) he had written on me after I left E Company. In those days, the rater did not have to show the OER to the rated officer, nor was his signature required. Macadamia, of course, had not shown the OER to me, or sent me a copy. I told Jerry Brown that I didn't care, because I wasn't staying in the Army. In recent years I became curious about this OER and the evaluation written by CPT Guill, which I also had never seen. I filled out the necessary form and sent it to the Army Personnel Records Center in Saint Louis MO, requesting copies of all OERs done on me in Vietnam. No OER copies were returned to me by the APRC. I have my original 201 File, which was sent to me in 1980 by the State Military Department when I got out of the Maryland National Guard. It contains other OERs going back to Fort Hood, but none from Vietnam. I know the OERs existed, so who pulled them from my 201 File? Macadamia condemned *Mister Hyde*, while Guill praised *Doctor Jeckell*, but they apparently did so with equal enthusiasm. Considering the sources, I would be proud to have *both* performance ratings in my military personnel records jacket.

The 2nd Platoon's motto was "Let's go get them Charlies!" Frank Korona told me it was a comment used by CPT Francis Powers, to conclude his OPORD briefing on 12 October 1970, the day he was killed. This motto was supplemented by "Second Platoon! Scunnion!" I did some serious bragging about the exploits of The Famous Second Platoon and so did my soldiers. We were not overly concerned with literal truthfulness in this public relations effort. I'm afraid that guys like The Mad Fragger and The Lifer probably got carried away and told some outrageous lies about the things we did. The other troops got into the spirit of this, in that they would talk about "*The* Second Platoon", even to soldiers from other battalions, although every rifle company in Vietnam had a 2nd Platoon. My guys became so invested in this that they started believing their own crapola, at least to the extent of keeping themselves pumped up. At every opportunity they went out of their way to act superior to the other platoons, probably irritating them to no end. Some of the outsiders probably believed a portion of the propaganda we generated about the notorious 2nd Platoon, or at least they wondered whether some of it might be true. The high morale in 2nd Platoon was maintained by our success, derring-do, pride, bonding and limited friendly casualties. I was not aware of it at the time, but Bob Swanson told me there was a platoon song which the guys sometimes sang among themselves, to the tune of Johnnie Horton's *The Battle of New Orleans*: "In 1971 we took a little trip, along with El Tee Dolan, down the famous Gaza Strip. We took a few LRRPs, and we took a few Cs, and we caught the bloody dinks down by the ocean breeze. We fired our 60s 'till the barrels melted down, but El Tee said to fire another round..." This ditty was probably one of Roger "Hillbilly" Webber's efforts. Roger kept a guitar in the rear and he was an accomplished musician, playing and singing for the guys when we were on stand-down. Paul Malonson's

2nd Squad called themselves "The Bounty Hunters" and had their own patch made up; it was dark purple and featured a hand, holding a severed VC head by the hair. Yeah! Second Platoon, Scunnion! Let's go get them Charlies!

We did not really have a battle cry. The closest thing to that was "CHIEU HOI, MOTHER F-ER!" (or *Chieu hoi, du ma'm!*, the same thing in Vietnamese) which my troops would scream at the enemy during every firefight. As noted previously, *chieu hoi* literally means "open arms", or colloquially, "come over to our side and join us". To hear the guys yelling that, plus the vulgar insult, at Charlie Cong while they were trying their best to kill him, always appealed to my twisted sense of humor.

There was an underlying dark side to our activities in the field. The ongoing environment of continuous violence and fear apparently brought out the worst in a few young men, who did not keep their animosity towards the enemy separated from their general anger and resentment, or whatever bubbled within them below the surface. I don't really know what motivated them, but the outcome was the kind of cruelty and cowardice which had been demonstrated against the villagers in the Song Ve Valley during my first outing with B Company. Another example of this was provided by a squad leader in my platoon, who left almost immediately after I took over. He appeared to be a normal and solid citizen, but after he departed I started hearing rumblings about cruel things he had done. Other soldiers described him as "vicious" or "mean". The most horrific story was that he had dropped a baby down a well and thrown a hand grenade in after it. I heard this from a couple of guys who claimed that they had heard about it, but who supposedly were not witnesses to the act. It became clear that anyone who had actually witnessed the baby's murder was not going to admit it. The stories seemed to have some credibility, because there was no reason to make up such lurid tales about that particular soldier. If they were true, he was obviously a sociopath. But there were other acts of cruelty or bullying which did not seem to have such a tidy explanation. In the Song Ve Valley, we found a litter of puppies, whose mother took off when we appeared, before anyone could shoot her. It was SOP to shoot village dogs in Indian Country, because the dinks used them as an early warning system. The villagers did not seem to resent this too much, because they would usually butcher the dog on the spot. Hamlet dogs seemed to know that we'd shoot them and they would immediately disappear after barking at a GI patrol. One of the guys said that the puppies should be drowned, so I told him to go ahead and do it; I did not hesitate about this, because it was a distasteful thing which was related to mission-accomplishment. A few minutes later, there was some laughter and commotion which drew my attention. The soldier who volunteered to drown the litter was holding the first puppy under water for a period of time and then pulling it out and laughing as the puppy gasped, sputtered and struggled for breath. I have no idea why he thought this was funny and there was just no excuse for that kind of cruelty. I raised hell with the troops who were involved in it and the litter was pardoned. The soldier who did this was not a bad kid or a psychopath, although he was somewhat immature and indifferent to the general plight of the Vietnamese. We were later on a patrol in the 515 Valley and I saw the same soldier pretend to stumble and throw his shoulder into a young mamma-san. He knocked her off a bridge into a wide stream. She had been carrying covered baskets of live ducks on a chogy stick and I got into the water to pull her and the baskets out. The young woman was dripping wet and furious. As I chewed him out, the laughing soldier tried to pass it off as an "accident", apologizing profusely to her, but I saw him do it and it was not an accident. It made no sense to deliberately antagonize the villagers, especially in that pacified area. SSG Wayne Wilson told me that after I went home, he discovered this same soldier and his buddy, holding a Vietnamese teenager by the ankles upside down over a well. They were interrogating him while threatening to drop him. Wayne ordered them to release the boy, who was completely terrorized.

They initially refused, insisting that he was Viet Cong. SSG Wilson believed that they really intended to drop the kid into the well. Both of these soldiers were young (about 20) and they were ruthless in combat. That is not necessarily a bad trait for combat soldiers, but grunts must know how and when to turn off their aggressiveness. This is probably the primary downside of fighting a war with teenage soldiers, who are naturally rebellious, unruly, full of raging hormones and sometimes lacking in judgment. Some of them need a strong leadership hand to keep them on track.

    I had grown up until the age of ten in Sparrows Point, Maryland, which was a "company town" completely owned and operated by the Bethlehem Steel Corporation. That was a pretty tough community in the 1950s and my mother often said that I had to fight my way home from school every day. That was somewhat of an exaggeration, but not much. I earned a reputation and the adults would say, "That Dolan kid really likes to fight", but it wasn't true. I fought only because I preferred getting thrashed to kowtowing to bullies. I probably lost as many fights as I won, but nobody really wins most fistfights anyway. The most important outcome was that, even in encounters with older kids where I got hammered, the bullies never came back for a second dose. From dealing with bullies nonstop in that tough steel town, I learned a few things about fighting. Although I was bigger than many other kids my age, I wasn't especially strong or agile, nor did I have any real boxing skills, but I made up for that through stubbornness and rage. When a fight started, I always let my temper run amok and I refused to give up no matter how badly I was battered. I learned that you have to use all possible means to inflict violence on your opponent. Once you've gained the upper hand, you must keep him on the ground and continue to punish him without mercy. If you don't do that, he is going to get up and he is probably going to hurt you. Those lessons learned on the mean streets of Sparrows Point were equally valid in the mean jungles of Vietnam. Willingness to inflict overwhelming violence on the enemy, along with ruthlessness and indifference to his pain, were not bad traits in a combat infantryman, in fact they were characteristics necessary for survival on the battlefield. But they had to be applied only to our opponents in battle, otherwise we became bullies, and the difference between bullying and terrorism is only one of degree. Aside from deplorably weak leadership, the atrocities committed at My Lai 4 in 1968 were probably attributable to bullying which escalated into terrorism. I believed that it was necessary to fight without remorse or compassion, but that this could be done with integrity.

Sometimes the troops played with the minds of the unsophisticated villagers in humorous ways. Roger Webber, who wore full dentures, would dumbfound the peasants by detaching his false teeth and sticking them out on his tongue, then pulling them back into place and grinning toothily. I also remember an elaborate pantomime put on by two of my soldiers in the Song Ve Valley, which they apparently ad-libbed. We had rounded up the adult villagers and were holding them in the center of the hamlet, where they wouldn't get into any mischief. None of them appeared to speak any English. The two soldiers were fooling around with a Starlight Scope, which made a slight whining noise when it was turned on. They'd turn it on and hold it up to the villagers' ears, so they could hear the sound, then switch it off. One of the mimes held the bulky scope like it was an oversized ray gun and pointed the eyepiece at his buddy, throwing the toggle switch. The other guy screamed, covered his groin with his hands as if the imaginary death ray would make him sterile, and ran away shrieking. Then the guy with the scope pointed it at the cluster of villagers, which resulted in cringing, wailing and general panic. The two soldiers spent the rest of the day guarding the detainees with the Starlight Scope, turning it on and pointing it at them if there was any talking or fidgeting. Abusive? Yeah, but it was pretty funny.

My best individual soldier and in some ways my personal mentor was our Kit Carson Scout, Huynh The Hy. I learned to trust him implicitly. He was older than the rest of us, in his early thirties.

Hy was quiet, cheerful, brave and he had a strong sense of humor. Hy's best friend in 2nd Platoon was Bob "Swanee" Swanson, another quiet and reliable guy. They spent a lot of time together in the bush, looking at pictures in magazines, talking softly with many hand gestures, trying to teach each other English and Vietnamese. When Hy walked "point", Swanee usually covered him as his "slack" man and at night they always slept near each other. They were sitting at a table in the Mess Hall at LZ Liz one day and Hy was listening to a transistor radio. The volume was turned down low, but the radio was playing Vietnamese music, which is clangy and discordant. A soldier from another unit, sitting at another table with some of his buddies, called out in a loud voice, "Hey! Turn off that #!@$% gook music!" Swanee got up and walked over to the soldier, bent down and said something in his ear which no one else could hear. The 2nd Platoon troops who were present braced themselves for a brawl. Swanee went back to Hy's table, sat down and loudly said, "Turn the sound up, Hy, I can't hear the music". Hy apparently understood what Bob Swanson said, because he turned up the volume, a slight smile on his lips and his eyes dancing. The mouthy soldier at the other table turned purple, but there was no brawl.

Swanee was selected as The 11th Brigade Soldier of the Month. He was sent to the rear and they dressed him up in new fatigues and shiny boots, to accompany the Brigade Commander as he performed his duties. But Swanson was an outstanding *grunt*, not a parade ground soldier. He did not enjoy being honored and 1SG Ruby kept putting him on guard duty every night. After several days and nights of almost no sleep, Swanee went AWOL from the Soldier of the Month gig and he returned to 2nd Platoon in the bush. They couldn't really punish the Soldier of the Month for returning to battle without permission, but the Brigade Commander didn't ask for him back either. Swanee was easy going and soft spoken, but he was not a pacifist. He beat the crap out of another soldier, after he saw him slap a crippled and elderly Vietnamese man. CPT Guill asked Swanee, "What happened to _____?" Swanson answered,

The Mad Fragger and Me

"I think a tree fell on him." The CO asked no more questions. After Bob Swanson later became a Squad Leader, he confronted another trooper who initially refused to comply with a legitimate order, but he was not aware that the wayward soldier had been a Golden Gloves boxer. He punched SGT Swanson five or six times, but he was so fast that Swanee couldn't lay a fist on him. The fight ended when SGT Swanson ignored the blows, grabbed the other guy and smashed his head against a rock.

Although the violence and cruelty of combat brought out the worst in some young men, it had the opposite effect on others. For example, SP/5 Thomas E. "Doc" Wright was a clumsy, conscientious, kindhearted and cheerful good-ole-boy from South Carolina, who was a pleasure to have in the platoon as our Combat Medic. Doc carried the heaviest ruck, always loaded down with extra medical supplies, which he used to hold his own MEDCAPs (Medical Civic Action Programs) for civilians out in the boonies. The Battalion Surgeon and the medics in his Aide Station used to do MEDCAPs sometimes on QL 1 with vehicular support, but as far as I know Doc Wright was the only medic to hold them out in the boondocks from medical supplies transported on his back, always with a waterproof cover over his rucksack to protect the contents from the elements. Doc was not very articulate and as a result, he sometimes came across as thickheaded, but he really wasn't. He had graduated from the Army's Medic School at Fort Sam Houston, which was a very tough program academically. Doc knew what he was doing, but he often got his words a little tangled up. He was telling SSG Wayne Wilson and me about some druggies dying in the rear area. They thought they were shooting up smack, but they had actually bought some "sterakine" from a drug dealer. We were trying to figure out what the heck sterakine was and Doc said, "You know, rat poison." He meant strychnine. SSG Wilson joked about Doc's butchery of the Queen's English by calling him "Our Comic Book Medic", but we would not have traded him for Doctor Kildare. I saw Doc Wright gently treating a Vietnamese infant, whose toes were raw and bleeding. I asked him what had happened to the baby's toes and he said rats had chewed the tips off during the night. I don't know how he figured that out, but I'm sure he was right. Everyone in 2nd Platoon *knew* that Doc *would* come for us, no matter what, if we were wounded. He went to each guy (including me) every Monday to distribute the huge orange malaria pills. He always insisted that we swallow the horse pills while he watched and we never had a case of malaria in the 2nd Platoon while Doc Wright was our medic. He always took care of everyone for all other medical and health needs in the same way. He was able to establish himself as our surrogate mother, insistent and fussing with us when necessary, but without ever really irritating anyone because he was so sincere and kind. Doc Wright was probably the most diligent and conscientious soldier I have ever known. I have heard that there is a special place in heaven, reserved only for Army medics and Navy corpsmen who served in combat with grunts. I believe it, because they are a special breed.

B Company also had a Chief Company Medic, SP/5 Bob Thompson, who was a real bird. His signature phrase was "Get back, Loretta" from the Beatles' song lyrics. He turned in his M16 and began carrying a half-dozen M72 Light Antitank Weapons (LAWs), plus a .45 pistol as his personal armament. Whenever our unit got in contact, Doc Thompson would chortle "Get back, Loretta", start popping open his LAWs and shooting them at the dinks. We never had any tanks to shoot at in Quang Ngai or Mo Duc provinces, but M72 LAWs were great for busting bunkers. They were also used to scare the enemy, because they made a deafening blast when they were fired and again when they hit. There was never any doubt about whether or not this weapon went off when you pressed the trigger. What we were doing apparently wasn't adventurous enough for wild medic Doc Thompson and he transferred out to a MEDEVAC/Dust Off unit. He later visited B Company and brought me a brand new Nomex flight suit, already tricked out with my name, rank and CIB. It fit me perfectly and I wore it in the rear area,

The Mad Fragger and Me

because it was loose and comfortable. The flight suit wasn't practical for wearing in the bush, nor could I take it home with me, but I appreciated the gesture of friendship. I still think about Crazy Doc Thompson whenever I hear the Beatles singing *Get Back* on the radio... Get back, Loretta!

"Wendy" and "Jim-Jim" were our two primary Speakeasies, or interpreters. Both boys were around 13 or 14 years old; or maybe 15 or 16. I don't really know, because it was standard practice for Vietnamese male teenagers to lie about their ages, to delay being drafted into the Army of the Republic of Vietnam (ARVN). Jim-Jim and Wendy preferred to go into combat with us, instead of fighting as soldiers in the ARVN forces. Neither of those names was real, of course. They adopted pseudonyms in an effort to avoid retaliation against their families by the Viet Cong and I have no idea what their real names were. They were provided with food, uniforms, field equipment, weapons and ammunition, but they were not paid for their services as interpreters. Our troops did give them some pocket money occasionally, but not much. Jim-Jim was the type of boy who would make any father proud. He was smart, courageous and had a sharp sense of humor. Working with Huynh The Hy, Jim-Jim was extremely helpful in interrogating civilians or detainees. He was a great John Wayne fan, would always be in attendance when any of his movies were shown on LZ Liz and he thought "The Green Berets" was the Duke's best film ever. Jim-Jim was a curious kid and asked a lot of questions about American life and culture, but he did not really believe me when I told him that many U.S. families owned color TVs, and two cars (*"Color TVs? Two cars? Oh bullshit*, El Tee"). When I left Vietnam, I asked SSG Wayne Wilson to try to look out for Jim-Jim. When the 1/20 Infantry stood down permanently, he took Jim-Jim with him to his new unit in the 196th Brigade. They were not initially welcomed, because SSG Wilson's new unit was not accustomed to working with Vietnamese scouts or interpreters. Wayne told them that he and Jim-Jim came as a package deal. They were ultimately accepted, but after awhile Jim-Jim went home on leave and he did not come back. Wayne Wilson later got word that the VC killed him.

One night I went to the helipad next to the TOC at LZ Liz, to watch an open-air movie with the 2nd Platoon guys. Besides a Hollywood film, this was the same night we viewed some Super 8 movies taken by Curly Schilling. Curly carried around an 8mm camera with zoom lens and he had fantastic footage of 2nd Platoon in the bush, most of it shot when we hadn't realized we were on Candid Camera. Curly had several of the small reels spliced together into one big one and the results, especially with the hilarious comments made by B Company troops as it was being shown, were truly entertaining. Curly's favorite subject seemed to be girlie-show dancers, but the films also showed activities in patrol bases, airborne shots from choppers, combat patrols and our guys engaged in various grab-ass antics. Curly was a biker and a hard knot, but a nice guy. These qualities and his dependability made him one of the most highly regarded combat soldiers in 2nd Platoon. He also had creative instincts and an eye for detail. His movies were visually arresting and they could have been used in recruitment ads for the Infantry. One film sequence panned across a green panorama of gorgeous mountain scenery from high ground, then abruptly stopped and zoomed in on a distant jungle clearing. Our outgoing patrol suddenly came in view, prowling through an opening in the jungle. One man after another appeared, then disappeared into the lush foliage, everyone obviously alert, properly disbursed and looking lethal. The effect was chilling, because of the contrast between the peaceful scenery and the heavily armed grunts, obviously looking for a fight. This segment of film inspired a spontaneous demonstration by the 2nd Platoon troops in the audience, who began shouting "Second Platoon! Scunnion!" and "Get them Charlies".

As I was leaving the movie show that night, I encountered my nemesis, Major William Saltz, who called me into the TOC bunker. I had grown a mustache when I was in the 4.2" Mortar Platoon and I kept it for awhile in B Company before shaving it off. My thick red mustache had grown beyond the corners of my mouth into a modest handlebar and the acting CO noticed it. Major Saltz told me that my mustache was not within Army regulations and he expected his junior officers to set a proper example for the troops. Several 2nd Platoon soldiers saw me standing stiffly in front of him, obviously getting my butt chewed, although they were not close enough to hear what was being said. The guys were crowded into the narrow TOC entrance and one of them, Jim Morgan, called out "Hey Tom! How's it going? We'll see you back on the bunker line, Tom"... then they walked away, laughing. I could feel my face heating up, but Major Saltz gave me an odd look which clearly communicated that he did not realize the troops were pulling his leg and busting my chops. I'd already had that prior collision with Major Saltz, when I pretended not to hear his radioed order to "sweep" in darkness, pouring rain and zero visibility. My excessive mustache and the über-familiarity of my troops apparently verified his already low opinion of me, because Saltz later commented to CPT Guill that I was a lousy line officer. (*Golly-boogers, Major! What do you expect from a '90 Day Wonder' Shanty Irishman?!*) This was the only time any of my soldiers had the nerve to directly address me by my first name. The gangsters were still snickering among themselves when I got back to the bunker line. I could see the humor in the prank even though I was the butt of the joke, so I laughed with them. (Jim Morgan was a National Guardsman, the only "NG" I encountered in Vietnam. He presumably had been placed on active duty for missing too many unit drills. He was more nervous than most troopers about going home in one piece, but he always did his duty.)

We had an excellent Platoon RTO (Radio-Telephone Operator) named Bob Scates, who was highly intelligent and very reliable. Those were the qualities everyone wanted in an RTO, so CPT Guill reassigned Scates to the Company CP Group when one of his RTOs went home. This was a critical slot and the loss of Bob Scates left a major void in the 2nd Platoon, which we could not immediately fill.

We tried a couple of guys, but they did not work out. I discussed the problem with SSG Wilson. We needed somebody with brains and initiative, who would remain calm when the Shinola hit the fan. Our Platoon RTO also needed to be physically strong enough to carry the radio and accessories, plus his personal gear. Sergeant Wilson said that we had a newbie who looked good for the RTO job and he gave me his name. We were on LZ Liz at the time, so I walked down to the bunker he was assigned to and asked for Richard Smith. PFC Smith came out of the bunker wearing a bushy Afro haircut, a non-regulation black mesh tee shirt and a braided "black power" bracelet. He was obviously cultivating a tough "affect", but he was articulate and muscular. After a brief conversation, I concluded that PFC Smith was mature and intelligent. I bluntly described the qualities I was looking for in an RTO. He seemed wary of the job offer, apparently because he didn't know a lot about RTO procedure. But I told him we would train him and he finally said he would give it a try. He turned out to be a quick study, steady under fire, cheerful and dependable. Richard Smith was from California and everyone called him "Bigfoot", but to SSG Wilson and me he was "Smitty". He became my constant companion and my right hand man, day and night, so we eventually became joined at the hip. Most of us were Rock 'N Roll Soldiers in those days and Smitty also fulfilled my music needs. He carried a portable tape deck and a good supply of Motown cassettes. I often asked him to play *Respect*, *Land of a Thousand Dances* and *What'd I Say?* ... Aretha Franklin, Wilson Pickett and Ray Charles were my favorite R&B artists.

    The Platoon CP Group consisted of Wayne Wilson, Bigfoot Smith, Doc Wright, Steve Speith and me. SGT Steve Speith was our Artillery Recon Sergeant, so he was called "Redleg" by everyone. This reflected a throwback Army tradition, because Union artillerymen wore red leggings during the Civil War. SGT Speith was the closest thing we had to a forward observer. He had a few cannon-cocker duties such as plotting Delta Tangos and advising me on available munitions/fuses. I usually called in contact fire missions myself, but he was there to back me up. Redleg basically functioned as an artillery consultant, extra rifleman and assistant Platoon RTO. He was also our platoon's barber, because he had been a ladies' hair stylist in civilian life. This civilian occupation might have inspired some ball-busting, but there was not much of that because everyone preferred to ask Steve for a haircut, instead of going to the battalion barber on LZ Liz. He did a much better job, expertly styling anyone's hair with only a comb and a pair of barber's scissors which he carried in his rucksack. Redleg snored terribly, so loudly that I can't find words to adequately describe what it sounded like. This was a serious problem because his snoring could give away our NDP location. SSG Wilson and I quickly broke him of that. We made him sleep between us at night and every time he started to snore, one of us woke him up, as rudely and abruptly as possible. His choices were either to learn to sleep without snoring, or to not sleep at all. Redleg was soon sleeping as quietly as a mouse.

The Mad Fragger was a fixture in 2nd Platoon, but I haven't explained how he got his alias. Gary Smith was cheerful, outgoing and likeable, but he was also somewhat anxious and eccentric. He had a vivid imagination, especially when he was alone in the dark. From the beginning of his tour, the other guys noticed that Gary habitually carried lots of M26 hand-frags in his pockets and rucksack, many more than anyone else. At the first hint of trouble, he would always start pulling pins and slinging grenades at the enemy, and he had a pretty good arm. In the middle of one dark night not long after he joined 2nd Platoon, he was guarding one of the platoon's NDP positions, alone. He suddenly went hot with all weapons on the guard position, blowing the Claymores, throwing frags, sending up illumination flares and firing the M60 machine gun at cyclic rate. By the time Platoon Leader Frank Korona scrambled to the guard position, Gary was frantic, yelling that a "monster" had loomed up out of the dark and tried to "get" him... "It was as big as a house and it was making weird noises, like a wild man or an orangutan! It was screaming 'Awrghh! Awrghh! Awrghh!' And the bullets were bouncing off its chest!" The position had been given away, so the platoon had to pack up in the dark and move to another NDP. Everyone was angry at Gary Smith for awhile, but they also wondered about his sanity. 1LT Korona started calling him "The Mad Fragger" and soon everyone was doing it. And of course, "The Night The Mad Fragger Fired Up the Orangutan" became *the* favorite war story in the annals of The Famous 2nd Platoon.

The Mad Fragger loved to talk to people, and to brag outrageously about the real or imaginary exploits of *The* 2nd Platoon. Despite his somewhat nervous nature, he did not lack courage and he would always come through in a crisis. It has been said that courageous men are not fearless, rather they are frightened men who are able to overcome their fears and perform brave acts. Gary Smith personified that definition of a courageous man. I've already described the events leading to his formal decoration for valor, but there were other minor incidents which also demonstrated his pluck. As a counterpoint to The Mad Fragger's cheery disposition, he had a somewhat volatile temper, which occasionally boiled over. To the amusement of the other 2nd Platoon guys who were sent with him on a special MEDCAP security detail, he lost his temper with an ARVN lieutenant in a hamlet on QL 1. The Mad Fragger had been flirting with a pretty Vietnamese girl, making the *Ti Hui* jealous. The ARVN lieutenant began yelling in Vietnamese, posturing aggressively in martial arts stances, and throwing karate kicks at The Mad Fragger. Our hero bravely waded through the flurry of kicks and beat the snot out of him. The Fragger was still fuming about being attacked by an ARVN officer when he returned from the MEDCAP detail.

One of The Mad Fragger's endearing qualities was that he carried an M203 grenade launcher, which he could shoot very accurately and with blinding speed. The guys who carried M203s occasionally challenged each other to shooting contests, which was good practice, but after awhile Gary Smith's superior skills stifled all such competition. The Mad Fragger's hands were a blur when he

The Mad Fragger and Me

shot his thumper and he would usually have several rounds in the air before the first one hit the ground, which added appreciably to the platoon's firepower. It was sometimes a challenge for our Platoon Sergeant to keep him supplied with enough M26 frags and 40mm HE rounds.

The other guys learned by experience to exercise caution, if they relieved The Mad Fragger on a guard position at night. A half dozen or more frags were always placed on the front of each guard position, with the Claymore clackers and hand-poppers. When it was his turn on guard duty, The Mad Fragger would flip all the clacker safety bails to the "off" position and reverse the caps on the parachute flares so they were ready to go. Then he'd remove all the wire jungle clips and straighten the pull-pins on the frags, carefully lining up the hand grenades within easy reach. If the next guy on guard picked up a frag and squeezed the safety spoon, the straightened pin would fall out from gravity and the weight of the pull ring. This happened to Bob Swanson one night and he couldn't find the pin by feeling around in the dark for it, to put it back in the grenade. He could not light a match or use a flashlight, so Swanee had to hold the safety handle against the side of the frag and wait for daylight to find the pin. It was useless to try to discourage The Mad Fragger from taking off the safety clips and straightening the grenades' pull-pins, because he *knew* he might have to repel the hordes of Viet Cong (and orangutans) which were lurking out there in the dark.

The troops hated to take the enormous orange weekly malaria pill, because it gave most of them the "trots", which was why Doc Wright always insisted that they swallow it while he watched. One of our fine young soldiers, who shall remain nameless, had taken his Monday morning pill and soon felt the urgent call of nature, so he walked off into the bushes outside our day laager, equipped with an entrenching tool and a packet of toilet paper. While he was having an especially severe attack of Ho Chi Minh's Revenge, behind him in the patrol base The Mad Fragger decided to practice his "fast draw" with his .45 pistol. When the shooting started, the other guy came shuffling rapidly into the perimeter in a panic, with his now soiled trousers still around his ankles. This resulted in a lot of laughing, hooting and catcalling. The 2nd Platoon may have been a Band of Brothers, but this does not mean that any one brother's embarrassment ever went unrecognized or unappreciated by his siblings. Doc Wright helped the unfortunate soldier clean up from his accident. I approached The Mad Fragger without saying a word, my hand in front of me, palm up, making a "Gimme" gesture with my fingers. The Mad Fragger handed me his pistol and then went to find something else to do.

One dark night, The Mad Fragger excitedly reported on the radio that he spotted an NVA tank moving towards us. (He apparently saw a palm tree swaying in the wind.)The Mad Fragger also woke up the whole platoon, but we were accustomed to him doing that kind of thing. He did not start shooting, perhaps having learned his lesson from the grief he took after the orangutan incident. But on LZ Liz, the TOC Night Duty Officer had monitored his radio transmission, so the Battalion Commander was awakened. Panic ensued on the firebase, because they thought an NVA Armor Regiment was attacking into Quang Ngai Province. I don't know whether the TOC Commandos saw the humor in the situation when the mistake was explained, but this incident added to The Mad Fragger's cachet within 2nd Platoon.

The Mad Fragger sometimes wore spectacles, which magnified his habit of blinking his eyes in an owlish way. He was of moderate height, slim and gangly. Except for his wide shoulders, his general appearance did not suggest that he was an athlete, but he had been a star player on his high school's basketball team back in Quincy, Illinois. His buddies, Swanee Swanson and Hillbilly Webber, were also skilled basketball players and they sometimes amused themselves by hustling unsuspecting black soldiers in rear area pick-up games. The Mad Fragger was "Smith" in my notebook roster, but I was in the 2nd Platoon for quite awhile before I learned his first

The Mad Fragger and Me

name. He invariably introduced himself by saying, "I'm The Mad Fragger" and everyone *always* called him that. Most grunt nicknames were apt for the person, or had a humorous connotation, but Gary Smith's moniker was a classic. He had a wry sense of humor and he was a practical joker, so I occasionally wondered if some of his antics were conjured up or exaggerated for our entertainment. He kept us laughing most of the time and he always laughed with us, even at himself. Despite his mild appearance and his sometimes peculiar behavior, he was a really good combat soldier.

Like The Fragger, our permanent M60 gunners, Arturo "Pancho" Ramirez and Mike "Wooly" Jones were also highly skillful with their weapons. Ramirez and Jones were like Mutt and Jeff iterations of the ideal machine gunner. Pancho was the smallest soldier in 2nd Platoon, but he carried the biggest weapon, an M60 machine gun, which weighed 23 pounds unloaded. Wooly was a strapping redhead from Iowa who *looked* like a 60 Gunner and he always carried a cool Bowie fighting knife, which had been made by his father aboard a U.S. Navy ship during WW II. The M60, or "Pig", was our go-to weapon whenever serious firepower was needed, such as to suppress the VC/NVA in a firefight. The gunner in the leading squad automatically moved forward with his Pig as soon as we got in contact, to knock back the opposition. There were two problems with the M60. One was its prodigious appetite, combined with the serious weight of its 7.62mm linked ammo. Squad Leaders always assigned other soldiers to carry extra ammo for the Pigs, but Pancho and Wooly managed to carry large amounts of it themselves. The second problem with the M60 was that it was somewhat temperamental. Some ex-GIs will tell you that the M60 machine gun was a heavy piece of junk which constantly jammed or broke down. Other veterans will sing its praises as one of the greatest squad machine guns ever made. The truth is that the Pig was a reliable and formidable weapon, but only if it was tended by a competent gunner. If it was carefully maintained and properly lubricated by someone who really knew what he was doing, the M60 would always work when it was supposed to work. Pancho and Mike were obsessive-compulsive experts who babied their weapons. I don't remember either of those guns ever jamming in a firefight. The M60 was theoretically a crew served weapon, unless it was attached to a pintle mount, such as in the doorway of a helicopter, to help offset its serious weight. But we never really considered the M60 to be crew served, because our 60 Gunners could always manage their weapons without any help. We never carried extra barrels because of their weight, preferring to hump more 7.62mm ammo instead. Pancho and Mike would shoot their M60s until the barrels glowed red and pour canteens of water over them to keep them in action. If a barrel got burned out, the hell with it, we'd just order a new one on the next resupply list.

My first encounter with Bob Mace occurred during my first mission with 2nd Platoon. PFC Mace turned out semi-naked for his squad's daily patrol. He was wearing only a brightly colored hippy headband, olive drab boxer shorts and jungle boots. I wondered why he bothered to wear the skivvies, because the effect would have been more dramatic without them, like an ancient Celtic warrior going into battle stark naked to terrorize his enemies. I advised Mace that he could not go out on patrol in his underwear. He tried arguing, "This is how we *always* do it in The 'Nam". I told him that there was a New Rule: On patrol, everyone is required to wear a shirt of some kind, jungle fatigue pants, boots and headgear, either a bush hat or a bandanna, all of which had to be subdued in color. I cited the need to camouflage Mace's white skin as explanation for The New Rule. He did put on some clothes, with a moderate amount of bitching, to save face with his Homies. One of my black soldiers offered his opinion that African-Americans should be exempt from The New Rule, because their skin color provided "natural camouflage". I said sweaty black guys also made good targets and there were no exceptions. On another occasion, PFC Mace was scheduled to go back to LZ Liz on the resupply helicopter for some reason. Unknown to us until the chopper landed, the Battalion S3/Operations Officer, CPT Arthur Parker, was also using the resupply bird to fulfill some tactical observation need. Parker was a stern, by-the-book taskmaster, which the troops mocked by always calling him "Captain America". PFC Mace was carrying an M203 grenade launcher that day. As he got on the resupply chopper with Captain America and it lifted off, one of the other guys said, "Hey El Tee, watch what Mace is going to do". As the bird gained altitude and banked, Mace launched three or four 40mm tear gas grenades into a large ville, about 300 meters away from our day laager. Dozens of Vietnamese peasants came scurrying out of the hamlet, coughing, choking, rubbing their eyes and running into each other, temporarily blinded by the CS gas. Helicopter always crews freaked out if grunts fired their weapons from choppers, even going into hot LZs. Bob Mace demonstrated an amazing level of loopiness when he fired that volley of CS gas grenades into a ville, from a chopper, in the presence of the grim and straight-laced CPT Parker. I howled with laughter along with the rest of 2nd Platoon, but that stunt got Mace busted. He was too much of a free spirit to prosper within The OD Machine.

One of my troopers sometimes behaved so strangely that I wondered if he was suffering from a serious mental illness. His real name is not important to this story, so I'll call him Brad Owens. During the 12 October 1970 battle at the old French concrete bunker complex, at the height of the raging firefight, everyone was hugging the ground in fear. Brad Owens casually strolled up to 1LT Frank Korona with his weapon tucked under his arm like he was out rabbit hunting and he said, "Hey El Tee, I think it's time to fall back", ignoring the storm of flying bullets. On another occasion, he demonstrated his craziness, while some 2nd Platoon soldiers were discussing the arming distance of 40mm HE grenades. Those grenades would supposedly not explode until they traveled a specific distance after being fired from a grenade launcher, but no one trusted that theory very much. Brad Owens told the other guys that an HE grenade had to travel 20 meters before it was armed and he immediately fired a 40mm round from his M203 into the ground in the middle of the group. Fortunately it did not explode and he commented, "See, I told you so" and he walked away. I once saw Owens shadowboxing with unseen demons in a hyperactive pantomime. I tried to talk with him, but he was incoherent and appeared to be hallucinating. He seemed a bit strange all the time, always marching to the beat of a different drummer, but he was never uncooperative. There were rumors that he was using a French "speed" drug called Obisital, but we never caught him with dope. Whenever Owens entered one of his manic phases, he was sent to the rear area for evaluation, but he always reported for field duty within a few days. I don't know whether the medical people ever gave him a thorough psychiatric evaluation. It might seem that having to cope with a possibly psychotic soldier was a challenge I didn't really need on top of everything else I was dealing with, but he was not really a problem. When Owens was not impaired by his psychosis (or drugs?) he was a good soldier, which was most of the time. None of the other guys ever complained about him, because he didn't bother anyone, he knew no fear and he would always hang tough in a firefight. He may have been an odd duck, but he was one of *us*. If he was schizophrenic, maybe he was really no more insane than the rest of us, or the situation we were all in.

We got a replacement I will call Ralph Hall (not his real name) and he came with a rumor that he was a druggie, although we never actually caught him using dope in the bush. The druggie reputation did not sit well with the other guys in the platoon. It became worse after SSG Wilson had to stop SGT Malonson from killing him, when he found Hall asleep on a guard position in the middle of the night. There are no secrets about events like that within a rifle platoon. We knew there was something going on with Hall because of that incident, and because he seemed to be sick all the time in the field. The result was that PFC Hall was not welcomed with open arms, although most other newbies usually were. The Mad Fragger

The Mad Fragger and Me

started picking at Hall on a regular basis, calling him a druggie and a slacker. Hall responded that The Mad Fragger was a racist. I don't know whether or not that was really part of the problem, but there was that kind of animosity between them. One day, they got into a loud confrontation, pushing and shoving each other, in a patrol base in the Dragon Valley. I stopped the NCOs when they moved in to break it up. I told Hall and The Fragger to go ahead and beat the hell out of each other. They were evenly matched, but they seemed surprised and disappointed that I was going to let them fight. They did more posturing and threatening than actual damage to each other, but we did break it up when they both grabbed weapons, a machete and an E-tool. They were never friends after that, but there were no more arguments or fights. Peer pressure sometimes worked wonders in solving personnel problems. Doc Wright caught PFC Hall using heroin in a rear area and threatened to turn him in, unless he did it himself. Hall did turn himself in, after Doc and Bigfoot Smith talked to him, making it clear that his drug use was not going to be tolerated. They were also concerned about salvaging him, which resulted in his referral to a substance abuse program, but he did not return to 2nd Platoon afterwards. Doc later received a note from Hall, thanking him for his intervention. I hope that Hall completed the detox program and got straightened out. He was an affable guy and he probably had a lot of potential. I try to remember that grunts who used drugs were really just kids who suddenly found themselves among strangers in a very frightening environment, but chemical means for coping with that were cheap and plentiful. However there were plenty of other guys who may have been equally scared by the crazy things we were doing, who had too much character to turn to drugs.

Two other soldiers were known pot heads. One of them claimed to be a cowboy. He always tried to project a cool "seasoned warrior" affect, but he was just a cocky goldbricker. I'll call him Pecos Bill, after another wholly imaginary cowboy hero. Pecos Bill was not with me very long and I don't recall where he went. He constantly invented excuses to go to the rear, so he may have finagled a job there, or a medical profile, to get out of the bush. A notation in an old field notebook indicates that Pecos Bill temporarily returned and was attached to 2nd Platoon on Nui Vong/Hill 103 at the end of my tour. The note says he was being given a Field Grade Article 15, but I don't remember what he did to provoke the disciplinary action, or whether I brought the charges against him. Pecos Bill's best buddy was SP/4 Orville Oddball, a counterculture wannabe. Oddball fancied himself as a hippy, and he played that part to the hilt, replete with longish blond hair, tinted granny glasses, peace tokens, colorful headband and "Heeey man" dialect. Pecos Bill and Oddball were self-absorbed and indifferent to the welfare of their comrades. As far as I know they did not smoke grass in the bush because we never caught them, but they sometimes disappeared in a rear area and turned up later, a little too mellow. One day, Oddball approached me in a day laager and he thrust his M16 into my hands. I asked, "What's this for?" and he responded, "I'm claiming CO status." I really didn't know what he was talking about and I said "What does that mean? Commanding Officer?" Oddball answered, "Nooo, man...I'm a Conscientious Objector, so I have to go back to the rear on backhaul, man." I told him I would send his rifle back to the rear and he could claim to be a conscientious objector, but he would remain in the bush while his application was being processed. He was shocked and he said, "Heeey man, you can't keep me out here without a weapon", so I responded "Well here, take your rifle then, make up your mind goddamn it." We went around and around on this, until he decided to stay in the bush *with* his rifle. Not long after that we were preparing to leave LZ Liz to return to the bush and Oddball's squad leader told me he was refusing to carry the squad radio as instructed. With the squad leader as a witness, I gave Oddball another direct order to carry the radio, then asked if he understood it was a direct/lawful order and if he was aware of the consequences for refusing to comply; this rigmarole was necessary to make formal charges stick. Court martial charges were filed against him for insubordination and Oddball was kicked out of B Company. They made him the full time LZ Liz "Shit Burner" while the charges were pending, which was the lowest of low jobs. The other 2nd Platoon guys laughed at him because of this, but Oddball didn't care, because he thought he was "getting over" on the Army. He ended up with a Field Grade (Battalion Commander's level) Article 15 punishment in lieu of court martial, a bust in rank and pay grade. This was just a slap on the wrist for refusing a direct order in a combat zone, but at least I got rid of him. He was still burning out latrine drums the last time I saw him, a job for which he was well-suited. Oddball did not have the backbone or character necessary to be a true member of The Famous 2nd Platoon.

There was a common element with soldiers who were suspected of using drugs, in that their fellow soldiers did not condone their drug use. A few 2nd Platoon members may have had casual attitudes about what other soldiers chose to do when everyone was partying in a rear area, but the druggies knew that no seasoned infantryman would tolerate their use of dope in the bush. In view of the magnitude of the drug problem within the Army, the size of our platoon and the high turnover rate from troop rotations, four or five soldiers who might have been druggies seems like a relatively small number.

Bravo Company humped in from The 515 Valley after one mission and we entered the west side of LZ Liz at the Four Deuce area. Dink, my former pet, came charging at us in a fierce display of aggression. I pulled my bush hat down to conceal my face and lurched directly at her, roaring and doing my best impression of Frankenstein's monster. She had her mouth around my lower leg and was starting to bear down, when she suddenly realized who she was biting. Then she let go, whining and wagging all over the place, apologizing profusely in dog language. She had shifted her affection pretty well to SSG Willard and she stayed with him, instead of following me to the bunker line. Later in my tour however, SSG

Willard told me that Dink was dead. She had bitten the Battalion Sergeant Major when he'd visited the Four Deuce area, and he'd had her shot. I had mixed feelings about that, because I understood why a vicious dog would not be tolerated on the firebase, but I also thought that our Sergeant Major was a jerk for other reasons. Apparently Dink thought so too. Mark Twain once commented that if there were no dogs in heaven, he didn't want to go there. I agree and I hope to see Dink wherever I go after this life.

The 11th Brigade's 59th Infantry (Scout Dog) Platoon had one war dog which dropped in his tracks and played dead whenever his handler casually inquired, "Hey Buster, would you rather be a Lifer or a dead dog?" The handler usually asked this question when there were brass hats around. I thought that scout dogs were an underutilized resource and it made sense to use them on "point", especially in dense jungle, so I regularly requested one. There were two additional types of war dog teams available to us, which were the mine/wire dogs and tracking dogs. A unit requested a mine/wire dog if it started to encounter booby traps in an area. Tracker teams were used to follow blood trails. The tracking dog was usually an affable Labrador retriever, because Labs have excellent noses and they will track silently, unlike hounds. A tracker team also included a scout dog (usually a German Shepherd) and second handler, plus a visual tracker, either American or Vietnamese, a total of three men and two dogs.

Scout dogs usually walked "point" with their handlers and were trained to "alert" silently when they smelled/sensed the enemy's presence, such as in an ambush. My favorite scout dog from the 59th Scout Dog Platoon was named Blitz, but his heart and soul belonged to Craig Valashek, his gutsy young handler. Craig told me that they tried to cross-train the scout dogs to detect trip wires and booby traps, but they were usually good at only one task. One problem with using dogs in the bush was that they did not tolerate the tropical heat very well. A platoon leader who was aware of that could slow down his patrols to compensate, the handlers always carried extra water for their dogs and it wasn't really a big problem. A few of the dog handlers didn't like to stay in the bush over night, so they would claim that their dogs were sick, or they forgot to bring dog food, or invent some other excuse, in order to go in on backhaul. I had to move our mountain NDP in the middle of one very dark night, because a handler could not control his dog, which began barking and growling until he was muzzled. Blitz was well behaved and Craig Valashek was conscientious, so we never had any such problems with them. I specifically asked for Valashek and Blitz whenever I requested a scout dog team, but they were not always available. Blitz was a handsome young black and tan German Shepherd. Unlike many war dogs, his gleeful and friendly personality had not been altered by military discipline. When we were in a day laager, Blitz was off duty and we could throw sticks for him to retrieve and pet or play around with him, but it was clear that he worshipped Craig Valashek, whereas the rest of us were just temporary playmates. Blitz LOVED to ride on helicopters and he would start cutting all sorts of wild capers whenever anyone yelled "Pop smoke", because he knew it meant a chopper was inbound.

The war dogs usually became devoted to their GI handlers and many of them were aggressive breeds. American units occasionally had to shoot a war dog if the handler was wounded, because the dog refused to let a medic come near his master to render aid. A sore spot with the dog handlers, who naturally became attached to their dogs like young men do, was that the war dogs were in Vietnam for the duration of their lives. This was supposedly because of a tropical canine disease called "Red Tongue" which the military allegedly did not want to bring back to the United States with the dogs. But the real problem was that the U.S. Army considered war dogs to be equipment and lobbying by GI Dog Handlers to change this policy fell on deaf ears. The more aggressive war dogs were euthanized when the United States pulled out of Vietnam in 1973. All other K-9 veterans were turned over to the South Vietnamese Army as surplus military equipment and left behind. These were disgraceful acts of treachery by the U.S. Army, in my opinion. The feckless generals who made these decisions apparently were not aware of the high esteem these dogs had earned from their human comrades. Because of cultural differences, the Vietnamese did not have the same affection for dogs as Americans did, so it is doubtful that any war dogs survived when the NVA overran South Vietnam in 1975.

Blitz was killed in action on 31 May 71. CPT Guill told me that Valashek and Blitz were working with another 11th LIB unit and Blitz was severely wounded when he tripped a booby trap. Blitz wasn't much good with mines/trip wires, as Craig had said. Blitz was apparently working off-leash, because SP/4 Valashek was not hurt. The unit they were working with called a dust-off chopper for Blitz. A veterinarian was not available, so Blitz was taken to an evac hospital, probably the 91st, where a regular physician/surgeon tried to save him. Craig Valashek was outside the surgical suite waiting for the outcome and the doctor came out and said "I'm sorry, but your dog died on the operating table". Craig's eyes filled with tears and a female Registered Nurse, an officer, said "Why are you crying? It was *just* a dog". SP/4 Valashek responded appropriately to this stupid comment, using colorful grunt language. As a result, the nurse filed charges against him for insubordination. When CPT Guill told me this story, I commented that we couldn't let SP/4 Valashek be punished for saying the same things we would have said to the bitch. CPT Guill said he had already talked to Craig's CO about it and the problem was being taken care of. Considering how the surviving war dogs were abandoned in 1973, I'm not sorry that Blitz was killed in action. At least he died doing what he was supposed to do, trading his life for the lives of combat infantrymen. Blitz was born a dog, but he died a soldier.

Chapter 11:

PEANUT BUTTER FRAGS

This narrative would not be complete without some attempt to describe what it was like to live and operate in the boondocks. The equipment and the tactics we used may be of some interest to the reader. Military operational practices or decisions occasionally impacted us in unexpected ways. Amusing incidents sometimes occurred, or practical jokes were played. I don't know how to describe life in the bush, except through a loosely connected series of thumbnail essays, vignettes and anecdotes. *Quang Ngai Tales*, if you will, with apologies to Geoffrey Chaucer. Please bear with me on this episodic journey. I will try to serve it up in a lively fashion.

Most of our days and nights were uneventful and tedious. Our diet was bland too. We became so tired of eating canned C rations that we tended to skip or minimize meals, but if resupply flights were delayed by weather or other circumstances, we sometimes had to subsist on *really* short rations. All of us were thin from the skimpy diet and constant exercise. We were on duty around the clock and we got real time off only when we went on Stand-Down, which occurred at three month intervals. Biweekly rotations to LZ Liz for perimeter security could not be considered as breaks from combat, because we were tasked with night ambushes, daylight patrols into the surrounding area and bunker guard duty. We were also burdened with KP and other fatigue details while at LZ Liz. We were actually in combat continuously for months, unlike soldiers in most prior wars. The tropical heat and humidity were oppressive and unrelenting. It was normal to feel clammy, damp or wet, because we sweated constantly in the steamy climate and regularly waded through flooded paddies or streams. We were always exposed to the elements. Jungle rot, boils or infected sores were common skin maladies. We often slept in rain and mud, or on rocky and uneven ground, always under siege all night by swarms of bloodthirsty mosquitoes. We were usually tired, footsore and achy, from humping through the paddies, or up and down mountains, with our heavy rucksacks. Keeping our bodies reasonably clean required considerable effort and we wore the same rank clothes 24/7, for two weeks at a time. Our funky jungle fatigues became faded, frayed and ragged, even while we wore them. Body odor was not a problem, because we all smelled equally rank. We looked like a gang of homeless, gaunt and dirty tramps, who had been conscripted and equipped by a Banana-republic army. Concurrent with our primitive existence in the hostile environment, there was always underlying tension because of the constant threat of booby traps and imminent enemy contact. Our only communication with loved ones at home was through APO/USPS mail. In that kind of situation, it might be expected that morale would suffer, but it never did. When soldiers are continually exposed to danger and mayhem, life itself becomes increasingly precious, so the joy of living and the value of friendships also increase exponentially. Simple group pleasures, such as unexpectedly finding a clean mountain swimming hole, or going with our whole gang to a second-rate floor show in a rear area, therefore became sources of indescribable glee. These circumstances resulted in a level of bonding and a sense of brotherhood which are difficult to describe. The grunts in my platoon were always uncomfortable and usually somewhat stressed, but most of them remained cheerful and optimistic in spite of that. Even more amazing, most of us were *proud* of the difficult, dangerous and thankless jobs we were doing.

During field operations, we roamed around and looked for signs of the enemy, mostly by patrolling. Active patrolling also discouraged the enemy from sneaking in to attack our patrol bases to some extent, although that did occur occasionally. Children regularly brought us unexploded ordinance or munitions, which we purchased with C Rations. We often picked up detainees and sent them to the rear for questioning by Vietnamese authorities. We sometimes found enemy booby traps, bunkers, tunnels, pieces of equipment, food caches and so forth. But none of that was very interesting. Every once in awhile, the poop would hit the fan and we'd be caught up in violence, excitement and chaos, as described in earlier chapters. The tedium was occasionally broken by minor enemy contacts which were not recorded in the S2/S3 journal. I remember once spotting a group of enemy soldiers moving together in tactical formation, but too far away to engage them. We also got sniped at occasionally, but those VC/NVA snipers were not very good shots and these events became routine. If we could tell where the shot(s) came from, we dealt with a sniper by calling in artillery behind him and then dropping it incrementally, to walk the explosions into his position. I was always amused by the discomfiture this tactic was probably creating for the little beggar. It was done to discourage sniping and to trigger possible booby traps, but it was also like saying, "So you want to shoot at us with your dinky little rifle? Look what I'm going to shoot back at you with."

There were many hazards in the bush, but not all of them were the result of enemy actions. Friendly-fire incidents were an ongoing source of potential disaster. Accidents occurred regularly, from the careless operation of vehicles, mishaps with aircraft, negligent handling of weapons or explosives and the use of unfamiliar equipment. Some accidental casualties were attributable to the 12 month rotational system, which always assured the presence of a certain percentage of inexperienced troops, who could not always be protected from their own foibles. A newbie battalion commander in another unit lost his life when visiting one of his companies in the bush, because he exited his hovering helicopter on the side of a mountain and ran *uphill* into the main rotor blades. Despite constant cautions to only cross in front of a chopper to get to the other side, a soldier occasionally tried to go around the back and ran smack into a tail rotor, which was always messy and lethal. A poncho which someone forgot to secure in a day laager could bring down a resupply chopper on top of a platoon, if it blew up into the rotor blades. GIs were killed while cleaning "unloaded" weapons, or because they were horsing around with them. The monsoon season in 1970 was especially hazardous, because of a secret military attempt to manipulate the weather by "salting" the clouds as a strategic measure. The cloud-salters apparently forgot that there were grunts living in the boonies, so this weather manipulation experiment resulted in widespread flash flooding and friendly drowning incidents in 1970. Our battalion experienced several emergencies and the loss of weapons and radios because of the unexpectedly severe 1970 monsoons. Frank Korona commandeered two sampans to rescue stranded B Company troops from rising flood waters on The Gaza Strip, in a fly-by-the-seat-of-his-pants operation. Another problem was exotic tropical diseases, most commonly malaria. We had been inoculated against typhus, bubonic plague, yellow fever, diphtheria and cholera, but there was no inoculation shot for malaria. In the rear areas, they sprayed to kill mosquitoes and soldiers slept under mosquito nets, but that did not occur in the bush. The prescribed malaria prophylaxis was weekly (giant orange) and daily (tiny white) pills, both of which had to be taken to prevent the two types of malaria. Drinking untreated water could also kill you. Simple infections could quickly become serious medical problems in the jungle; medics were kept pretty busy tending to blisters, lancing boils and disinfecting small cuts or abrasions. Tigers and poisonous snakes were always prowling or slithering around in the jungle. On a lighter note, there was a persistent rumor about "The Black Clap", a supposedly incurable venereal disease. The horrific symptoms varied according to who was telling the story, but they often involved certain body parts turning black and falling off. According to the rumor, any GI who came down with The Black Clap would be listed as Missing in Action and permanently quarantined in a medical facility similar to a leper colony, on a remote S/E Asian island, for the rest of his natural life. Anyway, it could be pretty dangerous out there, even without The Black Clap and Charlie Cong.

The Mad Fragger and Me

Our Areas of Operation (AOs) generally included the 515 Valley, Dragon Valley/VC Highway, the Song Ve Valley and the mountains adjacent to those areas, in Mo Duc and Quang Ngai Provinces. Our battalion had operated extensively in the Gaza Strip before I joined B Company, but that AO was dropped in 1971.The Song Ve Valley was a very hostile area and communication was uncertain there, because the mountains sometimes blocked our FM radio transmissions. There were no occupied hamlets in Dragon Valley, which was the closest thing we had to a free fire zone in the lowlands. None of our areas were formally designated as free fire zones, but all grunts knew there were no civilians in Dragon Valley or the mountains, so we fired-up anything that moved in those locations. Most valley areas were relatively flat, but they sometimes had low rolling hills. Valley areas contained active or abandoned rice paddies, broken by hedgerows and clumps of trees.

The forested parts of the mountains were probably the most treacherous areas for us, because they were infested with NVA and there were lots of places for them to hide. The jungle always seemed ominous because of its vastness, coupled with relative darkness beneath the treetop canopy. The lush jungle was shady, but usually hot and steamy, because no breezes could penetrate the foliage. Movement through the denser sections of the rain forest was often difficult, mostly because of the steep terrain. The edges of the jungle usually appeared to be impenetrable, and sometimes it was. But once inside the foliage it was often possible to move around without too much difficulty, because the upper tiers of the triple canopy denied sunlight to undergrowth on the jungle floor, except for ferns and similar plants which thrived in shade. Bamboo thickets and stands of elephant grass were consistently more difficult to penetrate and always required the use of machetes. The jungle areas of the mountains were a great equalizer for the NVA, because the difficult terrain and heavy foliage diminished the effectiveness of U.S. air superiority and artillery firepower.

Booby traps were encountered only occasionally in the 515 Valley, but they were common in Dragon Valley, in the Song Ve area and in the mountains. Experienced soldiers developed a sixth sense about when and where booby traps might be present, so we were then more cautious in our movements. We tried not to walk on trails, but dense vegetation, rough terrain and/or time constraints often forced us to use established paths in the mountains; this applied to the enemy as well. Effective point men developed an uncanny ability to spot trip wires or other signs of enemy mines on trails. I did not have those skills and I might as well have closed my eyes, stuck my fingers in my ears and marched along at quick time cadence like I was on the parade field. For this reason, I never walked point during daylight hours, but it didn't matter in the dark, when everyone was equally blind, so I occasionally led the way into an NDP. Otherwise, I positioned myself near the front of our platoon or squad patrol formations for navigation and control purposes, often right behind the point/slack team. On one occasion our point man spotted a trip wire and called me forward to show me, but I still couldn't see it, even when he pointed and I got down on my knees. The soldiers who were good at sensing enemy presence and spotting booby traps took pride in it and I never had any trouble finding someone willing to walk point. They probably got an adrenaline rush from performing this hazardous job, and they were certainly admired by the rest of us. A squad leader would often do it himself to protect his men if he had the required skills, notably Doug Landry and Keith Moore. Both of these squad leaders taught other soldiers how to walk point, which was like teaching a mixture of fine art and Voodoo. There was no Field Manual for this job and the skills were passed along from man-to-man, but some of it was instinctive. Keith walked point for 1st Squad regularly, rotating the job with his slack man Robby Robinson only occasionally, usually as a teaching opportunity. SGT Paul Malonson walked point occasionally, but he didn't do it all the time. He wisely delegated the job to Bob Swanson, because Swanee had a high skill level, plus the confidence and guts to do it. Country boys like Swanee, who had hunted and trapped in the mountains of Pennsylvania as a kid, were usually better point men than city boys from back on the block. Either Hy or The Mad Fragger covered Swanee on slack and Hy often rotated to the point position. Curly Schilling also walked point for 2nd Squad, with "Arthur Ambush" (SP/4 Moses Bush) as his slack man. When circumstances forced us to use a trail, the point man was focused on that, while the slack man scanned everything else to the front and sides, so they operated as a true team. This could be incredibly nerve-wracking, on some mountain trails in Indian Country. The platoon had a "lucky" point man's hat that got passed along as point men left the unit. It was a standard bush hat, but it was faded, frayed and bedraggled, with a blue and white Pabst Blue Ribbon Beer patch sewn on the top; Keith Moore is wearing it in some of my photos. The fact that we never took any casualties from booby traps, when they were occurring regularly in other units, was the best testament to the skills of the 2nd Platoon's point men.

The booby traps in Quang Ngai and Mo Duc provinces were always the explosive-type and we never encountered pungi stakes, tiger pits or other mechanical devices. The booby traps we found were often U.S. M26 grenades with the pull pins straightened and a trip wire attached, for a six second delay. Sometimes the pin was removed and the frag was placed inside an empty C-rat can to hold the safety spoon down; the trip wire would pull out the whole grenade, releasing the spoon. Another dink favorite was a petna-packed #10 can with a smoke grenade fuse, which exploded with no delay. We also encountered unexploded ordinance, tricked out with triggering devices. Other units found or tripped booby traps made of dud ordinance as large as 250 pound bombs. I heard of other units finding or tripping Bouncing Betties and toe-poppers but 2nd Platoon never encountered any of those while I led it. Most of the enemy devices were simple but clever. (One of their favorite tricks along Highway 1 was to remove the jungle clip and pull-pin from an M26 frag, then secure the safety spoon to the grenade body with a rubber band. It only took a few seconds to unscrew the cap on an unattended truck's gas tank, drop the grenade in and put the cap back on. The fuel in the tank would later weaken the rubber band and release the spoon, with spectacular results.) In the bush, we seldom tried to dismantle enemy booby traps, because it was possible to encounter a pressure-release trigger or other trick device. When we discovered unexploded booby traps, they were usually blown in place. This was typically done with the smaller devices by pulling the pin on an M26 frag, laying it next to the explosive and running for cover. We did the same thing to dispose of captured CHICOM grenades, which could not be backhauled. On larger stuff, such as booby trapped artillery or mortar rounds, we'd blow them with C4, nonelectrical blasting caps and time fuse.

Although I never developed the hypersensitivity of sight and hearing possessed by good point men, my brain, senses and instincts did become somewhat rewired. This probably occurred automatically because of my total immersion in the combat environment and a strong subconscious desire to survive. Most seasoned infantrymen experienced similar phenomena and this sensory reprogramming may be part of the reason some of us had readjustment problems when we returned home. I've already mentioned my ability to smell the enemy, which non-grunts usually do not believe, but it's really true. As another example, Nighthawk gunships often shot fairly close to our NDPs. Artillery batteries also routinely fired night-time H&I Missions (harassment and interdiction barrages) on sensor transmissions, or randomly on enemy trails. These battle sounds at night did not signal any danger to my platoon, so I therefore learned to ignore them, even when I was asleep. I would always sleep soundly through gunfire coming from helicopters, or artillery-type explosions. But I would be instantly awake and completely alert if someone whispered "El Tee", or if small arms were fired from our perimeter, because those things signaled imminent danger. On the other hand, your subconscious mind can play tricks on you if you lean too heavily on it. I once slept right through all the commotion when someone punched off a claymore mine outside of our NDP, even though concussion from the thunderous explosion should have levitated my body. I guess my sleeping brain thought it was a friendly art'y round.

We always moved in a "Ranger File", to minimize the chance of tripping an explosive device. Most other Army schools taught the use of flank security during tactical movements in those days, presumably a holdover from WWII tactics for moving large units, but we never did that in Vietnam. Moving in more than one file increased the odds of tripping a booby trap. Putting out flank security was clearly not a good thing if we got in contact, because friendly troops on the flanks would mask our lateral fire or become sacrificial lambs. In open terrain, in areas which were not heavily booby-trapped, we sometimes used a three man point team in a triangular formation at night, such as when moving into an NDP, to increase our immediate frontal firepower. The possibility of walking into an ambush was less likely than encountering a booby trap, but it was also a real possibility.

We set up our Night Defensive Positions in the dark, but usually on sites which had been previously reconnoitered during daylight hours. A platoon NDP consisted of three or four guard positions, more often the former, in a perimeter configuration. Our night perimeters therefore usually took the form of a triangle, or sometimes a square or a diamond, the exact shape being determined by the terrain feature on which we were set up. The squad leaders were adept at doing this and there was seldom any need for me to make adjustments to their NDP arrangements. Three or four Claymore mines were set up in a fan pattern to the front of each guard position, for command detonation only, never for trip detonation for safety reasons. Claymores were generally placed only about 10-15 meters out, to make it difficult for Charlie to creep in and turn them around on us. Because they were often set up much closer than the length of the firing cord, a perimeter guard always got his head down before he squeezed off a Claymore, to preserve his night vision and avoid the back blast. Trip flares were placed in front of the Claymores and additional flares were situated to cover any dead space, i.e., depressions or other defilade areas which could not be directly observed from the guard position. Squad leaders briefed their troops on the locations of the mines, flares and adjacent guard positions. The triangular NDP perimeters were not optimum, but we had a limited number of troops available for guard duty and we got away with it. An M60 machine gun was placed on each squad guard position on its bipod, along with a PRC25 radio and one Starlight Scope. Claymore clackers were consolidated on the position, arranged laterally in the order of mine placement. There were always several illumination hand-poppers and a pile of M26 hand frags on hand. The squad leader slept near the guard position, to be quickly available if something happened during the night. The size of the NDP perimeter varied according to the terrain and foliage. In open areas it was often possible to see surprisingly long distances, only by ambient light from the moon and stars, because of the clarity of the air. 2nd Platoon soldiers were very skillful at moving into an NDP location and setting up their mines and trip flares in the dark, making almost no noise. No lights were ever used at all. Smokers usually wanted a cigarette very badly after their 1½ to 2 hour guard stint, but they were required to do all smoking under a poncho. Even on the firebase, lighting a cigarette at night without precautions (a "sniper check") was not done by grunts. All NDP communications, including radio transmissions, were always whispered. Requests for SITREPS were sometimes answered, especially on night ambushes, by breaking squelch twice to signal "all is well". Radio volume was turned way down, in the "New Squelch On" mode, so they could barely be heard breaking squelch, even with an ear pressed against the handset. Artillery Delta Tangos were always plotted around the NDP and along avenues of approach, as a defensive measure.

There were only about 25 to 30 of us in the 2nd Platoon at any given time and only eight to twelve soldiers went out from our day laager on each patrol. For the most part, the enemy usually operated in small groups too, but not always. A lieutenant in D Company told me that his platoon spotted a North Vietnamese Regular Army unit, approximately 75 uniformed and heavily armed soldiers. They were boldly moving through an open area near the platoon's day laager in broad daylight. The D Company platoon was outnumbered three to one, so they stayed hidden and allowed the NVA to pass, close by but unmolested. I've often thought about that and wondered if I would have done the same thing, or tried to take them by surprise, with artillery and gunship support. I don't know, because the opportunity never arose, but I was aware that there was always a possibility of bumping into a large enemy force.

There were events driven partly by boredom, such as the day we sprung an ambush on a deer. On another slow afternoon, I unsuccessfully tried to burn a suspected NVA mountain sanctuary with white phosphorous artillery barrages; I learned from this exercise that a fire cannot be started in a rain forest. On another occasion, my platoon linked up with a South Vietnamese battalion in the mountains overlooking the Song Ve Valley and I had an interesting visit with the ARVN commander and his two USMC advisors, an SSG and a 1LT. They were the only Marines I ever saw in Vietnam, because most had been sent home prior to 1971. We escorted a sensor emplacement team into the same area on another occasion. The sensors were at that time considered to be very high-tech and top secret. They were battery operated electronic devices, designed to detect enemy troop movements from a remote monitoring location. They were thermal devices, triggered by body heat and ground vibrations. They could supposedly differentiate between groups of people and other mammals, such as herds of wild pigs. The sensor placement team leader, a sergeant, gave me a briefing on how they worked, but I no longer remember the details. I do recall that the sensors were cleverly designed. The antenna portion, which was still exposed after the devices were buried, was camouflaged with plastic stems and leaves, to appear exactly like indigenous jungle plants. Some models could be dropped from the air and were made to imbed themselves in the ground upon impact, except for the bogus plant/antenna portion. The preferred method of employment was to take them in on foot, so that the location could be determined more accurately; batteries were replaceable on that type.

Most Infantry lieutenants were in the bush about 3 or 4 months, sometimes less. Then they were given rear jobs, unlike the enlisted men who were usually out in the boondocks for many months. I was in the bush for about 6 ½ months, which was still not as long as most of my men. Some guys, like Bob Swanson, Paul Malonson, The Mad Fragger, Harold Weidner and a few others were in the bush for their entire 12 month tours, which was very stressful. Only a limited number of rear jobs were available for infantry enlisted men, but some of those jobs were given to slackers; it was sometimes better to send a loser to the rear than to try to cope with his shortcomings in the bush. Mandatory "levies" sometimes came down the pipeline for in-country schools, to alleviate shortages in specific Military Occupational Specialties. We naturally wanted to keep our best men, so soldiers who were troublemakers or suspected drug users were sometimes sent to in-country MOS schools. They were retreaded as Military Policemen, Snipers, or whatever other occupational specialty the in-country school turned out. Because of the early rear job rotation of lieutenants, just about the time that a platoon leader was fully getting his act together, he was reassigned to another job. This was counterproductive and it gave credence to the myth that rank has its privileges. In reality, rank had its responsibilities, but there were few privileges if a platoon leader was doing his job. I did not particularly enjoy it, but I did take pride in getting up in the middle of every night to take my bleary-eyed turn on guard duty, in the field or on the perimeter at LZ Liz. I also went on all 2nd Platoon patrols and performed other physical tasks as demonstrations of my leadership commitment to my men. This was somewhat self-serving, because I knew I wouldn't encounter resistance if I ordered someone else to do the same things.

Environmental factors in Vietnam were interesting, if only because they were so different and exotic. There were tropical animals, such as leopards, tigers, odd varieties of deer, wild boar and bizarre lizards. Up north, there were elephants. There were also various snakes (pythons, cobras, bamboo vipers and others) and monkeys. We often heard jungle cocks crowing in the jungle like domestic roosters, but we almost never saw them. All the wild animals were elusive and rarely spotted. Even the domestic animals, like water buffs, pigs, chickens and ducks, were unlike the ones we knew "Back in the World". The clarity of the air in Vietnam was phenomenal and especially obvious at night, because of the absence of air pollution. It was possible to see for long distances at night if any portion of the moon was showing, because of the light emitted by the stars and the moon. Many nights, I lay on my back against my rucksack frame and marveled at the thousands and thousands of stars I saw in the night sky, with shooting-stars almost continually visible all over the spectrum. The night sky in the United States probably looked exactly like that to my ancestors 200 years ago, before industrial air pollution obscured the view. The visual clarity of the air was favorably impressive, but the odiferous qualities were not. This was no doubt partially due to the absence of sewerage systems and the methods used to fertilize rice paddies, but also because of the continuous rotting of vegetation in the tropical jungles. Vietnam looked beautiful and exotic, but smelled terrible.

Grunts were inclined to fool around with jungle snakes, even though many of them were dangerous. One species of viper was called a "Two-Step", because that is how far a victim could go after being bitten. I saw photos of a huge python killed by 2nd Platoon, before I joined B Company. The troops said they boxed up the corpse in an SP carton and sent it back to their XO as a practical joke, because he was petrified of snakes. Doug Knight's guys also shot and killed a giant 12 foot King Cobra, which had been stalking one of their soldiers in a day laager. My 2nd Platoon soldiers caught a *live* python near another day laager. One of them grabbed the snake behind its head and desperately held on with both hands, while it writhed around and fought him. After a major struggle, several soldiers managed to stuff the huge python in a large mail bag. The snake quieted down when the bag was closed and it was given a ride back to the rear area on the backhaul chopper. There was considerable excitement in the rear area, when the mail bag was opened and the giant snake slithered out. Our Company Commander then received an angry radio call from the Battalion Commander. Randy Guill didn't know anything about it, of course, but he promised to do a complete investigation and get to the bottom of it. No one could remember who was involved in the prank. *Xin loi*, Battalion HQ.

I did not care for the attitudes of many REMF officers, who too often acted like jerks, but I certainly did not loath everyone who had a rear job. Most rear-area enlisted soldiers and junior NCOs served with complete honor and many had jobs which were critical to our well being. Some support troops, like truck drivers who traveled QL1, and Combat Engineers who built roads, did in fact go into dangerous situations on a regular basis. The contemptuous term "REMF" resulted from resentment, because grunts were often treated like the Army's bastard stepchildren. We were acutely aware that a Saigon-based Office Machine Repairman, MOS 41-J-10, got the same $35/month combat pay that we drew, which was not equitable. Grunts got no special compensation and we rarely received any acknowledgement for the hardships we endured on a daily basis. The use of the REMF label was highly variable and it was usually applied according to how far in the rear a soldier was located. To line company grunts, our forward firebase at LZ Liz was obviously a rear area, but soldiers who worked there thought of the 11th Brigade troops at LZ Bronco as REMFs. I've seen an artillery unit's website, where several photos of the barbed wire entanglement around LZ Bronco are bombastically labeled "The Front Lines", so they didn't consider themselves to be REMFs. Thousands of rear-area troops attended a Bob Hope show near Saigon, but 2nd Platoon was allowed to send only *two* grunts. SSG Wilson and I agonized over the impossible question of which two guys had made the biggest contribution to our platoon. We picked two soldiers' names at random after narrowing it down to more than a dozen candidates, but it was a toss-up and we should have been able to send more.

We did not hold ARVNs in high regard, because they usually did rear duty in our AO while we were out in the boondocks fighting their war and bleeding for them. When an ARVN unit did go into the field, they seemed timid, passive and reluctant to find or fight the NVA. We were in a convoy on QL 1 one day and, as our trucks crossed a bridge, an ARVN soldier guarding it fired a burst from his weapon into the water. I'm sure the ARVN guards on the bridge had done this previously, as a practical joke to make GIs duck and cower, but they shouldn't have done it to a convoy of grunts. Spontaneously, my 2nd Platoon boys immediately lit up both sides of the highway with automatic weapons and I had the pleasure of seeing frightened ARVNs (and civilians) diving for cover all over the place. None of them were hurt because my guys deliberately shot over their heads. But MACV (Military Assistance Command-Vietnam) had a cow over that incident. A Reply-by-Endorsement came down through channels, requiring our CO to explain why we were interfering with MACV's efforts to "Win the Hearts and Minds of the People". My soldiers sometimes pranked rice farmers, by shooting 40mm tear gas grenades along the ground upwind of a herd of water buffalo, which always created an instant rodeo when they got their snoots full of CS gas. Curly Schilling captured another caper in living color on Super-8 movie film: En route to Stand-Down, the 2nd Platoon celebrated our return from the bush by tossing all leftover smoke grenades out of both sides of our convoy, while we were motoring through several connected villages on Highway 1.

Tom Dolan

This pyrotechnical bombardment created huge billowing and swirling clouds of red, green, blue, yellow and purple smoke, to the dismay of the QL1 villagers and the vehicle drivers on the road behind us. My boys couldn't help it. The Devil made them do it. *Xin loi,* MACV.

Please note that there were some exceptions, but in general, I learned to have a low opinion of Ring Knockers. That was a nickname for graduates of West Point, the government school for spoiled boys on the Hudson River. Some of them had a habit of calling attention to their big U.S. Military Academy class rings by tapping them on tables or chair arms during meetings, hence the sobriquet. USMA graduates formed a tight ruling clique in the Army, euphemistically known as the WPPA (West Point Protective Association). The more numerous OCS and ROTC officers were just grist for the mills of West Pointers on their way to the top. Among themselves, West Point officers sometimes referred to OCS counterparts as "Ninety Day Wonders" and ROTC officers were similarly disparaged. This probably would have been regarded with dismissive good humor by OCS and ROTC officers, except that the leadership flaws within the WPPA membership were so obvious. At the lower end of the scale, some of the West Point lieutenants were good guys, but a noticeable number of them were narcissistic, entitled and conceited. I always wanted to ask the arrogant ones, "How can you take yourself so seriously, with so little justification?" Farther up the food chain, the WPPA colonels and generals usually talked tough, but they always tried to lead from the rear, which didn't help their credibility. The more senior Military Academy graduates called the shots from a sandbagged TOC, or from a safe 2,000+ feet in a C&C chopper, and many policy edicts spewed from air conditioned trailers in Chu Lai and Saigon. WPPA decisions were too often premised on "What is best for my career, in this situation?" rather than "How can we best accomplish this mission?"

We regularly received inane directives which were prompted by career path motives and political correctness, rather than by sound thinking. One of these was that not enough black troops had been promoted to E5, so <u>all</u> promotions from E4 to SGT would be restricted to African-Americans until further notice. This arbitrary order unfairly delayed the promotions of white and Hispanic SP/4s who were already doing sergeants' jobs as acting NCOs. Another directive stated that some inappropriate incidents involving U.S. troops had occurred in villes. We were therefore prohibited from entering and searching all villages, unless we actually observed enemy soldiers entering them with weapons. Even if that occurred, the platoon leader was required to get explicit permission from battalion HQ, before entering the ville. This Rule of Engagement seriously impeded our mission in The 515 Valley, which was saturated with small hamlets, by creating numerous sanctuaries for the enemy. Another directive stated that there had been too many accidents with M203 grenade launchers, so we were instructed to carry them with the 40mm portion unloaded until we got into actual contact. That was soon followed by another directive which proclaimed there had been too many accidental shootings with M16s, so we were instructed to carry them with the empty chambers until we were in a firefight. I'm *not* making up this stuff and it provides insight into how clueless some of our top commanders were about the realities of combat. This micromanagement in lieu of leadership was consistent with the Pentagon trends started by Robert McNamara. It prompted SSG Wilson to begin saying, "What are they going to do to us El Tee? Put us in the Infantry and send us to the bush?" Accordingly, we ignored these orders whenever we could, because it is always easier to get forgiveness than permission. I know it is not fair to condemn all of the Army's higher ranking officers and that there were honorable and intelligent men in the upper ranks. But they were conspicuously absent and remote, while I was trying to cope with difficult combat situations and occasional leadership problems in my platoon. The "guidance" I saw coming down from above was typically not helpful. Why didn't the good guys, who presumably also lived in the upper echelons, intervene when the dumbasses issued those ridiculous CYA directives? I decided that I did not want a career in an organization being run like that.

LTC Thomas Brogan, then our battalion CO, came out one day to visit CPT Guill, who was traveling with 2nd Platoon. After Colonel Brogan was dropped off in our day laager, his chopper took some dink automatic weapons fire as it was lifting off. The bird must have been hit, because it did not come back that day to pick him up. LTC Brogan unexpectedly had to spend the night with us in the bush, probably the only time he did that during his tour. Always gregarious, The Mad Fragger spotted Colonel Brogan's flashy nickel plated/pearl-handled .45 auto and brashly asked him if he could shoot it. Remarkably, LTC Brogan handed the pistol over to him. The Fragger blasted through a full magazine and started looking for more ammo, acting like he wasn't going to give it back, no doubt to pull Brogan's chain. He did return the weapon after I told him to quit screwing around with the colonel's pistol. While he was with us, LTC Brogan picked up Curly Schilling's M203 grenade launcher, hit the thumb latch and pulled the slide forward. He was shocked when a 40mm HE round popped out and he began berating Curly, saying "This thing is NOT supposed to be loaded". LTC Brogan, bless his heart, actually expected us to comply with that nutty directive which ordered us to carry the M203s unloaded until the stinky stuff hit the fan. Poor Curly had no idea what he was talking about, because I had not bothered to tell the guys about that directive after SSG Wilson and I decided to ignore it. (Sorry, Curly.)

One of the most despised military groups among grunts was the Army Security Agency, or ASA. These were the rear area soldiers responsible for monitoring our radio transmissions for procedural correctness and COMSEC (Communications Security). ASA wonks lived in a world of their own, far removed from actual combat. They continually picked at nits, under the guise of COMSEC. We regarded their activities as officious, silly and intrusive. We already knew that our operational COMSEC was about as good as it could be under the circumstances, although certainly not perfect. Squad/platoon leaders and RTOs went by the book as much as was practicable, because it was to our advantage to take COMSEC seriously. Deviations were usually minor and were almost always attributable to new radio operators, who were omnipresent due to troop turnover. ASA was also supposed to do intelligence gathering, by monitoring and decoding enemy radio traffic, but my experience with a stateside ASA unit indicated that they did this poorly. ASA veterans now fancy themselves as "Old Spooks & Spies", the hyperbolic *nom de guerre* of the Southeast Asia ASA Veterans' Association. According to their website, the "cover name" of the ASA Chu Lai group was the "Americal Radio Research Company-Provisional". But wait... weren't all ASA units called Radio Research Companies? Secretive, huh? Just like 007! Too funny.

Most of the channels on our AN/PRC25 FM radios were assigned to units, but the top of the band, at 7500 megahertz on the dial, was always unassigned. This was the "BS Push" and when somebody said "Meet me on Three-Quarter" it meant he was going to switch channels to 7500 MHz to pass along some gossip, play a favorite tune, or tell a bawdy joke. Assigned call-signs were never used on Three-Quarter and the talkers depended upon voice recognition or nicknames to identify each other. When I was on guard duty and heard someone say "Meet me on Three-Quarter" I'd usually switch channels to listen, because the transmissions were often hilarious. Army Security Agency became apoplectic about the outrageous things which were said "in the clear" on the Three-Quarter channel. Nobody transmitting on 7500 MHz paid any attention to proper radio-telephone procedure, but COMSEC was not really compromised, because the channel was used only for blathering, not for tactical communications.

For use on tactical radio channels, our Battalion TOC RTOs also published a "Brevity Code". This pseudo-cipher was invented to irritate ASA radio monitors, who had conniptions if somebody used an "unauthorized" code. The Brevity Code was a list of three digit numbers and corresponding phrases. It was a random collection of humorous sayings, with liberal use of F-Bombs and other expletives. If someone said "1-4-5" as part of his radio transmission, it decoded as "F-ing roast beef again". When someone said "1-1-2" it meant "Let me talk to the son of a bitch". "1-4-2" unshackled to "F-ing ASA". I don't know why it really mattered in a combat zone, but cursing in-the-clear on the radio was strictly prohibited and it was only rarely heard. If a platoon leader was in a firefight and he said "Where is that @!#$%& artillery?!", ASA would throw a tantrum about transmitting vulgarity on the air. What did they think they could do to him? Put him in the Infantry and send him to the bush? *One-Four-Two.*

    Encoding entire radio transmissions through a regular SOI (Signal Operating Instructions) code book was too time-consuming to be practical. Operating units were issued only two "SOI Extracts", one for call signs and the other listing radio frequencies. We also had clear plastic devices called "Whiz Wheels", which used daily code sheet inserts to shackle grid coordinates. Whiz Wheel inserts and SOI Extracts were classified documents, so RTOs carefully guarded them. Using proper radio-telephone procedure in Vietnam did not necessarily quash creativity. A request for a "Radio check" properly invoked a minimalistic response of "Roger, out". This meant, in verbal shorthand, that I hear you loudly and clearly and I assume you hear me the same. If that assumption was correct, the commo check was complete. Otherwise, the operator who requested the radio check would clarify, e.g., "I hear you weak but clear", or "I've got you broken and distorted". RTOs typically extended this conversation slightly by responding to a request for "Commo check, over" by saying, "Loud and clear, how me?" and the requesting station usually answered, "Same-same, thank you much, out." But frequently, "Loud and clear, how me?" morphed into "Lima Charlie, Hotel Mike?" by applying the ubiquitous phonetic alphabet. RTOs sometimes competed with each other to invent new radio language. Thus, "Lima Charlie" became "Lucky Chucky",

The Mad Fragger and Me

"Lemon Coke" or "Lickin' Chicken". One of the funnier variations I remember hearing was, "Lincoln Continental, How's Mom?"

The call-sign *Yankee-Three-Three* was assigned to a conscientious but somewhat verbose RTO who manned the radio on a small outpost at the South OP, located on a separate mountaintop next to LZ Liz. *Yankee-Three-Three* seemed to be on the battalion command net 24 hours a day and I wondered if he ever slept. His radio voice was unmistakable, because he sounded exactly like Elmer Fudd. His call-sign always came through as "Yankee-Twee-Twee" and the humor in his transmissions, intentional or inadvertent, was always enhanced by his slight speech impediment.

"Secure" radio sets were available only to Infantry Company Commanders, for communication with battalion and higher HQs. In the absence of secure radios and SOI encryption, substitute words were regularly used to describe things by radio. For example: "Funny paper" meant a map. "Mickey" or "package" meant a mechanical ambush. "Blue line" was a river or stream. "Packs" meant people, such as the number of passengers in a helicopter lift. "Push" was a radio frequency. "PZ" meant a helicopter pickup zone. "Hard ball" or "red ball" was a paved road, such as QL1. And there were many more. We knew that the VC/NVA were monitoring our radio traffic and you had to wonder how they interpreted those transmissions and the GI slang the RTOs used on the air.

For awhile, one of our Battalion COs was preoccupied with forcing grunts to wear flak jackets and steel helmets at all times. The fiberglass protective vests issued in 1971 were hot and heavy. The zippered fronts usually were left open because of the intense heat and they didn't offer much protection. They typically did not prevent wounds, but they did cause heat injuries. The bulky flak vests also made carrying a heavy rucksack, which was a necessity for grunts, almost impossible. The steel pot was the first thing you'd lose when you started running around in a firefight, or it could fall down on your face and bust your nose, because it had poorly designed suspension webbing and it did not come with a useful chinstrap. The Lifers may have had good intentions, but they never humped heavy rucksacks, or had to fire and maneuver in a firefight, so they didn't understand the problems with using this equipment outside of a firebase. Our LTC would usually observe us leaving LZ Liz, to verify that we were all wearing our steel pots and flak jackets. On one such occasion, after we were out of sight, I took a break in the first ville we came to in The 515 Valley. We checked in all our flak vests and steel pots with an elderly Poppa-San. He neatly lined them all up in his hootch and we picked them up a couple of weeks later when we humped back in to LZ Liz, paying him for his trouble with a few cans of C Rations. He seemed to be proud of the hat check job we'd given him. After awhile, probably because of spotty compliance, the Battalion Commander gave up on trying to enforce his flak jacket mandate. Most of the time, I carried my helmet on top of my rucksack, but it was just 6 pounds of dead weight. It was also difficult to secure the steel pot to the top of the pack. We were humping through the 515 Valley one scorching day when my steel pot fell off for about the third time. Hot and angry, I flung down my rucksack, picked up the helmet and threw it as far as I could into the middle of a thicket which Br'er Rabbit could not have penetrated. The next day, a couple of village kids proudly presented me with the helmet. I had to pay them for it with some C-rats, so as to continue winning their hearts and minds. There were no civilians around when I tossed my steel pot into the briar patch, and I have no idea how the kids found it. It had a black lieutenant's bar on the front, but no name on it. The damned thing was like an albatross around my neck and it seemed that I couldn't even throw it away. I later dropped the helmet down an abandoned well and it didn't come back to me again.

The 515 Valley was our favorite AO, because we seldom encountered booby traps there. As I had learned from Hy, it was entirely possible to plant explosive devices which were invisible. This always worked on our minds while we were moving around in heavily booby trapped areas, but it was a relief not to be too concerned about it in The 515 Valley. The villagers in that area were usually friendlier too, so we reciprocated. I sometimes took close up color photos of the mamma-sans and the girl-sans there. The developed pictures were handed out to the ladies when I again came through the same area and they were always thrilled with these little portraits. These people were so poor that it was hard to understand how they managed to subsist. We searched enough Vietnamese homes to know what they owned, which was almost nothing. Each family had a straw hut framed with bamboo, open windows and doorways, with sleeping platforms and dirt floors. Rice rats infested the huts. A family had one cooking pot and each family member had a rice bowl. They ate rice almost exclusively, flavored with *nuoc mam*, a very pungent fermented fish sauce, which had an offensive odor to Americans. We went fishing with hand grenades one day in a wide stream near Recon Hill and the villagers had a field day gathering the little fish which floated to the surface. They were too small to eat, so they probably went into a new batch of homebrewed *nuoc mam*. Each family member had one set of pajamas, flip-flops and a conical straw hat, which they wore every day. A family might also have a few chickens or ducks and a pig or two. Water buffalos, which were used to till the paddies, seemed to be community property. The people were abjectly poor and they clearly just wanted to be left alone.

We always had a lot of children hanging around us in the 515 Valley and the troops would joke with them, play games and generally entertain them. Some of them were no doubt VC spies, but my instincts indicated that most of the kids were not. Many of the older children were "Coke Kids", basically minor players in the Black Market."Coke" referred to Coca-Cola, not cocaine. These youthful entrepreneurs brought sandbags full of soft drinks and beers out to the hamlets on their bicycles and sold them for $.50 per can MPC. We bought Cokes, Pepsis or 7-Ups from them, because the only soft drinks we ever received through Army supply channels were warm cans of Fresca, the most disgusting drink known to man. The Coke Kids always carried a block of ice, wrapped in wood chips and burlap. They got the drinks icy cold by rapidly spinning the cans for a few minutes in a trough on top of the ice block. Upon request, the Coke Kids would bring other drinks or perishable food items the next day. The most requested item was crescent rolls, made of wonderfully tasty and chewy French bread, which was baked in a ville on QL 1. We were not supposed to buy local products like bread or bottled drinks because of the possibility of contamination or poison, but we purchased the French rolls anyway. They made indescribably delicious sandwiches, with C-ration spiced beef and hot sauce, or broiled pork slices and a little mustard. I had a heavy duty padded canvas tube strapped to the top of my rucksack, with a snap-on cover over one end. I scrounged it from the covert team which we escorted into the Song Ve Valley to plant electronic sensors. I usually carried C-Rat cans in the padded sensor case, but it also served as my cooler. At the end of a day, I'd occasionally buy a Coke or a couple of beers from the kids and pack them in the cooler with chunks of left-over ice, for a midnight snack on NDP guard duty. Prior to departing for the boonies from LZ Liz, I sometimes packed the canvas tube with ice from the mess hall, cans of C-Rat peaches and fruit cocktail. The melting ice cooled me off as it ran down my back and the chilled fruit was a real treat.

I got to know several of the children who lived in the 515 Valley and they found me every time our unit operated in that area. Two of them were small boys, about 8 to 10 years old. Thom ("taum") was a cheerful cockeyed optimist, who was intrigued that my name was the same as his, except for the slight inflection difference. His best buddy was T`he ("tay"), a grubby urchin who had neither mother nor father. T`he had somehow avoided going to an orphanage and he apparently survived on the charity of villagers in the area. The two boys were inseparable and they lived in a hamlet near "The Buddha Ville", which was dominated by a neat and colorful little Buddhist temple. T`he and Thom always showed up and clung to me whenever we laagered near The Buddha Ville, because I gave them C rations, candy and cigarettes. Thom could speak only a little English at that point, and T`he none at all, but we were still able to communicate because they were bright and inquisitive. A third kid I knew was a pretty girl named Soong (phonetic spelling). Soong was a vivacious teenie-bopper of about 13 or 14. She used her fluent English extensively, because like many teenage girls, she loved to talk. Soong dabbled slightly in the Black Market, but she was not a hustler like most of the other Coke Kids. These children were really no different than nice American kids of the same age and they were fun to have around. I hope they are alive and prospering somewhere, and maybe they are, because they were survivors.

The Black Market was endemic to Vietnam and we often encountered hoards of teenaged Coke Kids when we were being airlifted out of LZ Dragon on a CA. We were there one day and SSG Wilson ordered bush hats and hammocks from Coke Kids for several FNGs (F-ing New Guys) who had been assigned to 2nd Platoon. Bush hats could be obtained through supply channels in one size only, 6 ¼, which fit nobody, but they could be purchased new in any size for $5 (OD) or $6 (camo) MPC on the Black Market. GI jungle hammocks were not available except on the Black Market, for $10 each, brand new in the wrapper. When the Coke Kids came back with the bush hats and hammocks, the newbies balked at paying for them. They said, "We shouldn't have to buy back our own equipment after it was stolen by the Vietnamese". When SSG Wilson repeated this to me, we both knew they were right. By this time, the choppers were inbound and we had a near riot on our hands, with the teenagers wailing and raising a clamor about not being paid. We shouted "SOUVENIR!" and got on the birds. (Don't feel too sorry for the LZ Dragon Coke Kids, because they were pushy little beggars.)

There were many bootleg handguns available in Vietnam. I remember being offered a Victory Model S&W .38 Special revolver and a black market Walther P38 9mm pistol. But I preferred a .45

Tom Dolan

auto for its reliability, stopping power and fast reloading capability, the same reasons the U.S. Army had adopted it in 1911. My Remington Rand M1911A1 was exactly like the one my father bought for me through the Director of Civilian Marksmanship/NRA when I was 13 years old. I had a tan leather spring-retention shoulder holster at home for my personal .45. I asked my wife to take the holster to a shoemaker and have it dyed black, to simulate military issue. She mailed it to me and I used the holster until the tropical climate caused the shoulder strap to rot. In addition to my bootleg pistol, I started off with an M16A1, but after awhile I traded it in for an M203 grenade launcher. An M203 was a 5.56mm M16 rifle with a slide-action single shot 40mm grenade launcher attached to it, under the rifle barrel in place of the hand guard. This modification made two weapons in one, commonly called an "over and under" by the troops. (Arnold Schwarzenegger wielded an M203 in *Predator*.) The grenade launcher portion was marked "AAI" with a lightning bolt logo. I may have been the only person in Vietnam who knew what AAI stood for, because the original plant stood across the road from St. Joseph's Church in Texas, MD, where I served as an altar boy and attended elementary school. AAI was originally known as "Aircraft Armaments Incorporated", but the company now acts like that is a government secret. Before long, about every third grunt in 2nd Platoon was carrying an M203. CPT Guill ordered some of them turned in and redistributed, when he realized that almost all M203s were in my platoon. We also had an off-the-books 7.62mm M14E2 automatic rifle. Loaded 20 round steel magazines for an M14 are heavy, but someone had an OD canvas vest made up by a Vietnamese tailor, with magazine pockets all the way around it. The M14 provided great firepower and we sometimes carried it on mountain patrols instead of toting a heavy M60 MG. When CPT Guill mandated redistribution of the grenade launchers, I turned in my M203 and drew another M16. I then started carrying an M72 LAW for awhile. It finally became too much and I lightened my load. Wayne Wilson and I carried Starlight

Scopes, 6 volt batteries, binoculars, extra claymores, and other heavy stuff nobody else wanted to hump. Other than Doc Wright, we probably had the heaviest rucksacks in the platoon, but it was another opportunity to lead by example.

I encouraged my troops to fire their weapons on semi-automatic in a firefight, or to shoot in short bursts, but when the bullets started flying most of them went to full auto and held their triggers down. This was poor fire discipline, because everyone ran dry at the same time and there would be a lull in our firepower while everyone changed magazines. Despite the professionalism of my soldiers, this continued to be a problem, probably because the increased excitement of a firefight sometimes overwhelmed training. I seldom fired my rifle when we were in contact, because my real weapons were my map, compass, radio and the platoon itself. I was usually too busy trying to get artillery and gunships incoming, figuring out the situation, or maneuvering the platoon, to shoot at the Gomers. My weapon was nevertheless a comfort to me and it was important to have it next to me, because I was confident that I could hit anything I could see. Firefights or sounds of the enemy in the dark were always exciting and scary, but I was never overwhelmed with fear as long as my rifle was close at hand.

I was scrupulous, probably obsessive, about continually keeping track of exactly where we were, within the limitations of the 1:50,000 scale maps we were issued. Always knowing our precise location was the key to getting prompt fire support, avoiding friendly-fire mishaps and calling for dust-offs. I became an expert at land navigation by dint of continuous practice, but I promptly lost this skill level after getting out of the Army because I no longer used it every day. In Vietnam, I navigated mostly by terrain analysis, using the compass only to orient the map and to get rough directions for art'y adjustments. After awhile, I began using a small GI survival compass for this, which I wore with my Timex on a watchband made from a piece of rucksack strap. My larger tritium-illuminated lensatic compass was used only in the dark, or for precision plotting. A few of my guys were fairly competent at land navigation, but none would be considered experts. Surprisingly, SSG Wilson couldn't really read a map, but his attitude was "If you don't care where you are, you ain't lost." God and grunts loved the helicopter pilots, but not all of them were good at reading maps. When they were approaching us for an extraction or to bring resupply, they would usually fly into our general vicinity and call on the radio for us to "pop smoke" so they could find us. The pilot then identified the color of smoke and we verified it, so the chopper would not be suckered into the wrong LZ by the enemy. Lead pilots sometimes put us down in the wrong place during an insertion into a mountain LZ. I do not know if these were honest mistakes, or if they did it because they didn't like the looks of the designated landing zones, but they never told us that we were being dropped at an alternative LZ. It was usually not possible to fully orient myself to terrain features while I was sitting on the floor in the doorway of a rapidly maneuvering helicopter, so landing in the wrong location always drove me nuts. I did not immediately know why things did not quite look or feel right. I'd then get out my lensatic compass and shoot some azimuths to known terrain features to plot resections. If that wasn't feasible, I called an art'y battery for a marking smoke round, to help me figure out where I really was.

    Combat Assaults (CAs) usually started off like Chinese Fire Drills. We often departed from LZ Dragon, which had a lengthy and broad landing zone, flat like an air strip, on top of a plateau, which allowed an entire lift to depart together. A line company was often CAed into a single landing zone in the mountains, but several platoon-sized LZs might be selected in lowland areas. Prior to pick-up at LZ Dragon, we'd be told to plan on having X number of ships in Y number of lifts. This was apparently done to set up a practical joke, because the X and Y numbers were often changed at the last minute to create chaos in infantry units. Each Huey could carry about six grunts with equipment. We could not put two radios, two machine guns or two leaders in the same ship, because of the problems it would cause if that bird went down. It was also important to maintain unit integrity down to squad level. So when the numbers of helicopters or lifts changed, everyone had to regroup. Untangling that mess fell mostly on the Platoon Sergeant, because I always went on the first chopper and he went on the last one in a platoon lift. Helicopter Combat Assaults were adrenaline-pumping affairs, especially in the mountains, which were essentially free fire zones where the LZ could be "prepped". This was done whenever enemy presence was possible or expected, which it often was in the mountains. We circled the landing zone at a couple of thousand feet and watched the prep. There were no doors on the "slicks" and we always sat on the floor in the open doorways with our feet dangling, so the view was terrific. Despite the grab-ass beginnings of an airmobile assault on the ground, the rest of it was beautifully choreographed. Heavy barrages of artillery were brought in, on and around the LZ. As soon as the art'y was lifted, helicopter gunships swept through the LZ at low level and hosed down the surrounding jungle with rockets and miniguns. The troop-carrying slicks would swoop in right behind the last gunship pass and the door gunners on both sides of each ship in the first lift started firing their M60 machine guns. The pilots would usually just touch 'n go, so we only had a second or two to throw off our heavy rucksacks and jump out after them. The platoon in the first lift moved out into the edge of the jungle and secured the LZ for the rest of the Company. To simplify planning, the Bravo Company SOP was that the 2nd Platoon was the lead platoon in all combat assaults into company-sized LZs, and the last platoon out when the company was extracted. I was therefore always on the first ship in, or the last ship out. Early in our relationship, I complained to Randy Guill about 2nd Platoon taking the drag position during all extractions and he immediately started chewing me out for bitching about trivia. I told him the 2nd Platoon took pride in always leading B Company CAs, but when we were the last platoon extracted, the clean uniforms were always picked over before we arrived at LZ Liz. He needed to do something about *that*. He rolled his eyes, but he did not accuse me of petty griping again.

There were some odd or mysterious occurrences in Quang Ngai and Mo Duc provinces. These included occasional Salt & Pepper sightings. "Salt" and "Pepper" were the familiar nicknames for two American deserters who were rumored to have been fighting alongside the dinks, one white and one black. Artillery officers/NCOs at LZ Snoopy noticed the peculiar behavior and the odd attire of a black soldier who showed up in their mess hall. He was wearing ARVN-style tiger stripe fatigues with a nametag which read "Blackest Cong" and he was carrying a gasmask bag full of fragmentary grenades. They questioned him and didn't like his answers, which resulted in the probable capture of Pepper. The artillerymen locked up Pepper in a CONEX container until he was evacuated for interrogation, primarily to protect him from the wrath of some 1/20th grunts who happened to be present on LZ Snoopy. More than two turncoats were probably operating in the Quang Ngai/Mo Duc area, based upon the variations in physical descriptions of them. There were occasional sightings of a blond man wearing khakis, who was reputed to be a "Frenchman" but who was probably also a U.S. deserter. GIs who spotted the Frenchman always hesitated to pull their triggers, so he always got away. Another strange event was the discovery of a U.S. Marine's skeleton, buried on the North OP, a hilltop adjacent to LZ Liz, when the defensive positions there were being improved. Liz was originally a USMC firebase, but how did GI become buried there in an unmarked grave? Was he murdered? A soldier in another line company had a Zippo lighter engraved with his name and a motto, which he lost in the bush. A couple of months later, the same grunt killed an NVA soldier and found his own Zippo when he searched the body. How's that for a coincidence?

All smokers had Zippo lighters with their names engraved on them and mottos such as, "Yea, though I walk through the Valley of

The Mad Fragger and Me

the Shadow of Death, I shall fear no evil, for I am the baddest son of a bitch in the Valley." Based upon unit casualties there, I thought that the Valley of the Shadow of Death was probably a scriptural reference to the Song Ve Valley. Other memorable aphorisms were, "Believe in God, but have faith in your M16"... and "Nuke 'em till they glow, then shoot 'em in the dark". My battered Zippo is engraved with a CIB and an Americal patch. The other side is inscribed "Killing is my business. Business is good." ... followed by "LT T.E. Dolan" and "Religion: Infantry. Blood Type: OD". Not quite as pithy as "Have gun. Will travel", but that one was already taken.

When I called for helicopter gunship support, "Sharks" from the 174th Assault Helicopter Company usually came charging to our rescue. The "Guns" all had open red mouths with formidable looking white sharks' teeth painted on their noses, wrapping around the front doors. I just loved those Shark crews, because they were fearless and they always acted like they could not do enough for us. Shark crews flew "C" Model Huey heavy gunships, which were relatively slow, but Shark pilots maneuvered them like they were lunatic participants in a flying circus. The most notorious and beloved Shark gunships among grunts were *Easy Rider, The Grim Reaper* and *The Ace of Spades*. In addition to its name on both sides of the fuselage, *Easy Rider* had a red white and blue flag motif painted on her tail boom. According to contemporary legend, *The Ace of Spades* was named by the ship's original pilot, an African-American. If that's true, it demonstrated a politically incorrect sense of humor, not uncommon among flyers. Slicks from the same unit used "Dolphin" radio call signs. Dolphin and Shark were perfect call sign choices, because of the vaguely fish-like shape of the Hueys. Many slicks and gunships from the 174th AHC were shot down and destroyed while attacking the Ho Chi Minh Trail in Laos during *Operation Lam Son 719*, in February-April 1971. *Easy Rider, The Ace of Spades* and *The Grim Reaper* were <u>all</u> shot down during that brutal operation. (Photos of the recovered wreckage of *Easy Rider* are posted on the 174th AHC website... it is heartbreaking to see that once proud gunship in such a dilapidated state.) Huey PSYOPS choppers occasionally operated in our AO, dropping Chu Hoi leaflets. These were equipped with tape decks and blaring loudspeakers, used to broadcast propaganda messages to enemy forces in Vietnamese. A PSYOPS bird spotted our day laager one day and buzzed us several times, playing *We Gotta Get Outta This Place* and *I Can't Get No Satisfaction*. But *Gary Owen*, or the finale from *The William Tell Overture* would have been more apropos for The Famous 2nd Platoon.

    The only perk which grunts received was a periodic "SP", or Sundry Packet. It was a large cardboard carton which contained free personal items for grunts, the same things which were usually purchased by garrison troops at their PXs. Each SP box held 12 regular cartons of cigarettes (ten packs of 20 smokes each) plus smaller quantities of cigars, snuff, pipe and chewing tobacco. There was also chewing gum and climate-resistant candy, such as Good 'N Plenty, M&Ms, Jujubes, Life Savers, Chuckles, Tootsie Rolls and Tropical Hershey Bars (ugh!). An SP box contained supplies of soap bars, shaving cream, razors, double-edged razor blades, tooth paste and toothbrushes. There were other odds and ends, like corn cob pipes, pipe cleaners, boot laces, stationary, ballpoint pens, pencils, lighter fluid and Zippo flints. Whoever decided upon the SP contents and the quantities of each item did a very good job. I think the official distribution standard was one SP box per day for every 100 soldiers. Frequency of SP delivery was adjusted mathematically, based upon the number of soldiers in the platoon, so another Sundry Packet would usually arrive just when we were running out of stuff. The only thing the Army logistics personnel didn't nail down very well was the relative popularity of various brands of cigarettes. Most smokers requested Marlboro, Winston or Salem and there were never enough of those to go around. Someone in the logistics chain must have gotten a good deal on Kent cigarettes, which we always gave away to villagers because they tasted like dried monkey dung. The non-filter brands included Lucky Strike, Camel and "Red

The Mad Fragger and Me

Devils" (Pall Mall). There was usually a carton or two of less popular brands, such as Parliament, Kool, Old Gold or Raleigh. The Platoon Sergeant always did his best to distribute the cigarettes equitably and nobody bitched. The cigarettes in the SP cartons were supplemented by hard packs of four stale cigarettes which came with each C-ration meal and there was regular trading of those. It's hard to believe that the Army gave out so many free tobacco products to teenaged soldiers then, but it was a different world.

Most military leaders in those days agreed that regular mail delivery and good chow were the two biggest morale factors which are under the control of commanding officers. In the bush, we usually received resupply about every three days, so that was the frequency of mail call and one meal of hot A Rations. Taking resupply also meant backhaul of mermite and water cans, outgoing mail, administrative evacuation of soldiers going on R&R, and so forth. We therefore had two helicopter flights, in and out, of our patrol base/ laager on resupply days. This was not a problem when we were working in the lowlands or on defoliated mountaintops, but operations in heavy jungle areas complicated resupply considerably. We truly appreciated the efforts of our mess hall and S4 personnel to get a hot meal out to us, relieving the monotony of a constant diet of C-rations. The food was also pretty good, considering the difficulty of cooking it at a remote location and delivering it to us still hot. The hot A Rations came in mermite cans, which were insulated metal containers, each containing several aluminum inserts for different food items. Occasionally the backhaul flight was cancelled for one reason or another. This created a significant problem, because the already overburdened infantrymen had to haul around the empty 5 gallon water cans and insulated food containers until they were picked up by RS helicopter, perhaps days later. The metal containers were heavy, awkward and noisy to carry. The battalion commander and staff, of course, had no idea how much trouble this caused. This happened once too often to another rifle company. After receiving notice of backhaul cancellation, a platoon leader called the TOC and requested that a helicopter be sent out immediately, to pick up his empty mermite and water cans. The TOC denied the request and instructed him to carry the containers until the next regular resupply flight. The El Tee responded that he was going to blow them in place. The TOC reiterated the order to carry the cans until next the resupply run. The lieutenant told his men to drop a frag in each container, close the lids and run for cover. They blasted the cans to Kingdom Come, striking a blow for Truth, Justice and The American Way. Battalion HQ made more of an effort to backhaul empty containers after that episode, especially if you said the magic words, "I'm going to blow them in place".

One of our battalion commanders decided that if receiving a hot meal once every three days was good for morale, then having a hot meal every day was three times better. This is an example of how clueless our leadership could be. The constant helicopter traffic compromised our ability to sneak around in a tactical manner, because the dinks always knew exactly where we were located. This bad idea didn't last long, probably because it strained battalion support resources. I heard a similar story, probably true, about the commander of another battalion who really liked ice cream. He therefore ordered his S4 personnel to deliver ice cream in mermite cans to his troops every day. I don't remember ever getting ice cream in the field, but its absence was not a morale buster.

Living in the bush was not too difficult during the dry season. It was pretty much like being on a poorly equipped camping trip that went on a little too long. Camping out during the monsoons was truly miserable, but there was nothing to do except suffer through it. Living out of a rucksack did simplify things, because after you loaded up with rations and munitions, there wasn't much room for anything else. You didn't have to decide what to wear today, or tomorrow, or the next day, because you were wearing it when you went to sleep and you already had it on when you got up in the morning. The jungle rucksack itself was a great piece of gear, lightweight and simple with an aluminum exterior frame, much better than the over-engineered ALICE packs the Army issued later. We carried very little for personal comfort. Most grunts had either a hammock or an air mattress, but seldom both. The old Rubber Lady air mattresses were ominously coffin-shaped and it was hard to find one which was not dry rotted. Most grunts therefore gravitated to nylon jungle hammocks and slept directly on hard ground when there were no trees to sling hammocks.

Everyone experimented with his load bearing equipment, tinkering with it until he was satisfied. Some guys placed a piece of heavy C ration packing case cardboard in their rucksack frames, so lumpy objects in the pack would not dig into their backs, but most preferred to take more care in packing their rucks, to avoid that problem. Few grunts wore GI pistol belts, except perhaps to carry a flap holster and ammo pouches for a .45, but never with TA50 suspenders, which were not compatible with rucksack shoulder straps and frames. Grunts never used Army-issue ammo pouches to carry M16 magazines, because they were designed for use with pistol belts and suspenders, but I had one attached to the outside of my rucksack. It was used to carry my field notebook, ballpoint pen, grease pencil, signal mirror and a few other small items, plus two M26 frags in the carriers on the sides of the pouch. The 5.56mm stripper-clips came packaged in seven pocket bandoliers, made of thin cotton fabric. The cotton bandoliers were lightweight but strong enough to carry loaded M16 magazines. Two stripper-clip bandoliers would carry 14 twenty round magazines, or a combination of magazines and hand frags. Some soldiers carried extra magazines, especially the 30 round ones, in Claymore mine bags. I made frequent use of the heavy plastic bags from PRC25 battery packaging, to protect my camera, notebook and other small items that moisture would damage. RTOs always kept their radio handsets tightly "bagged" to protect them from rain; the heavy plastic raincoat did not inhibit transmissions in the least, even when the talker was whispering. For me, an essential piece of gear was an olive drab towel, which I always wore around my neck when humping the rucksack. The towel ends were tucked under the ruck's shoulder straps for extra padding during long humps. I also used the towel for wiping sweat from my face/neck and for keeping my spectacles clear.

We each had a waterproof poncho and a poncho liner, which was an ultra-light camouflaged quilt. Ponchos were used as shelters, not as rain garments. There were two types of poncho, including a lightweight rip-stop nylon version, which grunts always rejected because they were not completely waterproof. Infantrymen always carried the older, heavily rubberized version. Two ponchos were sometimes snapped together to make a two man shelter. In the jungle, a hammock could be tightly strung low between two trees, with a single poncho stretched just above it and tied to the same trees with boot laces. Each end of the poncho was then spread by sticks between the corner grommets, to form an "A" shaped roof. The four corners were tied off with boot laces to shrubs or stakes. A soldier could stay dry in this type of shelter, even in a heavy rain. They taught this form of hammock shelter at the Jungle Warfare School in Panama, with a mosquito bar suspended from the end-sticks, but grunts rarely carried mosquito bars in Vietnam. In open areas at night, we'd usually just roll up in our ponchos and poncho liners on the ground, to sleep in the rain; all grunts spent many miserable nights that way. If it was not raining, the poncho was used as a ground cloth. We slathered GI insect repellant on our exposed skin and pulled the poncho liners over our heads, to fend off mosquito attacks. The insect repellant was so strong that it would literally melt the paint off a hand grenade, and we quickly learned not to get it in our eyes, but bug dope didn't damage the lightweight material of a poncho liner.

I developed a really severe case of jungle rot on my feet, so Doc Wright sent me to the Battalion Surgeon. The doctor said the only cure was to come out of the field, which I couldn't do. He told me to regularly take off my boots and dry out my feet when we were in day laagers, but I was already trying to do that to the extent possible. I had a pair of Monsoon Slippers, which were lightweight ankle-high canvas slippers with thin rubber soles and Velcro closures, a neat piece of gear. I wore the Monsoon Slippers without socks in day laagers, but never in NDPs. I always wore my jungle boots at night, wet or not. Monsoon Slippers were hard to come by, so many guys had Ho Chi Minh Sandals to wear in day laagers. Ho Chi Minh Sandals were locally manufactured from discarded jeep tires and strips of inner tubes, standard footwear of the VC and NVA. All GIs carried an extra pair of socks and foot powder. Doc Wright checked everyone's feet regularly. No one wore underwear, because it caused chafing and jungle rot in the groin area, but we each carried thin cotton OD boxer shorts, to use as swimming trunks near villages. In the hinterlands, we often skinny-dipped in large bomb craters... or bathed from steel pots.

Everyone had some kind of waterproof container, often a small steel ammo can, for photos, letters from home, stationary, documents and a few other personal items, such as toothbrush, soap, razor, and camera/film. My waterproof container was a Tupperware box, which was about 14"X14"X4". It was perfectly sized to fit neatly inside my ruck against my back, light in weight and it stood up to extreme abuse for 6 ½ months. For nostalgia and good luck, I carried and used my Grandfather's old Gillette double-edge steel safety razor, even though it was almost as heavy as a framing hammer.

We mostly carried ammunition, water and food. While I had an M203, I wore a mesh and nylon ammo vest with 24 individual pockets for 40mm grenades. Someone found a footlocker in the rear which was full of experimental Colt-manufactured thirty round magazines, which worked reliably. I carried 7 loaded thirty round magazines, plus 14 loaded twenty round magazines and at least one bandoleer of 5.56mm rounds in stripper clips. For reliability, magazines were always loaded two rounds less than full capacity, so that came to 448 rounds in magazines and another 140 rounds in clips, for a total of 588 rounds of rifle ammo. I also carried three or more hand frags, of the M26 "lemon" type. The newer M67 baseball grenades were made in that size and shape, because all American boys know how to throw a baseball. But grunts would not accept baseball grenades, because of rumors that some of them had short fuses. Frags were always "cooked off" before throwing, so a short fuse was deadly. I always carried several smoke grenades, at least one Claymore with 6 volt lantern battery, 40 feet or more of det cord, a one pound block or two of C4, time fuse and both types of blasting caps. Iodine tablets could be used to purify water, but were used only in emergencies because they produced a terrible taste. We were usually resupplied with lukewarm potable water every three days. I had a 5 quart bladder canteen, three 2 quart canteens and a 1 quart canteen. That comes to 12 quarts of water, which alone weighed more than 24 pounds. I also had a Starlight scope, my Bethlehem Steel/Work Safely flashlight, a GI pocketknife, a Puma Folding Hunter, a .45 pistol with three loaded magazines and three days of C rations. There were assorted other things, such as a signal mirror, towel, a paperback novel (several came out in each mail bag) and a monsoon sweater. Sometimes I also carried a machete. All my gear, including weapon and steel pot, weighed well over 100 pounds, far too much according to backpacking experts. My rucksack eventually became so heavy that I needed help lifting it onto my back, or getting to my feet with it already on. I still have a strong memory of the searing pain in my shoulders, low back, knees and legs, from the exertion of humping my heavy ruck, especially in the mountains. But I carried it because I needed everything. One key to managing this load was to carefully pack the rucksack so it was balanced and most of the weight was as high as possible. The other key was to be young and fit from humping the bush every day. We were in the 11th Light Infantry Brigade, but "Light" did not describe the loads we carried.

    C rations deserve to be mentioned because we lived on them. C rations were "wet" canned Combat Rations, originally developed during WWII. They were designated for "infrequent" use by combat troops, because studies showed that a steady diet of canned food was tolerable only for short periods of time. The slightly improved versions issued in Vietnam were labeled MCI (Meal, Combat Individual) but everyone continued to call them C rations. They were still intended to be issued only for short time periods because of the monotony factor, but grunts in Vietnam subsisted mainly on Cs for months at a time. They were consistently bland and there was no effort by the Army Quartermaster Corps to make them more palatable. C ration meals were put up in standard cans, which were not as packable in rucksacks as the flattened rectangular cans previously used for K rations. Old soldiers griped about the demise of the flat rectangular cans, but standard round cans were cheaper to manufacture, so round cans prevailed. Wet rations in round cans were too bulky and excessively heavy, especially for already overburdened foot soldiers who were embroiled in tropical jungle warfare. Most grunts stacked the C-rat cans and repacked them in cushion-soled socks, to improve portability and reduce clanking. Soldiers were allowed three meals per day, but to minimize their burdens many grunts ate only one or two meals. Each complete meal weighed about 2.6 pounds. For a standard three day supply of food, it was easier to carry six meals (15.6 lbs.) than nine (23.4 lbs.). Infantry soldiers often went hungry, basically because military combat rations were not as light and portable as they should have been.

Each C ration meal box contained these items, individually packed in four cans, one tall, two short and one very short/flat: 1.) Main meal item, 2.) Crackers, with candy discs or cocoa, 3.) Fruit; or bread/desert. 4.) Cheese, peanut butter or jam spread. Except when we occasionally received some 1950s-series rations, there were the same 12 meals in each cardboard packing case. Everyone wanted the meals with pound cake or peaches, which were the tastiest things in a case. The Platoon Sergeant sometimes opened the cases upside down so the guys couldn't read the labels when they picked meals, but most of them knew the packing patterns anyway. On a practical level, there were really only 10 meals instead of 12, because nobody would accept *Ham & Eggs/ Chopped-Cooked*, which looked like coagulated beige dog food, or *Ham & Lima Beans*, which were always called "Ham and M-Fs". Those two items were unspeakably awful and were always thrown away, but QMC was not attuned to customer satisfaction, so the two abominable meals continued to be issued. A "B1 Unit" meal box contained fruit in a tall can, meat in a short can (e.g., *Boned Chicken*), crackers packaged in a short can with one of several types of chocolate candy discs and peanut butter. A B2 Unit provided meat in a tall can (e.g., *Franks & Beans*), crackers, dessert (fruit cake, pecan roll or pound cake) and processed cheese spread. A B3 Unit provided meat in a short can, white bread in a short can, crackers packaged with cocoa powder in a tall can and jam. The cheese, jam and peanut butter spreads were put up in small flat tins. The disc crackers were tasteless, reminiscent of 19th Century hardtack. The chocolate candy discs came in four types, none of which were very appetizing. The pecan roll tasted like processed sawdust, but the pound cake was surprisingly tasty. It was SOP to open unwanted rations, such as Ham & M-Fs, or the terrible fruitcake, and burn them in a fire at the day laager. But a prankster would sometimes throw an *unopened* can in a hot fire and wait for it to cook off. The resulting explosion was called a "Peanut Butter Frag", regardless of which food produced it. This gave rise to a standard admonition to bunched-up troops, "Spread out, one Peanut Butter Frag would kill all of you!" C ration peanut butter was so oily that it would readily light and tins of it were sometimes burned in firebase perimeter bunkers as smoky field-expedient candles. Most soldiers reached a point where they could only stomach the fruit and a few of the meats. My standard meal choices eventually became *Turkey Loaf, Boned Chicken* and *Beef in Spiced Sauce*. I could also eat the thick *Ham Slices,* or *Pork Steak Slices,* if they were broiled on a stick to burn off the grease. Peaches, fruit cocktail, pears and the delicious pound cake were my favorites. I became tired of apricots, pineapple chunks and apple sauce, but I occasionally ate them, or mixed them with other foods (e.g., ham slices with pineapple chunks) for variety. Some soldiers favored *Spaghetti, Franks & Beans* or *Beans with Meat Balls*. To cope with the blandness, nearly every soldier doused C-rations from a bottle of Louisiana Red Hot Sauce or Tabasco Sauce which was always carried in his rucksack. Each C-rat meal contained a plastic spoon wrapped in clear plastic. There was a sealed brown Accessory Packet in each meal, containing 4 cigarettes in a miniature hard pack, an OD book of paper matches, Chiclet chewing gum, toilet paper, salt, pepper, "Coffee-Instant-Type II", nondairy creamer and sugar.

    Some soldiers became jackleg gourmets by mixing ingredients creatively, but most of their concoctions are best left forgotten. C ration gumbo creations were so prevalent among grunts that the McIlhenny Company, maker of Tabasco sauce, published and distributed a *Charlie Ration Cookbook*, available by mail, free for the asking. Alas, the *Cookbook* was primarily a marketing ploy for Tabasco sauce, because its recipes frequently called for ingredients that grunts never had, such as butter. Supplemental food items were often sent to grunts from home, such as tea bags, canned Danish bacon, Minute Rice, small canned hams, dehydrated gravy, dried soup, Kool Aide, powdered lemonade, sardines, tuna, Spam, Vienna sausages, smoked oysters and various condiments.

    Occasionally we received LRRP rations (pronounced "lurp") which were originally produced for Long Range Recon Patrols. These lightweight freeze-dried meals came in foil-lined canvas pouches. Water was boiled in a canteen cup, dumped into the pouch and allowed to sit for several minutes to reconstitute the food. LRRP meal choices included Beef Hash, Beef and Rice, Beef Stew, Chicken and Rice, Chili Con Carne, Spaghetti with Meat Sauce and several others. LRRP rations were quite tasty, especially when jazzed with a little hot sauce. They were the type of rations infantrymen *should* have received routinely in Vietnam. LRRP rations came with a tropical chocolate bar or a dried fruit bar, lighter but not as palatable as canned fruit. The LRRP Accessory Packet was identical to the one which came with C rations. CPT Guill once discovered that the B Company Supply Sergeant had acquired a shipment of LRRP rations, but he was hoarding them in Chu Lai as REMF snacks, to supplement their three daily A-ration mess hall meals. It wasn't pretty. *Xin loi*, Supply Sergeant.

Everyone carried several tiny P38 can openers to open his C-rations, plus an old fashioned church key. Four P38s in individual paper wrappings were packed in every case of C rations. There were always plenty of church keys available; they had disappeared from common use Back in the Real World, but zip-top beverage cans did not exist in Vietnam. A canteen cup was a simple but necessary piece of gear, used for brewing hot drinks or cooking C ration hobo-hash creations. Meals were heated on little stoves made from an empty C-rat short can, perforated all around, top and bottom by a church key and fueled by heat tablets. Heat tablets were blue oval *Trioxane* chemical tablets. They burned hotly and gave off extremely noxious fumes, the tiniest whiff of which would cause the nose and eyes to burn severely. Small chunks of C4 plastic explosive were sometimes used as stove fuel. The C4 plastic explosive burned even more hotly than heat tablets and it was preferred by grunts as a cooking fuel for that reason. We tried to always maintain a supply of heat tabs and C4 explosive, to prevent cannibalization of our Claymore mines by the troops. They would break off the backs of the Claymores to liberate the C4, oblivious to the cost and the waste of ordinance. C4 was very safe to handle and it could be formed like putty into various shapes. C4 could be tossed around or set afire without concerns about it exploding, but it was *NOT* recommended that a soldier stomp on C4 if it was already lit, to put out the fire. It was formulated to explode only if subjected to heat and concussion at the same time, such as from the explosive force of a blasting cap.

The Mad Fragger and Me

I have only fragments of memories left about some events. On one occasion, I got into a pissing contest with a Cobra gunship pilot who shot for us after a minor skirmish, but now I can't remember what the dispute was about. I found two separate S2/S3 journal references to dust-offs for heat injuries of 2nd Platoon soldiers, but I have no explicit memory of related events. One of the heat casualties was a dependable and genial soldier named Don Braziel, who did not come back to us; I think he recovered and was given a rear job, but I'm not sure. On another occasion, my troops slaughtered, cooked and ate all of a villager's chickens and the old farmer was furious. I couldn't get too upset with them because a couple of resupply flights had been cancelled and we were subsisting on very short rations. I had to buy off the outraged farmer with MPC. I also have a vague recollection of a lieutenants' party in Dennis Ransdell's Chu Lai quarters, during which I got truly hammered and earned a world-class hangover.

I seem to have suffered a total memory dump of some events. Doc Wright recalls that we found the skeleton of an enemy soldier in a hammock, inside a hootch, on jungle high ground overlooking a valley. The dink's weapon and gear were also there, but Doc says we did not touch anything for fear that it was booby trapped. There was a deserted NVA compound nearby. Doc also says that we called in art'y, Willie Pete on the deck, to destroy the hootch and the compound. I do not remember any of that and I know that I would have been extremely reluctant to abandon a captured weapon, even if I thought it might have been booby trapped. So I deduced that the incident might have occurred while I was on R&R/leave, or after my DEROS date. But Doc specifically recalls that I was there and SSG Wayne Wilson remembers it the same way. Oh well, it *was* many years ago. Maybe I've seen too many *Night of the Living Dead* sequels, so my brain suppressed the creepy memory of a zombie soldier, reclining in his rotting hammock, waiting for the next full moon, or whatever the heck zombies get resurrected for.

Tom Dolan

I now wish that I had kept a diary and replaced my stolen camera to take more pictures, to keep my memory fresh. A list of LZ Liz bunker assignments near the end of my tour in an old notebook lists: <u>Bunker #4</u>: Goins, Krebsbach, Sanchez, Telamentes, Thomas, Lane. <u>Bunker #5</u>: Swanson, Dingleberry, Mace, Henry, Lowe, Phillips. <u>Bunker #6</u>: Jones, Lowery, J. Stephens , Weidner, Schmidt, Schilling, Malonson, Bush. <u>Bunker #7</u>: Dolan, Wilson, R. Smith, Wright, Rodriguez, Speith. <u>Bunker #8</u>: S. Stephens, Walton, Russell, Spieght, Ried, Evans. (G. Smith was on leave.) It is sad to admit it, but now I don't remember what some of those soldiers looked like.

Chapter 12:

GOING HOME

I mentioned that I was offered the job of Recon Platoon Leader, which I turned down to stay with the 2nd Platoon. This occurred near the end of my tour. Around the same time, our Battalion Commander told me I had been offered an interview for a rifle platoon leader's job with The Warlords. That was B Company, 123rd Aviation Battalion, the Americal Division's Aero-Scout Rifle Company. The Warlords essentially operated as the Commanding General's personal shock troops. "Warlord" was their radio call sign and official designation, but they were more commonly known by everyone in the Americal Division as "The Animals". Those guys were the real deal, gung-ho ruthless killers, with blood and rice paddy dirt under their fingernails, unlike the starchy and pretentious 75th Rangers. The Animals reportedly had the highest kill ratio of any similarly sized unit in Vietnam. They had their own dedicated helicopters, pilots and crews. They spent all their time, every day, looking for trouble and making combat assaults into hot LZs. Most of their officers were Regular Army, Airborne and Ranger qualified, so it was surprising that a plain vanilla OCS lieutenant like me was invited to join. I don't know how or why The Warlords got my name, but I was flattered by the invitation. I would have had to extend my tour in order to accept and perhaps apply for a Regular Army commission (mine was USAR). I was also tired of the stress of combat and ready to end the experience. So I declined, truthfully telling the Battalion Commander that I had decided to get out of the Army. Maybe that was a mistake. I really did like the Army, just not its politics and the lack of moral courage among some of its leaders.

After my final mission on Nui Vong, I said goodbye to CPT Guill at LZ Liz and returned to the B Company cantonment area in Chu Lai. I gathered my belongings, took care of clearance paperwork and picked up travel orders from Zip Onevelo. My imminent departure seemed to be fraught with bad omens. I saw an enlisted man wearing the jungle fatigue shirt I had brought with me from Fort Hood, which I immediately recognized because of the horizontal U.S. Army tape and the directly-embroidered collar insignia. He had ripped off my name tape, but he was wearing my lieutenant's bar, crossed rifles and other insignia. The new "lieutenant" played dumb when I confronted him about souveniring my shirt and doing a lousy job of impersonating an officer. When I cleared battalion HQ, I received a couple of meritorious service medals, but I noticed that there was no Air Medal, although I had accumulated enough CAs for at least two awards. The Battalion Awards Clerk said the orders were probably in transit to Brigade HQ for signatures and he would forward copies to my HOR, but of course I never received them. (I was also aware that our First Sergeant and Command Sergeant Major had both finagled Air Medals for themselves, although they never went on any Combat Assaults.) I discovered that my entire collection of VC/NVA souvenirs had disappeared from the Supply Room, stolen by REMFs. My old AWOL bag was still there, containing my grandfather's leather shaving kit and my whiskey flask. I also found the three casual civilian outfits and Weejun penny loafers which I had purchased in Hawaii. I had one tropical weight khaki uniform and an overseas cap, but my previously spit shined low-quarters were completely covered with thick green mold. The leather was ruined, but I had to clean and polish the shoes as best I could, because replacements were not easily available. For some reason, the sight of the moldy green low-quarters, which had originally been issued to me in Basic Training, had a profound impact on me. They seemed to be symbolic of something, perhaps a sad and ignominious end to my military career. Accordingly, I threw them away as soon as I got home.

    I went through the Cam Ranh Bay Repo Depot on my way home. As soon as I arrived in Cam Ranh, I purchased a large hard-side Samsonite suitcase at the PX. I repacked my personal belongings in the lockable suitcase. The dilapidated AWOL bag and a scrounged barracks bag were both tossed in a trash can. At Cam Ranh Bay, there was an impromptu reunion with many of my OCS classmates, the survivors who had not been killed or badly wounded and who were getting out of the Army. We all had the same Date of Rank and we therefore also had the same DEROS and ETS dates. Those of us who had chosen to leave active service were given the same two month "drop" from our two year commitments as part of Army downsizing, so we were leaving Vietnam about a month early from our original 12 month tours. We were in the Repo Depot for several days waiting for flights. There was continuous partying in the O-Club every day and in the officers' barracks every night. Lots of beer was consumed, while many outrageous war stories were told. We also talked about the guys who had been greased or dusted off to The World, all of whom someone seemed to know about, through the Jungle Telegraph or the Star & Stripes casualty lists. Ray Simmons commented about an OC 37-69 classmate who was killed in action, "I never liked him, because he wouldn't share his cookies from home in OCS". We all laughed, probably out of relief that we had survived. One night, the Cam Ranh Bay base was attacked by 122mm rockets and a nearby ammo dump blew up. Several very excited clerks with M16s, flak jackets and helmets burst into the officers' barracks, trying to evacuate us to a bunker. The clerks were met by a chorus of shouts, "Get the hell out of here! We're trying to sleep!"

The Army drug tested us, by ushering us into a small building, where we were required to stand in a row along a long trough and pee in little bottles, while a perverted looking PFC leered at us from his seat in a lifeguard chair, to make sure we didn't switch urine samples. This insulting treatment was infuriating, after all the crap I'd been through as a rifle platoon leader. I was <u>now</u> ready for rank to finally have some privileges and to be treated accordingly. Adding more insult to injury, the MPs met us at the airport with drug dogs to sniff us and our bags. The MPs searched through our luggage too.

Tom Dolan

They confiscated my tattered field map as an alleged "security violation" and they also took my Monsoon Slippers because they were "unauthorized" for stateside wear. A thieving MP tried to take a frayed NVA pistol belt which I'd had in my rucksack (instead of in the Supply Room) supposedly because I didn't have any "paperwork" on it, which was absurd. But I'd had enough by then, so I made a loud stink about it in blistering grunt language, demanding to speak to his OIC. The MP changed his mind, acting like he was making a major concession. I kept the belt and he missed finding my jungle hammock, which was folded up inside of one of the two jungle fatigue uniforms I was permitted to take home. The REMF Military Police therefore did not disappoint me, exceeding all expectations as assholes.

My 18½ hour flight to Vietnam in October 1970 had taken place all in daylight, but the flight home all took place in the dark. We again refueled in Japan. As a going home gift to myself, I purchased a new self-winding Seiko diver's watch in the Yokota Airport gift shop. My battered old Timex had taken a lickin' but it kept on tickin'. (Thanks for the advice, John Cameron Swayze.)

We flew into Fort Lewis, Washington, where we had to go through U.S. Customs in the middle of the night. My friend Sid Hopfer was on the same flight and he came out of another customs line, chuckling. I asked him what was so funny and he said the elderly customs agent who was about to search his bags noticed the 20th Infantry Regiment unit crests on the shoulder straps of Sid's TWs. He'd said, "Twentieth Infantry Regiment, huh? I was with 'Sykes' Regulars' in 1918, so go on through, lieutenant". Sid didn't even have to open his bags. (I still always get in the wrong line.) I stayed up all night in a Fort Lewis orderly room while the EM on our flight were out-processed, on top of the sleepless 18 ½ hour flight from Cam Ranh Bay. Everyone was given chits for a 24 hour steak house operated by the Army and I had a huge steak and egg breakfast around 0300, local time. The Army therefore gave me a traditional "Combat Breakfast" only after all combat was behind me. Officers were out-processed commencing at 0800, which took most of the day. After that, I went to the Fort Lewis Main PX to purchase a clean tropical weight khaki uniform and a set of ribbons to wear on the flight home. We were encouraged to travel in civilian clothes in those days, because of occasional incidents in air, bus or train terminals instigated by anti-war activists, but I was too cocky to hide in mufti. I had been awake for at least 48 continuous hours and I badly needed a shower and shave. So I shared the cost of a hotel room with OCS classmate and friend Jim Griffin, to get cleaned up and catch a few hours sleep. Griff was a former SSG/Drill Sergeant and he was returning from his second Vietnam tour, both in the Americal Division. After a sumptuous meal at the hotel with Griff, we said goodbye and I caught a direct flight from SEATAC Airport to Baltimore-Washington International. I noticed hostile vibes from only one civilian, a businessman who was seated next to me on the flight to Baltimore. Nobody spit on me or called me a baby killer.

I reviewed what I've written and I have not done a very good job of explaining how grueling life was for grunts, or the difficult strain of infantry combat. Oh well. Maybe you just had to be there to understand.

My transformation from a naïve 22 year old college boy to a callous and cynical 25 year-old combat veteran was thus completed. But no one was aware of it. And no one, not my wife, friends or family, really cared.

The Army released me from active duty effective 1 September 1971. I was in the inactive Army Reserve for about a year and I joined the Maryland Army National Guard in 1973. I was promoted to Captain there on 19 December 1973 and stayed in the Guard until 1980, when I became fed up with its politics and resigned my commission. I had some truly hilarious experiences in the MDARNG, but I think I'm finished writing about my military career. The problem with all the stuff that happened during those years was that it was anticlimactic and it paled in comparison to my experiences in combat. That is also unfortunately true of all my civilian experiences during my working life. I lived more uninhibitedly and I had more adventure, fun and satisfaction as a rifle platoon leader in Vietnam than at any time in my life since then. *Xin loi, El Tee.*

Epilogue

I found that the effort of remembering and writing down this personal history was cathartic, because I needed to get a few things off my chest. This project started as a vehicle to entertain my relatives and descendants, but it morphed into other things, including a critical commentary on Army leadership. It eventually became, primarily, a testimonial to the stalwart fighters of the 2nd Platoon. I decided to formally publish it mostly because these men have never gotten the recognition they deserved, for their patriotism and their service to our country. I omitted or changed a few names for obvious reasons, but this story is otherwise as accurate as I could make it.

During the 6 ½ months I was with Bravo Company, five of our soldiers were killed and more were seriously wounded, but those casualties were probably less than the deaths and injuries in other rifle companies during the same period. By objective military standards, Bravo Company's casualties were minimal, but that does not in any way diminish the tragedy for the families and friends of our fallen comrades, to whom this book is dedicated. Jim Califf, Fred Young, Steve Ast, Joe Johnson and Alex Quiroz were honorable young men who did not shirk their responsibilities as U.S. citizens, unlike the poltroons who ran away to Canada during the same era. This fact alone is sufficient reason to cherish their memories. These fine young men may be gone but they are not forgotten.

The reader may have correctly guessed that The Mad Fragger's grunt name in the title of this memoir is symbolic. Gary Smith was a very good combat soldier, but his moniker is in the title to represent *all* the enlisted soldiers of the 2nd Platoon, who could not be listed individually. Like The Mad Fragger, some of them were draftees and most of them would have preferred to be somewhere else, but that did not really matter. Never mind that the United States had conceded the war. They were already in Vietnam and they were embroiled in the ultimate competition, combat. They did not fight for the glory of it, or for the generals, or for the politicians, or for Grandma, or for anyone else outside of 2nd Platoon. They fought for each other. And they did that with honor.

We tracked down The Mad Fragger in early 2012, but a few months too late. Gary W. Smith died at age 61, on August 24, 2011, from an Agent Orange-related cancer. He too is a legitimate casualty of the Vietnam War, although he is not counted among the 58,000 American war deaths. Several others from my platoon suffered similar fates. A disproportionate number of us have been diagnosed with chronic illnesses attributed by the Veterans Administration to toxin exposure. This is not surprising, given our 24/7 immersion in the tainted environment. The Operation Ranch Hand records show that the nasty stuff was sprayed extensively in Quang Ngai and Mo Duc Provinces. We were not only walking around in Agent Orange residue, but we were also breathing it, laying down to sleep in it, and probably ingesting it with our food and water. Lobbying by the VFW, the American Legion and other misguided veterans' groups has resulted in some ex-sailors drawing Agent Orange disability benefits, because they once disembarked from their blue water ships for a day or two at some Vietnamese port city. Additional blue water sailors are now claiming that they were exposed to Agent Orange through their ships' water filtration systems, 60 miles or more offshore! I did not put my life on the line for *that* kind of freeloading. Raquel Welch had more time in-country than those bogus Vietnam veterans.

I was in Vietnam from October 1970 through August 1971. More than 6,000 GIs were killed in Vietnam during 1970, almost all of them U.S. Army troops. To provide modern context, less than 4,500 American troops were killed during the entire *nine* years of the Iraq War. Many people think that the Vietnam fighting was mostly over by 1971, but that is not correct. More GIs were killed in 1971 (2,357, of which 2,131 were in Army units) than in 1965, the first year of Vietnam ground combat for U.S. Marine and Army units. To provide another contemporary comparison, U.S. KIAs in

The Mad Fragger and Me

1971 exceeded the total number of American troops killed during the first *ten* years of our 21st century war in Afghanistan. The Vietnam War was more intense and lethal than later wars.

1LT Roger Mackintosh and 1LT Sidney Hopfer provided conflicting opinions to me about what Infantry combat was like, before I experienced it for myself. According to Mac, grunt life was like a long hunting/camping adventure at government expense, but Sid deplored the experience because of the horrors he had endured. Ironically, Lieutenant Mackintosh was later grievously wounded, but Lieutenant Hopfer ultimately survived the ordeal without a scratch. I hope I have communicated, by relating my own experiences, that both of them were truthful, although they had opposing perspectives. For me, it was a pretty violent 6 ½ month safari with Bravo Company, but my platoon dished out most of the mayhem.

I left Vietnam directly from a rifle platoon, which may have intensified the shock of the transition from active combat to civilian life. I felt badly about leaving Huynh The Hy, Jim-Jim and my GI comrades behind, in the sense that it seemed like an act of abandonment, even though I knew I had fully done my duty. By the time I left Vietnam in 1971, I believed that continuing the war was pointless, because I did not think that the South Vietnamese Army would ever be able stand up to the communists. I had only invested two years and eight months of my life in the war effort, but many thousands of other GIs had given their lives, or permanently lost various body parts and their dreams for the future, in the same cause. This terrible sacrifice by other soldiers tragically continued even after I came home, because the U.S. did not pull out completely until two years later.

By 1971, the most difficult leadership challenge faced by rifle platoon leaders and company commanders was that the war we were fighting had already been forfeited, as demonstrated by the withdrawal of American units. We knew this and so did all of our troops. Commencing with the 1968 Tet Offensive, the American news media preached that we were losing the war, parroting the propaganda generated by the North Vietnamese. This turned out to be untrue, but American soldiers had no way of assessing the larger picture and we had front-row seats for the continued violence. This situation was profoundly demoralizing and it probably resulted in increased drug use and deterioration of discipline. Many (or perhaps most) company grade officers responded to the war's forfeiture by trying to avoid contact with the enemy, which seemed like a logical plan. They hoped that this would allow them to bring their soldiers home unscathed, but the enemy still killed them at every opportunity. A few of us took the opposite approach and were not afraid to make the tiger growl by poking him in the eye with a sharp stick, but there were no strategic goals involved and we were just trying to survive by dominating the enemy on the battlefield.

The peasants clearly wanted to be left alone. They had nothing to begin with and they did not care whether the country was controlled by Saigon or by Hanoi. I doubt that they understood the differences between capitalism and communism. The ubiquitous rice farmers were constantly caught in the crossfire between us and the communists, so they seemed to support whichever side happened to be present in their village at the moment. I sometimes had an uneasy feeling that we might be fighting on the *wrong* side, when I reflected on the contrast between the hardnosed NVA troops and the lackadaisical ARVN soldiers. Perhaps it predated the influx of Americans, but an especially disturbing aspect was the corrupting influence that Western culture and affluence seemed to have had on the South Vietnamese. This was demonstrated by the Black Market, the thriving drug trade, the theft of military payrolls by ARVN officers, the political assassinations and the many other signs of rampant corruption. On the other hand, honorable people like Huynh The Hy and Jim-Jim seemed unaffected by the widespread fraud. The whole country was an enigma.

Nobody wanted to talk to me about Vietnam when I first came home, which was fine with me, because I was exhausted by the experience and wanted to put it behind me. I thought that no one could understand what combat was really like unless they had been in it. I also thought the United States had become mired in a mess, from which there was no honorable escape. I was angry about what I saw happening to *my* Army and I had no hope that the military hierarchy would fix it. (I was wrong, as evidenced by the U.S. Army's exemplary performance in *Operation Desert Storm* and subsequent wars. Some of my contemporaries, including West Point graduates who were eventually promoted into top leadership positions, recognized the leadership deficiencies and systemic problems in Vietnam... and dedicated their careers to correcting them.) Even now, people seldom bring up the subject of Vietnam with me, but if they do it is usually to ask me if I supported the war or was opposed to it. That is a meaningless question to a lowly Infantry soldier who was caught up in the middle of a shooting war. In that situation, you just hunkered down with your comrades and did your best to survive. Infantry soldiers always fight for their buddies, never for a political goal. Few soldiers in the bush really sympathized with the war protestors at home, but there wasn't much indignant outrage directed at them either, probably because many of us had ambivalent feelings about the war. We were also too busy with the urgent problem of staying alive to worry very much about the opinions of some soft college students and spaced out hippies at home. There was a consensus that anti-war radicals who openly encouraged the communists to kill American soldiers were treasonous scum, but other than that most of us were indifferent to the protests.

It's a strange admission, but I am *still* uncertain whether I supported, or was opposed to, the Vietnam War. The historical and political reasons for our involvement in Vietnam are tangled, difficult to fully understand and beyond the scope of this commentary. But the "Second Indochina War" was not simply a civil war which the U.S. stupidly blundered into, nor was it an illegal/immoral manifestation of U.S. imperialism, as the communists and their leftist American supporters would have us believe. A more accurate theory is that the Vietnam War was a proxy conflict, fought as a part of the Cold War, with U.S. and Communist Bloc prestige on the line. The reason usually given during the 1960s for our presence in Vietnam was honorable. We were there, under the "Domino Theory", to halt the spread of communism in Southeast Asia and to provide Vietnamese citizens with an opportunity for self-determination. A major fallacy in that concept is that communism may not be a bad deal for people who have nothing to begin with, especially if they don't give a damn about who is running things. Under those circumstances, it is doubtful that the desire of U.S. politicians to halt the spread of communism justified the commitment of American combat troops. On the other hand, the dominoes ultimately did not fall throughout all of Southeast Asia and many governments there remain free of communist domination to this day. The United States also won The Cold War, as of 1990. Therefore it is difficult to say, even with the clarity of 20:20 hindsight, whether I supported the Vietnam War or was opposed to it. There is a more appropriate and profound question about the war, which is more easily answered: Was the war in Vietnam <u>worth</u> fighting? It was not. It was not worth sacrificing the life of even one American serviceman who died there, or worth ruining the prospects of any soldier who was maimed in combat. This brings me inescapably to the conclusion that the Vietnam War should not have been fought by the United States. I *still* do not regret that I participated in it. No, I cannot really explain that. My friend David Cox often says that we are among the very few men from our generation who were privileged to have led an Infantry rifle platoon in ground combat. My lack of regret for participating in the Vietnam War probably has something to do with that. I can't really explain that either, but others who have done it know what it means.

    Truth is sometimes difficult to ferret out. Winston Churchill observed that accurate information in wartime is so precious that it must always be protected by a bodyguard of lies. Accordingly, false information has been used in war from the beginning of time in various ways, including propaganda. But deceptive information has seldom been used to demoralize and defeat the propagandists' <u>own</u> country, which would of course be treasonous. After I returned from Vietnam, I began to realize how activists were using lies and deceit in their antiwar crusade, abetted by the news media and an entertainment industry with the same agenda. Most of the false information campaign was directed against American combat soldiers. This may have been the foundation of their effort to prove to the public that the Vietnam War was "immoral" and "meaningless". The My Lai Massacre was a genuine abomination, but I knew from personal experience that incidents like that were rare. All Vietnam veterans were inferentially or directly accused of similar atrocities, but terrorist acts committed by the VC/NVA were never mentioned by the American press. The efforts and sacrifices of veterans were not appreciated and we were usually ridiculed for our patriotism. Hollywood propaganda against veterans was omnipresent and insidious. Watching reruns of old TV dramas and 1970s-vintage movies will confirm that Vietnam veterans were usually portrayed as war criminals, drug addicts, neurotics, psychopaths, bums and losers. Whenever a Vietnam veteran got into trouble, the news media always emphasized that aspect of his history, as if his bad behavior was a *fait accompli*. Because of the media bias and continuous misinformation, many American citizens became leery of Vietnam veterans. Because of the abuse from antiwar activists, veterans also became wary of civilians. A few well-publicized antiwar demonstrations had been staged in airports, which were widely broadcast on network TV news programs. That footage showed returning soldiers being assaulted by gangs of cursing and spitting antiwar demonstrators. As a result of these occasional confrontations, military authorities often recommended that servicemen travel in civilian clothes, to avoid unnecessary trouble. The airport demonstrations were not frequent, but they apparently caused many veterans to synthesize civilian behaviors into a common Urban Legend. According to the tall tale now told by an overwhelming number of Vietnam veterans, when they got off their Freedom Birds in various U.S. airports, all of them were spit upon and called "baby killer" by war protestors. I want to laugh every time I hear that implausible statement, but the underlying truth is not so funny.

Occasionally I have been asked about my opinion of various Vietnam War films. I think most of them are terrible, because they caricaturize and insult veterans. Some of them, like the *Rambo* series, are just silly. Probably the most absurd Vietnam War film I've seen was *The Deer Hunter*, which is loaded with ridiculous stereotypes and contrived metaphors. After I saw that tedious and overblown movie, I thought, "What the hell was that all about?", because it bore no similarity to the war I was in. Even the antlered deer which Robert De Niro's character passes up in the final hunting sequence is a phony, because there aren't any European Red Stags in the mountains near Pittsburg. A sign of the times was that *The Deer Hunter* was nominated for numerous Academy Awards and won the award for Best Picture of 1978! Another surrealistic motion picture which was just as bad, for similar reasons, was *Apocalypse Now*. In my opinion, *Platoon* did a wonderful job of conveying the spooky feel of a night ambush and the chaotic terror of close combat, but it was misleading and seriously flawed in almost all other ways. Oliver Stone, who was supposedly a combat infantryman, clearly shared the enlisted men's fantasy which was described to me by Shane Pinkston. Weak lieutenants such as the El Tee depicted in *Platoon* certainly existed, but they were not the norm. *Platoon* also created the impressions that black troops were cowards, drug use was acceptable among grunts, and atrocities were commonplace, but none of these things were true, at least not in my unit. Oliver Stone should have known better, so his vilifications and distortions are reasons to speculate about his motives, or his personal behavior in Vietnam. *Platoon* is probably

The Mad Fragger and Me

the single most seductive piece of propaganda ever put out by Hollywood, because its leftist messages are so cleverly concealed within the rousing action sequences. The USMC boot camp segment of Stanley Kubrick's *Full Metal Jacket* was terrific in depicting military hide-toughening. The rest of the film was not like the war I knew, but it depicted the Tet Offensive battle at Hue, which was unlike any fight I was in. The Randall Wallace film *We Were Soldiers* (based upon the book *We Were Soldiers Once...And Young*, by Hal Moore and Joe Galloway) came out in 2002. It is the most accurate movie depiction of combat infantrymen, from training in the U.S. through the actual fighting in Vietnam and contains none of the insulting stereotypes or leftist propaganda with which Hollywood is so enamored. Some dramatic license was applied, but it basically replicates the brutal Ia Drang Valley battle in a straightforward way. In the early 1990s, retired Lieutenant General Hal Moore met with the commanders of the NVA units his battalion had fought at Ia Drang Valley in 1965. They told LTG Moore that they had been stunned by the fanaticism in battle of the American infantrymen. The 1st Cavalry Division troops in the Ia Drang Valley fight were competently trained and well led, but they were cherries when that battle occurred. They nevertheless fought like demons, according to the NVA, who were hardened combat soldiers as a result of the First Indochinese War. This was also true of most other U.S. Army and Marine Corps units. That is the part of the Vietnam veterans' story which is almost never told.

Throughout the entire Vietnam War, U.S. leaders made a series of strategic and political blunders, which tended to offset American military successes. At the same time, North Vietnamese communists waged a brilliant political and propaganda war against the U.S., assisted by the antiwar elements of American society and our left-leaning media. It has been generally forgotten that the South Vietnamese Army, with massive American artillery and air support, badly mauled the communists during their all-out 1972 Easter invasion from the north. Despite many years of disinformation and denial from left-wing academics, an increasing number of historians now acknowledge that U.S. and South Vietnamese forces had decisively won the Vietnam War as of December 1972. American suspension of the peace negotiations in Paris and the renewed Christmas 1972 bombing of North Vietnam had pushed the communists to the brink of total capitulation, but most U.S. citizens are not aware of this. North Vietnamese leaders have quietly acknowledged that the Viet Cong had been annihilated in the South by U.S. forces. They have also admitted that North Vietnamese Army was demoralized and defeated, prior to withdrawal of the last U.S. combat troops in 1973. Concurrent with the final U.S. troop withdrawal, congressional Democrats pushed to outlaw all military assistance to South Vietnam, via the Church-Case amendment in 1973. That law eventually passed, with veto-proof bipartisan support from opportunistic congressmen who were worried about the impact of prevailing antiwar sentiment on their reelection campaigns. Congress also severely curtailed the president's authority to continue waging war, by passing The War Powers Act in the same year. Congressmen on both sides of the aisle proudly proclaimed that they had forced the Nixon administration to end the Vietnam War, but their ill-timed and counterproductive actions "snatched defeat from the jaws of victory". The already defeated communists were reinvigorated by these clear political signals from the United States. During the next two years, the North Vietnamese rebuilt their decimated military forces, with assistance from China and the USSR. The NVA again invaded South Vietnam in 1975, with their entire army led by Russian tanks, resulting in the fall of Saigon. The communists' victory in 1975 was attributable to the Church-Case amendment and to the War Powers Act. This final episode of the Vietnam War reflects a disgraceful betrayal of our South Vietnamese allies. American antiwar activists and career politicians were directly responsible for the defeat of South Vietnam and the loss of American prestige in Southeast Asia, not military veterans. I refuse to accept any of the shame which goes with that loss. Guess who <u>owns</u> the shame? All Vietnam veterans should feel vindicated by these facts, regardless of their other opinions about the war.

I had no nightmares while I was in combat, but I started having them soon after I got home. I did not remember my bad dreams upon awakening, but there was a residual aura which convinced me that most of them were combat-related. One of my disturbing dreams was apparently a recurring one, based upon a strong sense of déjà vu whenever I awakened from it, shaking and in a sweat, with my heart pounding. I ducked reflexively whenever fireworks exploded, a truck backfired or a thunderclap sounded unexpectedly. I did not have flashbacks, but in quiet moments my mind always wandered back to reflecting upon my war experiences and this occurred every day. I began to realize that my combat memories were more valuable learning tools than my other life experiences. We always referred to the United States as "The Real World" in Vietnam, but it seemed to me that infantry combat was far more vivid and real than civilian life. In battle, I learned more about leadership, human strengths/weaknesses, situation analysis and managing for results than I would have in any civilian occupation. Over a period of several years, the nightmares diminished and my reactivity to loud noises disappeared. I never talked to anyone about these things, because I thought that they were trivial and a normal part of readjustment. Our participation in the war defined the lives of Vietnam veterans and most of us have not been able to put it completely behind us, but that is not necessarily bad. It appears that all active combatants were changed to some degree by their experiences and some veterans were affected by the horrific episodes more deeply than others. All of us who were involved in actual combat probably experienced some degree of "Post Traumatic Stress", but for many of us this was a relatively minor problem and it did not become a "Disorder". I was not aware that it was happening at the time, but an alarming percentage of my soldiers *were* badly traumatized by our combat experiences. A significant proportion of them, including several who are now deceased, have suffered from severe Post Traumatic Stress Disorder. I don't think the emotional trauma could have been avoided under the circumstances, but I wonder how much their PTSD was exacerbated by the shabby treatment they received from their countrymen when they returned from Vietnam.

For the reasons outlined above, I had a feeling that I was disconnected from the rest of society when I first came home. I found it to be especially annoying whenever a friend asked what I'd been doing and abruptly changed the subject when I said that I'd been away in Vietnam. Even worse were the people who asked "Why didn't you go to Canada?"... which REALLY means, *What's the matter with you, are you STUPID?* I initially had trouble landing a decent job and some interviews went sour as soon as my Vietnam combat experience came up. This sense of alienation was probably even stronger for the younger soldiers who were re-entering The Real World. Most returning veterans reacted to this the same way we learned to deal with adversity in combat. We kept our heads down, coped with the situation and made the best of it. While we were trying to cope however, we were assailed by ridicule from others in society, because we had not dodged military service as they had done, while they pretended to have demonstrated higher moral values by opposing the Vietnam War. Returning combat soldiers knew that the stories of mental illness, unrelenting atrocities and widespread drug abuse among front line troops were exaggerated, but those myths still interfered with our unalienable right to the pursuit of happiness. Nevertheless, I think that most Vietnam veterans have no major regrets and we are proud of the sometimes difficult jobs we did while other citizens were evading military service. The injustices I experienced at the hands of society led me to this Philosophy for Life: *You should try to live your life in such a way so that you can tell any man, at any time, to go to hell.* I therefore now say this, to all of the effete, treasonous, pseudo-intellectual draft dodgers who gave Vietnam veterans a hard time: Go to hell and spark for eternity, you sorry sons of bitches.

Judging by casualty statistics, my experiences were probably tame compared to combat which was endured earlier in the war by other infantrymen, but it is hard to make battlefield comparisons unless you were actually *there*. Some of the most hair-raising war stories I ever heard, involving sapper attacks, dinks in the wire, snipers, rocket barrages, mortar bombardments, blood, gore and mayhem, were told by two enlisted buddies who were seated next to me on my Freedom Bird back to the USA. Listening to them, I wondered where they had been stationed, to have seen so much brutal and unrelenting combat. Suspicion arose when they began to gripe about having to sell their surf boards, because the Army refused to ship them home free as "hold baggage". At that point, I interrupted their conversation, to inquire about their military jobs and place of assignment in Vietnam. They had been Army cooks for 12 months, at the China Beach In-Country Rest & Recreation Center. War stories, by definition, contain some fiction, because veterans seldom let the facts get in the way of a good combat yarn, but unlike those R&R Center cooks, I have tried to tell my tale without embellishment. The events in this memoir are described precisely the way they occurred, or at least exactly the way I remember them.

As this is being written, 17 former B Company soldiers from 1971 are still alive and in regular contact with each other, including 13 who are veterans of the 2nd Platoon. We are still looking for a few of our other old comrades. Some "found" buddies have already gone ahead of us to the Final Stand-Down, but we do not really consider them as deceased. We carefully guard our memories of them, just as we all protected each other's lives many years ago, and somehow appropriately, they remain forever young in our minds. There have been several small reunions in recent years, with attendees coming from all over the United States. Some reminiscing has of course occurred, but spinning war stories really has not been the primary activity. We were simply delighted to again *be with* the best men we have ever known.

I wonder if old draft dodgers and war protestors hold reunions. Do they reminisce about their mutual cowardice? What do they talk about?

Tom Dolan
August, 2016

Glossary of Terms

Acting Jack: An acting sergeant

AC130: USAF fixed-wing gunship, called "Puff the Magic Dragon" by grunts. "AC" stood for Attack-Cargo; converted from C130 cargo planes.

AIT: Advanced Individual Training. MOS school, attended after Basic Combat Training.

AK 47: Kalashnikov-designed Soviet assault rifles, 7.62X39mm. The version with a collapsible wire paratrooper-style stock was called "AK50" by GIs.

AO: Area of Operations. An area blocked out in grid squares on a topographical map and designated for tactical operations by a specific unit.

Ao dai: Traditional Vietnamese female garment; silky trousers covered by an ankle-length high-necked dress, slit up both sides to the hip.

APC: Depending upon context, All Purpose Capsule (aspirin), Armored Personnel Carrier, or All Personnel Concerned.

ARCOM: Army Commendation Medal. Generally awarded for meritorious serve, but much more significant if awarded with "V" device, signifying a specific act of valor.

Article 15: A non-judicial punishment, imposed in lieu of court martial, under Article 15 of the UCMJ.

ARVN: Army of the Republic of Vietnam, i.e., the South Vietnamese Army.

ASA: Army Security Agency. A rear-area organization, whose members spent all their time monitoring radio traffic.

AWOL: Absent Without Leave.

Backhaul: second part of a resupply mission, to retrieve empty food containers, carry outgoing mail, turn in damaged equipment, etc.

Back in the World: The Continental U.S.A.

BA30: Military designation for a D Cell flashlight battery.

BCT: Basic Combat Training

Beaucoup: Mispronounced "boo-coo" by GIs. French, meaning "many".

Beehive: Anti-personnel rounds, loaded with steel flechette projectiles, shaped like small darts.

BMNT: Beginning of Morning Nautical Twilight. First light, when grunts "stand to" in the bush. Last light is EENT in military parlance, End of Evening Nautical Twilight.

Bouncing Betty: A small CHICOM antipersonnel mine. When triggered, it launched about 3 feet into the air and exploded, releasing shrapnel in all directions.

Call for Fire: Radio call format, used to request artillery or mortar fire, standardized to insure that all essential information is included.

CA: Combat Assault. Airmobile attack by helicopter.

Can cuoc: (pronounced "cahn-cook") civilian I.D. card, issued by the South Vietnamese government.

CAR15: The XM177E1 Submachine Gun. An experimental model ("XM") short-barreled version of the M16, with collapsible stock.

Cattle truck: Military tractor-trailer used as troop transports in BCT and AIT.

C&C bird: Command and Control helicopter.

Charlie (or Charlie Cong): a metaphor for the enemy, either Viet Cong or NVA.

Cherry: An inexperienced infantry soldier. A newbie, or FNG.

Chi-Com frag: Chinese-Communist hand grenade, similar in appearance to a German potato-masher, ignited by jerking a string inside its wooden handle. Chi-Com generally means "manufactured in China".

Church Key: A pocket sized beer can and bottle opener.

CIB: The Combat Infantryman's Badge, created in 1943. A silver musket on a rectangular blue background, with a silver wreath, worn above all other decorations on a soldier's uniform.

Chieu hoi: (pronounced "chew-hoy") Literally "open arms", roughly meaning to surrender to U.S. or ARVN forces.

Cherry: A new infantry soldier, inexperienced in combat.

Chogy stick: A flexible wooden or bamboo pole, used by women to carry baskets or bundles on both ends, on one shoulder. Heavier chogy loads resulted in a peculiar flat-footed rhythmic gait.

C4: A plastic high explosive.

Claymore: M18 antipersonnel mine, used extensively for perimeter defense and Mechanical Ambushes.

CMB: Combat Medical Badge, similar in prestige to the CIB.

CO: Commanding Officer. (Less frequently, Conscientious Objector.)

Command Performance: An event for which attendance was mandatory.

COMSEC: Communications Security.

CONEX: A heavy steel cargo container with a door on one side, 8'X8'X10', used to ship military equipment.

CONUS: Continental United States.

Cook off: SOP, to pull the pin on a frag and count to three before throwing, to prevent it from being picked up by the enemy and thrown back.

CP: Command Post.

Crocodile: To kill. (Also, "dust", "waste" or "grease")

CS: Military-grade tear gas.

CYA: Cover Your Ass.

Day laager: A daytime patrol base and temporary defensive position.

Dead Space: An area on the ground which cannot be observed or fired upon from a specific observation point, because of terrain contours or other obstructions.

Delta Tango (DT): "Defensive Target". Preplanned artillery fires, routinely plotted around an NDP or along anticipated enemy escape routes.

Tom Dolan

DEROS: Departure En Route Over Seas (date). The date a GI's tour in Vietnam was over.

DET cord: Plastic demolition cord, filled with explosive. DET cord was primarily used to cut down trees, or to link explosive charges.

Deuce 'n half: 2 ½ ton 6X6 truck. AWD, 5 speed manual transmission w/ Hi & Lo range axle, multifuel engine.

Di di mau (pronounced "dee-dee mow"): To sky up, cap up, or "get out of here".

Di huy (pronounced "die-wee"): Captain, who was also called "CO" if he was in charge of a line company.

Dink: Grunt slang for VC/NVA. Sometimes used as a racial pejorative for all Vietnamese, especially by rear-area soldiers. Probably derived from the Vietnamese term for a crazy person, "dien cai dau", always mispronounced "dinky dow" by GIs.

Dog and Pony Show: A TOC briefing put on by one or more staff officers, to impress a VIP visitor, accompanied by charts & statistics. The briefing officer usually used a long pointer, wielded smartly like a fencing foil.

Doughnut Dollies: Young female employees of the American Red Cross. They handed out cookies and Kool Aid to GIs, while playing silly games with them on forward firebases or in rear areas. These patriotic girls were pretty adventurous, but were sometimes unfairly disparaged as "Pastry Pigs" by grunts.

Drag: Last man in a movement formation, responsible for rear security.

DR: Delinquency Report. A written citation, issued by MPs.

Dumb Irish Trick: Any really stupid action by a person of Irish ancestry. Each year on March 17th, all persons are traditionally permitted to commit Dumb Irish Tricks if they are wearing green, regardless of actual ancestry.

E1 through E9: Enlisted pay grades. E5 and above were usually noncommissioned officers (NCOs).

The Mad Fragger and Me

Eleven Bravo: MOS 11B10 or 11B20. An enlisted Infantryman. The corresponding officers' MOS is 1542, Infantry Small Unit Commander.

El Tee: How lieutenants were usually addressed by EM, i.e., L-T. Also, ti huy ("tee-wee", 2LT) or trung huy ("trung-wee", 1LT)

EM: Enlisted men.

E-tool: Entrenching tool. A compact folding shovel, with a straight wooden handle.

ETS (date): End of Term of Service. The date a soldier was scheduled for discharge from the Army.

E8 CS Launcher: A 35mm, 16 tube portable tear gas launcher. Unpredictable, it sometimes fired itself.

FAC: Forward Air Controller. USAF officer who directs air strikes or artillery attacks, from a small fixed wing aircraft.

Fast-mover: F4 Phantom fighter-bomber. Loosely, any attack jet aircraft.

FDC: Fire Direction Center. Where the mathematical calculations for mortar or artillery fire missions are done.

Fire-for-Effect: Barrage fire, after the final artillery or mortar adjustment.

Fire up (or "light up"): To shoot at.

First Sergeant: The highest ranking NCO in a company-sized unit. The Top Soldier.

FNG: F-ing New Guy

FO: Forward Observer. Anyone who calls for and adjusts indirect fire or air attacks, from the ground.

Four Deuce: 4.2 inch (106mm) heavy mortar.

FPF: Preplanned Final Protective Fire, at very close range. Calling for the "FPF" means "Fire all available munitions, my defensive position is being overrun".

Frag: Fragmentary hand grenade, most commonly the M26 "lemon" variety.

Fragging: To murder an unpopular officer or NCO, with a fragmentary grenade.

FSB: Fire Support Base; aka, Firebase, Forward Firebase or Landing Zone. Semi-permanent base of operations for battalions or larger units.

FUGAS: Mixture of JP4 aircraft gasoline and diesel fuel in a 55 gallon drum, sometimes wrapped with barbed wire for increased shrapnel effect, command detonated by a C4 charge.

Gaza Strip: GI nickname for the lowland area running North-South, between Highway 1 and the South China Sea, in Quang Ngai and Mo Duc Provinces.

GT Line: Gun-Target line. The direction, in degrees or mils, from an artillery battery to the target.

Gunship: A fixed or rotary wing aircraft which was designed as, or converted into, an attack gun platform.

HE: High Explosive projectile. Used in the artillery call-for-fire, as in "HE Quick"... meaning high explosive ordinance with Super-Quick fuses.

HHC: Headquarters & Headquarters Company.

H&I: Harassment and Interdiction. Artillery barrages intended to interdict enemy movements, especially at night. Usually triggered by ground radar or electronic sensors, but sometimes fired randomly.

Hoi Chanh: An enemy soldier who had come over to our side, through the Chieu Hoi program.

Hootch: Any small dwelling or shelter.

HOR: Home of Record.

India Lima Lima: Illumination, provided by mortars, artillery or flares.

Indian Country: Enemy controlled territory.

Jeep: ¼ ton 4X4 vehicle; the 1960s variation was the M151A1.

Jody: In marching cadence calls, the metaphoric name of the draft dodger who dated your girlfriend, played with your dog, drove your car and ate your Mom's food, while you were away in Vietnam.

KCS: Kit Carson Scout. A Hoi Chanh who accompanied U.S. forces as a scout and advisor on enemy capabilities/ tactics.

KIA: Killed in action. Similarly, KHA, killed hostile action

Kimchi: The Korean national dish. Very hot, highly seasoned and fermented shredded cabbage.

Klick: Abbreviation for kilometer, i.e., 1,000 meters. About 0.6 mile.

La dai ("lah-die"): Come here.

Liaison Officer. An officer who coordinates activities between military groups, such as artillery and infantry.

Lifer: Disparaging term for anyone who was in the Army as a career.

Lifer Gear: A full kit of TA 50 web gear, with pistol belt, suspenders, bandage carrier, compass case, M16 ammo pouches, holster, canteen and other web accessories. Lifer Gear was never worn by grunts, because it interfered with carrying a rucksack.

LOACH: Pronunciation of the acronym LOH, for Light Observation Helicopter. Hughes OH-6 Cayuse.

LRRP: Pronounced "lurp". Long Range Reconnaissance Patrol. Also refers to freeze-dried rations developed for use by LRRP teams.

LZ: Landing Zone. Can refer to a permanent fire base, or to a field-expedient helicopter landing zone.

MA: Mechanical Ambush. Euphemism for a booby trap, using Claymore mine(s) modified for trip detonation. Also sometimes called an "Automatic Ambush".

MACV: Military Assistance Command-Vietnam.

Madam K: Vietnamese prostitutes; the term is of uncertain origin. Also called "boom-boom girls".

MEDCAP: Medical Civics Action Program. Medical treatment provided to civilians as a way of "winning their hearts and minds".

MEDEVAC: Medical Evacuation, by helicopter, also called a Dust-Off. MEDEVAC urgency was assigned by the leader on the ground: Routine, Priority or Urgent. Platoon leaders sometimes inflated the urgency factor by one level, to ensure prompt evacuation of a wounded soldier.

Tom Dolan

    Mermite cans: Heavy aluminum insulated food containers with hinged tops and three aluminum sleeve inserts.
    Miniguns: Electronic multibarreled Gatling-type machine guns, caliber 7.62mm NATO.
    Monsoon slippers: Lightweight, ankle high, OD canvas slippers with thin rubber soles and a Velcro closure strap.
    Monsoon sweater: Officially labeled "Sleep Shirt". Long sleeved OD pull over, worn for warmth during the monsoon season.
    Morning Report: Official roster, completed each morning in every company-sized Army unit, showing the status of each person in the unit; basis for payroll preparation.
    MOS: Military Occupational Specialty.
    MPC: Military Payment Certificates. Used as U.S. currency in Vietnam, instead of greenbacks.
    MP: Military Police.
    M2 Carbine: A variation of the M1 Carbine, with a selector switch and full-automatic capability.
    M2 Heavy Machine Gun: The "Ma Deuce", Browning, .50 caliber.
    M14: Improved version of the M1 Garand in 7.62mm, with detachable 20 round box magazine, first issued in 1960. The M14E2 version was capable of full automatic fire.
    M16: U.S. 5.56 mm assault rifle. The M16A1 version was standard issue in 1970-1971.
    M60: Standard U.S. light machine gun, 7.62 mm, belt fed, air cooled, with a quick-change barrel capability.
    Napalm: Jellied gasoline, used in bombs.
    NDP: Night Defensive Position.
    NCO: Noncommissioned Officer. Sergeant (pay grade E5) through Sergeant Major (pay grade E9). "Noncom".
    NCOIC: NCO In Charge
    Neca eos omnes. Deus suous agnoscet. (Latin): Kill them all. God will know His own.
    No bic: Piggin English for "I don't understand"

Nomex: A lightweight fire retardant material used primarily in flight suits.

Non gratum anus rodentum. (Latin) Not worth a rat's ass. Combat Engineer Tunnel Rats' Motto.

NVA: North Vietnamese Army.

Nuoc mam: ("nuk-maum") Pungent, fermented fish sauce, used to flavor rice.

Nui Vong: Hill 103 on U.S. maps, the site of an old French Foreign Legion Outpost.

Number one/number ten: Best/worst.

OD: olive drab color.

OD: Officer of the Day. Also called SDO (Staff Duty Officer). Administrative OIC of a unit during non-duty hours.

OER: Officer's Efficiency Report. A written performance evaluation.

OIC: Officer in Charge.

OJT: On the Job Training.

OP: Observation Post

OPORD: Operations Order.

Orderly Room: A cantonment-area administrative office, where a company's First Sergeant and Company Clerk worked.

PACEX: Pacific Exchange; the Army's answer to Sears & Roebuck catalogs.

PAVN: Peoples' Army of Viet Nam. Communist name for the North Vietnamese Army (NVA). Left-wing publications often give themselves away, by using the PAVN acronym.

PB: Patrol Base, or day laager.

PBO: Property Book Officer. The OIC of equipment records, usually a Chief Warrant Officer.

Peanut butter frag: Any can of food which explodes after it is thrown, unopened, into a hot fire.

Petna: Corruption of "PETN", a high explosive substance used in U.S. artillery shells and bombs. Often salvaged from duds by the VC/NVA for use in explosive booby traps.

Piastres: South Vietnamese currency, also known as dong.
PIO: Public Information Officer.
Pogue: Pejorative military slang word for a rear echelon soldier.
POV: Privately Owned Vehicle.
PK: Russian machine gun, caliber 7.62X54R. A superior belt-fed weapon, still in production as the PKM.
Platoon One: In the artillery call for fire, firing one gun in the battery.
PRC 25: A heavy backpack FM radio, the standard communications instrument in the Infantry. A visually identical version but with "secure" capability was the AN/PRC 77.
PSP: Paving, Special Purpose. A heavy corrugated steel paving material, often used for roofing material in bunkers.
PSYOPS: Psychological Operations, i.e., propaganda.
PTSD: Post Traumatic Stress Disorder. (Combat Medics' treatment regimen: Take two APCs with a hot toddy and go to bed with an attractive nurse.)
Puff the Magic Dragon: USAF AC130 cargo plane converted into a gunship, equipped with side-firing electronic Gatling guns and illumination flares. Capable of a very long time-on-target.
PX: Post Exchange. Army department store.
P38: a tiny can opener, often carried by veterans on their key rings as souvenirs of their military service. Four P38s were packed in each case of C Rations.
Q Company: Unofficial designation of the temporary unit which manned Nui Vong/Hill 103. This reflects a throwback Army tradition for naming provisional units "Q Company".
QL 1: Highway 1; the main North-South road through South Vietnam, one lane in each direction.
RA: Regular Army.
Rat Patrol: A night raid on a village.
Redleg: Grunt term for an artilleryman. Union artillery soldiers wore red leggings during the Civil War.

Recon Sergeant: An artillery buck sergeant assigned as a substitute for a lieutenant FO.

REMF: Rear Echelon M_F_: Anyone who was not a front-line infantry soldier.

Resection: Method of finding your location on a map, by shooting azimuths to two "known" terrain features, calculating the back-azimuths and plotting them on the map with a protractor. The point where the two lines intersect on the map is the location from which the azimuths were shot.

RF/PF: Regional Forces/Popular Forces, aka "Ruff-Puffs"; South Vietnamese militia units.

Ring Knocker (or Ring Banger): A Graduate of the West Point Military Academy. West Point graduates often called attention to their huge class rings by tapping them on some hard object, such as a table top.

RPG: In GI vernacular, a Rocket Propelled Grenade. Sometimes called a B40 Rocket. These antitank weapons are still in use around the world. The common version in Vietnam was the RPG 7.

RPG Screens: Sections of chain-link fence, erected in front of fixed fighting positions on firebases. These screens provided "stand-off", so incoming RPG rockets would explode against the fencing instead of entering the fighting position.

R & R: Rest and Recreation. A one week paid vacation to Hawaii, Taipei, Bangkok, Sydney, or Hong Kong, with free air transportation provided by the U.S. government. Other expenses were paid for by the soldier.

RS: Romeo-Sierra, i.e., resupply.

RTO: Radio-Telephone Operator.

Sappers: Elite NVA shock troops, who operated like commandos. Historically, "sappers" are similar to combat engineers. NVA sappers specialized in penetrating U.S. defensive positions and they used satchel charges extensively.

Satchel charge: Explosive charge, carried in a cloth bag, usually detonated with a pull igniter and time fuse. Used for blowing up bunkers or other structures; or as a weapon.

Scunnion: GI slang, meaning any action to inflict pain, death and destruction upon the enemy.

SDO: Same as OD. Staff Duty Officer.

Sergeant Major: The highest ranking NCO in a battalion or higher headquarters, pay grade E9.

Shackle: To encode numbers, using a "Whiz Wheel".

Shake 'n Bake: A graduate of the Army's 12 week NCO Academy.

Shelter half: One half of a canvas pup tent, which was issued to each soldier. They fastened together with either buttons or snaps, so it was necessary to buddy-up with somebody who had a similarly configured shelter half.

"Shot, over": Radio call from an artillery battery, to signal that rounds were on the way. Acknowledged by "Shot, out" from the FO.

Sic semper tyrannus (Latin): Thus always to tyrants.

SITREP: Situation report. Frequently requested by battalion headquarters at inopportune times, such as in the middle of a firefight. (My standard response: "We are kicking ass and taking names.")

Sky up: Cap up. Run. Move out smartly.

Slack: Second man in a movement formation. He was the bodyguard for the "point" man.

Slick: A lightly armed (2 M60 machine guns) Huey utility helicopter, used for carrying troops and cargo.

Snake: A night ambush, especially along a road.

Sniper check: To light a cigarette, or show any kind of light, at night.

Snuffies: Grunts; ground-pounders.

Soap round: A 5.56mm cartridge from which the projectile was pulled. The bullet was replaced with a wad of soap or candle wax.

Jujubes were sometimes used as faux bullets. Used to shoot rats inside of bunkers.

SOI: Signal Operating Instructions. A classified radio-operations booklet, containing each unit's assigned frequencies, call signs and ciphers/codes. Complete SOIs were never issued to small combat units in Vietnam, only "Extracts" with lists of unit call signs and assigned radio frequencies.

SOP: Standard Operating Procedure.

Souvenir/souveniring: To take, confiscate, or steal; from the French, reflecting their influence on the Vietnamese language.

Speakeasy: An interpreter, usually a teenaged Vietnamese boy.

SP: Sundry Packet. A box of personal supplies and goodies, such as tooth paste, soap, razor blades, cigarettes, candy, etc., issued regularly to grunts.

Stand-Down: A mini-vacation (3 or 4 days) for grunts, every three months. The term "stand down" was also used when a unit formally retired from battle and its colors were returned to CONUS.

Starlight Scope: A battery-powered night vision device, magnifying ambient light from moon or stars, producing images in shades of green.

STRAC: A model soldier; $\underline{S}$trategic, $\underline{T}$actical, $\underline{R}$eady for $\underline{A}$ction in $\underline{C}$ombat.

S1, S2, S3, S4, S5: "Primary" Staff Officers at battalion and brigade headquarters: S1/Adjutant-Personnel. S2- Intelligence. S3- Operations/Training. S4- Supply/Logistics. S5- Civil Affairs.

TA312: A hand-cranked, battery operated field telephone, used for communicating over longer distances. A voice-powered TA 1 was used over short distances.

TA50: Field web gear as a group, i.e., pistol belt, suspenders, ammo & first aid pouches, canteen, etc.

Ti Hui: Vietnamese for 2nd Lieutenant. (Trung Hui, 1st Lieutenant.)

TOC: Tactical Operations Center. A large bunker on the firebase, well lit, with charts, situation maps, banks of radios and phones, manned by multiple RTOs, various NCOs and officers.

TO&E: Table of Organization and Equipment. A printed list, showing authorized positions and nonexpendable equipment in a unit.

Toe-popper: A small booby-trap, made from a rifle or machine gun cartridge in a bamboo tube with a nail in the bottom. The device was buried in the ground and would explode when a GI stepped on it.

Top: Top Sergeant. Affectionate nickname for a First Sergeant or Sergeant Major.

Tracers: Small arms rounds which include a glowing element in each bullet, leaving a visible light trail. U.S tracers were red and Chi-Com tracers were green.

TWs: Permanent-press Tropical Weight khaki-colored uniforms. Usually purchased by officers and senior NCOs, to replace starched khakis.

UCMJ: Uniform Code of Military Justice. The statute on military law and disciplinary action. Article 31 of UCMJ is similar to the Miranda warning.

Wait-A-Minute Vine: Generic term for all jungle vines. Grunts called out, "Wait a minute" when they became entangled in them.

WIA: Wounded In Action. Similarly, WHA, wounded hostile action.

Whiz Wheel: A pocket-size encoding device with a rotating clear plastic dial, using classified daily insert sheets. Used by company and platoon RTOs to encode/decode grid coordinates, radio frequencies and other sensitive numbers.

Wilson Pickett: White Phosphorous art'y round, i.e., smoke, usually used as a marking round. White phosphorous was also called "Willie Pete". WP is incendiary and can be used as a weapon "on the deck".

WPPA: West Point Protective Association. Fictional organization, referring to USMA graduates.

Xin loi: (Pronounced "sin loy") Vietnamese for "Too bad", or "Sorry"; when said by G.I.s, it always meant "Tough shit".

XO: Executive Officer. A unit officer who was involved in supervising unit logistics and support services.

Young Lieutenant: Derogatory form of address, implying inexperience and lack of knowledge, used by other officers to deflate the egos of lieutenants who were overly impressed with themselves.

Fini- Doo (The End)

Printed in the USA
CPSIA information can be obtained
at www.ICGtesting.com
LVHW041343041024
792846LV00037B/362